Natural Born Celebrities

DAVID SCHMID

Natural Born
Celebrities

Serial

Killers

in

American

Culture

THE UNIVERSITY OF CHICAGO PRESS

CHICAGO AND LONDON

David Schmid is associate professor of English at the State University of New York at Buffalo.

The University of Chicago Press, Chicago 60637
The University of Chicago Press, Ltd., London
© 2005 by The University of Chicago
All rights reserved. Published 2005
Printed in the United States of America

14 13 12 11 10 09 08 07 06 05   1 2 3 4 5

ISBN: 0-226-73867-1 (cloth)

Library of Congress Cataloging-in-Publication Data

Schmid, David (David Frank)
  Natural born celebrities : serial killers in American culture / David Schmid.
    p.   cm.
  Includes bibliographical references and index.
  ISBN 0-226-73867-1 (cloth : alk. paper)
    1. Serial murderers—United States—Public opinion. 2. Crime in popular culture—United States. 3. Serial murders in mass media. 4. Fame. I. Title.

  HV6529.S32 2005
  364.152′3′0973—dc22

                                              2004026467

♾ The paper used in this publication meets the minimum requirements of the American National Standard for Information Sciences—Permanence of Paper for Printed Library Materials, ANSI Z39.48-1992.

CONTENTS

ACKNOWLEDGMENTS

Writing this book has been a long and sometimes difficult journey. I have been
helped by so many people along the way that I cannot possibly acknowledge
them all. The most I can do is to recognize those whose contributions have
been especially important. When I first began studying representations of
violence as a master's student at the University of Sussex, Jacqueline Rose
impressed upon me the seriousness and importance of such an endeavor.
While I was working on this project as a student in the Modern Thought and
Literature Program at Stanford University, Gil Sorrentino, Estelle Freedman,
and Sandra Drake were a wonderfully engaged and invigorating dissertation
committee. Equally important in their own way were Marie Brazil and Monica
Moore, peerless program administrators who steered me through threatening
bureaucratic thickets with their customary charm and efficiency. Since arriving at the University at Buffalo, I have been blessed by many supportive and
stimulating colleagues. Stefan Fleischer, Barbara Bono, Neil Schmitz, Bob
Daly, Mark Shechner, Alan Spiegel, Art Efron, Ruth Mack, Elayne Rapping,
and Tim Dean have all been extremely generous with their time and advice,
and the book is much better for their input. I would also like to thank my
superlative research assistant, Benjamin Joplin, for all his hard work on my
behalf. Outside of Buffalo, Erin Carlston has been for many years my closest
and most supportive friend, while my professional association and friendship
with Steffen Hantke has been crucial. Eric Hickey and Edward Ingebretsen

provided me with extremely detailed and constructive readers' reports, while the editorial staff at the University of Chicago Press, especially Douglas Mitchell and Timothy McGovern, have been models of professionalism and affability. I owe Susan Tarcov a particular debt of gratitude for her careful and inspired copyediting. My most important debts are those that I can never repay. My parents, Denis and Iris Schmid, can never be thanked enough for stressing the importance of education to their awfully lazy son. My brother, Antony, and his family, Mandy, Luke, and James, have been unfailingly generous and loving. My daughter, Lucia, was born during the most intense period of writing this book. I resented every minute this project took me away from her, but no writer ever had a greater inspiration than the thought of getting to spend as much time with this wondrous child as possible. As for my wife, Carrie, there are no words that can express my feelings for her. As a scholar, a teacher, a partner, and a mother she deserves all available superlatives and simultaneously renders them inadequate. This book is dedicated to her, with love and gratitude.

Idols of Destruction: Celebrity, Consumerism, and the Serial Killer

Fame, Fame, fatal Fame
It can play hideous tricks on the brain
But still I'd rather be Famous
Than righteous or Holy, any day
Any day, any day.
—The Smiths, "Frankly, Mr. Shankly"

The people's shudder of admiration for the "great criminal" is
addressed to the individual who takes upon himself, as in
primitive times, the stigma of the lawmaker or the prophet.
—Jacques Derrida, "The Force of Law"

To me violence had already been reinforced through time as a
means of being the star, center stage in this drama.
—Serial killer quoted in Eric Hickey's *Serial Murderers
and Their Victims*

Selling Murder

Online shopping is all the rage these days, and the murderabilia industry in particular, which specializes in selling serial killer artifacts, is booming. At Spectre Studios, sculptor David Johnson sells flexible plastic action figures of Ted Bundy, Jeffrey Dahmer, Ed Gein, and John Wayne Gacy and plans to produce a figure of Jack the Ripper in the future.[1] Serial Killer Central offers a range of items made by serial killers themselves, including paintings and drawings by Angelo Buono (one of the "Hillside Stranglers") and Henry Lee Lucas. For the more discerning consumer, Supernaught.com charges a mere $300 for a brick from Jeffrey Dahmer's apartment building, while a lock of Charles Manson's hair is a real bargain at $995, shipping and handling not included.

The sale of murderabilia is just a small part of the huge serial killer industry that has become a defining feature of American popular culture since the 1970s. A constant stream of movies, magazines, T-shirts, trading cards, videos, DVDs, books, Web sites, television shows, and a tsunami of ephemera have given the figure of the serial murderer an unparalleled degree of visibility in the contemporary American public sphere. In a culture defined by celebrity, serial killers like Bundy, Dahmer, and Gacy are among the biggest stars of all, instantly recognized by the vast majority of Americans. *Natural Born Celebrities* analyzes how and why serial killers became famous, what the consequences of that fame are, and what the existence of celebrity serial killers tells us about the roles fame and violence play in contemporary American culture.

Although the existence of famous serial killers predates the development of the murderabilia industry by many years, murderabilia is the logical place to begin my analysis because it represents a limit case in serial killer celebrity, that is, an opportunity to confront the consequences of the fame given to serial killers (both dead and alive) in its most egregious form.[2] Not surprisingly, murderabilia has been the focus of a sustained critique by the (usually self-appointed) guardians of "decency" in American culture. On January 2, 2003, the *John Walsh Show*, the daytime television vehicle of the longtime host of *America's Most Wanted*, featured according to its Web site an "inside look at the world of 'murderabilia,' which involves the sale of artwork, personal effects and letters from well-known killers." Featured guests included Andy Kahan, director of the Mayor's Crime Victim Assistance Office in Houston, Texas; "Thomas," who was horrified to find hair samples from "The Railroad Killer," the individual who killed his mother, for sale on the Internet; Elmer Wayne Henley, a serial killer who sells his artwork to collectors; Joe, who runs the Web site Serial Killer Central and sells murderabilia from a wide range of killers; and Harold Schechter, a professor of English at Queens College, City University of New York. Despite the program's stated intention to "look at both sides of the issue," the show was little more than a jeremiad against the murderabilia industry, with the majority of airtime being given to Andy Kahan and to the relatives of crime victims.

The program's bias was not lost on many of those who visited Joe's Serial Killer Central site and left messages on the message board on the day this particular broadcast of the *John Walsh Show* aired. Although some visitors shared Walsh's perspective,[3] others sympathized with Joe because of the way he had been treated on the show: "I as well saw you on the John Walsh show, you [showed] a lot of courage going on such a one sided show, and it was shit that they wouldnt let you talk, I would have walked off." But whether the comments were positive or negative, one thing was clear: the *John Walsh Show* had created a great deal of interest in the Serial Killer Central site. As one of the messages puts it, "I think that [if] anything else he [John Walsh] has put a spark in everyones curiousity . . . I have noticed that you have more hits on your page today than any others." Apparently, even the most explicit rejection and condemnation of serial killer celebrity finds itself implicated in (and perhaps even unwittingly encouraging the growth of) that celebrity.

John Walsh's attack on the murderabilia industry was another skirmish in a campaign that has been growing steadily since the late 1990s. One of the campaign's initial targets was the Internet trading site eBay, which was criticized for allowing serial-killer-related products to be sold online. In support of such criticism, conservative victims' rights and pro-death-penalty organizations like "Justice For All" organized an online petition against eBay (the petition can be found at http://www.jfa.net/petition.htm). In November 2000, BusinessWeek Online featured an interview with Andy Kahan in which he argued that the online sale of murderabilia should be suppressed: "The Internet just opens it all up to millions and millions more potential buyers and gives easy access to children. And it sends a negative message to society. What does it say about us? We continue to glorify killers and continue to put them in the mainstream public. That's not right" ("Underground"). Eventually bowing to public pressure, eBay decided to ban the sale of murderabilia items in May 2001, forcing the industry underground (M. Jones), where it continues to be pursued by the likes of John Walsh.

The celebrity culture around serial killers has developed so far that one can now purchase the nail clippings and hair of some killers, as if they were religious icons. But the ongoing debate around the ethics of murderabilia shows just how difficult it is to draw a neat line between those who condemn and those who participate in that culture. Despite John Walsh's censoriousness, for example, we have already seen how his show actually brought even more visitors to the Serial Killer Central site. Similarly, one could argue that few individuals have done more to disseminate information about violent crime in general and serial murder in particular to mainstream America than John Walsh. Of course, this information is presented in the unimpeachably moral context of fighting crime, but controversial features of *America's Most Wanted* such as the dramatic recreations of crime pander to the same prurient public interest in crime that the program simultaneously condemns.[4] An ABC News online article on murderabilia inadvertently highlights the difficulty of distinguishing a legitimate from an illegitimate, a normal from an abnormal interest in serial murder by quoting Rick Staton, one of the biggest collectors and dealers of murderabilia in the United States, who emphasizes that the people he sells to are not "ghouls and creeps [who] crawl out of the woodwork" but rather "pretty much your average Joe Blow." Even his family, Staton goes on to say, who profess to be disgusted by what he does, act very differently in practice: "The minute they step into this room, they are glued to everything in here and they are asking questions and they are genuinely intrigued by it . . . So it makes me wonder: Am I the one who is so abnormal, or am I pretty normal?" ("Killer").

The only way to answer Staton's question and to understand the serial killer popular culture industry it is directed toward is to assume, for the time being at least, an attitude of moral neutrality toward that industry. Rather than pronouncing the existence of celebrity serial killer culture to be either good or bad, instead I want to concentrate on the conditions that allowed for the emergence of that culture. In particular, I want to analyze how the concept of "fame" has evolved in ways that not only allow for the existence of criminal celebrities such as the serial killer but also make the serial killer the exemplary modern celebrity. In doing so, I will also argue that the fame of serial killers is absolutely central to understanding the varieties of cultural work they do in contemporary American culture.

Celebrity Diminished and Denied

In spite of the millions of words that have been written about serial murder, popular and academic studies alike are of very little use in explaining how and why serial killers have become celebrities. Popular treatments of serial murder are usually completely silent about the existence of celebrity serial killers, perhaps because to note the phenomenon would seem to necessitate some consideration of how popular treatments both contribute to and depend upon that celebrity. In fact, when the fame of serial killers is noted by the vast majority of popular cultural treatments at all, it is only to condemn it, as we have seen in the case of John Walsh. Condemnation not only is rhetorically satisfying but also avoids the potentially embarrassing topic of the imbrication of popular culture and serial killer fame.

We would not expect popular culture to provide self-conscious (and self-implicating) analyses of serial killer celebrity, but the absence of discussion about this subject in academic studies is more surprising. Despite the very important work that has been done in this field, work that has had a profound influence on my own analysis, academic studies of serial murder either take the existence of celebrity serial killers for granted or explain it in terms that preclude further analysis. Jane Caputi, for example, recognizes the fact that the serial killer has become a celebrity, but prefers to think of such killers as mythic, archetypal figures, as her analysis of Jack the Ripper indicates: "patriarchal culture has enshrined 'Jack the Ripper' as a mythic hero; he commonly appears as an immortal figure in literature, film, television, jokes and other cultural products. Such mythicization terrorizes women, empowers and inspires men, even to the point where some choose to emulate him, and participates in a cultural propagation of frequently lethal misogyny" ("American" 101). Caputi's focus on the importance of gender in understanding representations of serial murder has been invaluable, especially in the context of a mainstream understanding of serial murder that sees nothing significant about the fact that the vast majority of serial killers are men and the vast majority of their victims are women. Nevertheless, Caputi's emphasis on myth and her reduction of every aspect of serial murder to gynocidal misogyny disallow a nuanced analysis of the phenomenon, and in particular make it difficult to appreciate how the famous serial killer is the product of a very specific set of historical circumstances.

Although Mark Seltzer's approach to the subject of serial murder is almost diametrically opposed to that of Jane Caputi, he shares her relative lack of interest in the implications of the serial killer's celebrity. This lack is all the more surprising in Seltzer because the central concept in his approach to serial murder, "wound culture," lends itself so well to an analysis of the serial killer's fame: "The convening of the public around scenes of violence—the rushing to the scene of the accident, the milling around the point of impact—has come to make up a *wound culture*: the public fascination with torn and open bodies and torn and opened persons, a collective gathering around shock, trauma, and the wound" (1, original emphasis). It is immediately apparent from Seltzer's description of a "wound culture" what a prominent role a criminal like the serial killer would play in that culture. Indeed, Seltzer himself recognizes this fact when he refers to the serial killer as "one of the superstars of our wound culture" (2). After this single tantalizing reference, however, Seltzer does little to develop the implications of the serial killer's celebrity, partly because of his skepticism about whether the serial killer is truly motivated by the desire for fame (135). Revealingly, Seltzer argues that if the serial killer achieves celebrity at all, it is "a celebrity in anonymity: the most wanted man who is also a type of nonperson" (130). As I will demonstrate in chapter 1, I think this is an accurate way to describe the fame of a killer like Jack the Ripper who was never apprehended, but more recent serial killers have a far more specific, individuated form of celebrity that enhances the figure's ability to do the cultural work that is required of it.

Like Caputi and Seltzer, Philip Jenkins has relatively little to say about serial killer celebrity in *Using Murder*, despite providing a detailed and persuasive examination of both the serial killer's status and role in contemporary American culture and the particular importance of popular culture in establishing and maintaining that status. Jenkins recognizes that the serial killer is a celebrity, noting that "even death could not prevent [Ted] Bundy from achieving a high degree of postmortem celebrity" (55). Once again, however, Jenkins seems uninterested in pursuing the implications of this observation. This decision is particularly striking in Jenkins's case because appreciating the implications of the serial killer's celebrity is so helpful in elaborating upon one of Jenkins's most important insights: "A single instance of multiple homicide can be cited in support of divergent rhetorical messages, and none is self-evidently correct or objectively true . . . In the last decade or so, repeat homicide carried out over a period of weeks or months (*serial murder*) has come to be seen as one of the most pressing and widely discussed social problems; and the rich diversity of interpretations suggests the usefulness of the theme for various audiences" (2, original emphasis).

What Jenkins identifies as the susceptibility of serial murder to be "cited in support of divergent rhetorical messages" I want to describe as the "multiaccentuality" of serial murder.[5] The relationship of this multiaccentuality to celebrity consists of three distinct but related strands. First, the multiaccentuality of serial murder has played a major role in making serial killers celebrities. The fact that serial murder can be used to support such a wide variety of ideological agendas guarantees the adoption of serial murder by groups as diverse as policy makers, social/cultural critics, politicians, law enforcement personnel, true-crime writers, novelists, filmmakers, and so on. Second, as the serial killer's celebrity grows, the figure's multiaccentual potential grows alongside it, ensuring its adoption by an even wider variety of individuals and groups, which in turn leads to a further increase in celebrity, in a potentially infinite dialectical relationship. Third, the existence of celebrity serial killers is far from fortuitous. That is to say, the serial killer makes a particularly appropriate (even emblematic) celebrity because both figures inspire feelings of attraction and repulsion, admiration and condemnation. Even though the "normal" celebrity (for example, the film star) seems to be a wholly loved and admired figure, in fact the public's relation to the celebrity is also characterized by resentment, even violent hatred. Similarly (although it is the similarity of a mirror image: identical but inverted) the serial killer seems to inspire only condemnation and hatred. As we will see throughout this book, however, the public's reaction to the serial killer is also complicated by feelings of fascination, even admiration.

One of the most striking features of much contemporary discourse on serial murder is the fact that the complex public reaction to the serial killer is so often managed through the language of the gothic. As I will demonstrate throughout this book, comparisons of serial killers to a host of gothic monsters, including vampires, werewolves, and, of course, Frankenstein's monster, are legion and come not only from members of the public and critics (Judith Halberstam's work is especially notable here) but also from the killers themselves. What can explain the prevalence of ancient gothic metaphors in making sense of a figure who is in so many ways emblematic of American modernity?

In many ways, the gothic is enjoying an unprecedented boom in American culture, becoming "the *quid pro quo* for somber and disturbing moods, sites, events, and cultural by-products of latter-day America" (Grunenberg 210). As Edward Ingebretsen points out in his invaluable study, *At Stake: Monsters and the Rhetoric of Fear in Public Culture*, the purpose of the gothic is to produce fear, not only through the motifs of werewolf, vampire, and the like, but also by "the mythicizing of slashers, terrorists, lurking child abusers, and unnatural mothers" (22). Nicola Nixon suggests the particular form this gothic mythicizing takes with respect to serial murder when she details how extensively contemporary true-crime narratives draw upon the language of gothic monstrosity. In doing so, Nixon argues, true crime is symptomatic of a larger cultural tendency in the contemporary United States to turn serial killers into "real" gothic monsters: "That America thought it had horrify-ingly 'real' monsters instead of fictional demons is unquestionably reflected in the emergence and stunning efflorescence of eighties 'true-crime' books like Ann Rule's *The Stranger Beside Me* . . . and scores of other books about the so-called superstar killers" (220). While being cautious about the value of "broad generalizations about the Gothic," Robert K. Martin and Eric Savoy have summarized its role as a "negation of the Enlightenment's national nar-ratives" (5). In the American context, I believe that the gothic has been used frequently to counter the negation Martin and Savoy refer to. In other words, a large part of the appeal of the rhetoric of gothic monstrosity is that it enables us to express, in Karen Halttunen's words, "the incomprehensibility of mur-der within the rational Enlightenment social order" (*Murder* 48). Positioning serial killers as gothic monsters represents our attempt to salvage and locate a (national) community by defining what stands outside that community. In the process, gothic monster rhetoric demonstrates that serial killers, apparently so new and so threatening to the social fabric, are "not, after all, *new*, not really much of a surprise" (*Murder* 57, original emphasis). As we will see in chapter 1, these tactics are by no means limited to the contemporary United States. Commentators in Victorian Britain found the gothic to be an equally valuable repository of images when they tried to make sense of the apparently incomprehensible behavior of Jack the Ripper.

Martin and Savoy go on to cite Louis Gross's description of the "common thread" of the gothic as "the singularity and monstrosity of the Other: what the dominant culture cannot incorporate within itself, it must project outward onto this hated/desired figure" (quoted in Martin and Savoy, Introduction 5). The serial killer is the most recent incarnation of this singular and monstrous Other. Appropriately, bearing in mind that another defining feature of the gothic tendency in American culture is "the imperative to repetition" (Martin and Savoy, Introduction 4), the late-twentieth-century attempts to position serial killers as gothic monsters recall eighteenth-century attempts to cast incomprehensible murderers as monstrosities, as we will see in chapter 5. The fact that such repetitions are necessary suggests a "failure of repression and forgetting" (Martin and Savoy, Introduction 4).

Although the community attempts to cast the gothic monster (in whatever form) outside its bounds, such attempts are doomed to fail because these monsters exert equal parts repulsion and attraction, a fact that ensures their simultaneous abjection from and ingestion into the social in a process that is potentially infinite. Jeffrey Jerome Cohen has argued that "the monster also attracts. The same creatures who terrify and interdict can evoke potent escapist fantasies; the linking of monstrosity with the forbidden makes the monster all the more appealing as a temporary egress from constraint" (16–17). Moreover, Cohen goes on to argue, the "simultaneous repulsion and attraction at the core of the monster's composition accounts greatly for its continued cultural popularity" (17). We can see this complex combination of feelings at work in particularly vivid ways in American popular culture that addresses serial killers because these figures not only connote monstrosity but also personify another iconic American figure who inspires sharply contradictory feelings: the celebrity. Just as the monster is a strongly ambivalent figure, an "othered" being who seems strangely familiar, the same can be said about celebrities. The famous are simultaneously like us and completely other than us, inhabiting a different order of reality that we both desire and resent. Mark Edmundson has even argued that the "phenomenon of celebrity . . . has a streak of Gothic running through it" (88–89) that can be seen in the tabloids, the "Gothic underside of the pop-transcendence, celebrity phenomenon . . . [where] you meet the darker selves of the celebrities who have captivated you. You learn that they cheat, grub for money, trash their friends; they grasp like babies for whatever goodies roll by" (88). The famous serial killer combines the roles of monster and celebrity in a particularly economical and charged way, and this is why famous serial killers are such a visible part of the contemporary American cultural landscape.

With both the celebrity and the serial killer, therefore, we have a combination of an "official" approved narrative about what these figures mean, along with a hidden, disavowed narrative about the very same subject. The story I want to tell in *Natural Born Celebrities* is how this unstable combination of narratives about the status of the serial killer in contemporary American culture is managed in a variety of popular cultural forms. In order to tell this story, however, I want to repeat that it is necessary to tell another, deeply implicated, story: the changing nature of fame.

Defining Fame: Merit or Visibility?

Apart from reluctance to examine their own place in serial killer celebrity culture, perhaps another reason why most studies of the subject do not draw attention to the fame of serial killers is that the hegemonic definition of fame still assumes that it is an inherently positive category. According to this line of thinking, criminals in general, and serial killers in particular, are still more appropriately described as infamous or notorious rather than famous, as anti-heroes rather than heroes. In fact, the iconic status of serial killers in contemporary American culture is compelling evidence of the collapse of the difference between fame and notoriety. In particular, the decline of merit as a defining factor in fame means that nowadays to be famous and to be notorious are frequently the same thing.

Most writers on the subject agree that we have witnessed a sea change in the nature of fame over the past two hundred years. If in the past the ranks of the famous were peopled by those recognized for meritorious achievement, today the famous are the visible, rather than the talented. As Cathy Madison has commented, "In 1896 celebrities were leaders ... whose qualities we admired and aspired to; today celebrity means only someone whose name and face we know" (5). One now achieves fame not by performing meritorious acts or possessing outstanding qualities, but by being seen.[6] In turn, what it takes to be seen no longer has any necessary connection to merit but is determined by whatever gets the public's attention. Contemporary fame possesses a performative aspect that is quite new, as Leo Braudy explains: "Looking back over the history of fame, we can see how by the twentieth century the frames of achievement that had existed before—the audience of citizens, the audience of God, the audience of history—had been superseded by the more palpable and immediate audience for performance. Much more than the famous of any previous century, the famous of the twentieth century ... are *onstage*" (549, original emphasis). When fame first became associated with visibility in the early-nineteenth-century United States, the association was initially seen as positive. Braudy cites Frederick Douglass's comments on the portrait of Hiram Revels, the first black senator ("Pictures come not with slavery and oppression but with liberty, fair play, leisure, and refinement") in the context of asserting that "to be seen was to be free, to be heroic, to be American" (453). Once fame is characterized *primarily* by visibility rather than achievement, however, it no longer makes sense to distinguish between good and bad forms of fame. In a society where merit-based fame ceases to have any meaning, recognition and self-exposure are now believed to be absolute goods in themselves: "fame promises acceptability, even if one commits the most heinous crime, because thereby people will finally know who you are, and you will be saved from the living death of being unknown" (Braudy 562). When the essential factor about stars is whether they are broadly known, the way is open for notoriety to fill the gap left open by the disappearance of merit in definitions of fame (Fowles 7).[7] Or as Todd Gitlin writes: "Obviously, celebrity need not be admirable, merely spectacular. Hitler made seven covers of *Time*; Stalin, twelve. In the realm of celebrity, the fallen share center stage with the glorious, the evil with the good. The emotional glue that binds us to those we love to hate is not unrelated to the glue that binds us to those we love to love. The celebrity-making machinery capitalizes on this, and dissolves values in an acid bath of fame" (83). Under these circumstances, crime is no longer a bar to celebrity; indeed, it is as close to a guarantee of celebrity as one can find.[8] Thanks to the "morally neutral" nature of contemporary fame, "to be notorious or to be infamous may be no more than shortcuts" to fame, "more efficient uses of the machinery of fame" (Fisher 155). Perhaps this is the motive for those crimes committed by obsessed fans; as Mark Chapman found out when he killed John Lennon, by attacking the famous, you become famous.[9]

Given these developments, it is natural to ask whether it is still useful or accurate to distinguish between fame and celebrity. On one level, these categories seem as distinct as ever, fame remaining an honorific category with a long and glorious history, while celebrity seems a much more recent and debased category, usually because of its association with the mass media (Giles 3). Braudy, however, argues that we "might want to make distinctions between fame, renown, honor, reputation, celebrity, and so on—and have a good deal of moral reason to do. But we should also be sensitive to the way those lines have become blurred" (562). Indeed, some have argued that the supposedly clear dividing line between fame and celebrity has always been blurred. There is a sense in which fame and merit have never been more than loosely connected because "fame has, to some extent, always been regarded as essentially *amoral* and frequently undeserved" (Giles 4, original emphasis). Although the existence of famous serial killers might seem a perversion of the honorable history of fame, Tyler Cowen reminds us that "many of the supposed 'heroes' of the past were liars, frauds, and butchers to varying degrees" (65). On a related note, Chris Rojek has argued that it is becoming increasingly difficult to distinguish between celebrity and notoriety because, although notoriety usually connotes "transgression, deviance and immorality . . . today celebrity often involves transgressing ordinary moral rules by, for example, excessive conspicuous consumption, exhibitionist libidinous gratification, drug abuse, alcohol addiction, violence and so on" (31). Bearing this in mind, we might best interpret celebrity serial killers as continuous, rather than discontinuous, with the history of fame.

Although it would be a mistake to use the terms "fame" and "celebrity" interchangeably, clearly the two categories are closer today than they ever have been before. As David Giles argues, becoming famous today "beyond one's immediate field of excellence requires becoming a celebrity as well" (26).

Whether one is a Pulitzer Prize–winning author, a politician, a killer, or a failed contestant on *American Idol*, everyone today must be treated as a celebrity in order to be "legible" in the contemporary public sphere. Obviously, the collapse of the old distinction between fame and celebrity has not been widely celebrated; indeed, the conventional reaction to the "decline" of fame has been to present it mournfully as evidence of a broader cultural decline in modern America. In *The Image*, Daniel Boorstin's pessimistic account of what happened to the American Dream, he laments the modern tendency to degrade all fame into notoriety and finds this tendency encapsulated in the celebrity:

> *The celebrity is a person who is known for his well-knownness*. His qualities—or rather his lack of qualities—illustrate our peculiar problems. He is neither good nor bad, great nor petty. He is the human pseudo-event . . . He is made by all of us who willingly read about him, who like to see him on television, who buy recordings of his voice, and talk about him to our friends. His relation to morality and even to reality is highly ambiguous. (57–58, original emphasis)

For Boorstin, the celebrity embodies the superficiality that has come to dominate the public sphere in the United States. The celebrity's visibility stands in for, Boorstin believes, a chilling lack of substance in contemporary public figures, a lack of substance symptomatic of a culture that has come to prize image over reality. Christopher Lasch, like Boorstin, comments on the decline from fame to celebrity, but concentrates more than Boorstin does on this decline's impact on the American public: "The media give substance to and thus intensify narcissistic dreams of fame and glory, encourage the common man to identify himself with the stars and to hate the 'herd,' and make it more and more difficult for him to accept the banality of everyday existence" (55–56). Unlike Boorstin and Lasch, I am not interested in mourning the decline of fame; rather, I want to understand how and why it happened. As Lasch indicates, by promoting and publicizing stars, the media play a central role in defining what fame is and how it is disseminated.[10]

Media Technologies, Fame, and Violence

Regardless of their motivations, the ability of individuals who desire fame to realize their ambitions is partly dependent upon the media technologies available to them and the ability of those technologies to create and disseminate fame:

> Whatever political or social or psychological factors influence the desire to be famous, they are enhanced by and feed upon the available means of reproducing the image. In the past that medium was usually literature, theater, or public monuments.

With the Renaissance came painting and engraved portraits, and the modern age has added photography, radio, movies, and television. As each new medium of fame appears, the human image it conveys is intensified and the number of individuals celebrated expands. (Braudy 4)

Changes in fame over the past two hundred years have as much, if not more, to do with the development of the market economy for fame as with changes in why individuals desire fame.[11] The introduction of each new media technology therefore represents a decisive shift in both the types of fame available in a culture and the ability of that culture to disseminate fame. The introduction of printing, for example, by allowing for the possibility of a geographically dispersed reading public organized and, to some extent, unified by easily reproducible books, shattered the "old contrast between the good fame of the elite, whether spiritual or intellectual or political, versus the bad fame of common report carried by the tongues and ears of the vulgar crowd" (Braudy 267–68).[12] Although the changes brought about by the introduction of printing may be regarded as positive in the sense that they democratized fame, making it accessible to a larger number of people, Braudy implies that the price of this expansion was the disappearance of an older understanding of the famous as a distinguished, meritorious elite, rather than an undifferentiated mass.[13]

The erosion of the distinction between "good" and "bad" fame, and the concomitant emphasis on fame as a primarily visible phenomenon inaugurated by the introduction of printing, were both massively accelerated by the introduction of photography and film. In many ways, the establishment of the star as the organizing principle and of the close-up as the defining technique of the burgeoning film industry represents the apex of the idea that fame is a visible, rather than a meritorious, phenomenon. Crucially, however, technologies of mechanical reproduction such as photography and film not only demonstrate the increasingly visible nature of celebrity, but also guarantee that the aura of celebrity becomes more powerful. According to Walter Benjamin in his landmark essay "The Work of Art in the Age of Mechanical Reproduction," the art object loses its aura through being mechanically reproduced. Just the opposite is true, however, of the celebrity:

If great art loses its aura in the marketplace of mass impression, the individual life of the celebrity achieves an aura through mass reproduction . . . If the reproduction of the Sistine Chapel allows the artwork to be downwardly mobile, the reproduction (of the face, voice, gestures, personal habits) of the celebrity is often a case of upward mobility . . . the celebrity, "seen in the flesh," becomes more captivating the more he or she has been mechanically or electronically *reproduced*. (Ewen 93, original emphasis)

The combination of increased visibility and heightened aura go a long way to explain the enormous impact of the Hollywood star system when it emerged in the early years of the twentieth century, but the changing nature of fame orchestrated by developing media technologies was also conducive to making celebrities out of other groups, including criminals.[14]

Throughout American history, criminals have been the target of professional opinion makers, whether they be newspaper editors, television reporters, or documentary filmmakers, who all seek to make a point about the state of American culture (either pro or con) by making the criminal into an emblematic figure (Kooistra 40). Before the rise of the mass media, these opinion makers had to rely primarily on oral history to promote the renown of criminals. As a result, they could reach only a small audience. As the variety and scale of media technologies evolved, however, the opportunities for publicizing criminals expanded enormously, so that today, "the exploits of a criminal may be sung on records that will be broadcast by thousands of radio stations, dramatized in movies that will be viewed by millions, reported by a news service that will ensure a worldwide audience" (Kooistra 162). Such developments are one reason why representations of criminality now play a central role in the American mass media.

If the expansion of types of media technologies is an important factor in explaining the changing nature of fame and in giving criminals more opportunities to become famous, however, it would be the most reductive variety of technological determinism to suggest that the availability of media technologies is the only significant factor. In order to develop a better understanding of how criminals in general and serial killers in particular have become such widely known figures in contemporary American culture, I want to emphasize both the influence of how these technologies are used (rather than the bare fact of their mere existence) and also why there is such a high demand for stories of violence and death among the American populace.

Creating the Myth of the Serial Killer

Sensational coverage of crime has always had a prominent place in American popular culture, from the earliest forms of colonial popular literature, through the "yellow journalism" of the nineteenth century, to the true-crime book and slasher movie of today. The years since 1985, however, have seen a change in how the American mass media represent crime, a change that has important ramifications for the celebrity status of the serial killer. According to Richard Krajicek, during the late 1980s, newspapers and television news broadcasts lowered their editorial standards in order to compete with tabloid media such as *Hard Copy* and the *National Enquirer*. This "tabloidization" of the mainstream media has had an especially damaging impact upon the reporting of crime. Instead of detailed, objective stories about the crime problems facing the United States, now the mass media provide their audience with "raw dispatches about the crime of the moment, the frightening—and often false—trend of the week, the prurient murder of the month, the sensational trial of the year" (Krajicek 4). The tendency of crime news to focus on sex and celebrity trivia and to perpetuate inaccurate myths by presenting chaotic and ultimately false images of crime found its logical culmination in the media frenzy surrounding the O. J. Simpson case (Krajicek 9, 63).[15]

If increased attention to crimes involving celebrities was one consequence of the tabloidization of the American mass media in the 1980s, another was a newly prominent role for serial killers during this period. The serial killer became a dominant media figure not only because he personified the tabloid sensibility (all scandal, all the time) but also because he exemplified other important features of how the contemporary American mass media represent crime. One such feature confirmed by numerous studies is that the media routinely overreport violent crime. Although murder constitutes a tiny fraction of all crimes committed in the United States, murder and other crimes of violence dominate media reporting of crime. As a result, the incidence of lesser crimes is minimized, and the incidence and impact of violent crime are exaggerated enormously (Schlesinger and Tumber 184).

Media practices relating to the formation of "crime myths" make the situation even worse. The social construction of crime myths follows a recurrent pattern, whereby a few isolated criminal events and issues receive brief but incredibly intense media coverage. The intensity of the media coverage creates an equally intense reaction among mass media consumers, and as a result a few isolated events can quickly become defined as a major social problem (Kappeler et al. 4). The selection of crime problems is often limited to the most bizarre or gruesome act a journalist or investigator can uncover; the preference for the bizarre and gruesome is in turn determined by the competitive nature of modern media: "By culling unique and fascinating issues for public exhibition, the media ensures the marketability and success (viewers and advertising dollars) of a given media production" (Kappeler et al. 5). The combination of tabloidization, the overrepresentation of violent interpersonal crime, and a preference for the grotesque in the construction of crime myths has led to the rise of a media icon that Ray Surette has described as the "faceless predator criminal" ("Predator" 135), a figure who represents the American public's attempt to embody the seemingly omnipresent and anonymous threat of violent crime.

The rise of the serial killer is a product of the media's attempt to give a face to the faceless predator criminal. If a faceless criminal is a productive motif for media-created crime myths, even more public interest can be generated when we can give that myth a specific name, "serial murder," and then give that name an identifiable cast of characters, such as Ted Bundy, John Wayne Gacy, and Jeffrey Dahmer. According to Philip Jenkins, this is exactly what happened to serial murder in the mid-1980s, when the media, along with government agencies, law enforcement officials, and reform groups worked together to produce a "serial killer panic." The key elements of this panic were that serial murder was a qualitatively new phenomenon, that it was growing enormously, that there were a large number of serial murderers active at any given time, that serial murder was a distinctively American phenomenon, and that the crime had reached epidemic proportions, claiming four thousand victims a year. Although Jenkins locates the origins of the serial murder panic in a 1984 *New York Times* article, he emphasizes how smoothly different forms of media worked together to disseminate the myth, as well as how the myth established a few "representative" serial killers as household names: "The visual media strongly reinforced the concept of a new and appalling menace . . . Each of the major news magazines of the '60 Minutes' format had at least one story of this type, while a 'HBO America Undercover' episode was a documentary focusing on three well-known serial killers of the last decade: Ted Bundy, Edmund Kemper, and Henry Lee Lucas. Interviews with all three were featured, as were harrowing (and controversial) reconstructions, using actors" ("Myth" 55). Although Jenkins discusses the consequences of the serial killer panic at length, including its use as justification for a reorientation of federal crime-fighting funds toward serial murder and away from other forms of crime, he does not emphasize the fact that the panic made celebrities out of a large number of serial killers. The fame of serial killers, however, is not limited to the fact that they are culturally omnipresent in contemporary American culture or that promoting their fame has become a staple of American popular culture. If, as Braudy argues, the exemplary twentieth-century famous person "is especially the person famous for being himself or playing himself" (554), then it is not enough to say that serial killers are famous. Judging by contemporary standards of fame, the serial killer is the exemplary modern celebrity, widely known and famous for being himself.[16] This might seem to be a counterintuitive statement, because surely serial murderers are famous for what they do, not for who they are. In the serial killer, however, action and identity are fused. As we will see in more detail in chapters 5 and 6, every detail of the murderer's life story, everything that concerns who he is, contributes to an understanding of what he has done. The selfhood and murders of the serial killer thus become two sides of the same coin.

One consequence of the fame bestowed upon some serial killers is that such killers are increasingly aware of their status as celebrities, as public figures who have an audience and therefore the potential to capitalize upon their fame. Carl Panzram, a self-confessed murderer of twenty-one people, wrote a letter days before his execution to Henry Lesser, a prison warder to whom Panzram had entrusted his papers and miscellaneous writings. The letter suggests a highly developed awareness of the market for murder-related products:

> A bunch of these kind of newspaper clippings and my picture would go good to fill in the last part of the book. They would be very good because they would be both authentic and interesting. After all my part of the book to finish it off in proper style you as the author could write my wind up or epitaph with perhaps a picture of [me] after death or the grave or the Electric Chair. You write the Preface, use my writings for the book and your own explanations as the conclusions. This ought to make a hell of a good book. I have never seen or heard of one like it. It ought to have a big sale, with all of the interest that would be aroused by all of the papers publishing so much about me. (Quoted in B. King 192)

The fact that Panzram wrote this letter in 1929 suggests that the current market for serial murder represents the intensification of an interest in murder that is long-standing.[17] Many commentators on serial murder have been tempted to jump from noting serial killers' recognition of themselves as celebrities to arguing that the desire for fame serves as a spur to would-be serial killers. In particular, critics of the intense media coverage of serial murder have pointed out that the certainty of media attention sends a dangerous message to potential killers. Park Dietz, forensic psychiatrist and consultant to the FBI's Behavioral Science Unit, has argued that "the media help disseminate the message that it's good to be a serial killer . . . There are rewards to such violent behavior—loyal fans, marriage proposals, splashy headlines" (quoted in Davids 150). In a similar vein, Joel Black claims that potential serial killers can be motivated by a desire for celebrity, pointing out that their capture and subsequent trial give serial killers many opportunities to promote their renown (141–42).

While it is impossible to prove the causal connection that critics such as Dietz and Black argue for, the behavior of some serial killers is suggestive in this regard. The communications of David Berkowitz (aka "Son of Sam") with the *New York Post* during his yearlong murder spree in 1976–77 played a pivotal role both in Berkowitz's evolving self-definition and in his decision to keep killing.[18] Similarly, Ted Bundy's decision to conduct his own defense during his capital murder trial in Florida, even though it probably intensified the jury's negative feelings about him, enabled him to assume the starring role in a narrative of his own making.[19] Perhaps the most thought-provoking example of a serial killer's awareness of and desire for fame came in the midst of a series of murders committed in and around Wichita, Kansas, in the mid-1970s, when the killer, who called himself the "BTK Strangler," wrote to a local newspaper complaining about the lack of attention his exploits had received: "How many times do I have to kill before I get a name in the paper or some national attention?" (quoted in Braudy 3). Despite the suggestiveness of these examples, whether or not would-be serial killers are motivated by a desire for fame is ultimately undecidable; for this reason, I prefer to concentrate on an equally important question about which it may be possible to come to some more definite conclusions: why are so many Americans willing to support the culture industry that has grown up around the celebrity serial killer?

The Market for Death

In order to understand why there is such a vibrant market in contemporary America for representations of death in general and of serial murder in particular, we have to appreciate that the famous serial killer effectively and economically satisfies a double need, both halves of which have grown over the course of the twentieth century: the need for representations of death, and the need for celebrities. Where do these needs come from? We have already seen how the expansion of media technologies that began in the nineteenth century contributed to the scale, variety, and speed of dissemination of types of fame. According to Vicki Goldberg, these expanded media technologies also coincided with an increased need for representations of death as the reality of death receded from everyday American life. As the average American became less and less likely to be confronted with the brute reality of death in the form of dead bodies thanks to improvements in public health and the increasing sophistication of the funeral industry, Goldberg argues, there was a related increase in representations of death, an increase largely enabled by the development of new media technologies and fueled by people's desire to find other ways to manage their continuing anxieties about death now that death had been removed from the public sphere.[20]

Representations of death, especially aesthetic representations, are able to assuage such anxieties because "they occur in a realm clearly delineated as not life, or not real, even as they refer to the basic fact of life we know but choose not to acknowledge too overtly. They delight because we are confronted with death, yet it is the death of the other. We experience death by proxy. In the aesthetic enactment, we have a situation impossible in life, namely that we die with another and return to the living. Even as we are forced to acknowledge the ubiquitous presence of death in life, our belief in our own immortality is confirmed" (Bronfen, *Over* x). As paradoxical as it may seem, exposing ourselves to representations of death, even violent death, helps alleviate our anxiety about being claimed by such violent death. Consuming images of serial murder in carefully controlled settings (one can put down a book, turn off the television, or hide behind one's hands in a movie theater) might provide an effective way of managing anxieties about death. Whether or not this is so, the question remains: what does this have to do with a desire for celebrities? How is the need for representations of death and violence related to the need for celebrities?

Both celebrities and representations of death are potent means of resolving a variety of anxieties, ranging from a fear of death to concerns about what constitutes acceptable social behavior and worries about the decline of individuality in modern society. Jib Fowles has argued that the market for celebrities in general, and film stars in particular, arose as a result of the dislocating impact of urbanization on the American population, a process that began in the nineteenth century but reached a critical point in the early years of the twentieth century, just when the film industry had developed to the point where it was able to satisfy the public need for stars. Fowles argues that the move to the cities posed the question of public and private identity in a way that did not arise when people were part of long-established rural communities (Theodore Dreiser's Sister Carrie could be seen as an emblematic figure here). Faced by an unfamiliar and estranging urban environment, the new generation of city dwellers eagerly looked around for models of personality and found them, according to Fowles, on the screen: "Stars seemed to exude the perfected, confident behavior that unanchored city dwellers coveted . . . Performers offered various models of the well-integrated self, at a time of excruciating need, and when other well-wrought exemplars were not forthcoming. In a most revealing word choice, celebrated actors came to be called 'personalities'" (27). Even if we accept Fowles's argument that film stars were adopted as models of personality, there is clearly a big difference between asserting that the first generation of Hollywood movie stars resolved anxieties in their audience and arguing that criminals could do the same thing. Wouldn't criminals be more likely to create, rather than resolve, anxieties? The utility of stars, however, was not limited to displaying positive aspects of personality, but extended to exorcising negative emotions. One of the reasons why violence has become such a central part of American entertainment is that "by aggressing onscreen or onstage, stars perform the important psychological service of helping to vent anger" (Fowles 163). Violent stars thus help their audience to express hostile feelings without recrimination or consequence.

This variation on the well-established catharsis argument suggests how representations of death and violence performed by famous stars can serve an important triple function for an audience: managing anxieties about death, providing models of personality, and expressing negative emotions. The spectacle of film stars committing acts of violence also satisfies the double need I mentioned earlier, the need for representations of death and the need for celebrities. Movie stars such as Arnold Schwarzenegger and Sylvester Stallone, so consistent in their screen characters and so omnipotent over death in a large number of films, are a potent means of resolving anxieties about death and the strength of individuality in contemporary culture.

There is no reason to assume that only fictional representations of death and violence resolve anxieties. Although audiences feel less ambivalent about expressing their identification with fictional rather than actual serial killers, representations of real criminals can also serve a cathartic function for their audience, as Paul Kooistra argues in the context of explaining the appeal of the "heroic criminal": "narratives about [heroic criminals] serve a critical psychological function for those who read or write such tales . . . through such stories we may vicariously release rebellious feelings generated by the restrictions imposed by authority" (10).[21] However, as Kooistra acknowledges, this is an incomplete explanation because only certain types of criminals become heroes. Tellingly, Kooistra excludes serial killers from the category of "heroic criminal":

> While we undoubtedly find psychological release by vicariously experiencing the rebellious deeds of the lawbreakers, we choose to undergo this experience with a very limited number of criminals. We do not imagine ourselves dining with Albert Fish on the bodies of children he molested and then cooked; nor do we admire the handiwork of Edward Gein, who fashioned lampshades from the skin and soupbowls from the skulls of the women he killed . . . Certainly these criminals are fascinating, but we do not make heroes of them. (21)

Clearly, serial killers are not celebrated in the same way as heroic criminals such as Jesse James and Bonnie and Clyde because they lack the empathic dimensions of these Robin Hood–type outlaws. Consequently it is inadequate to assert that they resolve anxieties and act as models of personality in exactly the same way as "fictional" and "real" representations of other criminals. Yet stating these facts does not help us to determine why the serial killer has become such a dominant figure in American popular culture. What exactly is the appeal of the serial killer?

Producing and Consuming Mass Idols

In 1944, sociologist Leo Lowenthal published an essay entitled "Biographies in Popular Magazines," an essay he later reprinted as a chapter in his 1961 book, *Literature, Popular Culture, and Society*, under a new title: "The Triumph of Mass Idols." Lowenthal argued that biographies in popular magazines had undergone a striking change between 1901 and 1941, a change that Lowenthal believed signaled the emergence of a new social type. According to Lowenthal, the earlier biographies indicated that American society's heroes at that time were "idols of production" in that "they stem from the productive life, from industry, business, and natural sciences. There is not a single hero from the world of sports and the few artists and entertainers either do not belong to the sphere of cheap or mass entertainment or represent a serious attitude toward their art as in the case of [Charlie] Chaplin" (112–13). Sampling biographies in magazines from 1941, however, Lowenthal reached a very different conclusion: "We called the heroes of the past 'idols of production': we feel entitled to call the present-day magazine heroes 'idols of consumption'" (115). Unlike the businessmen, industrialists, and scientists who dominated the earlier sample, almost every one of 1941's heroes "is directly, or indirectly, related to the sphere of leisure time: either he does not belong to vocations which serve society's basic needs (e.g., the worlds of entertainment and sport), or he amounts, more or less, to a caricature of a socially productive agent" (115).

Although Lowenthal did not describe the change in these terms, with hindsight we can see that he identified what I described earlier as the shift from fame to celebrity, from merit to visibility, the emergence of a new kind of "well-knownness" personified by the film star. The "dream machine" that was Hollywood at the height of the studio system was organized around both "idols of consumption" and the act of consumption. As Samantha Barbas has argued, the film industry sold consumption to fans as a form of participation in the lives of their screen idols and in the world of the movies: "Capitalizing on fans' interest in stars, the film industry, with the help of publishers and advertisers, sold fans a variety of consumer products ... rather than become personally involved in the movies, fans might vicariously participate by purchasing the cosmetics and clothing endorsed by the stars" (5). Two emblematic aspects of modernity, consumer culture and celebrity culture, thus developed alongside each other and were connected most intimately in the persons of the movie stars themselves. For not only were the stars the objects of consumption, they were also consumers themselves, consumers par excellence. The stars' extravagant lifestyles, covered in exhaustive and loving detail by the mass media, took the phenomenon of "conspicuous consumption" identified by

Thorstein Veblen in 1899 to a new level, making them "idols of consumption" in both an active and a passive sense.

Lowenthal leaves his reader in no doubt that he sees the change from "idols of production" to "idols of consumption" as a serious decline: "If a student in some very distant future should use popular magazines of 1941 as a source of information as to what figures the American public looked to in the first stages of the greatest crisis since the birth of the Union, he would come to a grotesque result. While the industrial and professional endeavors are geared to a maximum of speed and efficiency, the idols of the masses are not, as they were in the past, the leading names in the battle of production, but the headliners of the movies, the ball parks, and the night clubs" (116). With Lowenthal in mind, one is tempted to describe the advent of celebrity serial killers as a further decline in the condition of American culture's "mass idols," but in order to decide whether or not that is the case we must clarify the serial killer's relationship to consumption.

Returning briefly to the murderabilia industry reminds us that celebrity culture and consumer culture intermingle just as complexly with serial killers as they do with film stars. Throughout the edition of the *John Walsh Show* that attacked the phenomenon of murderabilia, the show's eponymous host showed clips of *Collectors*, a recent documentary about the industry. *Collectors* is distributed by a small company named, appropriately enough, Abject Films, and on their Web site the film's director, Julian P. Hobbs, discusses some of the multiple connections between serial killing and consumerism. Hobbs points out that the serial killer is connected with consumerism in the most basic sense in that he has become a commodity, "a merchandising phenomenon that rivals Mickey Mouse. From movies to television, books to on-line, serial killers are packaged and consumed en-masse" (Abject Films). But as Hobbs goes on to argue, serial killers themselves can be seen as consumers, which implicates any representations of them in the same consumerist logic: "Serial killers come into being by fetishizing and collecting artifacts—usually body parts—in turn, the dedicated collector gathers scraps connected with the actual events and so, too, a documentary a collection of images" (Abject Films). Hobbs implies that no one (not even Hobbs himself) can avoid being involved with consumerism in relation to serial murder, even if one's reasons for getting involved are high-minded.[22]

In spite of the many reasons for the vigorous market in contemporary American culture for representations of death and violence I discussed earlier, consumerism alone is not enough to explain the appeal of the serial killer. Indeed, as Barbie Zelizer has argued in the context of discussing television journalistic celebrity, the "extension of celebrity status to different kinds of public actors" in recent years, an extension that has grown exponentially since Lowenthal's time, has invalidated some aspects of his argument (75). In particular, Zelizer claims, today it is "questionable whether the 'either-or' character of his argument remains as tenable today as it originally appeared to be" (75). In other words, despite the many ways in which the existence of celebrity serial killers is related to consumerism, it is unclear whether serial killers can be described as "idols of consumption" in Lowenthal's sense. In particular, what such a designation hides is the uncomfortable fact that many people do not particulate in serial killer celebrity culture solely in order to assuage their anxieties about victimization and death. The existence of famous serial killers also depends upon the fact that some people are fascinated with them, even admire them. No examination of the fame of serial killers could be complete without analyzing the reasons behind these more "affirmative" reactions to serial killers. In short, we need to consider why famous serial killers are often regarded as "idols of destruction."

Idols of Destruction

In the midst of the Washington, D.C., sniper shootings in October 2002, Twentieth Century Fox thought it wise to delay the release of their new movie, *Phone Booth*, which tells the story of a pedestrian who answers a public telephone in Times Square only to be told by the sniper on the other end of the line that he will be shot dead if he hangs up. A few days after Jeffrey Dahmer was arrested in Milwaukee in 1991, Paramount Pictures decided to pull all ads for their movie, *Body Parts*. Even though the studio denied that the movie's story bore any resemblance to Dahmer's crimes, they did acknowledge that the body parts littering the posters advertising the film were, under the circumstances, inappropriate. In 1978, an unknown perpetrator (who would later turn out to be Ted Bundy) killed two female students and attacked several others in their sorority house at Florida State University. The local affiliate of NBC had been planning to broadcast a TV movie, *A Stranger in the House*, a few days after the murders. The movie, a thriller about a psychopathic killer of sorority sisters, was quietly withdrawn from the schedule. Jane Caputi has referred to such moments as "slip[s] of the societal tongue . . . moment[s] of brief but unintended clarity" where we get a glimpse of how the "acceptable" ways in which American culture expresses its fascination with murder might be implicated with unacceptable actual incidents of murder (*Age* 51).

Sometimes we get more than a glimpse of America's fascination with murder; indeed, sometimes that fascination is presented as a full-blown media spectacle. At the 1992 Academy Awards, *The Silence of the Lambs* achieved something only previously accomplished by *It Happened One Night* in 1934 and *One Flew Over the Cuckoo's Nest* in 1975; it won Oscars in all five major categories: best adapted screenplay, best director, best actor, best actress, and best film. In a graphic demonstration of the film's popularity, the entire evening, beginning with the entrance of host Billy Crystal, straitjacketed and wheeled out on a hand truck to resemble the film's hero, Hannibal Lecter, was a celebration of *Silence* that confirmed its status as a modern American cultural icon. Much of the celebration focused on Anthony Hopkins's portrayal of Lecter. David Skal describes how Hopkins was "treated during the ceremony almost as a guest of honor, with an endless stream of flesh-eating jokes thrown in his direction throughout the evening" (382). Since 1992, the cult around Hannibal Lecter has continued to grow with the appearance of Thomas Harris's sequel, *Hannibal*, Ridley Scott's film adaptation of *Hannibal*, and Brett Ratner's prequel/remake of *Red Dragon*. So identified has Anthony Hopkins become with the role of Hannibal Lecter that the fulsome praise that has greeted Hopkins's performances in the role can reasonably be taken as relatively unguarded expressions of fascination with and admiration of Lecter himself, who was recently voted the top movie villain of all time in an Internet poll.

In an abstract sense, it seems both offensive and ludicrous to claim that American culture is not only repelled but also fascinated by serial killers. One does not have to look very far, however, to find ample confirmation of the claim. One should not, of course, minimize the differences between admiring the fictional character of Hannibal Lecter and admiring a "real" serial killer, but the difference is one of degree rather than kind. Characters such as Lecter allow for the free expression of feelings of fascination and admiration concerning serial killers that are more carefully concealed in other instances. And yet even this rule has exceptions. As Elliott Leyton has argued, "No one ever became famous by beating his wife to death in an alley; but virtually all our multiple murderers achieve true and lasting fame . . . During their trials, they will almost certainly be surrounded by admiring women who impress their affections upon the killer, radiating towards him little but admiration and love" (21–22). Even during the crimes themselves, some serial killers have felt and been influenced by the public's fascinated interest in them. After his arrest, David Berkowitz, the "Son of Sam," commented that "I finally had convinced myself that it was good to do it, necessary to do it, and that the public wanted me to do it. The latter part I believe until this day. I believe that many were rooting for me. This was the point at which the papers began to pick up vibes and information that something big was happening out in the streets. Real big!" (quoted in Leyton 206–7). It would be easy to dismiss such remarks as the product of a diseased mind, but as Leyton says, "Son of

Sam was not so very wrong when he thought the public was urging him on during his killing spree, for the media chronicled his every deed in a state of mounting excitement" (21–22).

Is it possible that serial killers are idols of destruction? Are some people attracted to their destructiveness? Perhaps so, but in a very specific way. In his essay "Critique of Violence," Walter Benjamin argues that the violent destructiveness of criminals inheres not necessarily (or not exclusively) in the deeds they commit but in what their deeds imply about an attack on the very principle of law itself. To support this claim, Benjamin emphasizes "how often the figure of the 'great' criminal, however repellent his ends may have been, has aroused the secret admiration of the public. This cannot result from his deed, but only from the violence to which it bears witness" (281). Benjamin then goes on to clarify his point by arguing that "in the great criminal this violence confronts the law with the threat of declaring a new law, a threat that even today, despite its impotence, in important instances horrifies the public as it did in primeval times" (283). The criminal's rejection of the law is horrifying but also exhilarating, hence the "shudder of admiration" mentioned by Jacques Derrida in the epigraph to this introduction, an admiration Derrida links explicitly to the criminal's claiming a "primeval" status as "lawmaker or prophet" ("Force" 40). The serial killer both outrages and thrills us by his seeming ability to stand outside the law, to make his own law, in a gesture whose ambivalent destructiveness and creativity mirror our ambivalent response to the killer, composed of both fear and attraction.

These are uncomfortable feelings to acknowledge, to be sure, but what could be more quintessentially American than a complex and ambivalent reaction to a violent criminal? As Stathis Gourgouris has pointed out, "If American society is paradigmatically founded on the primacy of law [the Bill of Rights], it is also *co-incidentally* founded on the phantasmatic allure of the outlaw—the Wild West, the frontier, and so on: the errant loner who forges his own rights, in some improvisational fashion, as he goes along" (135, original emphasis). Some may object to associating *Gunfight at the O.K. Corral* with *Henry: Portrait of a Serial Killer*, but any reader of Cormac MacCarthy's classic novel *Blood Meridian* will know that the realization of "manifest destiny" was, if anything, more violent and bloody than serial murder could ever be. Rather than drawing artificial and untenable distinctions between "legitimate" and "illegitimate" types of violence, I propose that we acknowledge that the serial killer is as quintessentially American a figure as the cowboy, and we should acknowledge this fact not least because the intrinsic Americanness of the serial killer has been a feature of writing about serial murder since at least the time of Jack the Ripper, some sixty years before the category of "serial murder" even came into being. In the words of a 1994 *National Examiner* headline: "Serial Killers Are As American As Apple Pie."

Christopher Sharrett has suggested that "perhaps the fetish status of the criminal psychopath . . . is about recognizing the serial killer/mass murderer not as social rebel or folk hero . . . but as the most genuine representative of American life" (13). Celebrity serial killers provide us with a way of acknowledging the truth of Sharrett's observation in a way that is not too destructive either of our self-image or of our image of America. Our complicated relationship with celebrities, affective as well as intellectual, composed of admiration and resentment, envy and contempt, provides us with a lexicon through which we can manage our appalled and appalling fascination with the serial killer, contemporary American culture's ultimate deviant. *Natural Born Celebrities* tells the story of that fascination.

Natural Born Celebrities

This book is divided into two sections, each locating serial murder in a variety of cultural and historical milieus. The opening section establishes a dual historical context for understanding contemporary American interest in serial murder, the first concentrating on the moment serial murder became defined as a particularly American crime, and the second solidifying the "Americanness" of serial murder in a way that is still extremely influential today. The second section updates the historical context by emphasizing how serial murder has been adopted and adapted by American popular culture in order to both focus and dissipate anxieties about the nature of celebrity, the relation between normality and monstrosity, and the place of violence in sexuality. Together, the two sections establish a narrative of serial murder that is both historically coherent and nuanced.

The first section, "A History of Serial Murder," establishes a genealogy of popular cultural interest in serial murder in a transnational and institutional context. In order to counteract the popular perception of serial murder as individualized pathology, this section emphasizes how serial murder has always been interpreted as a phenomenon with social dimensions that can serve recognizably social ends. In chapter 1, I revisit the Ripper case because it is still the most famous case in the serial killer "canon" and thus provides a logical starting point for anyone examining the fame of serial killers. I concentrate on the theories at the time of the murders that the Ripper was American. Although the British supported this idea eagerly because it allowed them to disavow any connection between violence and Englishness, American commentators proved surprisingly receptive to the possibility of an American Ripper, thus demonstrating two very different visions of the place of violence within what

Benedict Anderson has famously called the "imagined community" of the nation. The arrest of H. H. Holmes, the United States' first high-profile serial killer, in Chicago in 1894 suggested an even closer proximity between Americanness and serial murder. Nevertheless, commentators were still willing to consider the possibility that Holmes was a representative American of the post-frontier era.

My second chapter establishes a much more recent context for the fame of serial killers that is still relevant today. I interpret the FBI's response to the serial killer as the latest example of the Bureau's use of a variety of internal enemies over the course of its history (such as the gangster and the communist) and describe how an FBI somewhat chastened by Hoover-era crimes encouraged public panic about the figure of the serial killer in order to increase its funding and return its influence to former levels. I also explain how the FBI was able to maintain high funding levels and political influence when the American public interest in serial killers temporarily waned and the Bureau's reputation collapsed in the mid- to late 1990s.

In the second section of the book, "Serial Murder in American Popular Culture," I describe how serial murder, largely because of its synergistic relationship with the FBI, became a full-scale popular cultural phenomenon in the 1980s and 1990s. Chapter 3 examines how popular culture can trade on the fame of the serial killer only as long as it does not examine the reasons for that fame too closely. Although films such as *Seven*, *Copycat*, and *Natural Born Killers* self-consciously thematize celebrity serial killers, they do so in a way that allows their audience to disavow their own participation in making serial killers famous. My fourth chapter extends my analysis to the form of popular culture in which the influence of the FBI is still most visible. *Twin Peaks*, *The X-Files*, *Profiler*, and *Millennium* all feature FBI employee protagonists who are in the front line of battling serial killers. The tendency of these shows to conflate serial killers with demons and/or aliens, I argue, allows them both to emphasize the heroism of the FBI and to comfort their audiences with the thought that serial killers, despite what their mundane appearance suggests, are not of this world.

The final two chapters provide a detailed analysis of true-crime narratives, one of the most durable and successful examples of serial killer popular culture. In chapter 5 I argue that the otherworldliness of serial killers in television crime drama takes the form of a tension between normality and monstrosity in true-crime narratives. This tension is a structuring feature of such narratives and can be seen most clearly in the debates about whether the murderer is best understood as a representative member of the community or as a decidedly asocial, even monstrous, outsider. I demonstrate that although Puritan crime narratives attempted to treat killers as community members who needed to be reintegrated into the community, as the genre developed, the tendency to abject murderers and cast them out of the social became more and more pronounced.

My final chapter argues that true crime's tendency to define murderers as monsters explains the prominence of serial killers in contemporary true crime. Unlike any other study of the genre, however, this book emphasizes the extent to which monstrosity in true crime is often figured in sexual terms. In particular, through a discussion of Ted Bundy, Jeffrey Dahmer, and Aileen Wuornos, I show how true crime attempts to "exonerate" heterosexuality by emphasizing that Bundy is an anomalous straight man, not a representative one, while Dahmer and Wuornos tell us everything we (the implicitly straight reader of true crime) need to know about homosexuality and lesbianism.

Natural Born Celebrities analyzes the varieties of cultural work that serial murder performs, and this focus continues in the epilogue, which addresses how the figure of the terrorist has been conflated with the serial killer. In the aftermath of September 11, one might have expected the American obsession with serial murder to decline and to be replaced by a much more understandable preoccupation with the figure of the terrorist. In practice, however, the two categories are often used simultaneously, with Saddam Hussein, for example, being described as both a terrorist and a serial killer by the American popular press. Similarly, during the Washington, D.C., sniper shootings of October 2002, opinion was divided about whether terrorists or serial killers were responsible for the crimes; in the absence of facts, both possibilities were regarded as equally valid. But conflation with terrorism is not the sole fate of serial murder in post-9/11 America, for the flow of popular culture about serial killers unadulterated by any association with terrorism continues unabated. Moreover, the American public's relief was almost palpable when the D.C. snipers were finally arrested and turned out to be not terrorists but good old-fashioned serial killers. I conclude my study by arguing that the celebrity serial killer will continue to be a durable and highly visible presence in American popular culture because, paradoxically, thanks to the figure's long-standing presence on the American scene, the serial killer has a familiar and even comforting quality compared with the radical "otherness" of the terrorist.

PART ONE

A History of
Serial Murder

CHAPTER ONE

The Victorian Killer as Media Star:
Jack the Ripper and H. H. Holmes

From Hell and Back

On October 18, 2001, the film *From Hell* premiered in Los Angeles. Attending the glamorous event were its American stars, Johnny Depp and Heather Graham, the "shock rocker" Marilyn Manson, who wrote the music for the film, and its directors, Albert and Allen Hughes, the twenty-nine-year-old African American twin brothers previously responsible for the violent urban movies *Menace II Society* and *Dead Presidents*. Despite mixed reviews, the film had a good opening weekend, taking in $11.6 million and beating out Denzel Washington's *Training Day* for the coveted position of number-one film in the country. Bruce Snyder, president of distribution for Twentieth Century Fox, commented that "it is well positioned to capture moviegoers looking for Halloween thrills in the coming weeks," adding that the film "looked hip" and pointing out that 53 percent of the weekend's audience were aged under twenty-five ("Depp takes").

From Hell, featuring the work of some of the hottest people in the American film and music industries and attracting millions of the most sought-after demographic group in entertainment, centers on the British Victorian serial killer known as "Jack the Ripper." Based on the famous graphic novel by Alan Moore and Eddie Campbell of the same name, *From Hell* features Johnny Depp as Inspector Abberline, the man in charge of the investigation into the Ripper murders. Heather Graham plays prostitute Mary Kelly, the last of the

Ripper's five victims. One of the most controversial aspects of the film had been the choice of director. The Hughes brothers, best known for their gritty portrayals of contemporary African American urban life, were not the obvious choice to make a film about a British Victorian serial killer. The problem, it seemed, was not that the Hughes brothers were American but that they were black. Their blackness apparently disqualified them from having anything relevant to say about the putatively white space of late-nineteenth-century Britain. According to Albert Hughes, however, he and his brother were perfect for the job because "this is a ghetto story. It concerns poverty, violence and corruption, which are themes we deal with in our movies" (I. Sinclair).

It comes as no surprise that it was the Hughes brothers' blackness, rather than their Americanness, that was considered problematic because there is a long tradition, beginning during the murders themselves, of associating Americans with Jack the Ripper, in the form of both speculation that the Ripper himself might be American and contemporaneous American fascination with the case. Although most of the theories about an American Ripper were British in origin, few commentators in the United States rejected such theories outright. Indeed, many took a perverse pride in the idea that Jack the Ripper might be an American, perhaps feeling that the United States should lead the world in all things, including crime. *From Hell* is just the latest example of an American interest in Jack the Ripper that has proved to be just as intense and enduring as the British interest. Although the Hughes brothers used Martin Childs, the British Oscar-winning production designer for *Shakespeare in Love*, to recreate an authentic Victorian London, in every other respect *From Hell* is an American production.[1] Although the directors considered casting British actors Daniel Day-Lewis, Jude Law, and Sean Connery as Abberline, they eventually chose Depp partly because, according to Allen Hughes, "he has, like, 70 books on Jack the Ripper" (Salisbury).[2]

From Hell, however, differs in one important way from earlier examples of American engagement with Jack the Ripper. Whereas nineteenth-century Americans were often willing to consider the possibility that the Ripper might be American, *From Hell*, like the vast majority of recent Ripper-related popular culture, firmly locates the Ripper as British. Perhaps because Americanness and serial murder are now widely viewed as synonymous, twenty-first-century Americans are apparently much less willing to claim Jack the Ripper as one of their own than were their nineteenth-century counterparts.[3] By examining the nineteenth-century popular cultural response to the Ripper murders in both Britain and the United States, as well as the American reaction to the case of H. H. Holmes, the first high-profile American serial killer, in Chicago in the 1890s, I will emphasize the overdetermined connections between murder and national identity. In particular, I want to highlight the extent to which contemporaneous speculation about the Ripper's identity concentrated just as much on nationality, race, and ethnicity as it did on particular social groups (such as doctors or butchers) and on individual suspects.

Thanks in part to this emphasis on nationality, American commentators could not avoid discussing the delicate subject of H. H. Holmes's American-ness, a discussion that in turn necessitated an uncomfortable consideration of the relationship between violence and American identity. By reconstruct-ing these debates, I will demonstrate how the contemporaneous response to Jack the Ripper and H. H. Holmes, a response torn between ejecting these figures from the public sphere altogether and turning them into forms of lurid entertainment, inaugurates the ongoing debate about whether famous serial killers are the consummate insiders or outsiders of American culture.

Fear, Enjoyment, and the Ripper Industry

There is no denying the fact that a large part of the British public's reac-tion to the Whitechapel murders was abject fear and panic. Newspaper reports of the murders are filled with descriptions of anxious crowds at each of the murder scenes. After the murder of Annie Chapman, the Ripper's second victim, on September 8, 1888, *Reynolds Newspaper* reported that "the streets were . . . swarmed with people, who stood about in groups and excitedly dis-cussed the details of the murder . . . Great anxiety is felt for the future. While the murderer is at large, they cannot feel safe" (quoted in Paley 72–73). Part of the reason the public reacted so strongly to the murders is that they were so unusual. Although the East End of London in general, and Whitechapel in particular, had a well-deserved reputation for violence, murder was quite a rare event. In fact, out of the sixty-eight murders committed in London in 1886, and of the eighty committed in 1887, not a single one was committed in Whitechapel (Paley 70, 71).[4] Part of the reason, therefore, that the press and the public resorted to the language of gothic melodrama in describing the Ripper as a "fiend" and a "monster" is that they had very few other cases to compare with the Whitechapel murders.

And yet, alongside the frequent reports of fearful crowds can be found other reports of how people quickly capitalized upon the murders and found those same crowds eager to consume the murders as a media event. One of the most egregious attempts to cash in on the Ripper is described by Samuel Hud-son in a pamphlet entitled *"Leather Apron"; or, The Horrors of Whitechapel, London, 1888* published in Philadelphia in 1888. Hudson acknowledges that the "public uproar occasioned by these monstrous crimes naturally was widespread and intense" and gives the following example of how some profited from the uproar: "At 29 Harbury Street people were charged a penny to enter the yard in which the Chapman woman was murdered" (14). Business, apparently, was brisk. Charging people to view murder scenes was just one of the entrepreneurial possibilities opened up by Jack the Ripper. The crowds of sightseers who thronged Whitechapel were eagerly fed by local costermongers. A pavement artist thrilled onlookers with graphic representations of the murders, while a local woman did a lively trade selling swordsticks to members of the crowd.

The Ripper even inspired entertainments in other parts of England. At the hiring fairs in the Midlands in October 1888, "a penny at one bought three shies at a door with the object of bringing out Jack the Ripper or 'one of them from Whitechapel'" (Sugden 281). L. Perry Curtis has observed of the Victorians that "however upset they might be by the actual event [of murder], readers seemed to relish both the gruesome details of the crime and 'the moment of truth' when the jury returned the verdict of guilty and the judge imposed the familiar sentence of death by hanging" (83). In the Ripper case, the public was denied the catharsis represented by the trial and sentence, and so they had all the more reason to seek that catharsis by turning to popular culture.

Apart from the examples already mentioned, proprietors of waxwork museums were quick to see the possibilities offered by the Ripper murders. Some contented themselves with adding a few daubs of red paint to existing exhibits and offering the result as a tableau of the Ripper's victims, but others went to much greater lengths, as described by Montagu Williams, a local magistrate at the time of the murders:

> In the body of the room was a waxwork exhibition, and some of its features were revolting in the extreme. The first of the Whitechapel murders were fresh in the memory of the public, and the proprietor of the exhibition was turning the circumstance to some commercial account. There lay a horrible presentment in wax of Matilda Turner, the first victim, as well as one of Mary Ann Nichols, whose body was found in Buck's Row. The heads were represented as being nearly severed from the bodies, and in each case there were shown, in red paint, three terrible gashes reaching from the abdomen to the ribs. (6)

Williams describes how the building that housed the waxworks museum had gone through a number of incarnations in recent years (including, ironically, being used as a funeral parlor) but none of the businesses that had used the premises had enjoyed as much success as this "East End showman." The success of this establishment was duplicated by that of several similar entertainments in the area, Williams explains, and he regarded them as a sufficiently serious social problem that he led a successful campaign to have them closed down. He summarizes the testimony of a local trader concerned about the morally corrupting influence of these establishments on young men and women: "He said it was terrible to hear the jesting remarks that fell from the lips of young girls concerning the murders and other horrors that were illustrated inside and outside the shows" (10).

The presence of women at these shows suggests that they may have used these exhibits to distance themselves from the Ripper's victims, making themselves feel a little less vulnerable by underlining the fact that the Ripper killed other ("fallen") women and not them. These examples of the popular cultural appropriation of murder did not begin with the Ripper case, as Williams's description of another one of these shows illustrates:

> The Whitechapel murders were favorite subjects for representation; and while several showmen merely dabbled in these crimes, so to speak, one enterprising member of the fraternity dealt exhaustively with the whole series by means of illuminated coloured views, which his patrons inspected through peep-holes. Jack Sheppard, Charles Peace, and a host of other similar celebrities lived again on the canvas screens, and there repeated, before an audience of awe-stricken and admiring East End youths, some of the more daring acts of their graceless lives. (8–9)

These shows, popularly known as "penny gaffs," drew on a celebrity culture based on criminals that was clearly well established before the Whitechapel murders began. John Springhall has traced the origins of penny gaff theaters back to the early years of the nineteenth century, when they arose to satisfy a working-class desire for theater in the newly expanded towns and cities. From the beginning, well-known crimes provided theater owners with the opportunity for full houses and full wallets: "the famous 'Edgware murder' of 1836 whereby Hannah Brown, who took in washing, was killed then dismembered by her intended husband, James Greenacre, a much-married bankrupt, proved quite a windfall when dramatized for London gaffs and played to capacity houses for at least 10 months after the crime had taken place" (23).[5] Like the swiftness of the theatrical response to the murder of Hannah Brown, the speed with which the Whitechapel murders were turned into forms of visual entertainment is testament to the rich history of popular culture's use of crime for pecuniary benefit. The Whitechapel murders may have taken such opportunities to new heights, but they did not start them.

Unlike most other murder cases, which have a relatively short shelf life, that of Jack the Ripper continues to be a major presence in both British and American popular culture nearly 120 years after the murders, and it shows no signs of waning (see Colville and Lucanio). In particular, the Ripper plays a bigger role in London's tourist industry today than ever before. Not only can one go on walking tours and buy maps of "Jack's London," but one can also visit various Jack the Ripper exhibits, including (and here the connection with late-Victorian entertainments is particularly evident) Madame Tussaud's famous Waxworks Museum.[6] In 1980, Madame Tussaud's redesigned their Chamber of Horrors exhibit around the theme of the Ripper murders. Although the Ripper himself is not represented, there are several bloody recreations of his mutilated victims, and the exhibit as a whole is now arranged to resemble a "typical" late-Victorian East End street; dirty, fog shrouded, gloomy, and mysterious. Madame Tussaud's had resisted including the Ripper in the Chamber of Horrors for so long because of their policy of never inventing faces, which of course they would have had to do in the Ripper's case. Eventually, according to Judith Walkowitz, Madame Tussaud's was virtually forced into changing their mind: "By 1980 . . . Madame Tussaud's faced a dilemma: visitors (particularly children) were complaining that the Chamber of Horrors was not 'horrible' enough. 'People were just not finding it bloody enough.' By installing the 'Ripper street,' Madame Tussaud 'bowed' to demands for 'more gore'" (2). As Deborah Cameron has pointed out, the consequence of the Ripper's seamless integration into England's tourist culture is that "Jack the Ripper has been thoroughly sanitised, turned into a folk hero like Robin Hood. His story is packaged as a bit of harmless fun: only a spoilsport would be tactless enough to point out that it is a story of misogyny and sadism" ("That's Entertainment" 17). Bearing Cameron's point in mind, it would be easy but misleading to dismiss those who offer and those who consume popular cultural representations of the Ripper murders, whether now or in the Victorian era, as tasteless ghouls, bent upon ignoring "the actual significance of what Jack the Ripper did, and what sexual killers still do a hundred years later" (Cameron, "That's Entertainment" 17). While it is undoubtedly true that the version of the Ripper murders propagated by popular culture usually ignores, or makes light of, the possibility that the Ripper may have been motivated by misogyny, we cannot dismiss out of hand the waxwork museums, the walking tours, the films, the books, and the plethora of other objects inspired by the Ripper. Instead, we must confront the meaning of the Ripper's fame and ask why he has been such an object of fascination for so many and for so long.

At the time of the murders themselves, public fascination with the Ripper went far beyond viewing the murder scenes or attending a penny gaff performance. During the murders, and for many months after the murders had ceased, the police and press were inundated with thousands of letters claiming to be from Jack the Ripper, letters that gloated about previous crimes and predicted further crimes to come.[7] A significant portion of these letters announced that the Ripper had moved to another location, as in this letter received by the editor of the *Belfast Evening Telegraph*: "Dear Boss—I have arrived in your city, as London is too warm for me just now; so that Belfast had better look out . . . I have spotted some nice fat ones, that will work up well. I am longing to begin, for I love my work. Yours, JACK THE RIPPER" (quoted in Hudson 19). Although historians usually assume that all such letters were written by men, there is evidence that women also claimed to be Jack the Ripper: "At least one woman emulated the copycat activities of men and gained some notoriety from the case: at Bradford Police Court on 10 October 1888, a 'respectable young woman, named Maria Coroner, aged twenty-one, was charged with having certain letters tending to cause a breach of the peace; they were signed "Jack the Ripper"'" (Walkowitz 224). What motivated Maria Coroner and thousands of other letter writers to declare themselves publicly to be Jack the Ripper? Clearly, there was something about the Ripper (and the type of murderer he quickly came to represent) that appealed to thousands of otherwise ordinary people. One of the preconditions for that fascination is the fact that the Ripper was never identified. If Jack the Ripper had ever been apprehended and convicted, it is extremely doubtful that the case would have become as influential as it has.[8] The mystery of the Ripper's identity is the sine qua non of the Ripper industry, now as then, and as contemporaneous speculation about the Ripper's identity constituted a major part of that industry, it is to that subject that I now turn.

The Unbelievable Violence of Englishness

Most academic and pseudo-academic speculation about the Ripper's identity has focused either on types of suspects (a doctor, a midwife, a Jewish ritual butcher) or on individual suspects (Montague Druitt, Prince Albert, Aaron Kosminski, George Chapman). At the time of the murders themselves, although some speculation did focus on possible types of suspect (the doctor theory and the assertion that the murderer was a member of the West End upper-class slumming in the East End were two particularly popular theories), many theories about the Ripper's identity followed national, ethnic, or racial lines. Although it is now common to think of crime in national terms, with the United States figuring as the most crime-ridden country in the world, this was not always so. For example, in *Masters of Crime: Studies of Multiple Murders*, published in 1928, Guy B. H. Logan argues that murder has no nationality: "It is a mistake to suppose that every nation has its own particular type of murderer, that certain brands of crime are confined to certain races, that alien assassins are any worse or any better than our own. There are no national boundaries to crime. Humanity is inspired by the same motives the world over,

and in the depths of depravity to which, at its worst, it can sink, no country can cry shame upon another" (11). Ironically, given how assiduously the
British attempted to place the Whitechapel murders outside the boundaries
of Britishness, Logan refers to the Ripper murders as proof of his argument:
"The monster-murderer whose deeds we shudder at has had his parallel in
other climes . . . The truth of this was made manifest at the time of the 'Ripper' murders in London forty years ago. It then transpired that similar crimes,
inspired by the same blood-lust, perpetrated in circumstances almost identical, had taken place in Russia, in the United States, and in one of the South
American republics" (11–12). Commentators knew about these other crimes
at the time of the Ripper murders, but rather than taking them as evidence
that such murders can happen anywhere, instead they concluded from them
that Jack the Ripper must be a foreigner and had come to England to continue
his dreadful work. Contrary to Logan's argument that the serial killer is a cosmopolitan subject, the British media were obsessed with (re)nationalizing
the Ripper as distinctly non-English by figuring him as foreign and/or
American. In this way, they attempted to maintain a particular image of what
Benedict Anderson would term the "imagined community" of Great Britain
by picturing Jack the Ripper as a type of alien invasion.

When the Victorian press and public were faced with the Ripper murders
in 1888, they had multiple choices of whom to hold responsible for the crimes.
The choices they made were motivated by a largely unexamined assumption,
namely, that no Englishman could possibly have committed such vicious murders. When an attempt was made to justify the assumption of the necessary
foreignness of the Ripper, however, the evidence offered was tenuous, to say the
least. One letter writer to the London *Times* argued that there was no record of
an Englishman's ever having committed a series of such gruesome murders
and that therefore there was every reason to believe that an Englishman could
not have committed the Ripper murders. On a more amusing note, the same
writer went on to argue that "the celerity with which the crimes were committed [was] inconsistent with the ordinary English phlegmatic nature" (quoted
in Paley 147). In other words, the murders were committed with such speed,
daring, and energy that the perpetrator could not possibly be British.

Regardless of the weakness of the evidence, the assumption that the Ripper
could not be British was widespread, not only because of a deep-seated belief
in the essential decency of the Englishman, but also because of the conviction that criminality and foreignness were intimately related to each other.
For example, in *The Whitechapel Murders, or the Mysteries of the East End*, a
pamphlet published by the London firm of G. Purkess in the midst of the

murders and consisting of a strange combination of reproduced inquest testimony and fictional detective story, the anonymous author claims: "Brutality in the shape of bloodthirsty hacking was an aggravation for which English society, with all its sins on its head, declines to be responsible. When stories appear in the newspapers of atrocities on dead bodies we can generally boast that they are committed in a different latitude, and belong to a lower civilisation than ours. Such reflections as these naturally caused people at once to set down these atrocities to the credit of some ill-bred and ill-nourished foreigner" (4). Ronald Thomas has explored the grounds for this association of criminality and foreignness in late-Victorian England by analyzing Sir Arthur Conan Doyle's *Adventures* and *Memoirs of Sherlock Holmes* (1891–93), Havelock Ellis's landmark work of criminal anthropology *The Criminal* (1890), and Sir Francis Galton's *Finger-Prints* (1892). Thomas argues that not only are all three of these sources concerned with how to detect and arrest criminality but in all three cases "criminality is often associated with, and even defined by, the identifiable foreignness of the suspect's body. Criminal deviance became increasingly understood as an issue of national security, and, at the same time, criminal identity became inextricably linked with physiology and nationality" (659).[9] This developing relationship between criminality and foreignness was also energized by the long-established habit of describing murderers in gothic terms as fiends and monsters. Judith Halberstam has argued that the gothic monster is "the antithesis of Englishness" (*Skin* 14). Consequently, Halberstam goes on to argue, the "racism that becomes a mark of nineteenth-century Gothic arises out of the attempt . . . to give form to what terrifies the national community. Gothic monsters are defined both as other than the imagined community and as the being that cannot be imagined as community" (*Skin* 18). The xenophobia intrinsic to gothicized depictions of foreignness and criminality can be seen vividly in contemporary theories about the identity of the Ripper, with suspects being characterized as "other" than English, a difference marked on their bodies and by their nationality.[10]

For example, in the letters column of the *Times* of October 4, 1888, a writer who called himself NEMO claimed that the murders were the work of "a Malay, or other low-class Asiatic, coming under the general term of a Lascar, of whom, I believe, there are many in that part of London." NEMO went on to argue that such a person would appear normal, "but when the villain is primed with his opium, or gin, and inspired with lust for slaughter and blood, he would destroy his defenceless victim with the ferocity and cunning of the tiger" (quoted in Paley 146). Apart from such orientalist fantasies, there were also a large number of anti-Semitic diatribes aimed at that old scapegoat, the Jew.

As early as 1886, the *Pall Mall Gazette*, a popular London newspaper, was referring to "a Judenhetz brewing in East London" and warning its readers that "the foreign Jews of no nationality whatever are becoming a pest and a menace to the poor native born East Ender" (quoted in Fishman 144). Concern about Jewish immigration and the association between Jews and violence were heightened even further by the Lipski murder case in mid-1887, when Israel Lipski, a twenty-two-year-old Polish Jew, was found guilty of murdering fellow immigrant Miriam Angel, by pouring nitric acid down her throat.[11]

When the Ripper murders began in 1888, the belief that the murderer could not be English licensed open expressions of anti-Semitism and exacerbated racial tensions in the heavily Jewish area of Whitechapel. A case in point is the persecution of John Pizer, a Jewish boot finisher and one of the first serious suspects in the case. After the fourth murder in the series, suspicion focused on Pizer, a local Whitechapel character known by the nickname of "Leather Apron," with a reputation for harassing and bullying local women. For the press, "Leather Apron" was an ideal suspect precisely because dealing with a nickname rather than an individual person gave them carte blanche to demonize the Jews as murderers, as the following description published in the *Star* suggests:

> The distinguishing feature of costume is a leather apron, which he always wears, and from which he gets his nickname. His expression is sinister, and seems to be full of terror for the women who describe it. His eyes are small and glittering. His lips are usually parted in a grin which is not only not reassuring, but is excessively repellent . . . His name nobody knows, but all are united in the belief that he is a Jew or of Jewish parentage, his face being of a marked Hebrew type. (Quoted in M. Harris 42)

Given such an inflammatory description, when the police arrested Pizer he was nearly lynched by an angry crowd before the police managed to get him to a police station. Pizer's quick release due to lack of evidence did nothing to convince the prejudiced public that a Jew or other minority was not responsible for the murders, and in such an atmosphere, one can hardly blame the police officer who ordered the destruction of a piece of chalked graffiti found at the scene of one of the murders that read "The Juwes are The Men That Will not be Blamed for nothing," even though it may have provided a valuable clue to the Ripper's identity.

Given the level of xenophobia in late-Victorian Britain, the fact that Jews and other minorities were scapegoated for the Whitechapel murders comes as no surprise, but that Americans should be the focus of suspicion is striking. Sara Blair has argued that part of the cultural work done by the figure of the

Jew in Ripper narratives was "to embody more pointed threats to the continuity of a newly urgent Anglo-Saxon 'brotherhood,' forged between Britons and Americans in 'a larger patriotism of race'" (489). Despite the ways in which the racial idiom of Anglo-Saxonism was developed during this period as a way of forging links between the British and the Americans, however, any implication that the existence of this idiom somehow exempted Americans from suspicion of being the Ripper should be rejected as quite inaccurate. Although it is true that suspicion of Americans was not racialized in the same way as suspicion of Malays or Jews, there turned out to be grounds other than race for suspecting Americans.

An American Ripper in London

The first suggestion that there might be an American connection in the case came at the inquest into the death of Annie Chapman, the Ripper's second victim, when the coroner, Wynne Baxter, offered an explanation for why the murderer had removed the victim's uterus. Baxter began by assuming that "the abstraction of the missing portion of the abdominal viscera was the object" of the murder and went on to reveal that a subcurator of the Pathological Museum at "one of our great medical schools" had informed Baxter that "some months ago an American had called on him, and asked him to procure a number of specimens of the organ that was missing in the deceased. He stated his willingness to give $20 apiece for each specimen" (quoted in M. Harris 51). Baxter then went on to ask, "Is it not possible that the knowledge of this demand may have incited some abandoned wretch to possess himself of a specimen?" (quoted in M. Harris 54). Perhaps sensing that the reputation of the medical profession had already been damaged by reports that the murderer possessed some anatomical knowledge, within days the prominent British medical journal the *Lancet* attacked Baxter's theory, dismissing it as absurd. The press, however, did not dismiss the story out of hand, perhaps because of their dim view of doctors, but also because the story of an unscrupulous, acquisitive American resonated with the British public.

Whatever the reason, the possibility that the Ripper might be American was now established, and popular belief in this possibility was strengthened significantly by the publication of the infamous "Dear Boss" letter from an individual claiming to be Jack the Ripper on October 4.[12] The letter created a sensation not only because the phantom murderer now had a self-appointed name (assuming that the letter was actually written by the killer), but also because what the London *Times* described as the "brutal character" of the letter's language was "full of Americanisms" (such as "Dear Boss," "fix me," and "shant quit"). It was hoped that these linguistic peculiarities would be a clue to the murderer's identity (Evans and Skinner 170). Ultimately, these hopes were dashed, and it is still doubtful whether the "Dear Boss" letter or any of the other letters and postcards purporting to be from Jack the Ripper were actually written by the murderer rather than being the work of journalists eager to maintain improved sales of their newspapers.[13] Nevertheless, as a result of the letters, the belief that the Ripper could be American was widespread, so much so that future eyewitnesses tended to hear American accents and perceive American-style clothing in suspects in a way they probably would not have if the letters had never been written.[14] For example, Matthew Packer, the owner of a fruit and vegetable stall who had sold some grapes to Elizabeth Stride, one of the Ripper's victims, on the night she was killed proved more than willing to fall in with reporters' suggestions that the man who accompanied Stride spoke with a "Yankee twang" and was wearing distinctively American clothing, which consisted of a long frock coat and a soft felt "wideawake" hat (Sugden 225–27).

Some versions of Packer's evidence clearly incorporated press reports about the case, which illustrates not only how frequent newspaper reports of American suspects had become, but also the extent to which they were believed by people living in the East End and by the authorities. Public suspicion of Americans grew to the point that police even questioned three cowboys working at the American Exhibition in London, along with Richard Mansfield, an American actor who was starring in a London production of Robert Louis Stevenson's *Dr. Jekyll and Mr. Hyde* during the Ripper murders. Even though there was no evidence that connected Mansfield to the crimes, it was popularly believed that the Ripper was a "Jekyll and Hyde" type criminal, and Mansfield's portrayal of Stevenson's character was so convincing that it aroused suspicion and eventually led to the play's early closing.

What was the response of the American press to these accusations? Curiously, there were very few denunciations of the idea that the Ripper could be an American. Instead, U.S. newspapers often redirected the focus of discussion and implied American superiority over the British by emphasizing the awfulness of the murders and the wretchedness of the environment in which they were taking place. For example, the *New York Times* coverage frequently abused the British police, calling them "the stupidest detectives in the civilized world" ("News" 1) and criticizing them for "devot[ing] their entire energies to preventing the press from getting at the facts" ("Dismay" 1). Most peculiarly, the *New York Times* used the Ripper murders to criticize the British system of government. Discussing how the government's failure to catch the Ripper might lead to the dismissal of the home secretary, the *New York Times* of October 7, 1888, commented: "It seems odd enough to an

American mind to wreck an imperial Government because an abnormal sort of criminal killed some women in the slums and escaped detection, but this is one of the risks of a system which gives executive powers to certain members of the majority party in Parliament and places their tenure of office at the mercy of a yea and nay vote" ("Old" 1). In other cases, the differences between the United States and Britain in the matter of crime were stated more sharply, as when a New York correspondent commented that "nothing in the history of American crime can, for special and particular horror, be said to outmatch the East End butcheries" (quoted in Sugden 341). Even more characteristic is *The History of the Whitechapel Murders: A Full and Authentic Narrative of the Above Murders, With Sketches*, a pamphlet self-published at white-hot speed in 1888 by Richard Kyle Fox, the owner and editor of the American publication *National Police Gazette*, which frequently pointed out that there was no American analogy to what was happening in Whitechapel.[15] When attempting to describe the sordidness of Mitre Square, scene of the murder of Catherine Eddowes, the Ripper's fourth victim, Fox said, "I have been trying to think of some place in New York to compare with Mitre Square, and cannot do it" (21). In a similar vein, Fox said of Miller's Court, scene of the Ripper's fifth and final murder, that "misery is written all over the place—the worst kind of London misery—such as those who have lived their lives in America can have no idea of" (34).

In the coverage the *National Police Gazette* itself devoted to the Ripper murders, Fox was much more explicit in his denunciation of the London police, accusing them of a "want of efficiency that amounts to downright stupidity" ("Whitechapel" 2). In the same editorial, Fox also stated explicitly that such crimes could never take place in America: "It is safe to say . . . that no man, or organization of men, however adept in the perpetration of crime, could go about either of the great American cities committing murder after murder in spite of police vigilance, as the Whitechapel fiend has been doing" (2). In a similar vein, an article in the November 10, 1888, issue of the *New York Sun* quoted Superintendent Murray of the New York City Police as saying, "It would not be fair to draw any comparison between our policemen and those of London . . . because I have been informed that New York has no locality that corresponds in misery and crime with the Whitechapel district. I am confident, though, that no such crimes could continue under the system of the New York police" (*New York Sun*). These examples of American press coverage demonstrate how American writers did not need to deny the possibility of an American Ripper explicitly because they found ways to imply that America was in a more evolved state than Britain and was therefore unlikely to produce a monster like Jack the Ripper.

But if some parts of the American press were at pains to distance the United States from the possibility of an American Ripper, others embraced the idea, either by drawing attention to similar murders that were taking place in the United States or by discussing past murders that bore a resemblance to the Whitechapel killings (see M. Harris 90). At the height of the Ripper murders, the *Atlanta Constitution* contacted the London papers to inform them about a series of murders of black women that had taken place in Austin, Texas, in 1884. The *Constitution* encouraged the London papers in the belief that the Texas murderer could be the Ripper:

> His peculiar line of work in Texas was executed in precisely the same manner as is now going on in London. Why should he not be there? The more one thinks of it, the more irresistible becomes the conviction that it is the man from Texas. In these days of steam and cheap travel, distance is nothing. The man who could kill a dozen women in Texas would not mind the inconvenience of a trip across the Atlantic and, once here, he would not make any scruples about killing more women. (Quoted in Hudson 10)

Here we see the diametrical opposite of a denial that the Ripper could be an American. Indeed, the *Constitution* seemed willing to bend over backward to convince the British that the Ripper was an American, perhaps out of a misplaced sense of national pride.[16]

This same willingness to claim the Ripper as one of America's own continued to be a feature of American coverage of the case long after the murders themselves had ceased. For example, when Carrie Brown (known as "Old Shakespeare" owing to her fondness for quoting the bard when she was drunk) was murdered in a Ripper-like fashion at the East River Hotel in Manhattan in April 1891, American newspapers were quick to surmise that Jack the Ripper had moved (back) to America. But this case presented a problem for the American police. Having boasted that the Ripper would be apprehended within thirty-six hours if he ever came to America, the New York City police came under intense pressure to solve the murder. The *New York Times* was quick to remind Chief Inspector Thomas Byrnes of his boast: "There has not been a case in years that has called forth so much detective talent. Inspector Byrnes apparently feels that the murderer must be arrested, for Inspector Byrnes has said that it would be impossible for crimes such as 'Jack the Ripper' committed in London to occur in New York and the murderer not be found. He has not forgotten his words on the subject" (quoted in Colville and Lucanio 145). It actually took the police just under a week to name a suspect, and, like the British, they chose the easy option of scapegoating a foreigner for the crime.[17] Ameer Ben Ali, an Algerian Arab known as "Frenchy," was convicted of Carrie Brown's murder in July 1891 and served eleven years of a life sentence before it was determined that his conviction was flawed by manufactured evidence and perjured witness testimony and he was released.[18] The fact that as late as 1895 the *National Police Gazette* was still suggesting that "a Jack the Ripper" might be at large in New York ("Victim" 3) is testament to the intense American engagement with the Whitechapel case.

Dime Novel Rippers

American fascination with the Ripper found expression not only in extensive press coverage but also in a spate of dime novels about the case. In some respects, dime novels and journalistic reports on Jack the Ripper are connected for, as Michael Denning has argued, "many dime novelists were newspaper reporters and editors. Moreover . . . dime novel plots were often constructed out of the events reported in the daily and weekly newspapers of cities around the country" (24). The dime novels based on Jack the Ripper illustrate Denning's point and indicate that their authors drew inspiration from international as well as American crimes. In other respects, however, these fictional accounts need to be placed in a separate category from newspaper reports, because they had the freedom, denied to the press, not only to heap limitless scorn upon the British police but also to offer imaginative solutions to the Ripper murders that reveal a great deal about what was at stake, ideologically speaking, in assigning responsibility for the Whitechapel killings.

The dime novel entitled *The Whitechapel Murders; or, On the Track of the Fiend*, written by "Detective Warren" and published as part of the Cap Collier Library in December 1888, is the most insistent in its criticisms of the British police, who are invariably portrayed as bumbling fools. The detective hero in this case, with the impeccably American name of Clint West, joins forces with a French detective, Jules Henri (a move calculated to denigrate and upset the British even more), in a search for the Ripper, who they believe is a mad Russian. Ironically, although West and Henri are utterly contemptuous of the efforts of the British to capture the Ripper, the generic peculiarities of the dime novel require that they fail again and again to capture the Ripper themselves, despite having numerous chances to do so. "Detective Warren's" choice of a mad Russian villain is representative of one type of American fictional treatment of the Ripper case: the equation of criminality with foreignness is not denied but instead redirected away from America.

W. B. Lawson's 1891 dime novel, published as an entry in the Log Cabin Library and entitled *Jack the Ripper in New York; or, Piping a Terrible Mystery*, takes its inspiration, as its title and date of publication suggest, from the murder of Carrie Brown in Manhattan. Set in a district of the city that Lawson describes as "the Whitechapel of New York" (2), this novel, like that of "Detective Warren," berates the London police, praises the American police, and, like the New York City police themselves, pins the crime on a foreigner, the Algerian named "Frenchy."

Although these denials of an American Ripper and the construction of a suitably foreign Ripper are nothing if not predictable, an interesting variation on this theme comes in the form of A. F. Pinkerton's detective novel *The Whitechapel Murders; or, An American Detective in London*, published by the Chicago firm of Laird & Lee in November 1888, another example of the rapidity of the American response to the Ripper's crimes. Like his fellow dime-novel authors, Pinkerton was unconstrained by the need to stick to the facts of the case and so was free to come up with an inventive solution to the murders, and he did not disappoint his reader. In the course of a lurid and melodramatic tale, Pinkerton's American detective hero (who just happens to be in London working on another case) concludes that "the Indian princess, Wahconta, the daughter of In-yan-te-o-pa, the exiled chief of the Sioux, was responsible for the murders credited, by an intelligent public, to the mythical Jack the Ripper," either by killing the victims herself or by using her mesmeric powers to have Gyp Servosse, the detective's assistant, commit the murders on her behalf (124). Pinkerton's choice of perpetrator is interesting for several reasons. First, in making the Ripper a woman, Pinkerton tapped into a common vein of speculation during the murders that the crimes could have been committed by a woman rather than a man (a homicidal midwife was a particularly popular theory). Second, by making the Ripper Native American, Pinkerton not only drew on a long-established discourse of Indian savagery, while confirming the suspicion that the Ripper was American, but did so in a way that protected white male Americans from suspicion by making the Ripper an American "other."[19]

Richard Slotkin has described how, at the turn of the century, dime novels gradually changed their archetypal location from the western frontier to the untamed American city, and he argues that the dime novel's urban adventures "shared important structural features with the frontier romance. But when the corruption of civilization replaces wilderness as the scene of the drama, and the 'urban savage' replaces the Noble Red Man, Hawkeye is transformed from a saintly 'man who knows Indians' to a figure whose consciousness is 'darkened' by the knowledge of criminality" (139). Rather than replacing the wilderness with civilization, the Indian with the urban savage, and the "man who knows Indians" with the detective, in *The Whitechapel Murders*, Pinkerton finds a way to combine these features. His use of an urban location gives his story a modern feel, and yet his staging of the elemental confrontation between the white representative of the law and the Indian criminal moves the frontier romance lock, stock, and barrel into the metropolis.

Pinkerton's choice of an Indian perpetrator for the Jack the Ripper murders also intersects with British perspectives on the Ripper's identity. Although the British press did not claim that the Ripper was an Indian, Indianness was very much part of their metaphoric language of viciousness, so that W. T. Stead, the flamboyant and well-known editor of the *Pall Mall Gazette*, described the Ripper as a "Savage of Civilization" who was as capable of "bathing his hands in blood as any Sioux who ever scalped a foe" (quoted in Walkowitz 206). Similarly, a reporter for the radical newspaper the *Star* claimed that the Ripper was "stalking down his victim like a Pawnee Indian, is simply drunk with blood, and he will have more" (quoted in Curtis 123). Such descriptions serve the ideological aim that characterizes so much of the coverage of the Ripper murders in the British press, namely, distancing the Ripper as far as possible from a normative, implicitly nonviolent, sense of Englishness.

Reluctantly English Rippers

Englishness, however, was not entirely exonerated by British commentators. Evocations of Indian savagery appeared simultaneously with conceptions of Englishness that did acknowledge the possibility of British complicity with violence. In this respect, the images of vicious Indian killers provided a way for the British media and public to imagine the possibility of an English Ripper, rather than denying that possibility. In other words, the presumption of a foreign Ripper and the possibility of an English one were not always mutually exclusive, in at least two ways.[20] First, an English Ripper was thought possible because the anatomical knowledge apparently possessed by the Ripper could characterize not only a butcher, midwife, or surgeon but also soldiers who had served the Empire abroad and in the process acquired knowledge of certain ritual killing practices found in India and Africa (see W. G. Eckert, "Whitechapel"). As outlandish as this explanation seems, it had the advantage of allowing for the possibility that the Ripper was English, while at the same time implying that only an Englishman who had been exposed to the pernicious influence of foreign cultures could be capable of such atrocities as the Whitechapel murders.

Perhaps because it brought imperialism and violence into uncomfortable proximity with each other, the theory of the Ripper as homicidal soldier was not widespread; far more popular was associating foreignness and Englishness in a particularly pernicious way by presenting the East End of London as a foreign, savage land. Curtis has described the way in which Victorian writers

"Africanized" the East End by imagining it as an urban jungle filled with danger and sin and infested with savages (35). This vision of the East End as jungle was found not only in sensational journalism but also in the language of liberal reform. Henry Mayhew, writing in the mid-nineteenth century in *London Labour and the London Poor*, described the street folk as members of a "race" and a "tribe," and Gertrude Himmelfarb argues that these words were used "sometimes in the typical, loose Victorian sense of 'race,' in which the word might be used of any ethnic, national, religious, or cultural group, and sometimes in a biological sense" (324).

This racialization of the poor accelerated as the nineteenth century progressed. In 1890, in his best-seller *In Darkest England and the Way Out*, William Booth, evangelist and founder of the Salvation Army, took the jungle analogy to its limit: "As there is a darkest Africa is there not also a darkest England? Civilisation, which can breed its own barbarians, does it not also breed its own pygmies? May we not find a parallel at our own doors, and discover within a stone's throw of our cathedrals and palaces similar horrors to those which Stanley has found existing in the great Equatorial forest?" (11–12). Drawing on the language used by Henry Morton Stanley in his famous search for Dr. David Livingstone, Booth stressed the savagery of the average East Ender in order to emphasize the need for reform. The appeal of this vision of the East End lay not only in the way it allowed for the possibility of an English Ripper but also in how it confirmed well-established views about the degraded British working class while also exonerating the middle and upper classes from any association with the Whitechapel murders (especially important given the popular insistence that the Ripper was a member of the upper class slumming in the East End). The attempts of the British media and public to blame the Ripper murders on another nationality or race were not made in isolation. Rather, xenophobic and racist accusations leveled at the non-English coincided with conflicted attempts to imagine an appropriately "othered" English Ripper.

The Usual Suspects

Although the British press and public did make the effort to consider the possibility of an English Ripper, this was the exception rather than the rule. Foreign Rippers were considerably more attractive candidates, partly because their guilt could be asserted without conflicting with any part of English national identity. Indeed, one can argue that the popular sense of Englishness as decent and nonviolent was strengthened by the panoply of foreign Ripper suspects, including Americans. Speculation about an American Ripper continues among "Ripperologists" to this day and seems set to become an enduring part of the Jack the Ripper industry.[21] As the perception that Americans have a national proclivity toward violent behavior gathered strength over the course of the twentieth century, the examples of popular culture that placed the Ripper in America became more and more frequent precisely because America was felt to be the natural location for the Ripper. As Colville and Lucanio comment in discussing *Bridge across Time* and *Jack's Back*, two television movies about the Ripper, placing Jack the Ripper in America seems logical:

> Jack the Ripper haunting the streets of Lake Havasu, Arizona, in *Bridge Across Time* (because the city had acquired the old London Bridge) may stretch fantasy to absurd lengths, but his murderous actions seem somehow a natural part of an American environment if only for the frontier milieu of the Arizona desert. And if *Jack's Back* serves as a thinly veiled excuse for yet another film of gratuitous sex and violence, the film at the same time unwittingly incorporates a disquieting logic: if Jack the Ripper were to return, where could he more profitably ply his craft than in the streets of an American city. (136)

Jack the Ripper's celebrity clearly extends beyond the immediate time and place of his murders. As his popular cultural reincarnations continue to multiply, the Ripper becomes detached from a strictly British context and is transformed into a time-traveling supernatural being, technically able to visit any country at any point in history. But as Colville and Lucanio imply, the fact that Jack the Ripper so often ends up in contemporary America illustrates the now pervasive belief that America is the most violent country in the world, the most congenial place on the planet for a serial killer.

Although the belief that America is the natural milieu for murder might seem recent, in fact it has a long history. In 1894, just six years after the Ripper murders, the arrest of Herman Webster Mudgett, better known by the pseudonym H. H. Holmes, gave Americans the opportunity to debate the connections between Americanism and murder in much greater detail. The Holmes case was one of the first high-profile instances of serial murder in America, and the intense media and public interest in Holmes rapidly made him into a star of American popular culture. Holmes's fame forced Americans to debate whether a murderer was an archetypal or aberrational American in a way they had not done before.

H. H. Holmes as Representative American

One of the cornerstone events of the Chicago World's Fair in 1893 was Frederick Jackson Turner's address before the American Historical Association, "The Significance of the Frontier in American History." Distinguished, like the fair itself, not only by its scope but also by its ambition, Turner's address described the gradual extension of the frontier to the western coast of the United States as a series of movements, each one of which restaged the elemental clash between civilization and wilderness, each time developing qualities of rugged individualism and independence in the American settler. In Turner's hands, the frontier thus became a constantly reenergizing force in the production of American individualism, nothing less than the driving force of American history. But Turner was acutely aware that the very same individualism that enabled America to realize its "manifest destiny" could also be a destructive force if not harnessed properly because of that individualism's impatience with social convention. This dangerous possibility had never seemed more likely than when Turner delivered his address. Now that the frontier was officially closed, Americans had to face the challenge of how to harness the qualities that Turner celebrated in the cities:

> From the conditions of frontier life came intellectual traits of profound importance... That coarseness and strength combined with acuteness and acquisitiveness; that practical, inventive turn of mind, quick to find expedients; that masterful grasp of material things, lacking in the artistic but powerful to effect great ends; that restless, nervous energy; that dominant individualism, working for good and for evil, and withal that buoyancy and exuberance which comes with freedom—these are the traits of the frontier. (57)

Turner went on to argue that frontier traits would continue to exist despite the closing of the frontier. Indeed, Turner claimed, "the American energy will continually demand a wider field for its exercise" (57). The problem was that there were no longer "gifts of free land" whose taming would absorb this "American energy." Consequently, Turner concluded, Americans were living in a time of both unprecedented possibility and unprecedented risk because "the bonds of custom are broken and unrestraint is triumphant" (57). Although Turner could not have known it, less than two miles away from where he was speaking, a frequent visitor to the fair by the name of Herman Webster Mudgett, who would become better known as H. H. Holmes, was busy proving Turner's point about triumphant unrestraint.

In a building that would become known as the "Murder Castle," which combined Holmes's living quarters, several small businesses, and rooms for rent, Holmes was disposing of an untold number of individuals, many of whom were lodgers visiting the World's Fair and enjoying Holmes's accommodations, which were located conveniently near one of the entrances to the fair. After his arrest in 1894, and particularly as details of the extent of his crimes emerged throughout 1895, it became clear that Holmes embodied what Turner described as the "traits of the frontier." Undoubtedly possessed of "acuteness and acquisitiveness," a "practical, inventive turn of mind," and "restless, nervous energy," Holmes exemplified how these qualities could be used "for both good and evil" when "the bonds of custom are broken and unrestraint is triumphant" (57). The historian Richard Slotkin has used the influential phrase "regeneration through violence" to describe how "the Myth of the Frontier relates the achievement of 'progress' to a particular form or scenario of violent action" (11). Holmes is the realization of the dark side of frontier individualism, a man who, by defining progress in violent terms, was willing to use anyone to achieve his goal of self-(re)generation.

This, at least, is how Holmes looks to us today with the benefit of considerable hindsight. To those Americans reading the daily revelations about Holmes's crimes at the end of the nineteenth century, interpreting Holmes as a representative American was a far more threatening possibility. Holmes's representativeness was a possibility that could not be avoided, however, because he called to mind not only Turner's frontier values but also, as befitted someone who used multiple identities throughout his career, two figures with an even stronger connection to representative Americanness: the self-made man and his shadowy brother, the confidence man. The overdetermined response of Holmes's contemporaries to his crimes exemplifies a long-standing public ambivalence toward the acquisitiveness and assertiveness that defined the American ethic of success. Consequently, Holmes quickly became one of the most widely known figures of his day and provided Americans with an unparalleled opportunity to consider the role of greed, violence, and money in the formation of American nationhood.

H. H. Holmes and Jack the Ripper: Blood Brothers?

The cases of both H. H. Holmes and Jack the Ripper required their fellow citizens to look unflinchingly at how violence and national identity are interconnected. Despite having this important feature in common, however, there are also some significant differences that make Holmes quite distinct from the Ripper. First, unlike the Ripper's, Holmes's crimes did not come to light until after his arrest. Thus, although the Holmes case created a great deal of interest and concern, it did not generate the hysteria that characterized the public response to the Ripper crimes. Second, because Holmes was a viable suspect from the beginning of the case, there was no reason for the obsession about the murderer's identity that has marked the Whitechapel case from 1888 to the present day. Third, unlike the open-endedness that characterized the Ripper case with the perpetrator remaining at large, the Holmes case had a very definite conclusion. Holmes's passage through the judicial system imposed an easily comprehensible narrative upon the meaning of his actions, culminating with the decisive concluding paragraph of his execution. The sense of closure provided by his death meant that, although Holmes was undoubtedly a bona fide media star between his arrest in November 1894 and his execution in May 1896, after his death he was forgotten relatively quickly. While the continuing mystery of Jack the Ripper's identity enabled succeeding generations to project their fantasies and fears onto him, thus ensuring his survival in popular culture, Holmes's death at first glance seemed to dampen any long-term interest in the case. For most of the twentieth century, Holmes lived on only in the memories of true-crime aficionados, some of whom would occasionally try to resurrect the case as a classic of its kind, using that tone of admiration so peculiar to true-crime writers.[22]

In recent years, however, there have been numerous signs that a Holmes revival is under way. While interest in the case was kept alive by such books as Robert Bloch's novel *American Gothic* (1974),[23] David Franke's true-crime study *The Torture Doctor* (1975), and Allan Eckert's novel *The Scarlet Mansion* (1985), the most recent phase of the revival was inaugurated by Harold Schechter's *Depraved*, published on the centenary of Holmes's arrest in 1994 and part of an extremely popular series of books written by Schechter about famous American serial killers (including studies of Ed Gein and Jesse Pomeroy).

Since the publication of *Depraved*, interest in Holmes has taken a variety of forms, including numerous Internet retellings of the case (see Filippelli), *The Devil's Rood*, a bizarre novel written by four writing students and their teacher who call themselves "U.S. Five," and *H. H. Holmes: America's First Serial Killer*, a documentary by independent filmmaker John Borowski, for which Schechter served as the main source of expertise. Most recently, Erik Larson's book *The Devil in the White City* juxtaposes Holmes's crimes and Daniel Burnham's preparations for the World's Fair, implying that their temporal coincidence suggests more profound thematic similarities between these events. The renewed interest in Holmes is yet more evidence of the celebrity serial killer culture industry inaugurated by Jack the Ripper, but massively strengthened by the explosion of interest in serial murder that has characterized American popular culture since the late 1970s.

During the investigation into Holmes's crimes in the late 1890s, few sources compared Holmes to Jack the Ripper, except to mock what were regarded as inflated claims about the extent of Holmes's crimes.[24] In recent work on Holmes, however, it has become standard practice to associate him with the Ripper. Schechter refers to the Whitechapel murders as a way to provide context for what Americans would soon have to confront in the person of Holmes. Those citizens of Chicago who felt that the Ripper crimes were reassuringly distant, Schechter argues, "had no way of knowing that even at that moment, in the outskirts of their city, a psychopath who called himself H. H. Holmes was busily laying the groundwork for a murderous career that would rival, and in some ways outmatch, the atrocities of his English counterpart, Jack the Ripper" (*Depraved* 27). Reviews of Schechter's book eagerly take up this comparison, describing Holmes as a "contemporary of Jack the Ripper who made the British slasher look like a piker" and pointing out that Holmes got nowhere near the press coverage devoted to Jack the Ripper even though "his deadly compulsion racked up five times the number of victims."[25]

Such comparisons of H. H. Holmes and Jack the Ripper are based less on detailed analyses of any similarities between the two cases and more on the feeling that American serial killers are just as good as their British counterparts and should receive their fair share of publicity. Leaving this misplaced sense of national pride aside, is the comparison of Holmes with the Ripper justified? In spite of the differences between the Ripper and Holmes cases that I have discussed, there are also significant similarities. In both cases, the intense public response to the killers combined horror with fascination, even admiration. In both cases, the killers were quickly turned into popular cultural celebrities, drawing on a well-established market for representations of famous criminals. In both cases, there was a significant degree of open-endedness in the case that encouraged continued public interest in the killers. With Jack the Ripper, that open-endedness was the mystery of the Ripper's identity. With H. H. Holmes, despite the degree of closure given to the case by his execution, numerous questions remained unanswered, mostly concerning motivation, spurring a public interest in the case that lasted well after Holmes's death.

Paradoxically, for someone rapidly acquiring the reputation of being (in Schechter's words) "the first American serial killer," Holmes was never convicted of, or even charged with having committed, multiple homicides. Although Holmes's responsibility for the crime for which he was executed, the murder of his business associate Benjamin F. Pitezel, was proven convincingly, there was room for speculation about the most notorious aspect of the Holmes case: his activities in the so-called Murder Castle, a large structure Holmes had built on the corner of Wallace and Sixty-third streets in Chicago between 1888 and 1890. Designed to be a combination home, business venture, and lodging house, the building, when police began investigating it in July 1895, was found to be a concentrated example of every gothic cliché imaginable, with concealed closets, secret staircases, sealed rooms, corridors that led nowhere, and a basement filled with dissecting equipment, acid baths, and what appeared to be torture devices. Despite intensive investigation of the structure before it burned down in August 1895, it proved impossible to determine how many people had met their deaths in it or precisely how they had died. Holmes himself, in the last of his many confessions, claimed to have killed a total of twenty-seven people in both Chicago and a number of other places, but many were unconvinced by this claim, both because Holmes was being paid a handsome sum by a newspaper for this confession and because they preferred to let their imaginations run riot and attribute hundreds of murders to Holmes, turning him into the devil incarnate.

Although John Bartlow Martin has argued that the unanswered questions in the Holmes case make it "not wholly satisfactory" (85), I am not concerned about our inability to know the "truth" of the case. Rather, I want to focus on an aspect of the case that has been neglected by other writers: the public response to Holmes during his arrest and trial, and how much that response mirrors the reaction to the Whitechapel murderer, both in its combination of horror and fascination and in its obsession with what we might call the national representativeness of the killer.

Making a Killing

Although there was much disagreement among Holmes's contemporaries about what could have motivated such brutal crimes, it was generally accepted that the issue of motive could be reduced to two possibilities: greed or madness. Part of the reason there was so much debate about whether Holmes could be considered a representative American is that there is much at stake in deciding whether Holmes was motivated primarily by avarice or by pathology. If we choose the profit motive, the elements of Holmes that made him into an exemplary businessman come into focus; his murders then become imbricated with the many other swindles and moneymaking schemes that preoccupied him throughout his life. Even his most shocking murders, such as those of Alice, Nellie, and Howard Pitezel, the children of his business associate Benjamin Pitezel, can then be seen as part of an elaborate scheme of insurance fraud rather than as evidence of psychopathology. The advantage of this choice for contemporaries of Holmes was that it legitimated a tone of admiration that ran through many accounts of the case, because it allowed people to think of Holmes as a scurrilous, cunning, audacious rogue, rather than as a brutal serial killer. The disadvantage of this choice was that by asserting continuity between Holmes and other businessmen, and between Holmes and the moral imperatives of the Gilded Age, business as usual was necessarily called into question. Presenting Holmes as an especially avaricious entrepreneur entailed exploring the depth of meaning behind an apparently innocuous phrase like "making a killing"; one was forced to consider the possibility that Holmes was the nightmarish, perhaps inevitable, literalization of an economic culture that increasingly viewed people as one more kind of raw material. The difference, in other words, between Holmes and the captains of industry became one of degree rather than kind.

Those who would deny that Holmes was primarily a businessman must confront the fact that there is a considerable amount of evidence that his motives were economic and that murder was a natural progression for someone who had always regarded people in purely instrumental, rather than affective, terms. Almost invariably, Holmes murdered those whom he had taken out insurance policies on and/or those who compromised his financial security by threatening to tell the authorities everything they knew about his various illegal schemes.[26] Indeed, not only were the murders themselves economically motivated, but Holmes was always alert to the possibility of making more money from the products of the murders. On at least two occasions, Holmes had the bodies of his victims articulated into skeletons, which he then sold to doctors or medical schools. Even after his arrest, Holmes remained attentive to the financial opportunities created by his notoriety, both publishing his own version of events to compete with the flurry of books that appeared about him and, even with the shadow of the gallows hanging over him, negotiating with a newspaper to provide it with an exclusive version of his confession for thousands of dollars.[27]

Given the uncomfortable consequences of interpreting Holmes primarily as a businessman, there are several advantages to emphasizing madness as a motivation. Such an emphasis accentuates Holmes's difference from "normal" members of the community, making him into a monster rather than an Every-man. Although this might seem a risky maneuver in that a monster can be very frightening, creating a level of fear that is socially destabilizing, ultimately that fear acts as a force for social cohesion. Thinking of Holmes as a perverted monster places him safely outside the bounds of normality, reinforcing both our own sense of ordinariness and the ordinariness of the community, making that community a much safer and more desirable place to live.

Whether or not Holmes saw himself as a monster, he was more than willing to pander to the public's desire for monstrosity in his own writings. In an 1896 confession for which he received $10,000 from William Randolph Hearst for syndication rights, Holmes described himself and his actions in gothic terms, going so far as to claim that, since his imprisonment, his physiognomy had changed to the extent that he was coming more and more to resemble Satan: "Is it to be wondered . . . that even before my death, I have commenced to assume the form and features of the Evil One himself?" (quoted in Franke 184). Ironically, precisely at the moment that Holmes was presenting himself as a mad gothic monster (a view seemingly supported by the architectural peculiarities of the Murder Castle), he was providing perhaps the strongest evidence for his economic motives. Offering himself to his public as Evil incarnate, Holmes confirmed his awareness of the market value of murder by giving the public what it wanted.[28]

One alternative to presenting Holmes as either businessman or psychopath is to combine these perspectives. Mark Seltzer, in his discussion of Holmes, presents Holmes as both psychopath and businessman, seeing no need to choose between these two identities because financial schemes and murder schemes were always intimately related to each other in Holmes's life (212). Moreover, Seltzer does not see this combination of qualities as particularly unusual during this period because he claims that self-generation or self-making is an inherently violent process (219). Holmes can therefore be both Horatio Alger and Jack the Ripper, with those identities complementing rather than conflicting with each other.

Other writers on the case also present Holmes as both businessman and psychopath, not because they want to blur those categories but because this strategy gives the writer the best of both worlds. Holmes can be both thrillingly deviant and tediously ordinary, each category drawing a frisson from its proximity to the other. William Brannon, for example, describes Holmes as "a mass-murderer of the school of George Joseph Smith or Désiré Landru rather than that of Jack the Ripper or Peter Kürten: that is, a wholly amoral businessman rather than a death-obsessed psychopath; but there is no doubt that he took pleasure in killing and even came to practice it on occasions when no profit was involved—just as a hardheaded commercial writer may occasionally dash off something purely for his own entertainment" (71–72). With this explanation, Brannon is able to have his cake and eat it, too.

Although disposed to sensationalism, Harold Schechter occasionally tries to combine the two perspectives on Holmes in the same way as Seltzer, arguing, for example, that Holmes was motivated to build the castle partly out of entrepreneurial ambition and partly to satisfy his "dark desires" (*Depraved* 23). And yet, at other points in his account, Schechter contradicts this assertion, arguing that Holmes's business instincts were in conflict with his psychopathy: "Holmes possessed the sort of boldness, savvy, and boundless ambition that might well have earned him the financial success he so frantically craved. But the perversions of his nature made it impossible for him to employ his powers for legitimate ends" (72). This inconsistency is created by Schechter's desire to keep the categories of entrepreneur and psychopath as distinct as possible, despite abundant evidence that they were able to coexist quite comfortably in Holmes. For example, in an extraordinary letter written just before he was to go on trial for his life, Holmes gave his business associate John King very detailed advice on how to market Holmes's book, *Holmes' Own Story*, covering everything from what photograph to use on the title page to the best way to sell the book door-to-door.[29] In his desire to ignore the fact that Holmes was inextricably both murderer and businessman, Schechter is unperturbed by the fact that any evidence that Holmes murdered for pleasure is almost entirely speculative; he frequently argues that Holmes derived perverted pleasure from the murders (he even has him masturbating outside a room in which one of his victims is slowly asphyxiating), even though there is absolutely no reliable evidence to support this claim.

From Swindler to Fiend to Media Star

Compared with the extremes of much recent commentary on Holmes, most of the contemporaneous response to the man and his crimes was considerably more measured and less Manichean, genuinely seeking to make sense of a man who seemed simultaneously frighteningly different and disturbingly familiar. Newspaper reports about the case in the months following Holmes's arrest described him primarily as a swindler rather than as a murderer. This was perfectly logical, bearing in mind that Holmes was originally charged with fraud and was not indicted for Pitezel's murder until September 1895. The public response to Holmes at this stage was "fascination . . . flavored with a grudging admiration for the sheer audacity of the man" (Schechter, *Depraved* 199). Two events combined to change gradually the public's perception of Holmes. The first was the hiring of Philadelphia detective Frank Geyer in June 1895 to find the bodies of Alice, Nellie, and Howard Pitezel, all of whom Holmes had vigorously denied killing. Geyer's extraordinary achievement in foiling Holmes's labyrinthine efforts to throw any pursuers off his track is detailed in his book *The Holmes-Pitezel Case*. One of the smartest things Geyer did was to use the intense media attention being given to his search to his advantage. Geyer describes his method once the trail led him to Toronto:

> Seriously meditating as to the best method to pursue to arouse the citizens of Toronto, I then determined to meet the news-paper men, give them my views of the case, and explain to them my theories, so that the matter would be brought before the public, and the story of the disappearance of the children read in every household in the city . . . The next morning every newspaper published in Toronto devoted several columns to the story of the disappearance of the children. (222–23)

As a result of this tactic, on July 15, 1895, Geyer found the bodies of Alice and Nellie Pitezel buried in the basement of a house in Toronto that had been briefly rented by Holmes. Using similar methods, on August 27, Geyer discovered the remains of Howard Pitezel in a second house rented by Holmes in Irvington, a small town outside Indianapolis. Geyer's search for the missing children was front-page news throughout the summer of 1895. As concrete evidence of Holmes's crimes began to emerge, the tone of reporting also began to change, with "murderer" and then "fiend" replacing "swindler" as the most frequent term used to describe Holmes.

This change in tone was accelerated by the second development in the case, a development also triggered by Geyer's success. Four days after Geyer discovered the bodies in Toronto, Chicago police finally entered and began searching Holmes's "Murder Castle." Just as Geyer's search was closely watched by the media, the castle became the scene of an ongoing media frenzy for the month from July 19, when police first entered the building, to August 19, when the building burned down under mysterious circumstances. Press reports from the time give us a valuable window into public curiosity about the case. The July 29, 1895, issue of the *Chicago Daily News* reported what was a common scene at the time: a heterogeneous crowd trying to see the workmen excavating the castle's basement: "Cyclists, evidently away on a day's outing, dismounted and left their steeds in the alley back of the castle while they fought with the street gamins for advantageous loopholes in the wooden sidewalk, through which they could peep at the men digging in the soft mud of the cellar. By 9 o'clock fully 100 men, women and children were lying flat on the sidewalks above the cellar peering in through every conceivable crack or knothole" ("Detectives" 3). Every time one of the workmen appeared to find something, the crowd apparently went wild with excitement, as the news quickly spread that they had found another skeleton. In fact, very few bones of any kind were found in the basement, but it was still potentially a dangerous place. At one point, the combination of the large crowd and the extensive underground excavation led to the cave-in of part of the alley, with the result that the workmen were nearly crushed, and some of the crowd narrowly avoided falling headlong into the basement ("Detectives" 3).

Even though Schechter claims that the exploration of the castle changed public perception of Holmes from an "arch-swindler" to an "arch-fiend" "literally overnight" (*Depraved* 280), in fact it was a much more gradual process, with newspaper coverage remaining skeptical, especially in the *Chicago Daily News*. Even while the basement was being searched, the *News* claimed that there was no case against Holmes, and the July 27 issue criticized the excesses of press reports about the figure they still referred to as "Swindler Holmes": "Reporters are given free rein and with their imaginative faculties in good working order they concoct stories which not even the most gullible

of readers can swallow. Everything they write, no matter how absurd or man-
ifestly impossible, is published. A mighty sigh of relief will go up when this
era of Holmes idiocy is ended" ("Gone" 4).

Two aspects of the ongoing investigation in particular attracted press
ridicule. The first was the police habit of building a complicated case against
Holmes based on the flimsiest of evidence. In a "modern one-act melodrama"
entitled "Tracked to Earth" published in the July 30 issue of the *News*, two
bumbling policemen conclude that "D. D. Domicile" has done away with a
young girl named Cissy McNutty based on the evidence of a fingernail paring
and a fishbone they find in the castle's basement. The play concludes with a
parodic newspaper article reporting "Another Grewsome Find. Fingernail and
Fish-Bone. Prove Beyond a Doubt That Cissy McNutty Was Slain by D. D.
Domicile—History of the Blackest Crime Ever Committed" ("Tracked" 1).
Although the humor of the play is labored, it makes its point effectively.

The other aspect of the investigation often mocked by the press was the
police tendency to attribute an enormous number and variety of murders to
Holmes. Commenting on this tendency, the *Chicago Daily News* on July 31,
1895, reported the discovery of four hundred human skeletons in a cave in
Arizona and suggested that "perhaps these are the missing links in the Holmes
case" that the police were looking for (4). When the *Chicago Daily Tribune* on
July 29, 1895, related the details of an Indian massacre in the Jackson Hole
area of Wyoming and Idaho, they also included a cartoon of Holmes in his cell
protesting his innocence: "I am innocent: I had no insurance on any of those
settlers." The manner of Holmes's defense indicates not only how inflated
claims about Holmes's crimes were not taken seriously, but also that the reason
they were not taken seriously was precisely that Holmes was still seen primarily
as an economic criminal, an identity apparently inconsistent with mass murder.

This same assumption concerning the mutual exclusivity of an economic
motivation and wholesale murder can also be found in one of the earliest
books about the case, Robert L. Corbitt's *The Holmes Castle: The Only True
Account of the Greatest Criminal the Police Have Ever Handled*, self-published
in Chicago in 1895. Corbitt, a playwright, is also a good example of the lengths
people were willing to go to secure an advantage in the highly competitive
market of Holmes reporting. On July 24, Corbitt and an associate broke into
a storeroom in the castle while the police were still searching the building,
looking for material that would give their book about the case an edge over
their competitors'. Although the police forced Corbitt to turn over most of
the papers he found, he did manage to hide a bundle of letters and Holmes's
account book under a loose floorboard from where they were later retrieved and

smuggled out of the castle by another of Corbitt's associates. Despite Corbitt's claims to the contrary, the stolen materials are singularly lacking in revelations. Of more interest are Corbitt's reasons for thinking that Holmes did not kill the Pitezel children: "None but insane men commit murder without a motive. Holmes is not insane. The motive power of his life has been money. It is not reasonable to suppose he would kill the Pitzel [sic] children for any reason" (113). Corbitt could not have known when writing these words that Holmes had killed the children to ensure the success of his insurance fraud involving their father, but the counterposing of an economic motive with no motive at all is instructive and suggests that, despite the widespread coverage of the Jack the Ripper murders in the American press just a few years before, the idea of sexually motivated homicide was not particularly common at this time.[30]

Killers, Freaks, and Other Americans

Although some of Holmes's contemporaries were preoccupied with the issue of how to make sense of his crimes, others, especially those who would have recognized and admired Holmes's entrepreneurial drive and ambition, had a more practical response to the Holmes case. Just as proprietors of the "penny gaffs" in London quickly adapted existing waxworks exhibits to reflect the latest developments in the Jack the Ripper murders, so owners of dime museums in the United States shuffled their displays to make room for the latest sensation.

Capitalizing upon the fact that Holmes was to be tried in his city, one Philadelphia dime museum owner ran an exhibit consisting of "artifacts and photographs of Holmes, his victims, and his crime scenes. It included a large pile of human bones, a human skull, and a miniature replica of the Castle in Chicago" (Boswell and Thompson 46). We know that Holmes was aware of the existence of such entertainments because when he was interviewing prospective jurors for his trial (at that point he was serving as his own attorney), he expressed concern about the chances of finding unbiased jurors because so many had attended the dime museum (Franke 148). Chicago businessmen had been just as quick to exploit the Holmes case for financial gain. By August 5, 1895, just two weeks after police began searching the castle, C. E. Kohl and George Middleton's Clark Street Dime Museum was advertising "H. H. HOLMES! Come and See a Lifelike Representation in Wax of this Most Noted Criminal."[31] The ad went on to tell prospective customers that "the most skilled artists in America" had spent weeks modeling "a perfect counterfeit presentment of this alleged WHOLESALE MURDERER OF MEN, WOMEN AND IN-NOCENT CHILDREN!" Not surprisingly, the word "alleged" was printed in the smallest possible type to attract the largest possible number of customers.

The next logical step was to turn the castle itself into a tourist attraction. The first hint of efforts to do so comes in a newspaper report of a crowd of onlookers at the castle, which included the proprietors of a dime museum who were trying to negotiate a lease for the building. The *Chicago Daily News* reported confidently on August 8 that "the Holmes 'castle' will not become a public museum for the gratification of the morbidly inclined" but would instead be rebuilt to be used as flats and offices ("Castle" 1). Just two days later, however, the *News* carried an advertisement announcing, "The castle of the wholesale murderer (so-called) is now open for inspection." For just fifteen cents, people could enjoy what the ad described as "The Sensation Of The Day" (2). But it was not to be. When the castle was destroyed by fire on August 19, the impresario's dreams went up in smoke, smoke that was suspected, but never proven, to be the work of an arsonist.

It is tempting to dismiss the dime museum exhibits and the murder castle tours as cynical attempts to exploit the morbid appetites of the crowd, attempts mirroring those made in the aftermath of the Whitechapel murders. Although such attractions are obviously exploitative, I also believe them to be important sources of evidence about how Holmes's fellow citizens attempted to understand and process the meanings of his actions. On May 8, 1896, the day after his execution in Philadelphia, the *Chicago Times-Herald* reflected on the meaning of Holmes: "To parallel such a career one must go back to past ages and to the time of the Borgias or Brinvilliers, and even these were not such human monsters as Holmes seems to have been. He is a prodigy of wickedness, a human demon, a being so unthinkable that no novelist would dare to invent such a character. The story, too, tends to illustrate the end of the century" (quoted in Schechter, *Depraved* 278). The meaning of Holmes, this report implies, is twofold: he personifies the continuation of an ancient (putatively European) history of corruption and violence, but he is also emblematic of modernity. Although the *Times-Herald* does not specify exactly how Holmes illustrates the end of the century, if we take a closer look at the Holmes dime museum exhibits, we will see how Holmes is the latest episode in a long-standing and conflicted American engagement with freaks, criminals, self-made men, and con men, figures that have far more in common than we might think.

Pathologies of Self-Making

The fact that the Holmes exhibit in Kohl and Middleton's Dime Museum was advertised along with "Prince Lutgard, The Famous Oklahoma Midget" and "A Great Dwarfs' Convention" suggests how easily Holmes was integrated into the already established elements of the dime museum. This is partly because, as Andrea Stulman Dennett has argued in her history of the dime museum, it was common practice to exhibit waxworks of famous criminals next to the varied assortment of freaks that were the dime museum's bread and butter. The juxtaposition of Holmes and the dime museum freaks, however, also suggests that visitors were encouraged to view Holmes the "arch-fiend" as yet another freak, thus disavowing any potential connection between Holmes and the viewer of the exhibit.

There is little doubt that part of the cultural work of the dime museum's freak show was to reassure the spectator of his or her own normality. As Rosemarie Garland Thomson has argued, "the figure of the freak is... the necessary cultural complement to the acquisitive and capable American who claims the normate position of masculine, white, nondisabled, sexually un-ambiguous, and middle class" (quoted in R. Adams 31). It is difficult to see, however, how Holmes could be said to occupy the position of "freak" in the same way as Siamese twins, dwarves, and bearded ladies. Despite Holmes's attempts to give himself a Satanic physiognomy, it is likely that those who visited the Holmes dime museum exhibit were struck by their disturbing similarity to Holmes rather than by their comforting difference from him. This similarity between exhibit and viewer is physical in the sense that it is based on Holmes's lack of "freakish" physical attributes, but it also much more profoundly ideological, a function of what Mark Seltzer has described as "the manner in which the psycho is *nothing but representative*: not similar to someone or something but *just similar*" (127, original emphasis). While rejecting the label of "psycho" as a useful way of understanding Holmes, I believe that Holmes's similarity to a range of archetypal American figures can help explain the overdetermined popular cultural reaction to him.

For example, if the concept of "freakishness" fails to explain the appro-priateness of exhibiting Holmes in dime museums, a much more promising connection arises when we remember that the father of the dime museum was P. T. Barnum. Between 1841, when Barnum opened Barnum's American Museum on the corner of Broadway and Ann Street in New York City, and 1868, when the museum was destroyed by fire, Barnum succeeded in trans-forming museums from failing antiques into a major new form of amusement and thus provided the prototype for the dime museum (Bogdan 35). More important, Barnum wrote one more chapter in a famous life characterized by humbug, deception, the love of money, self-promotion, and tireless self-reinvention: all qualities that would have made him an exemplary figure to someone as ambitious and acquisitive as Holmes.[32] For all his emphasis on self-invention, however, Barnum himself was merely the latest example of an American archetype with a long and complex history: the self-made man.

The career of H. H. Holmes usefully encapsulates both the promise and the anxieties created by the figure of the self-made man.

In his landmark 1965 study, *Apostles of the Self-Made Man*, John Cawelti argued that "Benjamin Franklin was not the first self-made man, but certainly he was the archetypal self-made man for Americans" (9). Like so many others, Holmes was undoubtedly inspired by the example of Franklin's meticulous self-examination as detailed famously in his memoirs. The extent of Holmes's dedication to this ideal can be gauged by the fact that even when he was in prison, he still aspired to a Franklinian program of self-improvement, as this excerpt from his prison diary entry for January 1, 1895, suggests: "The New Year. I have been busy nearly all day in prison formulating a methodical plan for my daily life while in prison, to which I shall hereafter rigidly adhere" (quoted in Franke 140). Holmes's program included exercise, reading, academic study, and vegetarianism, with each day ending the same way: "I shall retire at 9 p.m. and shall as soon as possible force myself into the habit of sleeping throughout the entire night" (quoted in Franke 140). At first glance, the fact that such admirable sentiments came from someone awaiting trial for fraud and murder might seem like a sick parody of the Franklinian ideal of the self-made man. In fact, Holmes was never more representative than when he encapsulated a century of anxieties about the concept of self-making. In particular, Holmes personified the replacement of an earlier concept of self-making defined by character building with a self-made man defined more by morally relative financial acquisitiveness. For how could Holmes's life be described more accurately than as a ceaseless quest for money, regardless of questions of character, morality, or ethics?

While there is much truth to this characterization of Holmes's life, it is unlikely that he would have inspired the degree of interest he did among his contemporaries if he had been seen merely as a perversion of the American ideal of the self-made man. Although it is true to say that "Holmes personified everything that had gone wrong with the country. He symbolized all the hollowness and corruption at the heart of the American 'success ethic'— what the poet Walt Whitman decried as 'the depravity of the business classes'" (Schechter, *Depraved* 279–80), we must also account for the fact that the public response to Holmes was made up of fascination and grudging admiration as well as condemnation and disgust. In order to understand this ambivalent mixture, we must examine the relation between the self-made man and another closely related American archetype: the confidence man.

Karen Halttunen has traced the first use of the term "confidence-man" to 1849 in New York City, but she claims that a figure recognizable as a confidence man goes back even further and is dominant in "the vast literature of advice on personal conduct published in America after 1830" (*Confidence* xiv). Ironically, Holmes began life as a part of the intended audience for such advice literature because he was the kind of person most in need of protection from the con man: as a young man from the small rural town of Gilmanton, New Hampshire, Holmes came to the city like so many other innocent young men to make his fortune. As Halttunen points out, however, "in warning the American youth not to be seduced by the evil confidence man, antebellum advice manuals were cautioning him above all not to become a confidence man himself" (*Confidence* 33). We cannot know whether Holmes ever read any of the advice manuals Halttunen refers to, but what is clear is how closely Holmes came to resemble the archetype described by such manuals: "Instead of acting in open daylight, pursuing the direct and straight-forward path of rectitude and duty, you see men, extensively, putting on false appearances; working in the dark, and carrying their plans by stratagem and deceit" (quoted in Halttunen, *Confidence* 33). When one considers Holmes's long and complex career as a swindler, bigamist, thief, and speculator, no word sums up that career better than what was taken to be the chief defining feature of the con man: hypocrisy.[33]

Nothing could seem more different from the upstanding character of the self-made man than such descriptions of con men, and yet these two figures became increasingly blurred as the nineteenth century progressed. Over time, anxieties about how young men could do business in the "world of strangers" that constituted the modern American city without resorting to hypocrisy dovetailed with concerns about how "self-making" was being defined in increasingly financial and morally relativistic terms. What united both kinds of anxiety was the usually unspoken perception that, like it or not, hypocrisy worked in modern America. In other words, unscrupulous business practices tended to be the most profitable, and, inevitably, profitability took precedence over scruples.

This is not to say that Holmes's crimes were seen merely as a particularly flagrant example of bad business practices. Clearly, moral relativism in late-nineteenth-century America had not gone that far. With that said, we should also note that by the time of Holmes's arrest, the figure of the confidence man had almost entirely disappeared from conduct manuals, thanks to "the growing acceptance of the idea that the young American on the make had to become a kind of confidence man himself in order to succeed" (Halttunen, *Confidence* 205). Holmes was such a fascinating figure to his contemporaries because he personified the "mainstreaming" of the confidence man. Behind all the rhetoric of condemnation, there lurked in the ambivalent response to Holmes what Gary Lindberg has described as the confidence man as "a covert cultural hero for Americans" (3). Although they were shocked by Holmes's actions, late-nineteenth-century Americans recognized that he was motivated by desires they all shared to some extent.

Investing in Serial Killers

"Investment" is a particularly useful term to describe the contemporaneous public engagement with the figures of Jack the Ripper and H. H. Holmes because it both highlights how public interest in these men had psychological and economic dimensions and reminds us how quickly public fascination with serial killers was articulated with previous forms of mass entertainment and turned into a durable popular culture industry of its own. I have demonstrated in this chapter that these early versions of a celebrity culture organized around serial killers were driven by a complex mixture of fascination and horror. Both sides of this mixture could be indulged by turning serial killers into popular cultural products; by converting the murders into forms of entertainment, late-nineteenth-century Americans and Britons could work through their fascination with these figures in more or less socially legitimate ways.

Strikingly, these popular cultural investments were not affected by whether the killer's identity was known or unknown. Although the mystery of the Ripper's identity undoubtedly explains the figure's much longer popular cultural presence, the fact that Holmes's identity was known did not limit the extraordinary range and intensity of responses to his crimes. Jack the Ripper and H. H. Holmes together established the fact that serial killers could be read as condensed symptoms of the social, thus allowing for the establishment of a wide-ranging culture industry organized around them. If we now turn to an examination of the FBI's use of the serial killer, we will see an even more complicated series of interactions between celebrity criminals, popular culture, and both institutional and individual investors in serial murder.

CHAPTER TWO

Defining the Enemy Within:
The FBI and Serial Murder

Jack the Ripper Meets the FBI

In October 1988, in an event marking the centenary of the Whitechapel murders, a two-hour television program entitled "The Secret Identity of Jack the Ripper" was broadcast live from Los Angeles. Hosted by British writer and actor Peter Ustinov, the program included experts in London at the crime scenes themselves and at Scotland Yard, the headquarters of London's Metropolitan Police. Apart from Jack the Ripper himself, the star of the show was FBI agent John Douglas, then head of the Investigative Support Unit at FBI headquarters in Quantico, Virginia. Douglas had been invited by the program's producers to put together a psychological profile of Jack the Ripper. According to Douglas, he decided to accept for two reasons: "First, I thought the profile might be useful in training new agents. Second, it's difficult to resist matching wits, even a century later, with the most famous murderer in history" (Douglas and Olshaker, *Cases* 20). After reviewing the murders themselves and a large number of possible suspects, Douglas concluded that Jack the Ripper was an asocial white male, perceived by others as a quiet, shy loner, and proba-bly with a heavy-drinking promiscuous mother (64–65). Based on this profile, Douglas concluded that the Ripper was most likely a twenty-three-year-old Polish Jew by the name of David Cohen "or someone very much like him" (90).

For obvious reasons, there is no way of judging the accuracy of Douglas's profile, but its accuracy is irrelevant next to the fact that the FBI was invited to profile, in Douglas's words, "the most famous murderer in history" one hundred years after the murders took place. Douglas's participation in this television show illustrates the continued public interest in and celebrity of Jack the Ripper, but it also indicates just how central the FBI has become in producing the "official" definition of serial murder. Bringing the FBI and Jack the Ripper together made perfect sense. Each of the two, famous in and of themselves, could further enhance the fame and authority of the other. The FBI could confirm the Ripper's foundational place in the pantheon of serial killers, while Jack the Ripper provided further legitimacy to the FBI as the ultimate source of expertise on serial murder. As a result of this exchange, the celebrity status of Jack the Ripper and other serial killers was maintained, while at the same time the FBI agents, frequently described in glowing terms as "profilers" or "mind hunters," became celebrities in their own right.

This chapter will examine how the FBI achieved this position of unquestioned authority in defining serial murder by reconstructing how and why the FBI introduced the serial killer to contemporary America in the 1970s and 1980s. Although the official version of this story presents the FBI as disinterested defenders of the public good, selflessly protecting the helpless American public from the "epidemic" of serial crime, in fact the Bureau's definition and subsequent ownership of serial murder were almost entirely self-interested. In claiming exclusive ownership of serial murder and in using popular culture to both publicize and reinforce its reputation as the unquestioned source of expertise on serial crime, the FBI was behaving in ways that had characterized the organization since its earliest days. The first part of this chapter therefore analyzes how the Bureau, throughout its long history, has consistently cultivated a symbiotic relationship with the popular culture industries by defining multiple versions of "the enemy within," enemies that allowed the FBI to position itself at the center of the struggle against violent crime in the twentieth-century United States.

For the most part, this strategy has worked extremely well for the FBI, allowing it to rehabilitate its image whenever it was damaged by other Bureau activities. The FBI has made extremely sophisticated use of popular culture to publicize its self-image as the nation's premier crime-fighting organization, uniquely equipped to control and bring to justice the enemies within it has assiduously cultivated, such as the gangster, the communist, and, as I will show in the second part of this chapter, the serial killer. Although the serial killer demonstrates the Bureau's sophisticated ability to use the enemy within to achieve heights of public respect and political influence it had never enjoyed before, there are limits to the Bureau's ability to control this process. The disastrous decline of the Bureau's reputation through much of the 1990s, along with the related temporary waning of public interest in serial murder, presented the FBI with a dilemma: where could it find an enemy that could make as big a contribution to the Bureau's status as the serial killer? The FBI's use of figures such as the serial killer stands as the prime example of how political institutions and popular culture can coexist in a symbiotic, mutually beneficial relationship through the production and manipulation of celebrity social deviants.

What's in a Name? The Emergence of Serial Murder

In order for any individual or institution to develop an agenda around serial murder, the term "serial murder" must exist. Who first introduced the term, under what circumstances, and to achieve what ends? Although FBI personnel have frequently claimed to have coined the term (Ressler and Schachtman, *Whoever* 32–33), in fact "serial murder" as a term preexists such claims by several decades. It would be more accurate to say that the FBI popularized and regulated the use of the term to the extent that even if, technically speaking, they did not "invent" serial murder, they do, in a very real sense, "own" the concept. We can demonstrate these points by returning to the subjects of the previous chapter, Jack the Ripper and H. H. Holmes.

Even though Jack the Ripper has been retrospectively designated the first serial murderer, with Holmes being the first American serial murderer, their contemporaries did not think of them as serial killers because the concept of serial murder did not exist. Even though there had been notorious examples of what we would today call serial murder in America before Holmes, such as the Boston teenager Jesse Pomeroy, convicted in 1874 of a series of extremely brutal child murders, the Holmes and Pomeroy cases were compared with each other very infrequently, if at all. The Ripper murders were covered even more extensively in the United States than Pomeroy's crimes, but despite the fact that these killings took place only a few years before Holmes's arrest, there were very few comparisons of Holmes with Jack the Ripper, as I demonstrated in the previous chapter. Although Holmes's contemporaries saw him as a representative figure in many ways, there was apparently no consideration of the fact that Holmes might represent a new type of murderer.

In *The History of Sexuality*, in the context of discussing the "new persecution of the peripheral sexualities" (42), Michel Foucault discusses the significance of the moment when a new "type" of individual is generated from acts that previously could potentially have been committed by anyone:

> This new persecution of the peripheral sexualities entailed an *incorporation of perversions* and a new *specification of individuals*. As defined by the ancient civil or

canonical codes, sodomy was a category of forbidden acts; their perpetrator was nothing more than the juridical subject of them. The nineteenth-century homosexual became a personage, a past, a case history, and a childhood, in addition to being a type of life, a life form, and a morphology. (42–43, original emphasis)

While I am categorically *not* suggesting that homosexuality and serial murder are substantially connected in any way (indeed, it is this very assumption that I will critique in chapter 6), I do believe that Foucault's understanding of how a type of individual can be generated out of what were previously amorphous acts describes accurately the gradual development of the concept of "serial murderer" over the course of the twentieth century.

The aptness of the analogy is further confirmed by Jeffrey Weeks's comments on the significance of the "creation" of the homosexual. Weeks argues that "this new concern with the homosexual person, both in legal practice and in psychological and medical categorization," marked a crucial change from what had gone before "because it provided a new subject of social observation and speculation" (102). Once the serial killer became a type of person, a new form of behavior became visible, along with a typical perpetrator of that behavior, in ways that had previously been impossible. Judges, prosecutors, defense attorneys, doctors, psychiatrists, psychologists, and the police could now "see" serial killers in a way they could not have done before because the serial killer was now a recognizable, legible type. Although the process of typifying the serial killer was decisively accelerated and mobilized by the FBI, it was a process that had, in one way or another, been ongoing for some sixty or seventy years by the time the Bureau got involved.

The evolution of the concept of serial murder is difficult to reconstruct with any degree of specificity. It is easier to present some symptomatic examples of the much larger group of concepts that were used at one time or another to describe acts that would come to define serial murder, and to show how those concepts were gradually and in a broadly (but not neatly) linear fashion displaced by the growing influence of the term "serial murder." As I mentioned earlier, this was a process that had barely begun at the time of the Whitechapel murders and the execution of H. H. Holmes, partly because of the extreme rarity of such crimes. There is evidence from the early years of the twentieth century, however, to support the conclusion that "multiple homicide was first noted, defined, and studied in the U.S.A." (P. Jenkins, "Serial" 378).

According to Philip Jenkins in his study of serial murder in the United States between 1900 and 1940, the biggest influence on an emerging notion of multiple homicide was the crimes of Jack the Ripper. Although the influence may have taken a few years to become visible, Jenkins notes that "in 1903, the

New York Times reported a mutilation murder in terms suggesting that the word 'Ripper' was now being used in a generic sense" ("Serial" 384). Although the concept of "Ripper murders" occurred with great frequency over the next few decades, it was soon joined by a number of other concepts that all claimed to describe the same behaviors, so that the field had become quite crowded by the time the FBI entered the fray.

In his 1928 study *Masters of Crime*, Guy B. H. Logan used the term "multiple murder" with reference to Jack the Ripper. Writing in 1929, L. C. Douthwaite titled his book on the subject *Mass Murder* and emphasized how different the "mass murderer" was from "the average assassin" (v). According to Douthwaite, "There is no type of criminal so utterly impervious to the sufferings of others and so sensitive to his own as the *genus* mass murderer; it is one of his most marked, as it is one of his least understandable, characteristics" (222). By 1949, the psychiatrist Frederic Wertham was still using the term "mass murderer" to describe the most celebrated example of the type during that period, Albert Fish, who was executed at the age of sixty-six in 1936 for a series of child murders.[1] Although "mass murder" would turn out to be probably the most popular and enduring way to describe such crimes until the advent of the term "serial murder," it was by no means universally accepted. "Thrill murder" was a concept that had been around at least since the Leopold and Loeb case of 1924, while William F. Kessler and Paul B. Weston offered the terms "pattern murder" and "psycho murder" in their 1953 book *The Detection of Murder*.

This terminological confusion started to become a little clearer with the publication of *Murder by Numbers* by Grierson Dickson in 1958. Dickson was not only the first writer on the subject to acknowledge terminological difficulties in the field but also the first to mention the concept of "series murder." Having acknowledged the multitudinous ways of describing a group of murders, Dickson proposed an alternative form of classification:

> What we need is a simple rule-of-thumb division which must obviously be primarily based on quantity, so as to cover murderers who were successful for at least a time . . . Three quantitative divisions which cover the whole field in self-explanatory terms are single-murder, group-murder and series-murder. The last two are often bracketed together under some such loose term as multiple-murder, or, more popularly, mass-murder. But the divisions which should be bracketed together are clearly not the last two but the first two. (12)

Dickson then went on to argue that, having described the field as a whole, we should "restrict our researches to series-murderers who, of all types of criminal, constitute the gravest menace to civilized society" (13). Dickson criticized the tendency to include "series-murder" within the looser and more imprecise terms "multiple murder" or "mass murder," but ironically, given the subsequent influence of the concept of "series-murder," Dickson found that term equally inadequate: "We shall find it convenient to drop even our accurate but clumsy name of series-murderer, and to replace it by adding—with all due modesty—a new word to the English language: the word multicide" (13). Unfortunately for Dickson, the term "multicide" did not catch on, but neither did the term "series murder."[2] In fact, it was not for another eight years that a sustained treatment of series murder (now called by its modern name, serial murder) appeared in John Brophy's *The Meaning of Murder.*

First published in England in 1966, the American edition of *The Meaning of Murder* appeared in 1967 and contained a remarkably detailed discussion of serial murder that replicated in many ways what would become the hegemonic FBI definition of the crime, but did so a full ten years before Bureau involvement began. Brophy began by rejecting "mass murder" as a satisfactory way of describing a large number of murders committed over an extended period of time. "Serial murder" was a much more persuasive term, Brophy explained, because of what he described as the "essential character" of the crime: "repetition at intervals of time" (166). Having resolved terminological difficulties to his satisfaction, Brophy went on to install Jack the Ripper as "the most famous of all serial murderers" (189) and to distinguish serial murder committed for gain from serial murder motivated by psychopathy. Perhaps the most admirable aspect of Brophy's discussion, however, and the thing that really sets him apart from other writers on the same subject, is his lack of dogmatism. Despite having presented a very detailed and generally persuasive classificatory system, Brophy concluded his discussion by arguing: "Classifications of murder, though useful, are never so absolute and clear cut as they appear . . . Perhaps the only quality which all serial murderers have in common is the sustained purpose to murder. It is this which reveals them indisputably as abnormal and marks them off from murderers who may plead in mitigation that they killed on impulse, under provocation, or because circumstance brought them to a certain place at a certain time" (196). Because we have become so used to the idea that the FBI invented and has practically exclusive ownership of the concept "serial murder," it is surprising to find such a detailed and carefully articulated discussion of the crime a full decade before the FBI started its work on the subject. How did the FBI manage to place itself in this position of practically unquestioned authority? What were its reasons for doing so? And how did its definition of serial murder facilitate the Bureau's aims? The first step in answering these questions is to understand that the FBI's approach to serial murder was just the latest example of the Bureau's habit of creating a variety of public enemies and then defining itself as the only effective way to deal with those enemies. From the time the Bureau was founded in 1908 to the present day, this habit has been a remarkably consistent feature of how the FBI operates.

The Gangster and the G-Man

Throughout the many peaks and troughs of the Bureau's reputation, the FBI has always been intensely concerned with its public image. From cooperating with a reporter's request by producing the first "Ten Most Wanted" list in the 1950s, to introducing the Disney-designed tour through FBI Headquarters in Washington, D.C., to the long list of television programs, radio shows, comic books, and feature films made with the cooperation (and frequently under the strict control) of the Bureau, the FBI has long been keenly aware of the importance of a positive relationship with the popular culture industries.[3] But this was not always so. Even though the Bureau of Investigation was a contentious organization from its earliest days, it did not demonstrate an understanding of the importance of public image until J. Edgar Hoover took over the organization in 1924.

When the Bureau of Investigation (the word *Federal* was added in 1935) was founded by Attorney General Charles Joseph Bonaparte in 1908, it was in the teeth of opposition from many members of Congress, who feared that any federal police force would degenerate into the kind of secret police organization then terrorizing czarist Russia. Over the next few years, the Bureau seemed determined to prove its detractors right, as it acquired a reputation under Director William Burns for hunting down Bolsheviks, anarchists, and German sympathizers during World War I (C. S. Clark 322). This ignominious period in the Bureau's history culminated with fierce criticism of its role in the disastrous Palmer raids of the 1920s, which attempted to round up and deport hundreds of foreign nationals considered to be political subversives. Even though the twenty-four-year-old Hoover, then a special assistant in the Justice Department, played a key role in helping Attorney General A. Mitchell Palmer collect intelligence on, and then bring cases against, thousands of supposedly anti-American individuals, he was able to survive the controversy that erupted when many of the cases were overturned on legal grounds. When Hoover became director of the Bureau of Investigation in May 1924, he saw the wisdom of keeping a low profile. He ceased all intelligence-gathering activities and limited himself strictly to investigations of federal law.

The Bureau's reappearance in public life was largely the product of Attorney General Homer Cummings's well-publicized "war against crime" in the 1930s, a war that drew much of its rhetoric and inspiration from the larger discourses of federalization that animated the New Deal politics of the Roosevelt administration (Potter 1–9). If, during the early years of the Depression, there was a significant degree of public sympathy for the gangsters, who were popularly seen as Robin Hood outlaws, robbing the banks that had immiserated so many working people, as the 1930s wore on, public opinion took a more negative turn. The kidnapping of Charles Lindbergh's baby son in 1932 was an important turning point, both because it sharpened the public's intolerance and fear of criminal activity and because the local police's incompetent handling of the investigation increased calls for a national police force to handle such complicated and wide-ranging cases. Senator John J. Cochran of Missouri, for example, stated on the Senate floor that only "fear of Uncle Sam" could control crime (quoted in Powers, *G-Men* 12).[4]

Hoover and Cummings capitalized on such public feelings by emphasizing again and again that the country was in danger from an armed criminal underworld and that drastic action at the federal level was needed to repel this new threat. Just as the Bureau was to do with serial killers in the 1970s and 1980s, they placed particular emphasis on the mobility of gangsters like John Dillinger and criminals like Bonnie and Clyde as a way of explaining why a national police force was needed. The FBI argued that local forces were ill equipped to keep up with such mobile criminals. What was needed was a federal agency that could easily traverse state borders to catch the mobile killer. The public, convinced that violent crime was rising rapidly and becoming a serious social problem, was very receptive to the idea that crime fighting (along with many other areas of public life) should now be addressed at a national, rather than local, level. Consequently, they responded enthusiastically to Cummings's suggestion that the Division of Investigation (formed by combining Hoover's Bureau of Investigation with the Prohibition Bureau and the Bureau of Identification), under the direction of Hoover, should head the war against crime.

The intense publicity given to the threat of gangsters and to the FBI as the solution to that threat paid dividends in May 1934 when the first of nine major crime bills passed unopposed through Congress (Jeffreys 60). For the first time, the Bureau's agents were given the power to arrest and apprehend suspects and were allowed to carry firearms at all times while on duty. In addition, the Bureau's jurisdiction was expanded dramatically, with new federal crimes including killing or assaulting a federal officer; extortion involving interstate commerce; kidnapping with no ransom demand; crossing state lines to escape prosecution or avoid giving testimony; robbery of any bank operating under federal rules; and interference with interstate commerce through violence, intimidation, or threats (John Douglas, *Guide* 52–53). The result of these developments was that the FBI grew from a relatively small organiza-tion into a major crime-fighting weapon, whose congressional appropriations more than doubled in less than three years (Jeffreys 60).

The sharp growth in the Bureau's institutional and public profile in turn led to increased public awareness of the FBI's crime-fighting efforts. In fact, so enthusiastic was the public's response to Hoover and the Bureau that Homer Cummings soon found himself displaced as the focus of the war against crime, as an avalanche of popular cultural representations, epitomized by James Cagney's portrayal of a heroic FBI agent in the 1935 film *G-Men*, represented FBI agents in general and Hoover in particular as the answer to the problem of violent crime (Powers, *G-Men* 45–50). In this way, the "G-man" mystique was born, an image that had its roots in the older popular cultural figure of action detective heroes such as Nick Carter and Frank Merriwell, and that portrayed FBI men as brave, moral, efficient, and ruthless upholders of the law. The mystique reached its peak not so much when John Dillinger was shot and killed outside the Biograph Theater in Chicago on July 22, 1934 (an event to which the media were invited by the FBI), but rather when Hoover used the publicity generated by that event to mythologize the Bureau as an implacable and infallible crime-fighting machine. Films such as *G-Men*, therefore, both contributed to and were a reflection of the Bureau's ability to parlay the huge amount of positive publicity given to its crime-fighting activities into both political influence and even more financial and institutional growth (Powers, *Secrecy* 217–18).[5]

The iconic status of the gangster as the "enemy within," then, demonstrates the way in which the FBI was able to use such "supercriminals," with the enthusiastic cooperation of the popular culture industries, to promote itself as the most important and effective crime-fighting organization in the country. By convincing the American public that the country was being overrun by homicidal, fiendishly cunning gangsters, the FBI was able to make itself look heroic whenever it apprehended one of these criminals. In the process, the FBI formulated a pattern that we will see again in its use of the serial killer: establishing (even exaggerating) a criminal problem in order to offer itself as the only solution.[6]

To imply, however, that the Bureau's manipulation of popular culture was invariably deliberate and always successful is to oversimplify this complex rela-tionship. In order to understand properly the Bureau's relationship with pop-ular culture, we need to complicate this picture. To begin with, the fit between the Bureau's self-image and popular culture's image of the Bureau was not al-ways perfect. Indeed, Hoover initially found the "G-man" image as much of an irritant as a boon, because he felt it misrepresented and oversimplified the collective, bureaucratic, and technological nature of the organization he had built (Powers, *G-Men* 94ff.). Consequently, Hoover frequently tried to counteract the action-oriented, individualistic G-man image through competing forms of popular culture, including action pulps, comic books, and radio programs that publicized Hoover's own understanding of the FBI.

In an attempt to compete with the various G-man pulp comics on the market, for example, Hoover endorsed a pulp called *The Feds* in 1935. Although as lurid in style as its competitors, *The Feds* was not as appealing. Because it was trying to provide a more wholesome and responsible alternative to the action detective formula that dominated the other pulps, *The Feds*, rather than featuring fictional detective adventures, instead concentrated on detailed nonfiction essays describing various aspects of the Bureau's operations (Powers, *G-Men* 174). But the real problem with *The Feds* was that "instead of giving young readers an action hero to identify with in formula adventures, the magazine gave them the boss of the action heroes. Even more unpardonably, the magazine told the kids that they ought to look up to Hoover because he was a great teacher. Kids did not buy pulp magazines for a chance to identify with teachers" (Powers, *G-Men* 175). Because of such missteps, *The Feds* folded in 1937, after less than two years on the market.

The fate of *The Feds* typified Hoover-endorsed popular culture initiatives, which were all complete flops because they failed to give the public the violent action they craved. Hoover eventually realized that it was easier and more profitable to let the G-man image work on the Bureau's behalf, even agreeing to have himself cast in that role in newspapers and magazines. If Hoover's dominant public image up to this point had been that of a master supervisor of a complex law enforcement organization, the creation of his G-man image meant that he had to get out from behind the desk and be photographed holding not only a bewildering variety of guns but also other appropriate man-of-action objects, such as fishing rods and tennis rackets (Powers, *G-Men* 183). More substantially, the desire to project the right image also got Hoover out into the field to make arrests, something he had been repeatedly criticized for never having done. Between 1936 and 1939, Hoover organized and led several high-profile raiding parties to arrest a variety of gangsters and bank robbers, beginning with the former Ma Barker gang member and last big-name bandit at large, Alvin Karpis, in April 1936 (Powers, *G-Men* 178). These raids were often uncomfortable combinations of genuine FBI operations and carefully choreographed publicity stunts. Nevertheless, they had the desired effect, turning Hoover into a major celebrity in a way that had previously been unthinkable.

If Hoover allowed himself to assume a starring role in popular cultural representations of the FBI, however, he continued to view his celebrity as a necessary evil. Consequently, when the mass media occasionally bestowed celebrity status on other members of the Bureau, Hoover was incensed, partly because he felt that singling out individuals misrepresented the collective nature of the organization, but also because he felt that popular cultural promotion of individuals other than J. Edgar Hoover threatened his absolute control over the FBI. For example, when Agent Melvin Purvis, who hunted down John Dillinger, killed Pretty Boy Floyd, and also played a prominent role in several other gangster cases of the period, became a celebrity, Hoover first reprimanded him and then hounded him out of the FBI (Powers, *G-Men* 127ff.). By using such extreme methods, Hoover felt that the correct moral would be drawn from the spectacle of gangster deaths: that they were the product of the efficient running of a well-organized FBI, not of acts of courage on the part of individual agents.

The spectacular success of the Bureau in exploiting the phenomenon of the gangster to promote its own image and institutional authority made a huge impression on Hoover, so much so that he spent the rest of his career looking for figures that would fit the role of "the enemy within" as well as the gangster did. Sometimes, as in the 1950s when he demonized American communists, Hoover was able once again to strike a chord with the American public in a way that profited the Bureau both financially and ideologically (Powers, *Secrecy* 284, 289–90). At other times, as with Hoover's paranoid and obsessive persecution of Martin Luther King Jr. and the antiwar movement in the 1960s and 1970s, the FBI found itself out of step with public opinion, and the reputation of the Bureau suffered accordingly.

The real damage came after Hoover's death in 1972. While he was alive, Hoover's power to intimidate was such that he was able (to some extent, at least) to keep a lid on criticism of the Bureau and also control public access to the Bureau's secrets. With Hoover gone all that changed, and the revelations about the Bureau's conduct that came out throughout the 1970s completely destroyed the Bureau's reputation, so much so that all attempts at popular cultural rehabilitation (such as the television show *Today's FBI*, which premiered in 1981 and featured painfully sensitive, emotionally open, and politically liberal FBI agents) were in vain. Historian Richard Gid Powers, writing in 1983, understandably described the Bureau's reputation as fatally wounded; indeed, it was hard to see how the FBI could ever recover (*G-Men* 289). But just as the Bureau had been able to repair its reputation in the 1930s after the damage done by the Palmer raids in the 1920s, so in the 1980s it was able to bounce back from the damage inflicted by the revelations of the 1970s. Help for the Bureau was just around the corner, and it came from a most unlikely source: the serial killer.

The FBI Claims the Serial Killer

We have become so accustomed to thinking of the FBI as the unquestioned source of authority on serial murder that to emphasize this fact seems redundant. According to Robert Ressler, however, who is perhaps the single most influential figure in constructing the Bureau's perspective on serial murder, at one time the FBI was almost completely uninterested in "murderers, rapists, child molesters, and other criminals who prey on their fellow men" (Ressler and Schachtman, *Whoever* 38). Ressler states that such crimes were seen as the responsibility of local law enforcement agencies, not federal agencies. Ressler himself, who joined the FBI in 1970 after working in the U.S. Army's Criminal Investigation Division, made an important contribution to the change of emphasis that led to the Bureau's focus on crimes such as serial murder by organizing the first FBI-sponsored research study of serial murderers, the Criminal Personality Research Project, in 1979. Largely owing to Ressler's efforts, within ten years the FBI went from having no official interest in serial murder whatsoever to being the preeminent source of expertise on the subject.

To understand how this transformation came about, we need to look at how the FBI defined serial murder. Although the FBI had studied serial murder (although not always using this term) since the 1970s, its work did not become well known until October 26, 1983, when the Justice Department held a news conference in Washington, D.C., to "disclose some of the findings from . . . preliminary research into . . . the problem of 'serial murders,' killings by such people as Jack the Ripper or the Boston Strangler" ("35 Murderers" A17). This news conference is important for two reasons. First, it marks the point when the concept of "serial murder" came to the attention of the American public as a whole for the first time. Getting the public's attention and then convincing them that serial murder was indeed a serious problem that deserved their attention were the preconditions for everything else that the FBI wanted to achieve with respect to this crime. Second, the news conference determined that the direction of future public policy and mass media discussions of serial murder would be favorable to the FBI's goals by defining the nature and scope of serial murder in highly specific and partial terms.

In its article on the news conference, the *New York Times* stated the Justice Department's definition of serial murderers as "those who kill for reasons other than greed, a fight, jealousy, or family disputes" ("35 Murderers" A17). This definition represents the beginning of a pattern that became more sharply defined in the days and weeks following the news conference—the gradual equation in the public mind between serial murder and sexual homicide, often accompanied by the most extreme forms of sexual sadism. The sexual dimensions of serial murder were not referred to explicitly in the Justice Department news conference but were a prominent feature of the explosion of journalistic treatments of serial murder that followed the news conference. For example, in a January 1984 *New York Times* article entitled "Officials Cite a Rise in Killers Who Roam U.S. for Victims" (an article that recapitulated many of the themes of the Justice Department news conference), reporter Robert Lindsey cited "many officials" who thought the increase in serial murders was "linked somehow to the sweeping changes in attitudes regarding sexuality that have occurred in the past 20 years" (7). Lindsey went on to quote Captain Robbie Robertson of the Michigan State Police on the same subject: "I think you'll find sex as the dominant factor in almost all the serial murders" (7). The fact that Lindsey described Robertson as "one of the nation's foremost investigators of such crimes" gave such statements considerable authority.

Similarly, in an August 1984 article published in the popular science magazine *Omni*, Dan Kagan argued that serial killers shared "a powerful, overt sexual component. They may rape and then kill, or kill and then have sex with the victim. They may be child molesters who kill children after abducting them for sex. They may be homosexuals who kill their anonymous partners after sex" (20). Although Kagan's list of what he described as "nightmare images" sounds quite various, in fact articles such as those by Lindsey and Kagan contributed to making the dominant popular definition of serial murder extraordinarily narrow.

Logically, the crime of serial murder should include any offender, male or female, regardless of motive, who kills over time, normally with some type of pattern to their killing, in terms of motive, victim selection, and/or type of weapon used (Hickey 8). But since 1983, the assumption that serial murder can be unproblematically equated solely with sexual homicide can be found in more or less explicit form in practically any discussion of serial murder, whether in the mass media, an academic treatise, a public policy document, or a psychological study of an individual offender. The equation of serial murder with sexual homicide is especially common in law enforcement work on the crime, as the title of the 1988 landmark FBI-sponsored study of serial murder, *Sexual Homicide*, suggests. This concentration on sexual homicide means that public discussion of other forms of serial murder is largely absent, as Eric Hickey has noted: "Although many offenders actually fall into the serial killer classification, they are excluded because they fail to meet law enforcement definitions or media-generated stereotypes of brutal, blood-thirsty monsters. The 'angels of death' who work in hospitals and kill patients, or nursing home staff who kill the elderly, or the 'black widows' who kill their family and relatives also meet the general criteria for serial killing except for the stereotypic element of violence" (7). The Justice Department definition of serial murder represents exactly this type of exclusion. By discounting a motive such as greed in serial murder, the Justice Department automatically excludes from its definition most female serial murderers, who typically kill family members or lodgers for financial reasons. As Hickey estimates that such murderers represent 17 percent of the 203 American serial murder cases occurring between 1795 and 1988 that he studies, this is a significant omission.

The concentration on sexual homicide raises the question of why so much attention has been given to one type of serial murder, while other types have been rendered practically invisible. One answer to this question claims that sexual homicide is the most significant type of serial murder, both because it is the most common type and also because it involves such extreme violence visited upon the bodies of its victims. While both these points are valid, they do not fully explain the almost complete absence of other forms of serial murder from public discussion.

The focus on sexual homicide and the lack of attention paid to other forms of serial murder reinforce an extremely limited and distorted image of what serial murder is, who commits it, who is victimized, how they are victimized, and why they are victimized. This distorted image of serial murder, moreover, increases the public's level of fear and their sense that society is under siege, partly because the crimes are so vicious, and partly because the victim selection of this type of serial murderer seems so random. Third, this level of fear, if not panic, makes the public more responsive to the idea that massive federal involvement in serial murder is the only way something can be done about this problem. Increased federal involvement in turn ensures that the FBI's perspective on serial murder becomes more and more influential, to the point where it comes to seem like the only rational approach to the problem. In other words, the FBI's approach to serial murder has been practically identical to its approach to the gangster earlier: define a crime problem in the most extreme terms possible, generate a siege mentality among the American public, and then offer the FBI as the only feasible solution to the problem.

In pointing to how the federal law enforcement bureaucracy benefited both ideologically (from having its perspective on serial murder become dominant) and materially (from gaining increased federal funds to fight serial murder) from the equation of serial murder with sexual homicide, I may seem to be suggesting that the FBI deliberately manipulated the public image of serial murder to achieve its own aims. However, I do not believe one needs to attribute intentionality to the FBI or federal law enforcement in general in order to understand how serial murder presented it with a unique opportunity to expand both its material resources and the scope of its jurisdictions.

Such an extension of federal law enforcement influence had been resisted by civil rights activists in the 1970s in the wake of post-Hoover-era revelations about the Bureau's counterintelligence operations against large numbers of American citizens, because there was concern about giving the FBI this type of power once more. Serial murder thus gave federal law enforcement the opportunity to re-present their requests for expanded funding and jurisdictional powers, but this time under the banner of fighting serial murder, a subject that no sensible politician would want to oppose publicly (P. Jenkins, *Using* 57). In fact, the construction of serial murder as an explicitly federal crime was part of a larger effort by the Reagan administration in the early 1980s to extend federal jurisdiction to a number of serious crimes that before were the exclusive property of local law enforcement agencies (Ressler and Schachtman, *Whoever* 105–6). I will discuss exactly how the FBI benefited from the increased public attention to serial murder through the creation of new law enforcement institutions later in this chapter, but for now I want to note that the identification of serial murder with sexual homicide was just one element in the effort to persuade the American public that federal involvement was the only way to stop the "epidemic" of serial murder.

The second element in this effort also appears in the 1983 Justice Department news conference, when the Justice Department distinguished mass murderers "whose killings all occur in one spot," from serial murderers, who "often cross city and state lines, making detection more difficult" ("35 Murderers" A17). Emphasizing the mobility of serial killers repeated a feature of the FBI's image of the gangster in the 1930s. Just as it had done with the gangster, the Bureau emphasized the roaming serial killer both to frighten the public and to position itself as the logical answer to the problem of serial murder. Once again, this feature of the Justice Department's version of serial murder was breathlessly propagated by journalistic treatments of the subject. Robert Lindsey, for example, summarized the views of Seattle police investigator Robert Keppel on the issue of mobility: "Mr. Keppel said that such killers tended to be highly mobile, ready to move quickly to another town after committing several killings that might lead to their detection" (7).

The thought that a serial killer could take advantage of the nation's freeway system and of the lack of communication between police departments within a state or between states made it seem that no one was immune from the risk of serial murder. How real this risk is for the vast majority of Americans is an open question. Some have indeed claimed that everyone is at risk (Egger, "Working" 352), but it is more accurate to say that some groups (principally prostitutes, hitchhikers, transients, and homeless people) become victims of serial murderers far more than other groups.

The idea that all serial killers are highly mobile offenders provided the FBI with a ready-made justification for the involvement of federal law enforcement authorities in the tracking and apprehension of serial killers. It is not surprising, therefore, to find that in congressional hearings conducted on serial murder a few months before the Justice Department news conference, much was made of the mobility of serial offenders. The true-crime writer Ann Rule's testimony before the Senate Subcommittee on Juvenile Justice was typical in this regard: "The thing that I have found about the serial murderers that I have researched, they travel constantly, they are trollers, while most of us might put 15,000 to 20,000 miles a year on our cars, several of the serial killers I have researched have put 200,000 miles a year on their cars. They move constantly. They may drive all night long. They are always looking for the random victim who may cross their path" (U.S. Senate 14–15). Even though the figure of 200,000 miles Rule gives would mean that such serial killers would have to drive an average of 550 miles a day every single day of the year, such absurdities did not prevent the image of the highly mobile serial killer from quickly becoming as pervasive and accepted as the image of the serial killer as sexual sadist, and much work on serial murder accepts as incontrovertible truth the mobility of the serial murderer (see, for example, Holmes and De Burger 30, 31; Cameron and Frazer 156). Such accounts tend to give great weight to cases such as those of Ted Bundy, who killed in Washington, Colorado, Utah, and Florida, and Henry Lee Lucas, who claimed to have killed in practically every state in the country (P. Jenkins, *Using* 64, 65; Kappeler, Blumberg, and Potter 55–56).

The image of the mobile serial killer, however, does not tell the whole story. Three types of mobility characterize serial killers: there are those who travel, those who never leave the local area or state in which they start killing, and those who kill exclusively in their home or their place of employment (see Hickey 17). It has been estimated that the highly mobile serial killer accounts for approximately a third of all serial murder victims, while a majority of serial killers operate in a specific place or area and do not travel (Hickey 80, 81; P. Jenkins, *Using* 45–46). This suggests that the Justice Department and the FBI hugely overestimated the percentage of mobile serial killers as a way to justify their own involvement in this particular crime. Once again, one does not have to assume intentionality to note how this emphasis supported the argument that federal involvement was the only effective way of stopping serial murder.[7]

Apart from equating serial murder with sexual homicide and stressing the mobility of serial killers, the other significant element in the way the FBI defined serial murder was its estimate of the scale of the crime. At the October 1983 news conference, Roger Depue, then-director of the FBI's Behavioral Science Unit, said that "his office wanted to study all the open murder cases in the country [because] 28 percent of the nation's roughly 20,000 homicides went unsolved and . . . the percentage ha[s] been rising in recent years" ("35 Murderers" A17). Depue clearly implied that there was an equivalence between the number of serial murders and the number of unsolved murders being committed each year. This suggestion was quickly taken up and disseminated by the mass media, and Depue's implication was soon transformed into the unambiguous claim that serial killers were responsible for 4,000 (roughly 28 percent of 20,000) victims a year. This number, along with the Justice Department estimate that there were some thirty-five serial killers active in the United States at any one time, did more than any other piece of information to galvanize public feeling about serial murder, almost to the point of absolute panic.

The Justice Department and the FBI's reaction to this panic was to revise this figure of 4,000 at a later news conference, suggesting instead that serial killers were responsible for the deaths of closer to 540 victims a year (P. Jenkins, *Using* 68–69). Despite this correction, however, the figure of 4,000 has remained influential to this day. Even though, like Rule's estimate that serial killers traveled 200,000 miles a year, the figures of 35 serial killers and 4,000 victims were absurd (each killer would have to have murdered an average of 114 people a year), one can still find the figure of 4,000 victims widely quoted in popular discussions of serial murder. Although there is undoubtedly some overlap between serial and unsolved murders, there are also obvious differences between them (for example, many "unsolved" murders are subsequently solved and turn out not to be the work of serial killers at all). Even Ressler, who rarely criticizes the FBI in his writings, admits to the Bureau's role in propagating the erroneous 4,000-victim figure and thus contributing to the panic and exaggeration about serial murder in the mid-1980s: "In feeding the frenzy," Ressler says, "we were using an old tactic in Washington, playing up the problem as a way of getting Congress and the higher-ups in the executive branch to pay attention to it" (*Whoever* 229–30). Ressler softens the admission by implying that the Bureau's reasons for contributing to the panic were altruistic. As we will see shortly, there are good reasons to contest a view of the FBI as an altruistic organization.

Apart from the one attempt to replace the figure of 4,000 annual serial murder victims with 540, the Justice Department and the FBI were not exactly eager to correct the mistaken impression of the scale of serial murder they had created. After all, the exaggeration of the scale of serial murder was consistent with federal law enforcement's hyperbolic definition of serial murder as extreme sexual sadism, a definition that was seemingly intended to instill the maximum amount of fear in the American public. Consumers of mass media representations of serial murder were meant to see the serial killer as a ravening sexual sadist, roaming across America in an endless quest for blood, leaving thousands of victims in his wake. The exaggeration of the scale of serial murder was thus just as useful to federal law enforcement as the emphasis on mobility and sexual homicide were in achieving its goal of increased resources and power (P. Jenkins, *Using* 49, 50).

Serial Killing and the Federal State

The fact that the popular cultural industries embraced and disseminated the FBI's definition of serial murder so quickly and comprehensively suggests that this definition dovetailed neatly with broader patterns of thinking about crime and violence that were current in the United States during the 1980s. In a 1986 article, "Sexual Killers and Their Victims," Ressler and his co-authors explained that the law enforcement typology of serial killers "is based on discrete, verifiable concepts and behavior. It does not rest solely on controversial statements of motivation derived from a complex theory of subconscious motivation" (306). Ressler went on to say that "to hypothesize that a serial murderer killed a young woman to destroy his internal female identification with his sister is cumbersome and cannot be substantiated by crime scene evidence or other data available before his capture and evaluation" (306). In its hostility toward psychological explanations of criminal behavior and its emphasis on the apprehension and conviction, rather than the study and treatment, of serial murderers (see Ressler, Burgess, and Douglas, *Sexual Homicide* 10), the FBI perspective both reflected and contributed to the punitive attitude toward criminals that characterized the law and order emphasis developed by the Reagan administrations of the 1980s.

While it is debatable how much therapeutic perspectives on violent crime (in which the focus is on why the perpetrator behaves as he does, what events in the perpetrator's early psychic and/or physical life influenced his later behavior, and how that behavior can be treated or cured) have ever been dominant, the law enforcement perspective on serial murder clearly locates psychological speculation at the bottom end of a hierarchy whose pinnacle is occupied by verifiable (and therefore, it is implied, objective) crime scene data. Psychological evidence is always subordinate to this kind of data.

That this type of hierarchization was typical of the Reagan era as a whole is suggested by the founding in 1981 of the Task Force on Violent Crime by Attorney General William French Smith. According to Roger Depue, "The task force was to make recommendations regarding what might be done to curb the rapid growth of violent crime and to reduce its adverse impact on the quality of American life" (2). The recommendations that emerged from the task force certainly did not emphasize prevention of violent crime or the treatment of its perpetrators. Instead, the tendency was to recommend more punitive sentences and the building of more prisons, a policy that continues to this day. The FBI's definition of serial murder has to be understood within this larger context of President Reagan's desire to "get tough" on violent crime in general.

The rewards the FBI gained from increased public attention to serial murder were not only ideological (having their perspective on the crime become dominant) but also institutional: namely, the founding of the National Center for the Analysis of Violent Crime (NCAVC) and the Violent Criminal Apprehension Program (VICAP). Both the NCAVC and VICAP owe their existence to the mid-1980s public panic about serial murder that I have already discussed, but there were also two more specific influences—the attorney general's 1981 Task Force on Violent Crime, and the July 1983 Senate hearings on serial murder. The task force asked each agency of the Department of Justice to prepare a report on what contribution it could make to reducing violent crime. FBI Director William H. Webster concluded that the Bureau's Training Division, located at Quantico, Virginia, was the logical resource for ideas on this subject, and within the Training Division, the Behavioral Science Unit (BSU) began to prepare a report for the attorney general (Ressler, Burgess, and Douglas, *Sexual Homicide* 100).

Since the mid-1970s, the FBI had conducted at first unofficial and then Bureau-sponsored research into personality profiles of incarcerated sexual killers. The Task Force on Violent Crime gave the Bureau the opportunity to present an official request for the establishment of a national database that would contain information on all solved and unsolved serial homicides, the aim being to "identify and apprehend the most violent of all criminals in society today—the serial murderer" (Howlett, Hanfland, and Ressler 18). This request was the immediate origin of VICAP. VICAP was conceived of as one division of the NCAVC (the other divisions being Research and Development, Profiling and Consultation, and Training), and the structure and responsibilities of the NCAVC were conceptualized jointly by the FBI, state and local law enforcement agencies, and the Department of Justice agencies of the National Institute of Justice, the Office of Justice Assistance, and the Office of Juvenile Justice and Delinquency Prevention (Webster 1).

In April 1983, Senator Arlen Specter, chair of the Subcommittee on Juvenile Justice of the Senate Judiciary Committee, wrote to the Bureau's director,

William Webster, requesting from him his assessment of the need for NCAVC, where it should be located, and how much it would cost. Three months after sending this letter, Specter chaired the Senate hearings on serial murder, in which all significant decisions regarding the NCAVC were made. By the time Webster responded to Specter, the NCAVC was a fait accompli. The Senate hearings are a perfect example of how the law enforcement definition of serial murder was implemented in the interests of acquiring new federal funding for the FBI (P. Jenkins, *Using* 59, 60). The expert witnesses who testified before the subcommittee were unanimous in painting the most terrifying picture of serial murder possible—it was a crime of vast proportions, characterized by extreme sexual sadism, committed by highly mobile offenders who could be tracked down and apprehended only by federal institutions such as NCAVC and VICAP. The true-crime writer Ann Rule's testimony touched on all these issues: "The serial murderer is a man who travels continually. He is a troller who encounters his victims in a random and senseless manner, killing those he perceives to be vulnerable, simply because he is obsessed with killing for its own sake ... The serial killer seldom knows his victims before he seizes them. They are strangers, targets for his tremendous inner rage. He is ruthless, conscienceless, and invariably cunning" (U.S. Senate 20). When asked by Senator Paula Hawkins of Florida whether she thought VICAP would have affected the Ted Bundy case, Rule claimed that "VI-CAP would have saved 14 to 15 young women's lives at least" (18). John Walsh, who would later become the host of the FBI-sponsored show *America's Most Wanted*, was even more vehement in his support for VICAP, pouring scorn on any potential privacy concerns: "Now, there is a concern about a VI-CAP system in the missing children's bill about personal freedoms and invasion of privacy, et cetera, et cetera. Well, believe me, the women who are murdered by these people and the children, their privacy is invaded to the maximum. I think people have had it" (28).

In the face of such forceful unanimity, and spurred on by the desire to be seen to be doing something effective about violent crime, the Senate had no hesitation in recommending the necessary funding for VICAP and the NCAVC. Webster's letter was almost superfluous and simply confirmed conclusions that had already been reached—yes, there was a need for the NCAVC, he stated, and it should be located at FBI headquarters in Virginia. The estimated cost for the first two years of the NCAVC of $2,985,000 (U.S. Senate 8) was seen as a small price to pay for taking decisive action against a social problem as severe as serial murder. The NCAVC was established as a pilot project funded by the National Institute of Justice in June 1984. President Reagan considered this to be such a significant step in his fight against violent crime that he personally announced the establishment of the NCAVC at the 1984 National Sheriff's Association Conference. In October 1985, the total cost of the NCAVC was absorbed into the annual budget of the FBI, making it safe from possible changes of political administration at the federal level (Depue 5). VICAP became officially operational on May 29, 1985, and immediately began to enter the first of hundreds of profiles of possible serial murder cases that local law enforcement agencies required assistance with.

History Repeating Itself: The G-Man and the Mind Hunter

As a result of these developments, the FBI of the late 1980s and early 1990s bore striking resemblances to the Bureau of the 1930s: once again, the Bureau had succeeded in reestablishing its reputation in the wake of damaging scandal. In their rush to be seen fighting serial murder, politicians and pundits forgot any qualms they may have had about the Bureau's previous questionable use of power and resources and showered the organization with money and praise. By the time follow-up congressional hearings were held in April and May 1986, arguments for the necessity of federal involvement in the crime of serial murder that had been offered tentatively by the FBI in 1983 were now parroted by politicians as unquestioned truths. The FBI had firmly cemented its central role in fighting serial murder. Seen in this light, the founding of the NCAVC and VICAP was a stunning success for the FBI, extending its resources and responsibilities, and members of the Bureau readily admitted this.[8] In a special issue of the *FBI Law Enforcement Bulletin* devoted to the NCAVC, Richard Ault Jr. noted how the "changing image and mission of the FBI in the past 10 years have provided the NCAVC with an unparalleled opportunity to dig into the foundations of violent and nonviolent crimes with the hope of discovering clues about the behavior of offenders that can be applied in a practical fashion to investigations" (8).[9] But although members of the FBI were eager to discuss how the NCAVC provided multiple opportunities to extend their jurisdiction, they were much less forthcoming about whether its new institutional powers had actually succeeded in reducing the incidence of serial murder and increasing the numbers of arrests of serial killers.

In spite of the note of official optimism concerning how well the NCAVC was working during this period, the evidence suggests that the FBI had good cause to be reticent about the success rate of programs like VICAP. Soon after the institution of the program, it became clear that many local law enforcement authorities were not taking the time and effort to do the extensive VICAP paperwork, and so the VICAP forms were redesigned to make them easier and therefore quicker to complete (Howlett, Hanfland, and Ressler 17, 18). Very rarely, however, did the FBI hazard a guess as to how many cases the

VICAP program had significantly helped in solving. One exception to this general point can be found in Ressler, Burgess, and Douglas's *Sexual Homicide* (ix–x), but even here the estimate concerned the number of cases where profiling helped focus the investigation, rather than those in which profiling substantially helped solve the case. Some critics of the federal response to serial murder pointed out that many recent high-profile serial murder cases, such as those involving Jeffrey Dahmer and Joel Rifkin, did not involve the FBI at all, for the simple reason that no one knew Dahmer and Rifkin were serial killers until they were both arrested on unrelated matters.

But despite the fact that many serial killers were still arrested by accident, as it were, and despite the difficulty of assessing the effectiveness of the NCAVC and VICAP, the reputation of the FBI as a source of expertise on serial murder continued to flourish for the first part of the 1990s. Why was this? Part of the explanation lies in the overwhelmingly laudatory tone of popular cultural representations of the FBI. This hymn of praise to the Bureau reached its apex in the response to the film version of *The Silence of the Lambs*, but this response was itself a continuation of earlier positive reviews of FBI work on serial murder in general, and on the effectiveness of the investigative technique of psychological profiling in particular.

The significance of psychological profiling lay in the fact that it quickly became the most visible and well-known sign of the professional expertise of the FBI in the area of serial murder. Psychological profiling is based on the assumption that crime scenes can be analyzed and made to yield evidence concerning the psychological state of the perpetrator of the crime. This information can then be written up into a profile that serves as an investigative aid for the local law enforcement agency working on the crime, as a way of narrowing its list of potential suspects. Partly because of the writings of the FBI itself, which identified profiling as being especially appropriate in cases of serial murder because such crimes often "appear motiveless and thus offer few obvious clues about the killer's identity" (Douglas and Burgess 10, 11), and partly because of sympathetic journalistic coverage and popular cultural representations, profiling came to be seen as an almost magically effective method of tracking down serial killers, thus playing a crucial role in increasing the Bureau's influence in defining serial murder.[10]

Just as their hunting down of gangsters in the 1930s produced the image of the FBI agents as the "G-men," so profiling serial killers in the 1980s produced an analogous image: the FBI agent as "mind hunter," "uniquely qualified to deal with the serial murder menace" (P. Jenkins, *Using* 70). This image of FBI agents was a prominent part of *The Silence of the Lambs*, and it achieved the dual purpose of showing the human face of FBI bureaucracy (thus encouraging public identification with that bureaucracy) and reducing the complex social dynamics of serial murder to a simplistic morality tale of a fight between the good FBI agent and the bad serial murderer (thus reinforcing the public's sense that something tangible was being done about serial murder).[11] Although the extremely flattering "mind hunter" image of the FBI agent was a prominent feature of media coverage around the time of *The Silence of the Lambs*, the image itself had been used by the media for years preceding the release of the film. In a 1986 *New York Times Magazine* article entitled "The FBI's New Psyche Squad," for example, Stephen Michaud described the work of the profilers with great enthusiasm: "Working largely from police reports, autopsies, photos, and the like . . . they ferret out strictly behavioral clues to the identities of Unsubs [unknown subjects, a Bureau term for suspects] and produce multipage, typewritten analyses, often in startling clarity and detail" (40). The frenzy around the release of *Silence*, therefore, was the culmination of well-established media habits.

The atmosphere of media adulation that surrounded the Bureau during this period meant that comments about the limitations of psychological profiling from those most closely associated with the method tended to be ignored. For example, in their 1980 article on lust murder, Robert Hazelwood and John Douglas stated that "what can be done in this area is limited, and prescribed investigative procedures should not be suspended, altered, or replaced by receipt of a profile" (22). Once again, however, such an explicit statement of the limitations of federal law enforcement's impact on serial murder was relatively rare. As more and more media coverage described profiling as a practically infallible method for apprehending serial killers, the FBI apparently became more and more disinclined to correct this erroneous impression, preferring instead to ride the wave of publicity.

Such publicity took various forms and came from people both inside and outside the FBI. In her autobiography, *Special Agent: My Life on the Front Lines as a Woman in the FBI*, Candice DeLong describes the Behavioral Science Unit (BSU) profilers in reverential terms: "It was the dawn of the art/science of profiling, the most systematic analysis of crimes and their perpetrators ever attempted in history. I was lucky enough to train under the masters at the Bureau's celebrated Behavioral Science Unit and could now and then dream that I was helping to advance the field" (7). In his book about veteran profiler Roy Hazelwood, *The Evil That Men Do*, Stephen Michaud works even harder to create a cult of personality around the mind hunter, giving the following purple description of when he first met Hazelwood: "When I located Hazelwood that night in Des Moines, he was seated alone at a low table, savoring a nonfilter Lucky Strike and a sparkling glass of iced gin, habits he has since reluctantly abandoned. Roy's gaze was obscured by the amber lenses in his aviator frames—a look he'd acquired in Vietnam—and he was bathed in a haze of blue cigarette smoke" (3). One would never guess from such intensely noirish popular cultural depictions of the profiler that there have been many criticisms of the effectiveness of psychological profiling, and again they come from both inside and outside law enforcement circles. In *The Riverman: Ted Bundy and I Hunt for the Green River Killer*, homicide detective Robert Keppel is less critical of the concept of profiling per se than of how it has been practiced by the FBI: "We couldn't wait to hear what gems of wisdom would come from the BSU's agents, most of whom were only self-proclaimed experts in murder investigations and had never investigated one lead in an actual murder case. The FBI were the kings of follow-up but couldn't solve a crime in progress" (114–15). Keppel's comments are indicative of a long-standing tension between local police officers and the FBI, a tension that has constituted a very practical obstacle to VICAP's effectiveness.

Less vituperative but equally damaging are those critiques of the FBI version of profiling that come from profiling experts working outside law enforcement. Works such as Grover Maurice Godwin's *Hunting Serial Predators: A Multivariate Classification Approach to Profiling Violent Behavior*, D. Kim Rossmo's *Geographic Profiling*, and Janet L. Jackson and Debra A. Bekerian's edited collection *Offender Profiling: Theory, Research, and Practice* all represent the burgeoning field of profiling studies, and most of them begin by distancing themselves from and defining themselves against the FBI's conception of psychological profiling. Although in the twenty-first century, such criticisms have come close to discrediting the Bureau's profiling approaches completely, back in the 1980s, psychological profiling and the FBI both enjoyed high levels of prestige.

So solid was the Bureau's reputation during the 1980s, in fact, that once it and the Justice Department had succeeded in winning federal funding for the NCAVC and VICAP, the subsequent performance of these institutions in controlling serial murder was apparently irrelevant. Hard facts about whether the incidence of serial murder was going down, and if so, how much of this decline was due to federal law enforcement efforts, took second place to maintaining the public's belief that the FBI had everything under control and that the expansion of its institutional power was having the desired effect upon the "epidemic" of serial killers.

This perfect example of the triumph of image over substance resulted from the mutually reinforcing relationship that had developed by this point between federal law enforcement, the news media, and popular culture, as described by Philip Jenkins: "The Justice Department formulates the image, which is transformed and publicized in fiction, which in turn shapes public attitudes and expectations; while the news media present stories that respond to these images and stereotypes. In turn, the investigative priorities of bureaucratic agencies are formed by public and legislative expectations, which are derived from popular culture and the news media" (*Using* 223–24). Although Jenkins was undoubtedly correct to claim that the representation of the FBI's involvement in serial murder in the popular cultural media is important in maintaining the Bureau's public reputation, Jenkins, writing in 1994, could not have known of the catastrophic collapse in the Bureau's reputation that was to unfold over the latter half of the 1990s. The FBI went from a position of unquestioned influence and authority to reeling from one scandal to another partly because it became overreliant on serial murder as the basis of its reputation. As a result, the Bureau was left floundering when the American public's priorities shifted and interest in the serial killer temporarily waned.

From Quantico to Hollywood

Given the Bureau's long-standing obsession with its public image, popular cultural representations of the FBI have become an object of study within the FBI itself. In an article published in the *FBI Law Enforcement Bulletin* entitled "Crime-Time Television," Scott Nelson discussed television programs such *The FBI*, which ran from 1965 to 1974, and *Today's FBI*, a product of the early 1980s (2). These shows, whose current equivalents are such programs as *America's Most Wanted* and *Unsolved Mysteries*, profiled actual FBI cases and invariably portrayed the Bureau in a positive light as an effective and powerful crime-fighting organization. As I have already indicated, the majority of positive representations of the FBI during the 1980s and 1990s focused on psychological profiling, and an especially clear example of such work can be found in H. Paul Jeffers's book *Who Killed Precious? How FBI Special Agents Combine High Technology and Psychology to Identify Violent Criminals*. The subtitle left no doubt as to Jeffers's attitude toward the FBI. In fact, his book was completely uncritical of the Bureau in general, and of the work of the Behavioral Science Unit (BSU) in particular, enthusiastically describing the near-miraculous effectiveness of the psychological profiles drawn up by the BSU.

Jeffers's enthusiasm frequently led him into absurdities. For example, he discussed a serial murder case that was, to all intents and purposes, solved when investigators discovered a credit card slip with the name and address of the murderer's father in a plastic bag that was left covering one victim's head. Jeffers insisted, however, that the BSU profile played a crucial part in tracking down the killer, when it is clear that, without the credit card slip, the profile alone would have been useless in identifying a particular suspect (21). Jeffers's work was typical of popular cultural representations of serial murder and of the FBI as a whole during this period. Rather than attempting to understand the social and psychological forces that produced serial murder, and what the actual incidence of this crime was, the popular cultural media instead contented themselves with focusing on the drama of the serial killer's apprehension, conviction, and imprisonment/death. In other words, popular culture generally accepted the judicial process, a process apparently orchestrated by the FBI, as a satisfactory interpretive framework for serial murder.

At first glance, one of the most well-known popular cultural representations of serial murder, Thomas Harris's *The Silence of the Lambs*, also seems to satisfy itself with the law enforcement perspective on serial murder, but Harris avoided the extremes of either attacking the FBI or viewing it completely uncritically. This is one reason why his work made such a strong impression on the American audience of popular culture. Jenkins discussed the significance of Harris's work for establishing the "mind-hunter" image of the BSU and for popularizing the investigative techniques and methods of the FBI, "thus providing the FBI's violent crime experts with invaluable publicity and unprecedented visibility" (*Using* 73). What Jenkins said about Harris's work was even more true of Jonathan Demme's 1991 film version of *The Silence of the Lambs*, a film that illustrated how much influence the FBI had over both its self-presentation and the representation of serial murder.

In the avalanche of publicity that followed the release of *Silence*, it was reported that, as part of their preparation for their work on the film, Demme himself, as well as two of his leading actors, Scott Glenn and Jodie Foster, visited the FBI Academy at Quantico, Virginia, to learn about how the Bureau worked and how the BSU tracked down serial killers (Goodman 64). John Douglas, a profiler at the BSU, played for Glenn a cassette tape of "teenage girls being tortured in the back-seat of a Los Angeles van by a pair of rapist thrill-killers" (Goodman 70). Glenn claimed that he instantaneously dropped his opposition to the death penalty, saying that "the experience in Quantico changed my mind about that for all time" (70). Foster, meanwhile, met with Special Agent Mary Ann Krause, who "like Clarice [Foster's character in the film] is a shy, soft-spoken Southerner" (64). Krause became Foster's model for her character, Clarice Starling. Apart from providing professional expertise on serial murder, the Bureau also agreed to let the Academy grounds at Quantico be used as a set in the film.

With this degree of cooperation between Demme and the FBI, it should come as no surprise that his version of *The Silence of the Lambs* reflected (and, in the process, massively strengthened) the Bureau's perspective on serial murder.[12] Demme's film replicated the image of the FBI as the unquestioned source of expertise on the subject of serial murder. Demme, following Harris, actually went further than this by making the law enforcement figures into the heroes of the film, thus automatically enshrining the law enforcement perspective as both rational and uncontested. For these reasons, members of the FBI had good reason to be pleased with Demme's work. John Douglas, a BSU agent who was featured prominently in film-related publicity, commented that *Silence* "did more for the FBI than any real case . . . It was tremendous" (quoted in R. Kessler 223). *The Silence of the Lambs* was wonderful publicity for the Bureau, giving them and their perspective on serial murder a level of visibility and authority they could never have achieved themselves.

That *The Silence of the Lambs* provided such a boost to the FBI's authority over serial murder is somewhat ironic when we consider the fact that Demme's film (like Harris's book) contained a major implied criticism of the Bureau. Although for much of the film, the resources and investigative techniques of the FBI are seen in an unproblematically positive light, a major exception to this emphasis comes at the point when the FBI receives an address for the man they suspect is Buffalo Bill, Jame Gumb. The FBI immediately heads off to the address in a plane bristling with high-tech weapons and gadgetry, while Clarice, seemingly left out of the hunt, is out in the field tracking down leads. However, it is in fact Clarice who eventually finds and kills Buffalo Bill, whereas the official face of the FBI, despite all its sophisticated resources and technology, goes to the wrong address and arrives at the right address only when it is all over. What we see here is an exception to the praise and admiration lavished on the FBI and its ability to fight serial murder. There was apparently a part of both Harris and Demme that wanted to leave space for the valorization of individual pluck and initiative, for the working out of the intuitive hunch that often cannot be accommodated within the bureaucratic structure of an organization like the FBI.

Bearing this point in mind, we might wonder why this view of the FBI law enforcement machine as fallible and imperfect did not make more of an impression upon the film's audience. The answer, I think, is that this moment in the film was truly an exception. Demme's *The Silence of the Lambs* as a whole not only consistently supported the FBI worldview, but by means of the final scene of the movie, Clarice's graduation from the FBI Academy, closed any gap between the movie's protagonist and the institution of which she was a part. If we as viewers wished to identify with Clarice, therefore, we found ourselves necessarily identifying with the FBI as well. *The Silence of the Lambs* thus offered a critique of the law enforcement perspective on serial murder and then almost immediately neutralized that critique by reinstituting the very same perspective. It is through mechanisms such as these that popular cultural representations of serial murder have consistently validated and thus strengthened the FBI's perspective on this crime.

From Hollywood to Waco

When one looks at the position of the FBI in the early 1990s, basking in the limelight of its association with *The Silence of the Lambs*, it is hard to imagine that its reputation for almost magical effectiveness in fighting violent crime could ever be assailed. And yet, in just a few years, the Bureau's reputation would be in ruins. At first glance, the reasons for the Bureau's fall from grace in the latter half of the 1990s are self-evident. The scandal surrounding the inefficiency and corruption of the FBI's once-vaunted criminal investigation laboratory undoubtedly sullied its reputation for technical expertise (Gibbs 30). Moreover, the deaths of unarmed members of Randy Weaver's family at Ruby Ridge in 1992, and the Bureau's murky role in the events leading up to the disastrous conclusion of the 1993 Branch Davidian episode in Waco, clearly reactivated the image of the FBI as a brutal opponent of civil rights, not just among paranoid right-wing survivalists, but among large numbers of Americans (Klaidman and Isikoff; Norganthau). While not denying the importance of these incidents, I want to consider a number of other factors in the rapid decline of the Bureau's reputation and to analyze what role serial murder played in this decline.

The first sign of trouble after the euphoria around *The Silence of the Lambs* had died down was a growing realization among members of the FBI that popular cultural attention to the Bureau's activities was a double-edged sword. Despite the publicity bonanza the Bureau reaped from *Silence*, many within the FBI were unhappy with the film. Ressler, for example, in terms that echoed Hoover's unhappiness with how popular culture portrayed his FBI, argued that the problem was not that the film unfairly criticized the FBI, but rather that it gave an unrealistic depiction of how the FBI would pursue a serial killer case. The FBI, Ressler pointed out, would never send an academy trainee like Clarice Starling into the field on such a high-profile case; nor would the members of the Behavioral Science Unit be directly involved in hunting for the serial killer—that would normally be left up to the police (Achenbach 6).

In his autobiography, *Whoever Fights Monsters*, Ressler returned to this subject and drew a clear distinction between Thomas Harris's book (which Ressler advised Harris on) and Demme's film (which he did not). Ressler argued that the film was much more exploitative of the FBI, and that if the Bureau allowed the FBI Academy to be used as a set, they should have been more careful about checking the content of the film (273, 274). Ressler then went on to bemoan the flood of misleading and sensationalized publicity about the FBI and the BSU that the success of the film had spawned. Ressler saw this second wave of media coverage of the Bureau as less accurate than the first, which occurred in the early 1980s, and he also lamented the fact that the FBI seemed to be going along with the irresponsible lionizing of themselves as supersleuths (263, 264).

There are indications that profilers other than Ressler were also sensitive to both the negative and the positive aspects of the publicity generated by *Silence*. In their 1993 book *Murder in Mind: Mindhunting the Serial Killers*, Steve Clark and Mike Morley suggested that the FBI's decision to change the term "psychological profiling" to "offender profiling" was partly determined by a desire to disassociate itself from the Hollywood image of the "mind hunter." This sense that the mind-hunter image was starting to become a liability and an embarrassment is confirmed by Clark and Morley's description of a bizarre incident that took place in Sydney, Australia, in 1992, at the beginning of a weeklong conference entitled "Serious Social Offenders": "As the opening speech ended and the applause died down, the organizing press office made a tacky request. With great effort they had secured a life-size cut-out of 'Hannibal the Cannibal' from the film *Silence of the Lambs*. Now they embarrassingly cajoled the FBI group, who had spent most of the past year trying to separate hard fact from Hollywood fiction, to pose for photographs, with 'Hannibal' in the centre of their group" (192). Quite apart from the embarrassment of being shadowed by Hannibal Lecter, the Bureau, and in particular its profilers, had another problem to deal with: in addition to the criticism of its profiling techniques that I have already discussed, the FBI's definition of serial murder came under more and more frequent attack in the years following the release of *Silence*. The attack on the Bureau's conclusions about serial murder was made on multiple fronts. Some questioned the claim that serial murder was of "epidemic" proportions and that it was on the rise, arguing that it was impossible to estimate numbers of either murderers or victims with any degree of accuracy (Egger, "Serial" 29). Others called into question the connection between "unsolved stranger murders" and "serial murders," arguing that a significant portion of these stranger murders would turn out to have been committed either in the course of a felony or by someone known to the victim (Kiger 41–42). Still others criticized the narrowness of the FBI's equation of serial murder with male, sexually sadistic, mobile homicide, offering instead a much more inclusive definition of the crime (Keeney and Heide 16, 20).[13]

Although such criticisms did damage the Bureau's reputation for expertise on serial murder, the FBI had another problem that in the long term would have much more serious consequences. The many similarities between the way the Bureau used for its own ends the gangster in the 1930s and the serial killer in the 1980s and 1990s should not obscure one very important difference between these two instances; whereas the Bureau was able to profit from the "G-man" mystique for many years, even after the era of the gangster had ended, its ability to reap the benefits of the "mind-hunter" image was relatively short-lived. Understanding the reasons for this difference takes us back to the agent Hoover hounded out of the Bureau in the 1930s, Melvin Purvis. Whatever one thinks of the shabby, even brutal, way in which Melvin Purvis was treated by the FBI, in one sense Hoover was undoubtedly right to dispose of Purvis because in this way all the credit for the suppression of gangsters went to the organization rather than the individual. In the absence of Hoover's brutally effective management style, the long-term beneficiary of the serial killer panic and the associated "mind-hunter" image has not been the Bureau but rather individuals who used to work for the Bureau, such as John Douglas and Robert Ressler. These men have managed to negotiate lucrative publishing contracts for themselves by establishing reputations as independent experts whose knowledge and status are enhanced, but not constrained, by their former association with the FBI. The benefits for the FBI of being associated with these individuals are minimal.

The FBI and Its Others

Of all the FBI agents who have attempted to parlay their Bureau careers into an independent existence, John Douglas has probably been most successful in establishing an autonomous professional identity for himself. In a series of best-selling books—*Mindhunter* (1995), *Journey Into Darkness* (1997), *Obsession* (1998), *The Anatomy of Motive* (1999), *The Cases That Haunt Us* (2000), and *Anyone You Want Me to Be* (2004)—Douglas has relentlessly mythologized his FBI career, portraying himself in inflated terms as almost the sole originator and champion of the Bureau's psychologically based attempts to fight violent crime in general and serial murder in particular. At the same time, Douglas has repeatedly asserted, in both subtle and obvious ways, his difference from dominant Bureau ideologies and practices, painting himself as a maverick doing his best to fight crime within the constraints imposed by a bureaucratic, hidebound organization.

Not content with mythologizing his Bureau career, Douglas has also attempted to extend his expertise (and the prestige of psychological profiling— the two are always intimately connected in Douglas's work) by providing profiles of cases he was never involved in. As we saw at the beginning of this chapter, these cases included some of the most famous murderers of the past, not only Jack the Ripper but also Lizzie Borden and even Othello! This tendency is most evident in Douglas's 2000 book, *The Cases That Haunt Us*, where revisiting other cases and applying the Bureau methodologies Douglas developed are the premise of the entire book. Douglas analyzes not just famous cases from the past but also contemporary cases that he has consulted on since leaving the Bureau, such as the JonBenet Ramsey murder case, where his profile of the murderer apparently exonerated JonBenet's parents. Douglas's involvement in such cases is frequently accompanied by an acknowledgment of a possible tension between his FBI work, presumably done for the benefit of the organization or the nation as a whole, and his post-FBI work, presumably done for the purposes of self-promotion or money. Consequently, Douglas gets quite defensive about the suggestion that he sells his services indiscriminately to the highest bidder. Whatever his motives for doing so, be they self-interested or altruistic, Douglas has attempted to extend the "mind-hunting" model as far as possible and has thus proved himself to be a worthy successor to the power- and image-hungry G-man of the 1930s.[14]

Much the same might be said of Robert Ressler, whose post-FBI books, *Whoever Fights Monsters*, *I Have Lived in the Monster*, and *Justice Is Served*, show a striking degree of similarity to those of John Douglas. Like Douglas, Ressler writes both of his FBI career and about what he has done since leaving the Bureau. In *Whoever*, Ressler, like Douglas, tends to give himself the lion's share of the credit for the FBI's development of psychological profiling (indeed, one of the most entertaining features of Douglas's and Ressler's work is their obvious intense dislike for each other), while in *I Have Lived* he discusses his post-Bureau career in terms very similar to Douglas's, describing the consulting he has done in cases that have taken him all over the world, while also sharing Douglas's defensiveness about taking money for his services.

Although Ressler does not review past murder cases and profile them in as much detail as Douglas, in *I Have Lived* he does offer some comments about Jack the Ripper, which indicates that he, like Douglas, is concerned to emphasize the portability of the profiling technique. Finally, Ressler also tends to see himself as a bit of a Bureau maverick and takes particular pleasure, now that he has retired from the Bureau, in beating the FBI at its own game. Clearly, Ressler enjoys his image of himself as a lone international sleuth. Even though both his books, as I indicated earlier, contain complaints about the media's misrepresentation of the FBI in general and himself in particular, it is hard to take his complaints seriously, as he clearly enjoys and is ready to make use of any kind of publicity. In *I Have Lived*, for example, Ressler complains about being trapped into an embarrassing photo shoot by a British tabloid newspaper. His stance of dignified offense, however, becomes less persuasive when we realize that he uses one of the "offending" pictures as an illustration in the book, along with a picture of a grinning Ressler with the infamous life-size Hannibal Lecter cutout! While Ressler's criticisms of how the FBI has both contributed to and profited from the culture of celebrity that surrounds serial killers are sound, he seems unwilling to confront the extent to which he is part of the same dynamic. Indeed, he has exploited that culture much more vigorously than his former employers.

Although the Bureau does not really benefit from the publicity that former agents like Douglas and Ressler have managed to attract to themselves, at least it is not embarrassed by that publicity. Despite their mild criticisms of the Bureau's procedures and priorities, Douglas and Ressler essentially support the organization, and the worst they could be accused of is what would have been seen as a serious crime in J. Edgar Hoover's eyes: directing attention away from the Bureau's achievements to their own individual achievements. Far more damaging to the Bureau's long-term reputation, however, have been those agents whose criticisms of the Bureau have been sharper and more sustained.

A good example of such criticism came in 1992 when FBI agent Paul Lindsay published his first novel, *Witness to the Truth*. Part of the reason the novel caused so much consternation among the Bureau's hierarchy was that Lindsay was still an active FBI agent when the novel was published, making it much more difficult to dismiss him and his book as the ravings of a disgruntled former employee. Far more serious than Lindsay's active agent status, however, was the image of the FBI contained within the novel. Lindsay portrayed the FBI as a thoroughly corrupt, inefficient, and bureaucratic organization, run by "suits" with no experience of fighting street crime, who devote themselves to advancing their careers at the expense of the "humps," the street agents such as Lindsay's protagonist, Mike Devlin, who actually do the grunt work of investigating and solving crimes. Lindsay's description of Devlin's supervisor sums up the theme of much of the book: "L. John Fauber's career profile was becoming more common in the FBI management ranks. Out of training school he had been assigned to white-collar crimes in Omaha, Nebraska. The *Manual of Administrative Operations and Procedures* states that, without exception, an agent must have two years' investigative experience before he or she becomes a Bureau supervisor. The only exception to this is if he or she is an exceptionally gifted ass-kisser which is the exception to every Bureau rule" (16). Faced with such a harsh characterization of the organization, the Bureau responded in an appropriately punitive manner. As if it was stuck in the 1930s, with Lindsay as a latter-day Melvin Purvis, the Bureau investigated Lindsay and threatened him with dismissal (Rosenbaum 122–24). Even more embarrassing for the Bureau, Lindsay was one of the best agents in its Detroit field office, with a particularly impressive reputation for investigating cases of serial murder.[15]

The fact that the FBI was so eager to punish the kind of agent so recently lionized by the popular media showed how seriously it had lost its way when its publicity started turning negative. As much as the Bureau did not want to face up to the fact, there was no doubt that Lindsay's cynical view of the FBI's shortcomings was fast becoming received wisdom as the 1990s progressed. The problem was not just that individuals such as Douglas and Ressler, rather than the Bureau, benefited most from the serial killer panic; the problem was also that the panic itself was relatively short-lived.

The serial killer frenzy that gripped American popular culture in the first half of the 1990s seemed to be winding down by the decade's end, as suggested by the relatively lukewarm response to *Hannibal*, the sequel to *The Silence of the Lambs* (characteristically, Ridley Scott's version of *Hannibal*, as well as the Harris novel it was drawn from, both contained jaded pictures of a highly corrupt, overly bureaucratic FBI). The relative fading of the serial killer from public awareness meant that the FBI was losing the figure that, in a sense, had been its greatest ally since the 1980s, thus leaving the Bureau desperately seeking another figure who could occupy the role of "the enemy within" as compellingly as the serial killer did.[16] Even worse from the FBI's point of view, as the 2002 conviction and imprisonment of FBI agent Robert Hanssen for espionage suggests, the FBI itself has become, for many, "the enemy within."

Snatching Victory from Defeat

Even though the FBI's reputation was shattered during the second half of the 1990s, it is precisely that fact that creates a striking contradiction in the FBI's history during this period. Although the Bureau's representation in popular culture and the news media had never been worse, and although its public reputation suffered accordingly, during the same period the Bureau, under the directorship of Louis Freeh, enjoyed unprecedented growth. During the Clinton administrations, the FBI's annual budget grew by 25 percent (to $2.9 billion), and it added 3,600 new employees to its payroll (C. Clark 315). Moreover, this expansion of resources was accompanied by the federalization of such a large number of crimes, and the concomitant expansion of the FBI's responsibilities, that even Louis Freeh, who as director aggressively supported expansion of the FBI, expressed concern that the situation has gone too far (Freeh 194–95).[17] Ironically, during a period when the FBI lost its preeminent position of expertise and authority over serial murder, it was able to grow at a pace even greater than during the 1980s, when its ownership of serial murder was one of the prime engines of its growth.

How can we explain this contradiction? Part of the answer lies in the subsequent history of VICAP and the NCAVC after the creation of these programs in the mid-1980s. Despite the fanfare that accompanied their debut, there is evidence to suggest that VICAP and the NCAVC were allowed to wither and die fairly quickly. Indeed, in *The Riverman*, Robert Keppel describes his opposition to locating VICAP at the FBI when the program was still in its planning stages:

> I knew that housing the VICAP unit within the FBI meant the certain death of the program. First of all, promises of financial backing are just that, promises. After all the hoopla about VICAP died down, would the FBI's commitment and resources dry up? Furthermore, civilian police investigators would not systematically submit murder cases to an FBI VICAP unit because distrust of the FBI had long been institutionalized. In some quarters, there was flat-out refusal from local police departments to cooperate in any fashion with the FBI. (156)

After the program was opened up, a lack of cooperation from police departments so widespread that even the FBI had to acknowledge it confirmed the second half of Keppel's prediction, but what about the first half? In his history of the FBI, Ronald Kessler states that by the mid-1990s, the Behavioral Science Unit was severely underfunded and had to turn away 100 to 150 profile requests a year owing to a lack of staff. Kessler quotes John Douglas as saying, "We're doing all we can to keep our heads above water . . . We should be doing written profiles. Instead, we have to do it verbally just to keep up with the demand. If this were a business, we would have a lot more resources" (234). One might speculate that after the BSU had served its purpose in attracting positive publicity to the Bureau, it was allowed to languish.

And yet additional evidence suggests that the underfunding of the Bureau's "mind hunters" in the 1990s was not a Bureau decision. According to James Greenleaf, the associate deputy director for administration at the FBI, for several years the Bureau asked the Office of Management and Budget for more money to expand the profiling program: "We have asked for more profilers, and it's been cut out of the budget" (R. Kessler 235). Regardless of the valuable publicity serial murder and profiling gave the FBI throughout the 1980s and into the 1990s, by the mid-1990s it had clearly been decided that such publicity was superfluous, both because profilers were no longer prominent popular cultural figures and because the previous belief that there was a connection between positive popular cultural publicity for the FBI and funding for the Bureau no longer applied. In other words, we are led back to the puzzle of why the collapse of the Bureau's public reputation in the 1990s coincided with a massive growth in the FBI's resources and responsibilities.

The first thing to say about this puzzle is that its apparent intractability should not be overstated. As we will see in the epilogue, the FBI continues to use and to benefit from the latest version of "the enemy within," and the use it has made of the linked figures of the serial killer and the (domestic/foreign) terrorist is just one aspect of the complex role of the serial killer in post-9/11 American culture. With that said, the current state of the FBI poses the same puzzle as that of the 1990s FBI. In the wake of the terrorist attacks of September 11, 2001, the FBI has continued to be criticized for inefficiency and corruption as much as if not more than ever. Responding to the report of the 9/11 investigation commission, for example, the *New York Times* editorialized that "the FBI has been politically out of control, poorly organized and ineffective for a long time, and some critics may ask whether, with all the mounting evidence of its incapacity, it should be allowed to continue in its present form at all" ("Failed").

As a significant measure of how much things have changed since 9/11, however, now the most frequent source of criticism is not that the Bureau is encroaching on citizens' civil liberties but that it is not doing so aggressively enough. In February 2003, for instance, the Senate Judiciary Committee complained that "FBI officials as high-ranking as the director were ignorant of the surveillance law, and were still applying a too-stringent standard for those FBI agents seeking warrants to watch individuals under suspicion" (Tapper). And yet, despite the fact that criticisms of the Bureau are perhaps more vitriolic now than ever before, these criticisms have had no impact on the FBI's resources and responsibilities, both of which continue to grow exponentially as a result of such legislation as the Patriot Act of 2001.

Perhaps one way to make sense of this contradiction is to argue that the FBI's ability to liberate itself from the consequences of public and political criticism is a sign of just how successful it was in using such phenomena as serial murder in the 1980s. In other words, the FBI's contribution to the hegemony of what Richard Tithecott has called "dominant policing discourses" has led to its present prosperity. Tithecott argues that such policing discourses, which he says are used both inside and outside the police community, "describe a world threatened more by inexplicable horror than by various forms of medically and legally defined insanity" (15). When we recall the Bureau's skepticism toward conventional psychological assessments of such phenomena as serial murder, along with its concerted efforts to create a public image of serial killers as monstrous and terrifying as possible, we can see what a profound contribution the FBI made to the "policing discourses" Tithecott speaks of. By popularizing an image of the serial killer as a monstrous, sexually sadistic, highly mobile monster, the FBI both contributed to and demonstrated the necessity and validity of the policing discourses.

Tithecott goes on to argue that a consequence of the increasing dominance of policing discourses is "an intensification of what might be called a cultural 'policing mentality'" (16). Although Tithecott does not provide a detailed gloss of what he means by "policing mentality," I believe his phrase describes the prevailing atmosphere in the early years of the twenty-first-century United States very accurately. Thanks in part to the prevalence of the cultural policing mentality, today's public sphere is increasingly dominated by an unstable combination of fear, paranoia, and a forced acquiescence to authority. In such an atmosphere, criticisms of how the FBI (or any other federal institution) operates are a matter of supreme indifference and certainly no reason for jeopardizing the Bureau's access to the funding it needs to do its increasingly complicated and wide-ranging job. In such a context, terror of the serial killer who dominated the cultural landscape of the United States in the closing decades of the twentieth century can seem positively benign compared with the fear inspired and carefully orchestrated by the shadowy figure of the terrorist.

PART TWO

Serial Murder in American Popular Culture

CHAPTER THREE

Natural Born Celebrities:
Serial Killers and the Hollywood
Star System

Violence is cinematic . . . It's like putting mustard on a hot dog.
—Filmmaker Abel Ferrara

Film, Violence, and Stardom

The existence of famous serial killers in contemporary American culture brings together two defining features of American modernity: stardom and violence. Not surprisingly, therefore, film is unique among popular cultural media in its potential to shed light on the reasons why we have celebrity serial killers because it is a medium defined by the representation of acts of violence and by the presence of stars. One of the founding figures of the medium, Thomas Edison, seems to have had a long-standing interest in violence and was also attentive to the ways in which fame could be used in conjunction with the representation of violence. One of the earliest phonograph recordings he produced featured an actor reading the confessions of H. H. Holmes (Schechter and Everitt 185), and one of his first kinetoscopes showed the execution of Mary, Queen of Scots. Although the depiction was not entirely convincing, the audience was shown the executioner swinging his axe and Mary's head rolling onto the ground (Goldberg 49). Film's preoccupation with the representation of violence continued in the first narrative movie, Edwin Porter's *The Great Train Robbery* (1903), which showed a beating victim thrown from a moving train and climaxed with the massacre of the train robbers (Prince, "Graphic" 2). Such examples underline Vicki Goldberg's point that from its very beginnings, cinema "laid claim to a more extensive and intimate view of death" (49).

The representation of violence is so central to film that one can even periodize the history of the medium by tracing changes in how it has represented violence. Constructing this history also allows us to track the evolution of the market for serial killer movies. Fierce debates about the social consequences of film have been a constant feature of the medium, and more often than not this debate has focused on the supposed consequences of filmic representations of violence. Before 1930, filmmakers were technically free to include as much violence in their films as they wished, as long as they could weather the resulting controversy. In 1930, however, in a gesture of self-regulation in the face of concerted censorship efforts, the film industry passed the Production Code, and from that time until 1966, when the code was revised, the possibilities for the depiction of graphic screen violence were restricted. The 1960s modification of the code, which was largely a response "to the more liberal and tolerant culture of the period, particularly the revolution of social mores tied to the youth movement" (Prince, *Screening* 6), enabled the production of tougher, more violent, and more controversial films such as Arthur Penn's *Bonnie and Clyde* (1967) and Sam Peckinpah's *The Wild Bunch* (1969).

As Stephen Prince has noted, it is thanks largely to the efforts of filmmakers like Penn and Peckinpah that graphic screen violence, a new and highly controversial feature of 1960s cinema, has now become a pervasive feature of contemporary filmmaking, "We cannot, it seems, go to the movies today and avoid for very long the spectacle of exploding heads and severed limbs, or escape the company of the screen sociopaths who perpetrate these acts" (*Savage* xv). Although the serial killer undoubtedly plays a dominant role in today's ultraviolent cinema culture, he is by no means an anomalous figure either in the history of film or in the landscape of contemporary film. Rather, the serial killer takes his place alongside such figures as gangsters, vigilantes, and cyborgs in the heavily populated pantheon of contemporary film's violent protagonists.

Like violence, stardom has played an equally important role in film from the earliest days of the medium. Richard deCordova dates the emergence of a recognizable star system in American cinema to the early years of the twentieth century and argues that "the star system has been central to the functioning of the American cinema as a social institution" (1). The centrality of stardom to film has both textual and economic dimensions. Textually speaking, once the star system became well established in Hollywood during the late teens and 1920s, stars functioned as a principle of narrative coherence and stability, both in individual films, which told the story of the star protagonists, and in the larger context of a series of films, as particular stars developed a coherent star image that allowed them to be typecast in recurring roles.

The textual coherence represented by the star was always simultaneously an economic coherence. As Cathy Klaprat has argued, "Stars established the value of motion pictures as a marketable commodity. In economic terms, stars by virtue of their unique appeal and drawing power stabilized rental prices and guaranteed that the companies operated at a profit" (351). Stars were economically central not only to the film industry itself but also to the satellite industries that grew up around Hollywood and that devoted themselves assiduously to circulating images and information about the stars, whether in the form of entertainment magazines, gossip columns, or fanzines.

Stars not only were important to the development of film, however, but also made a crucial contribution to the development of the modern celebrity system in general. Before the advent of film, the building of the celebrity system had an improvisatory and primitive quality (Schickel, *Intimate* 45). Film gave celebrity new layers of discursive and institutional complexity in the process of creating the modern concept of stardom, as Emanuel Levy explains: "Stardom has neither been exclusive nor confined to film. The entertainment world in the United States (theater, ballet, opera) has always been centralized and star-oriented. Nonetheless, because film is a mass production medium, on a bigger and more standardized scale than the live, performing arts, it has magnified the star phenomenon to a system of huge proportions" (32). The contribution of film to the development of the modern celebrity system, a system unparalleled in both its reach and profitability, is just one way in which the medium prepared the ground for the emergence of celebrity serial killers. Another equally important influence is the complex network of associations between the medium of film and seriality. Part of the reason that film has played such an important role in the articulation of stardom is that it seems to promise the completion of a concept that is otherwise incoherent, as John Ellis has indicated in his description of the star image: "The star image is . . . an *incomplete* image. It offers only the face, only the voice, only the still photo, where cinema offers the synthesis of voice, body and motion. The star image is paradoxical and incomplete so that it functions as an invitation to cinema, like the narrative image. It proposes cinema as the completion of its lacks, the synthesis of its separate fragments" (93, original emphasis). Unlike presentations of the star in photos, writing, and radio, where elements of the star are offered in pieces and without movement, film seems to offer the tantalizing possibility of presenting what Ellis describes as "the completeness of the star," a completeness only hinted at by the fragmented nature of other media (94). However, as Ellis goes on to argue, the film medium is unable to complete the star image because the cinematic image and the film performance both rest on what Ellis describes as "the photo effect, the paradox that the photograph presents an absence that is present" (93). Rather than experiencing the absent-presence of the star in film as frustrating, the film audience responds to this perpetual sense of incompleteness with an optimism that perhaps next time the star image will be completed. As a result, stardom becomes implicated in serial structures (one form of which is the sequel), where the audience hopes that "maybe in the next film I'll have access to the star's complete personality."

Although Ellis's account makes the film audience seem rather gullible, it has the virtue of illustrating how films can become involved in serial patterns and how those patterns are connected to the articulation of stardom. Evidence suggests that connections between seriality and stardom in film go back many years. In the early teens, the fame of such stars as Mary Pickford was built from a series of films. In this context, a "series was a group of films that featured a particular actor or actress and was marketed to exhibitors as a package" (P. M. Cohen 137). At first glance, there is no reason why these associations between seriality and stardom should necessarily lead to the phenomenon of famous serial killers, and yet it should come as no surprise to learn that serial patterns are especially prominent in films about serial murder, as critic Amy Taubin has pointed out in her discussion of slasher movies:

> In such films serial killing is a function not of character, but of the internal narrative structure and motifs (the piling up of bodies one after another). Even more importantly, it is a function of the relationship of each film both to its sequels and to all the other serials in the genre. It is the killer's ability to rise from the dead in film after film—rather than his appearance, his physical strength or even the extreme sadism of his actions—that demonises him. Thirty years of these films have primed audiences to bind the words "serial" and "killer" into the image of a superhuman monster. "He's back!" "Coming Again this summer!" ("Killing" 16)

As Taubin indicates, serial killer movies not only make seriality as both theme and structure a defining feature of film but also use that seriality to promote the celebrity of the filmic serial killer, enabling movie psychos such as Freddy Krueger in *A Nightmare on Elm Street*, Jason Voorhees in *Friday the 13th*, and Michael Myers in *Halloween* to become the famous stars of their own long-running and extremely profitable series of movies.

Although these "slasher movies" of the 1970s and 1980s signaled the beginning of the modern obsession with seeing serial killers on film, they by no means inaugurated audience interest in the subject. Serial killers have been appearing on film since at least 1926, when a young Alfred Hitchcock released *The Lodger*, his movie about Jack the Ripper. Since that time, there have been numerous landmarks in serial killer movies, from Fritz Lang's classic study of psychopathology, *M* (1931), to Hitchcock's paradigm-shifting *Psycho* (1960).[1] Regardless of the richness and variety of film's long-standing preoccupation with serial killers, however, the vast majority of these representations tend to share an interesting feature: an unwillingness to broach, even obliquely, the subject of famous serial killers. A lot of films depend either explicitly or implicitly on the existence of a serial killer celebrity culture, but the vast majority of these films do nothing to acknowledge the existence of this celebrity culture. To some extent, this silence partakes of a more general silence in the film industry on the subject of violence in film. As journalist Bernard Weinraub has pointed out, "the one issue over which the Hollywood hierarchy has direct control and responsibility—violence in films—has left industry executives uncharacteristically silent . . . Left unspoken is a tenet that Hollywood executives are almost reluctant to acknowledge: violence sells" (28). The success of serial killer films in particular demonstrates the "salability" of violence to contemporary film, but this is not a subject that filmmakers and industry executives are going to comment on unless they absolutely have to. When they do, their tone is usually defensive because they are under attack from the self- or government-appointed culture police concerned about the deleterious social influence of violent films.

What we might call (with apologies to Thomas Harris) "the silence of the films" with respect to the fame of serial killers is more than an example of the medium's overdetermined relationship to violence. It is also another instance of a phenomenon I discussed in the introduction: both popular cultural representations of serial murder and studies of those representations have had remarkably little to say about the fame of serial killers because to do more than acknowledge the existence of that fame cursorily might make it necessary to discuss one's own imbrication with and contribution to that fame. In the case of film, however, that reluctance is particularly acute because of the importance of "identification" to the medium.

Identifying (with) Serial Killers

In the introduction, I discussed the delicate issue of whether the fame of serial killers in contemporary American culture is due partly to the way they inspire feelings of fascination, perhaps even admiration, as well as revulsion in many people. According to Simon Watney, "the question of identification— its nature and its conditions—lies absolutely at the heart of the film star phenomenon" ("Stellar" 112–13), and so film returns us to the issue of the fascination exerted by serial killers and to the following questions: can we explain the existence of famous serial killers by claiming that many people "identify" with those killers in the sense of admiring them and wanting to be like them? To what extent does an audience's identification with a film star provide a model for understanding contemporary American culture's identification with the serial killer?

In thinking through the relationship between the audience and the film star, it is tempting to follow the example of many film critics and explain the profound impact of the film star image in contemporary popular culture in terms of wish-fulfillment or imitation. In his classic early study of stardom, Edgar Morin argues that "the spectator psychically lives the exciting, intense, amorous, imaginary life of the movie heroes, i.e., identifies himself with them" (95). In other words, one could argue that audiences identify with film stars and serial killers in the sense of wanting to be like them and that these figures therefore reflect the desires of their audience.

The vast majority of academic and popular criticism of violent movies in general and serial killer films in particular usually follows Morin's lead and criticizes such movies for encouraging/facilitating sadistic (male) viewer identification with the killer. The assumption of the centrality of viewer sadism has been a particularly prominent feature of feminist criticism of the slasher movie, and in *Men, Women, and Chainsaws*, her groundbreaking reevaluation of the genre, Carol Clover provides a trenchant critique of this assumption: "I do not . . . believe that sadistic voyeurism is the first cause of horror. Nor do I believe that real-life women and feminist politics have been entirely well served by the astonishingly insistent claim that horror's satisfactions begin and end in sadism . . . horror's misogyny is a far more complicated matter than the 'blood-lust' formula would have it" (19). Clover proposes as an alternative the possibility that "male viewers are quite prepared to identify not just with screen females, but with screen females in the horror-film world, screen females in fear and pain" (5). The critical furor that greeted the publication of Clover's book supported her argument about "the official denial of such identification" (5) and had the virtue of stressing what should have been an obvious point: that structures of cinematic identification are enormously complex and cannot be schematized easily, if at all.

Much the same might be said of Steven Shaviro's important work in *The Cinematic Body*, which in many ways extends Clover's analysis by arguing for the constitutive role played by masochism, passivity, and abjection in the act of film viewing. Not only does Shaviro reject the claim that desire for sadistic mastery of the image is the motivating force in film viewing, but he actually relocates sadism in the filmic apparatus itself, rather than in the viewer's gaze: "Images literally assault the spectator, leaving him or her no space for reflection . . . When I watch a film, images excite my retina, 24 times a second, at a speed that is slow enough to allow for the impact and recording of stimuli, but too fast for me to keep up with them consciously. Perception has become unconscious. It is neither spontaneously active nor freely receptive, but radically passive, the suffering of a violence perpetrated against the eye" (50–51). Shaviro's work not only has interesting ramifications for whom the audience is likely to "root" for (or identify with) in a serial killer film (suggesting, for example, that we are much more likely to see ourselves in the victim, the focus of passivity and masochistic suffering) but also suggests that the reason many people watch serial killer films in the first place is to subject themselves to fear rather than voyeuristically participate in the incitement of fear.

As important as the work of such scholars as Clover and Shaviro is, however, and as sympathetic as I am to attempts to make our understanding of cinematic identification more complex, there is another side of the story that comes from insisting upon the importance of generic distinctiveness. As Daniel O'Brien says, "Aside from vastly increasing the number of applications to the FBI Academy, *The Silence of the Lambs'* box-office success helped pave the way for a new horror sub-genre, the high-class serial killer movie" (125). Clover has argued for highlighting the connections between the maligned genre of the slasher movie and the more respectable genre of the serial killer movie and has claimed that movies such as *Blue Steel* and *The Silence of the Lambs* "come awfully close to being slasher movies for yuppies—well made, well-acted and well-conceived versions of the familiar story of a female victim-hero who squares off against, and finally blows away, without male help, a monstrous oppressor" (232). It is helpful to be reminded of such continuities, especially because many serial killer films made after and dependent on the mainstream success of *Silence* have routinely disavowed the very "slasher" connections that Clover mentions, but it is equally important to insist upon the differences between slasher movies and serial killer films. The iconic status of the character Hannibal Lecter indicates that serial killer movies such as *Silence* tend to feature more complexly individuated protagonists who therefore attract a greater share of audience identification than the faceless, practically anonymous killing machines of the slasher movie. Although I agree with Clover and Shaviro that structures of audience identification are fluid and multiple in all types of movies, I would argue that identification with the victim is more likely to be a feature of slasher movies than serial killer movies.

Similarly, although I would contest the simplistic equation of identification with imitation or emulation, it must be acknowledged that serial killers, much like film stars, do have fans, and this suggests the possibility that the existence of celebrity serial killers is indeed partly a result of the way in which consumers "identify" with these killers in the sense of wanting to be or think like them. There is certainly ample evidence to suggest that contemporary American interest in serial murder is not exclusively condemnatory. One thinks, for example, of the crowds of women who attended the trials of Richard Ramirez (aka "The Night Stalker"), Ted Bundy, and a number of other male serial killers, many of whom made concerted efforts to communicate with these killers. One thinks of the continuing saga of Charles Manson and his ability to attract new adherents after over thirty years in prison. One thinks in particular of the men described in Devon Jackson's article "Serial Killers and the People Who Love Them," one of whom says, "If people weren't interested in serial killers . . . wouldn't everybody just be watching *Look Who's Talking Now?* You need variation in the culture. You need to have the sickness. There's a part where I can relate to what they went through" (29). The picture Jackson provides of men bonding around their shared enthusiasm for serial murder exemplifies Jeffrey Goldstein's point that "violent entertainment appeals primarily to males, and it appeals to them mostly in groups" ("Why" 215), but it also indicates that no matter how we think of what "identification" means in relation to serial killer celebrity culture, there is no doubt that it plays a foundational role in the facilitation of that culture. Moreover, there are reasons to believe that identification plays a more complex and important role in serial killer films than in all other existing forms of serial killer popular culture:

> Success in solving the case is wholly dependent upon the novice's ability to identify fully with the killer, to learn (like any good detective of the genre) to desire what the other desires, to inhabit the place of the other's identifications. In narrative terms, identification is as much a plot device as anything else; identification both sets this drama of serial killing in motion and provides the ultimate resolution. (Fuss, "Monsters" 191–92)

Although Diana Fuss is describing what Clarice Starling must do to track down Buffalo Bill in *The Silence of the Lambs*, what she says applies to serial killer films in general. Such films are nearly always premised on a person's ability to identify with the serial killer in the sense of learning to think like him, coming to see the world through his eyes. This type of identification is often presented in these films as dangerous, because it can lead to the violent cancellation of one's own identity; but only in this way, these films suggest, can the serial killer be apprehended.

Structures of identification in serial killer movies can also be violent in quite another sense because, as Fuss suggests, identification is itself a form of serial killing:

> Viewed through the lens of psychoanalysis, "seriality" and "killing" denote the defining poles of the identificatory process . . . At the base of every identification lies a murderous wish: the subject's desire to cannibalize the other who inhabits the place it longs to occupy. But as Freud also reminds us, identifications are at best "partial" and "extremely limited"; they must be continually renewed and serially reenacted, for the ego's appetite is voracious and unappeasable. Identification is an endless process of killing off and consuming the rival in whom the subject sees itself reflected. ("Monsters" 192)

Whether identification is present as a means of self-destruction or as a violent attack on others, serial killer movies tend to mobilize cinematic structures of identification in particularly intense and specific ways. In films such as *Seven* and *Natural Born Killers*, these identifications are heightened even further by the presence of film stars playing serial killers; in such instances, the curiosity that a film audience is encouraged to feel about the personality of the film star is overlaid by the American public's enduring fascination with "what makes a serial killer tick?" As a result, these films are appealing because they potentially offer the satisfaction of a dual and related curiosity on the part of the spectator about celebrities and killers, but this satisfaction can come about only if these films can discipline effectively the unstable structures of identification they generate.

As we will see, the dangers of identification that Fuss hints at are sometimes horrifically realized in serial killer movies, but mainstream Hollywood films about serial murder usually bring the potentially dangerous aspects of identification under control by giving their viewers a way to disavow their involvement with the serial killer characters; indeed, this disavowal is the secret to the success of these films and perhaps to the success of celebrity serial killer popular culture in general. Of course, disavowal is not limited to serial killer movies. Thomas M. Leitch has argued that the disavowal of violence has become a generalized feature of American films, especially as those films have become more and more violent: "For as representations of violence grow more clinical or shocking or disgusting or threatening, American films have developed an immensely sophisticated battery of techniques to disavow the power of the very images they are displaying onscreen" (1). Leitch provides a detailed discussion of the techniques of disavowal used by contemporary American films and summarizes them in the following terms: "Violence can be rendered acceptable to a sensitive audience by being ascribed to an evil Other, or by being justified in rational terms, or by being limited in its effects, or by being stylized through narrative conventions or rituals that deny its consequences, or by being rendered pleasurable through appeals to aestheticism or masochism or eroticism" (6). Film uses these techniques, according to Leitch, to deny personal responsibility—both the responsibility of the agents of violence and the responsibility of those who watch and enjoy the representations of violence.[2]

While Leitch is undoubtedly correct to draw attention to the pervasiveness of the disavowal of violence in American film, I would argue that such disavowal is particularly complex and intense in serial killer movies, partly because what is being disavowed is not only one's complicity in the acts of violence one sees onscreen, but also one's involvement in a much larger serial killer culture industry that extends well beyond the bounds of the screen. Thus, although films such as *Seven, Copycat,* and *Natural Born Killers* seem to acknowledge their, and their audiences', implication in the popular culture that has made serial killers famous, these films never explore that implication to a degree that would make the audience feel uncomfortable. By either killing the serial murderer or suggesting that the true source of villainy lies elsewhere, these films let their audiences off the hook, letting them enjoy the fame of serial killers within a moralistic framework that relieves them of pursuing the implications of that enjoyment. In spite of their apparent self-consciousness about the problems inherent in making stars out of serial killers, these films ultimately remain silent about those problems and thus reap the benefits of that stardom.

Filming Serial Murder

Given Hannibal Lecter's status as the "most prominent celebrity serial killer of the twentieth century" (Mizejewski 159), it is surprising to note that the theme of the serial murderer as celebrity is almost completely absent from what has become the ur-text of the modern serial killer movie, *The Silence of the Lambs* (1991). Although, as Martin Rubin has argued, the success of the film "reconfirmed the continuing status of the psychokiller as superstar" ("Grayness" 48), the film itself does not address the issue of the fame accorded to serial killers. While Buffalo Bill has newspaper articles about his murders in his basement, his methods of self-realization are essentially private and do not depend upon acknowledgment from others. Lecter is far more attuned to his own lofty position in the pantheon of serial killers, which is why he is offended when Clarice Starling, a mere FBI trainee, is sent to interview him. Lecter, however, does not seek fame. The closing scene of the film, in which a disguised Lecter sets off in pursuit of Dr. Chilton, reminds us of nothing so much as a reluctant celebrity eager to avoid the paparazzi. If the star system is more or less absent in the film itself, however, *The Silence of the Lambs*, as an enormously successful commodity, was thoroughly imbricated in the star system, sparking a furious debate about the consequences of according fame to serial killers. For this reason, serial killer movies after *Silence* are unavoidably responding, albeit implicitly, to the fame of their influential predecessor.

Responding to the influence of *Silence* is a particularly complicated issue in the case of *Hannibal* (2001), *Silence*'s much-anticipated and controversial sequel. One of the most striking features of the orgy of publicity that accompanied the release of *Hannibal* was the complete absence of any discussion of the one issue that had dominated the response to *Silence*; namely, the consequences of according fame to serial killers and what that fame suggested about the state of contemporary American culture. Instead, media outlets concentrated on the extremely protracted and complicated production history of *Hannibal*, with much time being devoted to the question of why so many of those associated with the fabulously successful *Silence*, such as Jodie Foster and Jonathan Demme, declined to participate in the sequel.

The apparent lack of concern about the fame of serial killers, as evidenced by the response to *Hannibal*, may have something to do with the fact that, as Peter Bradshaw has suggested, "the moral anxiety of the '90s has receded," but the absence of comment is above all convincing evidence of the sea change in public attitudes wrought by *The Silence of the Lambs*. After the success of that film, and after the initial fuss about it had died down, the fame of serial killers became an accepted part of the contemporary American cultural landscape, so much so that at least one movie magazine used the occasion of *Hannibal*'s release to review the "Top 10 Cinematic Psychos" of all time, a category that probably did not even exist before Hannibal Lecter's appearance (see Jim Douglas).

Perhaps the fact that the existence of famous serial killers is now taken for granted explains an equally puzzling feature of *Hannibal*. Despite the enormous success of *Silence*, despite the cultural omnipresence of Hannibal Lecter, and despite the fact that even within the world of the film, Lecter is a widely known and notorious character, there is nothing in *Hannibal* that even gestures toward thematizing Lecter's fame and what it may suggest about the fame of serial killers in general. This is not to say that the film avoids the subject of fame altogether. What prompts Lecter to get back in touch with Clarice Starling, after all, is her newfound (and unwanted) fame after she is suspended from the FBI. Similarly, as Linda Mizejewski has pointed out, Lecter's subsequent pursuit of Starling is familiar to us from reading other such narratives about crazed fans stalking those they are obsessed with: "Lecter begins by sending her mail, and then small gifts; he starts to follow her and spy on her while she is jogging; he breaks into her car just to sniff the air and gain approximate physical contact. He exemplifies, in short, the obsessive fan who becomes the stalker and the trespasser" (168). Despite the ways in which the film version of *Hannibal* alludes to the theme of fame, however, it studiously avoids the subject at the most important point, thus generating a notable absurdity. *Hannibal*'s audience is asked to believe that Hannibal Lecter, indubitably one of the world's most famous criminals, has been living for ten years in Florence, a city crawling with American tourists, and yet has never been recognized. This was a feature of *Hannibal* derided by several critics (especially because in Thomas Harris's novel version of *Hannibal*, Lecter has plastic surgery to alter his appearance), and even Anthony Hopkins felt compelled to address the subject: "The theory I've come up with is that he's so daring, he didn't give a toss about [getting] caught. He flaunts his presence" (Bernstein 61). It is an elegant explanation, but it is also utterly implausible, and its implausibility underlines the irony of the fact that the most famous filmic serial killer of all is of little use in an examination of how serial killer movies have thematized the relationship between fame and serial murder.

Because it is, technically speaking, a prequel, *Red Dragon*, the latest installment in the Lecter film saga, is untroubled by any such implausibilities regarding Lecter's celebrity status. We see the beginning of the Lecter legend with Lecter's arrest (a scene in none of Harris's books), and so the film is seemingly absolved from having to examine the subject of fame, despite the fact that the film would never have been made if Lecter were not already a famous character.[3] *Red Dragon* does have problems of its own, however, problems largely caused by its complicated relation to its predecessors. Although it is a prequel, as critic David Ansen pointed out, "the aim is clearly to make it look as much as possible like a sequel to [*Silence of the Lambs*]: the production designer, Kristy Zea, replicates Lecter's Gothic prison cell, and Anthony Heald is once more on hand to play the smarmy Dr. Chilton" (68). A film like *Red Dragon* is so dependent on its famous predecessors that it cannot possibly stand alone, but this dependence can quickly become a problem in itself: "[*Red Dragon*] will no doubt keep the franchise rolling in dough. But the fact it now *feels* like a franchise is dispiriting: the thrills seem awfully familiar. Hopkins does get the ferocity back into Lecter. What he can't do (no one could now) is surprise us" (Ansen 68, original emphasis). Apparently, not thematizing serial killer celebrity explicitly does not save some films from being victimized by the variabilities of that celebrity. So what would constitute an "effective" filmic approach to serial killer celebrity culture? In what follows, I will discuss a number of different films that I will group into three different approaches to serial killer fame: the skirmish, the all-out attack, and the outmaneuver.[4] I will conclude by arguing that outmaneuvering serial killer fame by producing what amount to "anticelebrity" films is by far the most effective way of thematizing the fame of serial killers.

Skirmishing with Fame: *Kalifornia*, *Seven*, and *Copycat*

Unlike *The Silence of the Lambs*, this first group of films "skirmishes" with the subject of serial killer fame, using it to point up their moral message but not really engaging with the theme in a truly detailed or self-critical manner. Dominic Sena's 1993 film *Kalifornia* is typical in this regard. The film stars David Duchovny in a role he completed immediately before beginning work on *The X-Files*. Duchovny plays Brian Kessler, a young writer obsessed with serial killers to the point where he bores all his friends with his constant tirades on the subject. At the beginning of the film, Brian's opinions about serial killers are notably liberal. While his friends feel that serial killers are evil and should be killed, Brian argues that "most of these poor people suffer from severe chemical brain imbalances . . . The answer is research and treatment under hospital-supervised conditions. Not the electric chair." Brian is in the process of working on a book about serial murder but is unable to complete the proposal because he feels that his knowledge of serial murder is "merely" academic. Brian hits on a solution to this problem one night when he takes his lover Carrie to a local abandoned warehouse where a woman committed a series of murders. While Carrie, who is a photographer, takes photos of the scene, Brian has a flash of inspiration about how to write his book: "With your pictures and my writing it's a book . . . A book on some of the most infamous murders in American history. I want to go where they lived and where they killed. And I want you to take the pictures and I'm going to write the text."

The remainder of the film dedicates itself to destroying what are taken to be Brian's naive opinions about serial killers, a naïveté made worse by his irresponsible contribution to the culture of fame surrounding serial killers. The agent of destruction is Early Grayce (played by Brad Pitt), a redneck serial killer whom Brian meets when looking for someone to share the driving and gas expenses during his and Carrie's planned road trip to California. Although Brian and Carrie are initially unaware of Early Grayce's violent history, when he starts to victimize them, Brian is forced to acknowledge that his opinions about serial killers were completely misinformed. In a process that highlights the theme of class conflict that runs throughout the movie, the subproletarian Early teaches the bourgeois Brian the rules of Early's world. Ultimately, Brian learns his lessons so well that he is able to kill Early and thereby save both himself and Carrie. Nothing is learned from this experience, however, and we do not get the sense that Brian's initial naive point of view has been replaced by authentic knowledge about serial killers. Indeed, at the end of the film, Brian says explicitly that "I'll never know why Early Grayce became a killer. I'll never know why any of them do. When I looked into his eyes I felt nothing. Nothing."

At the same time as exposing Brian's liberal delusions about serial killers, *Kalifornia* also critiques the celebrity culture that Brian and Carrie were both drawing on and contributing to through their proposed coffee table book on famous killers. In fact, the viewer is not sure what Brian is punished for most: his naïveté or his voyeuristic fascination with serial killers. To have serial killer celebrity culture exposed as a fantastic and irresponsible fraud is a comforting message for *Kalifornia*'s viewers. Although Brian is duly punished for his voyeurism by having a traumatic confrontation with the reality of serial murder, the film implies that we recognized the truth all along and that we would never be so naive or participate in the celebrity culture around serial killers. This is the advantage that films such as *Kalifornia* see to merely "skirmishing" with fame: one gets to occupy both the low ground and the high ground simultaneously by both contributing to and decrying the culture industry organized around famous serial killers.

Seven is another film that gets to have its cake and eat it too by skirmishing with the subject of serial killer fame. It does so more subtly than *Kalifornia*, however, because the connection between serial murder and fame does not arise until the film's conclusion, although it then plays a crucial role. The movie tells the story of a killer who dispatches victims in the manner of the seven deadly sins. Thanks mostly to the character of Lieutenant Somerset (played by Morgan Freeman), the audience is encouraged to interpret these murders as a morality tale, the killer's sermon on the degeneration he sees everywhere in contemporary society. Throughout the majority of the film, the killer remains (literally and figuratively) a shadowy figure, but that changes when he gives himself up. What is particularly shocking is that the killer turns himself in midway through the series. Having killed people who he felt represented the sins of Gluttony, Greed, Sloth, Lust, and Pride, the killer still has Envy and Wrath to go. His decision not only raises the question of the killer's motivation but also forces the audience to confront its own desire for narrative resolution, to have the series completed. We know this completion can come about only through more murder, and so the closing scenes of the film unfold in an atmosphere composed of equal parts suspense and guilty desire (Dyer, *Seven* 33–34).

When being questioned by Somerset and Mills (Brad Pitt), the killer (Kevin Spacey) initially emphasizes his own unimportance, preferring instead to place the emphasis on his deeds and what they represent. When Mills asks the killer what makes him so special that people should listen to what he has to say, he replies, "I'm not special. I've never been exceptional. This is, though. What I'm doing. My work." The killer's apparent lack of desire for personal glory is underlined by the fact that he uses the name "John Doe," the classic cipher of anonymity (in fact, he uses the name "Jonathan Doe," which makes his embrace of anonymity more teasing and oblique).

As the questioning progresses, however, the audience begins to suspect that Doe's pride in his deeds, and his certainty that they will live on in public memory, have at least as much to do with his own desire for fame as his desire to teach a moral lesson. When Mills taunts Doe by saying that in two months no one will remember what he has done, Doe claims, "You can't see the whole complete act yet. But when this is done, when it's finished, it's going to be . . . people will barely be able to comprehend it, but they won't be able to deny." The impression that Doe's messianism is fueled by a sense of himself more as a celebrity than as a teacher is strengthened by several details from a later conversation, such as when Doe says, "What I've done is going to be puzzled over and studied and followed forever." He then goes on to tell Mills that he should be grateful to him, because thanks to Doe, Mills will be remembered forever. It is clear that Mills and Somerset believe that Doe's motive is personal aggrandizement, and this is why Mills taunts Doe by telling him, "You're no Messiah, you're a movie of the week. A fucking t-shirt at best."

But if Doe really is motivated by a desire for fame, what are we to make of the fact that his scheme concludes with his own death at the hand of Mills? If Doe truly desired fame and the worship of fans, would he not want to live so that he could enjoy the impact of his actions? Rather than contradicting the argument that Doe is motivated by a desire for fame, his willingness to die confirms his commitment to being a star. As Marianne Sinclair has argued in *Those Who Died Young: Cult Heroes of the Twentieth Century*, "When they died, their images changed—death gave me a different perspective of their achievements, lending them a retrospective aura of pathos they did not possess to the same extent when they were alive" (9). Doe has learned well the lessons of James Dean, Marilyn Monroe, and Bonnie and Clyde. He knows that contemporary American culture reserves its most exalted iconic status for those who refuse to linger and instead go out in a blaze of glory. His death is therefore a perfectly appropriate way of satisfying his desire for immortality.

Seven leaves unanswered the question of whether Doe receives the fame he desires because we never see the response of the media or the public to the completed series of murders. In another sense, though, the film itself is the answer to that question. Before and during the filming, nervous studio executives pressured the director, David Fincher, to film an alternative ending in which Doe kills Mills's dogs rather than his wife, fearing that the scripted ending would be too bleak for the audience. Ultimately, it was Brad Pitt, or more precisely, the influence that Brad Pitt's star power gave him, that ensured the original ending was adhered to (Dyer, *Seven* 21). Pitt's instincts proved to be correct. The film was a huge hit, partly because it did not shy away from the awkward subject of the audience's desire for more murders, and partly because it did not pursue the implications of that desire. To put it another way, there was no reason to show the public reaction to Doe's murders because *Seven*'s success constitutes that reaction. The very fact that *Seven* grossed over $300 million worldwide and was Blockbuster's number one video rental for 1996 was proof enough that Doe's predictions about the fame his actions would bring him were uncomfortably accurate.

In a nicely postmodern gesture of self-referentiality, the most suggestive confirmation of John Doe's star status came from the makers of *Seven* themselves, as indicated by their 2001 release of the DVD version of the film. Although the original version of the film featured two major stars, initially *Seven* was marketed in such a way as to deemphasize the fame of its star actors. According to Chris Pula, head of marketing at the distributors New Line, the "star of the movie was the crime. Brad and Morgan were the co-stars. Yes, their names were there. But we showcased the crime, the seven deadly sins" (Matzer S14). In this sense, serial murder, rather than a serial killer, was the initial star of *Seven*.[5] Apparently, this situation had changed by the time the DVD version of *Seven* was released. As if acknowledging the enthusiastic audience response to John Doe, the DVD's packaging was designed to resemble John Doe's notebooks, complete with photo clippings and bloody smudges. In addition, the DVD included a feature called "John Doe's World," where viewers could view his photo gallery, his reading list, and his thoughts on the seven deadly sins. If the original incarnation of *Seven* avoided the subject of John Doe's stardom, the more recent packaging of the film confirmed what was always obvious: the serial killer, not the crime, and definitely neither Brad Pitt nor Morgan Freeman, is the film's biggest star.

Although *Copycat* stays more within the territory of the slasher movie than *Kalifornia* and *Seven*, giving us an almost supernatural and thoroughly demonized serial killer, it too explores the uncomfortably close relationship between the killer and his audience while ultimately relieving the audience from feeling fully implicated in this relationship. *Copycat* also shares *Seven*'s emphasis on the killer's desire for fame, but in *Copycat* that desire takes on a suggestive intertextual dimension.

The film begins with noted criminologist and serial killer expert Helen Hudson (played by Sigourney Weaver) giving a public lecture on serial murder. Immediately after the lecture, Hudson is attacked in a bathroom by Darryl Lee Cullum (played, in an extraordinary example of off-casting, by Harry Connick Jr.). Although Cullum is prevented from killing Hudson (and is subsequently convicted and imprisoned), Hudson is so traumatized by the attack that she develops a severe case of agoraphobia. One year after these events, a series of murders takes place that Hudson realizes are modeled after famous serial killers of the past, so that one murder is based on the Boston Strangler, another on the Son of Sam, another on the Hillside Stranglers, and so on. As the plot unfolds, and the killer's attention focuses more and more on Hudson, it becomes clear that the killer (who uses the name "Peter Kürten," a German serial killer of the 1920s) is inspired not only by "real" serial killers but also by Darryl Lee Cullum, the fictional serial killer role model provided for him by the film.

The extent of Kürten's dedication to Cullum becomes clear in a scene from the end of the film, when Kürten kidnaps Hudson in order to recreate meticulously Cullum's attack on her. Before commencing the attack, Kürten reminisces with Hudson about when he first saw her, at the public lecture that opened the film: "God, Helen, I remember watching you on that big screen. Your red dress. You looked huge." In the context of disagreeing with Walter Benjamin's assertion that "the effects of the cinematic apparatus necessarily lead to the shriveling of aura," Barry King argues that the "filmed image of the actor, especially the leading player, and its insertion in an articulation of filmic time and space that prioritizes a person-centred schema of causality, can be argued to increase the massivity of the actor's presence" (155–56). Kürten's memory of the size of Hudson's filmed image is a practical example of the cinematic apparatus's tendency to "massify" the visual image, and it is clear that Kürten is threatened by this "massivity." Almost as if he had read Laura Mulvey's work on the scopophilic gaze, Kürten intuits that the way to counteract his feeling of inadequacy in the face of that massive image is to reclaim the gaze by filming his attack on Hudson. When Kürten looks through his own lens at the powerless Hudson, he is able to cancel out the previous hugeness of Hudson's image: "But look at you now."

The presence of the movie camera is also motivated by Kürten's highly developed awareness of the fame given to serial killers, and Hudson's comment earlier in the film that Kürten "wants what those killers got—fame, the power to terrify us" is amply confirmed during his attack on her. After taunting Hudson about her powerlessness, Kürten says, "But look on the bright side, Helen. I am going to make you the world's most famous victim. Guess what that makes me." Kürten is able to predict his fame with some confidence because of his awareness of the huge market for representations of serial murder. At one point, he says to Hudson, "Did you know, Helen, that more books have been written about Jack the Ripper than Abraham Lincoln?" His attack on Hudson literalizes Kürten's willingness to participate in this savagely competitive market economy and makes his comment on the existence of this market even more mocking: "It's a sick world, isn't it, Helen?"

Despite his position of seemingly unassailable power, the film ends with Kürten dying at the brink of realizing his ambition to kill Hudson, shot four times in extreme slow motion by the police officer MJ (played by Holly Hunter), the last shot blowing out the back of his head. Why is Kürten dispatched in such extravagantly bloody fashion? Earlier, I discussed the fact that serial killers, like movie stars, have fans. Obviously, Kürten, with his specialized knowledge of the canon of serial killers, is such a fan, as are those individuals who are still writing to Darryl Lee Cullum at the end of the film, vying to be his next disciple. In a more oblique sense, however, this film's audience also consists of fans. Not only does our presence in the movie theater or our rental of this film identify us as being interested in serial murder (whatever that means, and here we touch again on the thorny issue of identification), but if we recognize the names of the serial killer role models that Kürten draws upon, we may feel even more implicated in the star system that has developed around serial killers. Assuming that we feel conflicted by such implication, the gory slow-motion death of Kürten gives us a perfect opportunity to disavow our involvement, as we enjoy the spectacle of one of the bloodiest killings in the film. In this way, *Copycat* both invites the audience to contemplate its own imbrication in making stars out of serial killers and lets it off the hook by conveniently removing a troubling source of spectatorial identification. This pattern of engagement and retreat defines the skirmish approach to serial killer fame.

Attacking Fame: *Natural Born Killers* and *15 Minutes*

Seven's John Doe provides us with a convenient way of describing how *Natural Born Killers* and *15 Minutes* go about attacking fame. When asked to justify the extremely sadistic nature of his murders, Doe replies: "If you want people to pay attention, Detective, you can't just tap them on the shoulder anymore. You have to hit them with a sledgehammer. Then you'll find you have their strict attention." In *Natural Born Killers* (*NBK*), that most sledgehammer-like of directors, Oliver Stone, attacks what he sees as the root of the evil that is serial killer fame: the media. To some extent, Stone's attention is welcome because the media are more or less invisible in *Kalifornia, Seven,* and *Copycat*. By contrast, *NBK* examines the subject of media investment in serial murder very thoroughly, and so it seems likely that it has the potential to offer a more rigorous interrogation of the nature of the American public's fascination with the serial killer superstar. *NBK*, however, lets its audience off the hook even more insidiously than the "skirmish" films do, and this is why the so-called satire Oliver Stone attempts in this film is such an abject failure.[6]

Stone has described *NBK* as equal parts road movie and prison movie (Courtwright 29). In the first half of the film, Mickey and Mallory Knox (played by Woody Harrelson and Juliette Lewis) drive down Route 666 like Bonnie and Clyde on speed, killing everyone in their path and riding on a huge wave of publicity and adulation. Mickey and Mallory are captured and imprisoned halfway through the film; the second half of the movie is organized around a post–Super Bowl interview Mickey does with Wayne Gale (played by Robert Downey Jr.), the host of a tabloid TV show called *American Maniacs*. For some unknown reason, the interview is broadcast to the rest of the prison population who, inspired by Mickey's eloquent defense of murder, tear the prison apart. In the ensuing chaos, Mickey and Mallory escape, along with Wayne Gale, whom they subsequently kill so they can live happily ever after.

The root of the problem with *NBK* emerges (appropriately enough) when we consider the phenomenon of copycatting. Almost as soon as the film was released, reports started to come in of copycat crimes supposedly inspired by *NBK*.[7] This phenomenon provoked a critique of Stone by the novelist John Grisham, who argued that films should be treated like any other product, and suggested that Stone could and should be sued under product liability laws because of the damage his product has done (Shnayerson 100). Although Stone has defended himself eloquently against the censorious implications of this argument, I want to emphasize how this controversy highlights *NBK*'s participation in the same exploitative logic used by the media that the film ostensibly critiques. Through a series of decisions (or mistakes, if you prefer) Stone produced a film whose mimesis of the worst excesses of the mass media celebration of serial murder is so perfect that it is impossible to tell the difference between the unself-conscious original and the ironic postmodern copy.

The critique of the film I am offering is considerably blunted if one assumes that the heavy-handedness of Stone's critique was entirely self-conscious. Several critics have tried to argue that *NBK*, rather than being failed satire, is in fact a knowing and brilliantly original duplication of media exploitation of serial murder (see L. Gross, "Exploding" 8; Riordan 513). Although Stone's stated intentions about *NBK* give some evidence for the film's self-conscious duplication of media excesses, there is far more evidence to support the claim that Stone intended the film to be a satiric exaggeration, rather than a duplication, of the media's coverage of crime. For example, in the context of discussing his decision not to depict the violence naturalistically in *NBK* (as he had done in *Platoon*, for example), Stone says in his introduction to the novelized adaptation of the film: "what I set out to do was satirize (i.e., reflect through exaggerating, distorting with dark humor for effect) the painful idea that crime has gotten so crazy, so far out of hand, so numbing and desensitizing, that in this movie's Beavis and Butthead 1990s America crimescape, the subject approaches the comedic, as does the media which so avariciously cover it" (10).

Why was Stone unable to achieve what he set out to do? Part of the reason can be seen in a comment that Stone makes in the same introduction: "When we set out to make *Natural Born Killers* in late 1992, it was surreal. By the time it was finished in 1994, it had become real" (7). Stone is referring here to a cluster of events that received intense media coverage and that he includes in a montage at the end of *NBK*: the trial of the Menendez brothers and of O. J. Simpson, the Tonya Harding–Nancy Kerrigan controversy, and the Rodney King beating.[8] One could argue, then, that *NBK* fails as a satire of the media's obsession with violence simply because it found itself outpaced by events, many of which seemed at least as bizarre as the story of Mickey and Mallory. But *NBK* also fails to shed critical light on the ways in which serial killers are made into stars because of certain ill-advised decisions Stone makes.

The first decision is his choice of target. It is almost impossible to satirize the tabloid television genre effectively because it is already so over-the-top to start with. Stone's version of a tabloid television show, *American Maniacs*, and how such a show might represent and capitalize upon the media frenzy surrounding Mickey and Mallory, exemplifies this problem by its inability to critique actual tabloid television shows such as *Hard Copy* and *Inside Edition* in a substantive fashion.[9] Rather, Stone is limited to exaggerating even further the defining features of a genre that is already ridiculously exaggerated. As a result, *American Maniacs* is simply a regular tabloid show, only more so, a fact that gives Stone's critique a mimetic rather than genuinely critical relationship to the object of criticism. Of course, one could again argue that the self-conscious perfection of the mimesis is the aim, but if Stone's only aim is to confirm our sense that media coverage of crime can be irresponsible and exploitative, *NBK* is less than groundbreaking, to say the least.

The second problematic decision Stone makes concerns the role of Mickey and Mallory in the film. Stone has argued, quite persuasively, that in contemporary American society, figures such as Mickey and Mallory are bound to "capture the hearts and minds of Americans looking for a human face" (11). There's no doubt that *NBK* does a very good job of showing the degree of that public investment in Mickey and Mallory (although the movie does a terrible job of exploring what motivates that investment). The problem, however, is that Stone seems equally invested in his killers. Despite the fact that they murder over fifty people, Mickey and Mallory are easily the most sympathetic characters in the film. Stone's excessive investment in his serial killer hero and heroine indicates his unwillingness to recognize *NBK*'s "own complicity in the culture of celebrity and the indulgence in violent spectacle that it wishes to attack" (Creekmur 100); it also suggests that Stone is interested in exploring other issues in this film besides that of media satire. Stone confirmed this in an interview with Gavin Smith when he said, "The underlying philosophy of this film is not the media satire, but the concept of aggression in this century versus compassion and love" (11). Contrary to what one might expect, it is the media that represent aggression for Stone, whereas Mickey and Mallory, the star-crossed and misunderstood young lovers on the run from Mallory's abusive family, represent the power of love, a love so powerful, indeed, that it survives the end of the film, even if Wayne Gale does not. If the death of the killer provides some degree of closure in *Kalifornia*, *Seven*, and *Copycat*, that closure is represented in *NBK* by Mickey and Mallory's murder of the media, Stone's real villain, personified in the form of Wayne Gale.[10]

Gale's death indicates the nature and extent of *NBK*'s critique of the media, as Caryn James has argued: "It's too easy to suggest . . . that television is the Devil . . . A sophisticated depiction of television must portray the attraction as well as the repulsion it evokes. Television wouldn't be an overwhelming influence, after all, if people didn't love to watch it" ("What" 13). Rather than explore the intricacies of the relationship between the media and the public they serve, Stone is content simply to demonize the media. By killing Wayne Gale, Stone allows the members of his audience to both maintain their admiring identification with Mickey and Mallory and receive the comforting impression that they have liberated themselves from the manipulativeness of the media. This deeply cynical, one-sided, and ultimately dishonest conclusion about how the mass media represent serial murder speaks volumes about the depth and effectiveness of the satire in *NBK*.

Like *NBK*, *15 Minutes* targets the exploitative excesses of tabloid television. Although its approach to the subject is somewhat different, it is plagued by the same problems *NBK* struggles with. Perhaps learning a lesson from Stone, *15 Minutes'* director, John Herzfeld, wisely chooses not to emulate the visual style of a tabloid news show. Instead, Herzfeld stays within the familiar territory of the thriller, with its clear distinction between good guys and bad guys. Herzfeld's good guys are New York City cop Eddie Fleming (Robert De Niro) and arson investigator Jody Warsaw (Edward Burns) who spend the film chasing the bad guys, Emil Slovak (Karel Roden) and Oleg Razgul (Oleg Taktarov). Slovak and Razgul are recently arrived visitors to America from Eastern Europe, and they (Razgul in particular) have a starry-eyed quasi-immigrant vision of America, as not so much a land of milk and honey as a land of fame, a place where anyone can become famous for any reason what-soever.[11]

Slovak and Razgul set about proving their theory by having Slovak commit a series of extremely brutal murders (including the murder of Eddie Fleming), which Razgul films. Having completed their masterpiece, Slovak and Razgul then sell the results to Herzfeld's final bad guy, Robert Hawkins (Kelsey Grammer), the host of a local television tabloid show, *Top Story*. Even though Hawkins professes to be a good friend of Eddie Fleming's, he cannot resist the temptation to show Slovak and Razgul's tape on his show, triggering widespread revulsion but also huge viewing numbers. Convinced that the extremity of his crimes means that any American jury will find him not guilty due to temporary insanity, Slovak turns himself in, only to be killed by his erstwhile partner, Razgul, who is resentful at his friend's receiving all the limelight.

As this summary indicates, *15 Minutes* is not quite as "sledgehammerish" as *NBK* in its critique of celebrity in general and serial killer celebrity cul-ture in particular. On one level, Eddie Fleming is presented as a somewhat unscrupulous character because of his apparent addiction to being a celebrity cop. In this respect, his murder by Slovak and Razgul might seem to be an example of a celebrity groupie getting his just desserts. We see another side of Fleming, however, when he explains to Warsaw how useful his celebrity has been to him in doing his job successfully. Although Fleming's remarks smack of self-justification, it is significant that Herzfeld, unlike Stone, does not dis-miss fame altogether. It is also significant, bearing in mind Stone's decision to have Mickey and Mallory still alive and well at the end of *NBK*, that Herzfeld decides to have Fleming/De Niro, one of his main characters and by far the biggest star in the movie, murdered nowhere near the end of the film. Eddie Fleming's murder thus could potentially be taken as evidence of Herzfeld's self-conscious refusal to let the power of stardom dictate the structure and outcome of his film.

Although Herzfeld's "attack" on criminal celebrity certainly had potential, the vast majority of reviewers felt that it did not realize that potential, and the film was absolutely savaged by many critics. John Zebrowski of the *Seattle Times* described the film as "two horrifyingly bad hours that should stand as a reminder to keep Hollywood away from big issues or anything else it can put in its mouth and choke on," while Chuck Rudolph of *Matinee Magazine* claimed that "there have been few media criticisms that are as hypocritical and inane."[12] Many of the reviews commented that it was hypocritical of Herzfeld in particular to offer a critique of tabloid television's treatment of crime. Herzfeld, after all, had made his reputation with the made-for-television "docudramas" *The Preppy Murder* (1989), about Robert Chambers's murder of Jennifer Levin, and *Casualties of Love: The Long Island Lolita* (1993), one of the many films made about Amy Fisher's shooting of her lover's wife. Such a pedigree should not necessarily exclude Herzfeld from making a film like *15 Minutes* (after all, he clearly has firsthand experience of tabloid TV exploitativeness), but it did seem a little ungrateful of Herzfeld to turn round and bite the hand that had fed him up to this point.

Other critics pointed out that Herzfeld's "hypocrisy" was not limited to his trashing the tabloid TV culture that he had risen from but also extended to *15 Minutes* itself. As Jan Stuart from *Newsday* put it, "The filmmaker tries to eat his cake and have it as well, giving his audience ample servings of what we presumably want while slapping our wrists for it at the same time." While Herzfeld wants us to disapprove of Robert Hawkins's decision to air the graphic killing of Eddie Fleming on his tabloid show, the film itself is filled with such graphic killings, the most egregious of which involves Slovak's murder of a seminude prostitute whose body Herzfeld lingers over almost lovingly. As David Edelstein perceptively remarks, "Herzfeld's disgust at tabloid ethics might be genuine, but his own ethics are nothing to crow about. He uses violence as a turn-on" (Edelstein).

While the critical firestorm unleashed by movies like *15 Minutes* and *Natural Born Killers* is, by and large, justified, I want to contest the unspoken assumption of many of these criticisms that the way these films both participate in and criticize the celebrity culture around violence is a serious contradiction in these films, or a sign of their failure. While it is important to challenge the hypocritical way in which these films give the audiences both the thrill of famous serial killers and the means to distance themselves from acknowledging their desire for serial killers, I do not believe that this characteristic of these films is something that can be avoided altogether because it is absolutely essential to their structure. There may be less offensive and contradictory ways of "attacking" the fame of serial killers, but all too often what appear to be less egregious examples of this type of film are simply those films that have developed more efficient ways for the audience to disavow its involvement with the serial killer celebrity culture it is simultaneously enjoying. In other words, hypocrisy is not a contradiction in these "attack" films; it is their raison d'être.

Only by "outmaneuvering" celebrity by emphasizing the serial killer's ordinariness can one make films that criticize serial killer celebrity culture effectively.

Outmaneuvering Celebrity: *Man Bites Dog* and *Henry, Portrait of a Serial Killer*

Even among aficionados of serial killer movies, *Man Bites Dog* and *Henry* have a special, disturbing status. In an essay that addresses the positive pleasures of violent film viewing by discussing why women might enjoy watching such "new brutalist" films as *Reservoir Dogs* and *Pulp Fiction*, Annette Hill states: "Of all the target films, the two films which people said were the most challenging (*Man Bites Dog* and *Henry, Portrait of a Serial Killer*) were the most 'realistic' in their depiction of violence" (148). What does "realistic" mean in this context? What is it about *Man Bites Dog* and *Henry* that makes them more "disturbing" than any other serial killer films?

Man Bites Dog (*MBD*) succeeds where *Natural Born Killers* and *15 Minutes* fail; it is able to satirize effectively the media's construction of serial killers as stars. Released in 1992, *MBD* is the first feature by three young Belgian filmmakers who got to know each other in film school. Filmed over two and a half years for the staggeringly low sum of $15,000, it tells the story of a serial killer named Ben who is being filmed by two documentary filmmakers, Rémy and André. As the film progresses and the murders accumulate, the relationship between Ben and Rémy and André becomes more and more intimate. First, when Rémy and André run out of money, Ben agrees to finance the film. Slowly but surely, Rémy and André become more and more involved in the murders themselves, gradually crossing the line from observers to participants. This process culminates in the most horrific scene of the movie, when Ben and the film crew rape and then murder a married couple. Ultimately, all three are killed by unknown assailants in apparent revenge for Ben's murder of another serial killer known as the Nightingale. In the process, as Scott Rosenberg has indicated, *MBD* forces its audience to consider a number of uncomfortable questions: "It forces you to think, at length and without evasion, about the symbiosis between TV 'reality programming' and the crimes it records—and, on a larger scale, between filmmakers and the violence they exploit. Does observing a violent act amount to condoning it? What about recording it rather than stepping in to stop it? And if observing and recording violence does implicate us, then what are we supposed to do—turn our eyes away?" ("New" D2). It is partly *MBD*'s unflinching attention to these questions that makes it a more effective critique of the media's investment in serial murder, but a large part of *MBD*'s success also comes from the fact that it was filmed outside America: it does not address American culture, and it does not feature any major Hollywood stars. I realize that all these factors make *MBD* very different from the other films I have discussed, but I want to consider the possibility that it is precisely these differences that make a successful critique of the serial killer star system possible.

Consider, for example, the absence of stars in *MBD*. Because film stars have such strong intertextual identities, we are inevitably reminded of other roles they have played when we see them in a particular film. Sometimes these associations can help the film, as when Sigourney Weaver's simultaneous status as both the hunter and the hunted of the serial killer in *Copycat* reminds us irresistibly of her character Ripley in the *Alien* movies.[13] In other cases, though, these intertextual associations can be more disruptive. The casting of *Cheers* alumnus Woody Harrelson as Mickey Knox in *NBK*, a decision to some extent forced on Stone, so that he could get $35 million from the studio to make the film rather than $10 million (see Hamsher 104–5), and even more the casting of urbane lounge singer Harry Connick Jr. as depraved serial killer Darryl Lee Cullum in *Copycat*, are both ineffective examples of off-casting. In these cases, the intertextual baggage carried by other aspects of these stars' careers made their work in these films less persuasive than it might have been. *MBD*, whose main characters are played by the unknown filmmakers themselves, has none of these problems, and this is one reason why its critique of media complicity is more effective. The absence of stars and their intertextual baggage allows *MBD*'s message to emerge more clearly.

Apart from the anonymity of *MBD*'s actors, the lack of money available to the filmmakers was another important ingredient in the film's success. A severe shortage of funds forced the filmmakers to shoot the film (and especially the episodes of violence) in a no-frills, naturalistic manner. This decision was not only financially expedient, however, but also thematically appropriate. Unlike *NBK* and *15 Minutes*, whose target was the role of tabloid television in the making of serial killer superstars, *MBD*'s critique focuses on the documentary genre, with its supposed commitment to objectivity and distance. The choice of documentary was the perfect way to chart the gradual breakdown of the barriers that separated the makers of the film and the subject of the film. Although both Wayne Gale in *NBK* and the filmmakers in *MBD* end up joining forces with serial killers, *MBD*'s depiction of this process is both more persuasive and more disturbing, first because it happens incrementally, and second because it is never implied that this shift can be explained by the filmmakers' mental disturbance.

The emphasis on the normality of the killer and the filmmakers in *MBD* is the final ingredient in the film's success and is illustrated by a scene in the film that takes place immediately after Ben shoots another serial killer named the

Nightingale in an abandoned building. While standing over the Nightingale's dead body, Ben suddenly realizes that other people are lurking in the darkness of an adjoining room. When Ben orders them to come out, what emerges is a mirror image of Ben's colleagues: another film crew who have been following the Nightingale and filming his exploits, just as Ben is being filmed. The presence of a second film crew, engaged in exactly the same activity, suggests not shared psychosis but rather the fact that the filming of serial killers is a business activity, the attempt to generate a salable commodity. This economic emphasis is confirmed by Ben's motivation for being a serial killer. Unlike the killers in the other films I have discussed, whose motives are left mysteriously vague or who are presented as insane, Ben is presented as a businessman. Serial killing is how he earns a living, which is why, as he explains at one point, he rarely kills children: because it is not financially remunerative.

This emphasis on killing and the filming of that killing as being "all in a day's work," as it were, gives *MBD* a degree of self-consciousness that is quite distinct from the self-consciousness that characterizes *NBK*. Stone's film is conscious of itself only as a supposedly avant-garde art object. Its loudly advertised status as satire, Stone would have the audience believe, protects both the film and the audience from being implicated in the irresponsible celebration of serial murder that characterizes the rest of popular culture. *MBD* is under no illusion that it can distance itself neatly from the irresponsible popular cultural exploitation of serial murder. Its emphasis on the economics of serial killing underlines the extent to which this film participates in the same market for images of serial murder as does any other example of popular culture. Because of the film's self-conscious status as product, the audience of *MBD* is not allowed the luxury of distancing itself from what it sees. If the film's status as product is highlighted, then so is our participation in the dynamic of consumption that makes the film a successful product.

Because the audience of *MBD* is forced to confront its imbrication in the market for images of serial killers, it is much more difficult for us to demonize the film's characters and thus place them at a comforting distance from ourselves.[14] This close relationship between character and viewer is hinted at in the original title of the film. *Man Bites Dog* is the title the filmmakers came up with for the film's release to an English-speaking market. It has the virtue of snappiness, but it has none of the suggestiveness of the film's original French title, *C'est arrivé près de chez vous*, which can be translated into English as *It Happened in Your Neighborhood*. The title is taken from a section of the Belgian national newspaper, *Le Soir*, that concentrates on local news (Klein 23). By problematizing the audience's desire to distance itself (in this case, geographically rather than psychologically) from its participation in the film's events, this title exemplifies the way *MBD* presents the media's making of the serial killer into a celebrity as an ordinary, gradual, almost banal process. Rather than "attacking" the fame of serial killers head on, *MBD* instead approaches the issue obliquely and gradually and can thus avoid the problems associated with *NBK* and *15 Minutes* by "outmaneuvering" serial killer fame. This is a much more effective way of critiquing the phenomenon of famous serial killers than the monotonal heroes-and-villains logic of the other films I have discussed.

The differences between *Man Bites Dog* and mainstream Hollywood serial killer films highlight how unlikely it is to find an American film featuring serial killers that interrogates the relationship between serial murder and celebrity in a substantive way. In any film produced for the American market, it is more than likely that the status of serial killers as stars is either not called into question at all, or presented in such a way that the film's audience is always left with a loophole, a way to avoid feeling implicated in the serial killer's rise to fame. Are there any exceptions to what seems to be a rule about American films? In closing, I want to discuss *Henry: Portrait of a Serial Killer* (1986), a film that suggests that the absence of stars rather than the nationality of the film might be the determining factor in whether a film is able to offer an effective critique of serial killer celebrity. Although *Henry* does not explicitly address the relation between fame and serial murder, with Henry remaining an anonymous figure throughout the film, in other ways *Henry* seems to contradict my claims about serial killer movies made for the American market in that, rather than giving its audience a way to avoid feeling implicated in watching acts of serial murder, it instead forces its audience to consider its implication even more intensely and uncomfortably than *Man Bites Dog*. Significantly, however, *Henry* has far more in common with the Belgian independent film than it does with the Hollywood blockbusters I have discussed.

In the first place, *Henry* is definitely not a Hollywood film, both in the sense that it refuses the prevailing ideologies of the Hollywood serial killer film and in the sense that it was made outside of Hollywood, not by a major studio but by a small independent film company, MPI home video, based in Chicago and owned by two brothers, Waleed B. and Malik Ali. Moreover, like *Man Bites Dog*, *Henry* avoids the complications of casting star actors in its lead roles by instead relying (for budgetary reasons) on local talent, predominantly from the Organic Theatre Company, one of Chicago's top off-Broadway-type theater groups (Bouzereau 200). But far more central to the impact and importance of the film than the location and the cast is the attitude with which director John McNaughton approached the project: "The device was to pull

out the fantasy and make it real . . . If you make it real, they'll believe it. When
you leave the theater after *The Texas Chainsaw Massacre*, you may have night-
mares, but you don't really believe that Leatherface is going to come flying
round the corner and chase you down the street with a chain saw. You can
have your thrill and walk away from it. With *Henry*, there's nowhere to run"
(quoted in Bouzereau, 203–4).[15] Defining his aim explicitly in opposition
to the Hollywood tradition of representing serial killers as exemplified by
the slasher movie, McNaughton instead attempted to make a film that would
confound the stereotypes associated with filmic serial killers. McNaughton
succeeded beyond his wildest dreams, as the official response to the film indicates. When McNaughton sent *Henry* to the Motion Picture Association of
America (MPAA) to be rated, he did not anticipate serious problems. There
was relatively little nudity in the film, and, although violent, *Henry* was deliberately not intended to be a gore fest in the slasher tradition (McDonough
44).[16] The MPAA, however, sent *Henry* back with an X rating because of
what it described as the film's "disturbing moral tone." The normal practice
in such situations is for the MPAA to specify to the producer and director
what the offending scenes are, so that they can cut them out. In *Henry*'s case,
however, the whole film was damned (McDonough 44). Unlike *The Silence
of the Lambs*, which achieved multiple-Oscar acclaim and made millions of
dollars, *Henry*, as a result of its rating, could be released only on a very limited
basis. It received critical praise, becoming a cult classic, but widespread public
attention continues to elude it. Even now it is impossible to get a copy of *Henry*
from most video stores, as they refuse to stock it.

The MPAA's response to *Henry* raises an interesting question. What did
it find so "disturbing" about this film that was apparently not present in the
mainstream Hollywood films I have discussed? To take *The Silence of the
Lambs* as an example, the success of Demme's film (and other films like it)
depends on how well Demme is able both to generate audience identification
with his serial killers and to discipline that identification when it becomes too
threatening. Unlike *Henry*, whose "hero" literally drives off into the sunset,
unmolested and undetected by any law enforcement figure, *Silence* makes
sure that the serial killer gets his comeuppance when Buffalo Bill is killed
by Clarice. But this is obviously only half the story, for *Silence* also contains
its own "sunset" scene (a scene not in Harris's novel) when Lecter walks off
to keep his dinner appointment with Dr. Chilton. The success of *Silence*,
therefore, and the reason it did not disturb the MPAA, is that it gives its
audience the best of both worlds: Buffalo Bill's death allows the audience to
disavow any identification it may have formed with the serial killer characters,
and yet that very same identification is adroitly maintained by the prospect

that Hannibal Lecter, in every sense the more acceptable serial killer in the movie (because he is more educated, urbane, and witty), is still at large and thus available for an equally successful sequel.

The death of Buffalo Bill is one reason why audiences, along with the MPAA, are undisturbed by the thought that Hannibal Lecter is still loose, but there is a second reason why the sight of Lecter walking off to commit new murders upset the MPAA less than the sight of Henry doing exactly the same thing. The disruptive effects of the continued presence of Lecter are somewhat alleviated by the insistent, one might say pervasive, presence of law enforcement in *The Silence of the Lambs*. If the FBI fails to recapture Lecter, it does get Bill, and the prominence of Clarice Starling as a protagonist ensures that the audience goes a long way toward internalizing the law enforcement perspective of serial murder as their own. In *Henry*, however, law enforcement is not fallible or partial, it is completely absent. The suggestion that the audience lives in a world in which serial killers often do go uncaptured, in which they experience no obstacles to committing their murders unless they make a stupid mistake or have some bad luck, is what the MPAA and the other guardians of culture in America would find most truly disturbing about *Henry* (P. Jenkins, *Using* 108).

While the absence of law enforcement in *Henry* undoubtedly makes Henry's continued presence more unsettling than Lecter's, there is a final explanation for the MPAA's intensely negative reaction to the film, an explanation that makes the producers' consternation about the rating board's response somewhat disingenuous. Although *Henry* contains less graphic violence than most R-rated movies, it is an incredibly intense film; in particular, more than any other serial killer film, it insists on the audience's complicity with what it is watching on screen. As a result, the audience is left with no way to disavow its identification with *Henry*. As McNaughton says, there is nowhere for the audience to run, and this is by far the most disturbing aspect of the film.

In part, *Henry* manufactures audience complicity by lulling the audience into a false sense of security. At first, McNaughton encourages his audience to feel some sympathy for Henry by not showing his killings and by carefully nurturing an image of Henry as an underdog. The first murder shown in detail—the death of a fence who was trying to sell a television to Henry and his accomplice, Otis—is given both motivation and an implicit endorsement: the man was rude to them (Kehr, "Heartland" 61). By this point, the audience feels the temptation to cheer what Henry does, partly because of a familiarity with other "justified" killings in action movies such as *Rambo* and *Die Hard*. Immediately after this scene, however, Henry and Otis brutally murder an entire family, and suddenly, just as when Ben and the filmmakers rape and murder the married couple in *Man Bites Dog*, the viewing experience gets much more uncomfortable. In *Henry*, however, the level of audience discomfort is intensified even further when we realize that the murder of the family that we have just witnessed was shot on video, a video made by Henry and Otis on a stolen camcorder, and that Henry and Otis are watching the video along with us. For McNaughton, the choice to shoot this scene on video was entirely deliberate: "With film you believe in the surface illusion, but with video you don't. We knew that by using that video image, it would make that act seem absolutely, terrifyingly real" (Bouzereau 202). The greater degree of realism was not an artistic end in itself, however, but rather chosen in order to force the audience to confront some disturbing questions, as McNaughton explains: "You think this is graphic . . . but you're sitting here watching it, waiting to be entertained. Now what do you think about yourself, and what do you think about watching this kind of violence on the screen?" The brilliance of *Henry*, and the reason it disturbs the conventions of serial killer movies so profoundly, consists of giving the audience what it wants, but in such a way that its desire for violence is unmediated either by any frames that suggest that desire is justified or by any loopholes that allow the audience to indulge that desire and simultaneously disavow it.

Such a sophisticated and unflinching attention to the audience's complicitous role in the viewing of violence sets *Henry* apart from the vast majority of American-made serial killer movies. Indeed, in its unwillingness to let its audience off the hook in any way it surpasses even *Man Bites Dog*, whose audience is able to fit Ben's death within a schema of retribution and poetic justice, no matter how ambiguous. As we move through the following chapters, it will become more and more clear that *Henry* is truly an anomalous example in the popular cultural treatment of serial killers. The vast majority of popular cultural representations of serial murder is premised on allowing the customer to simultaneously enjoy and disavow his or her identifications with serial killers; this duality plays a major role in allowing serial killers to be thought of as celebrities. *Henry* shows us an alternative possibility, but it is truly an exception to the rule.

Serial Killers on Film: "Strong" versus "Weak" Violence

The public debate about film violence in the contemporary United States is dominated overwhelmingly by conservative politicians, religious groups, and think tanks, all of whom parrot the same simplistic analysis whose essence can be expressed in the following equation: film violence = everything that is wrong with the world. According to this point of view, the existence of film violence is evidence that American culture is in a state of advanced decline, a decline whose consequences can be seen in teen suicide, high school shootings, robbery, murder, and numerous other forms of social and cultural malaise. In a characteristically overheated announcement, Michael Medved, one of the chief ideologists of the conservative viewpoint, has argued that "tens of millions of Americans now see the entertainment industry as an all-powerful enemy, an alien force that assaults our most cherished values and corrupts our children. The dream factory has become the poison factory" (3). Not surprisingly, Medved regards the "glorification" of serial killers that he sees in contemporary American culture as one of the greatest challenges facing Americans today:

> Anyone who doubts that Hollywood actively promotes this fascination with evil should consider the crowd of agents and producers who immediately swarm over any mass murderer the moment he (or she) is apprehended. In January 1991, for instance, Florida police arrested a filthy, overweight, alcoholic prostitute with a bloated and sadly battered face on charges of murdering six male customers. This case of Aileen Carol Wuornos instantly set off what the Los Angeles Times described as a "frenzy" among Hollywood writers and producers, with more than a half-dozen production companies (including CBS Entertainment and Carolco Pictures) competing for the rights for her story. For today's ugliness-obsessed entertainment industry, the cruelty of her crimes, combined with the seediness of her circumstances, created an irresistible combination. (212)

There are sound reasons for deploring and resisting the cynical exploitation of public fascination with serial murder that we can find in the popular cultural industries; indeed, I address this very subject with regard to Aileen Wuornos in chapter 6. Little except righteous anger, however, will be produced by Medved's wildly exaggerated and deeply paranoid account of the imminent collapse of Western culture under relentless attack by the godless bosses of popular culture machines. Rather than tarring all serial killer films with the same condemnatory brush for turning killers into celebrities, as critics such as Medved are wont to do, a more productive approach is to find a way of discriminating between more or less effective filmic treatments of serial killer fame.

A good way to start is to note not just the ubiquity of violence in contemporary film but also the preponderance of a particular type of violence: "Graphic violence is now embedded in contemporary cinema as a formulaic element, endlessly repeated, and often removed from any recognizably human context. It solves story problems by providing talented as well as mediocre filmmakers with an easily-assembled, if mechanical narrative structure. It also substitutes for thought and reflection" (Prince, *Savage* 241). When one considers such blockbusters as the *X-Men*, *Matrix*, and *Terminator* film series, so short on plot and so long on glossy, balletic violence, it is hard to disagree with Prince's observation. The problem with the frequency of movies that enshrine this type of cinematic violence is not that they provoke acts of imitative violence or numb their audiences to the consequences of violence but that they "falsify the nature of violence itself. The truth is, Americans *don't* want to see genuinely violent movies, movies that offer a full accounting of the costs and consequences of violent acts in the real world" (Rosenberg, "Heightened" D7, original emphasis). By insulating their audiences from the "costs and consequences" of violence, the vast majority of contemporary films establish a peculiarly dissonant harmony between two of the most foundational aspects of film: violence and stardom. The majority of the biggest stars in the medium have always tended to be associated with violence, but today more than ever before the largest amounts of stardom tend to go to those stars most closely associated with violent films.

Let me reiterate at this point that we are talking about a very particular type of violence, a violence that insulates its viewers from having to deal with the consequences of that violence by giving them an "escape hatch . . . [an] assurance that involvement can be avoided" (McKinney 108). Devin McKinney refers to such violence as "weak," by which he means violence that is "used only as a device: something a crowd pays for when it goes in [to a movie theater], but not when it comes out" (103). By contrast, according to McKinney, "strong" violence refuses "glib comfort and immediate resolutions" (100).

Applying McKinney's distinction between "strong" and "weak" violence to serial killer films, the most egregious examples of "weak" violence are slasher movies. Despite the thought-provoking work of critics like Carol Clover, there is still a sense in which films like *Halloween* and *Friday the 13th* have all the hallmarks of "weak" violence: a refusal to show the consequences of violence, a lack of effort to create empathy for the victims of violence, and multiple ways for the audience to feel uninvolved with the violence. Using the same standards, the films I discuss under the headings of "skirmishes" with and "attacks" on fame, *Kalifornia*, *Seven*, *Copycat*, *Natural Born Killers*, and *15 Minutes*, can also be categorized as employing "weak" violence. The reason these films fail to provide a detailed and honest analysis of serial killer celebrity culture is that they are too busy insulating their viewers from feeling implicated in that culture while at the same time entertaining them with examples of that culture. Although the majority of these films articulate an impeccably liberal disapproval of celebrity serial killers, their disapproval is ultimately unconvincing because they depend too uncritically upon the very celebrity culture that they purport to denigrate and repudiate.

By contrast, I would describe *Man Bites Dog* and *Henry: Portrait of a Serial Killer* as examples of "strong" violence. These films are effective interrogations of our fascination with serial murder because neither of them provides "glib comfort and immediate resolutions" (McKinney 100). Instead, they are focused on forcing their viewers to contemplate their own reflection in the filmic exploits of serial killers. Thanks to their unflinching and all too rare attention to the ways in which the viewer's relation to serial killers is a compound of fear and fascination, *Man Bites Dog* and *Henry* do not need the "big message" that films like *15 Minutes* yell at their audiences until they are hoarse.

CHAPTER FOUR

Out of This World: Aliens, Devils, and Serial Killers in Television Crime Drama

> 10:25 commercial break. Again an Eveready ad (they reproduce like rabbits, like batteries in series), again previews for a news story following the film at 11:00 ("Overkill: The Real Story," with real-life footage of Wuornos), again ads for tomorrow night's 11:00 news story ("Go Inside the Mind of a Killer"), an ad for this week's episode of the series *In the Heat of the Night* (about a killer sniper) and *Top Cops*. These ads running and rerunning in my mind, I realize that the term *series* is its own plural.
>
> —David Hirsch, "Dahmer's Effects"

Television presents serial murder in more forms than any other popular cultural genre, partly because, as David Hirsch's quote in the epigraph implies, of the huge amount and range of crime-related programming it features. What Hirsch also alludes to is the fact that seriality is a defining characteristic of the televisual medium, present in concrete forms like the drama series and in more abstract forms, such as the series of advertisements that punctuate an evening's television viewing. And like the bunny in the Eveready ad, seriality is breeding like crazy. Serial killers play a prominent role in the profusion of seriality on television, making frequent appearances in documentaries, news coverage, made-for-television movies, drama series, "reality TV" shows, televised trials, and many other genres, thereby demonstrating the extent to which the adage "If it bleeds, it leads" has become the motto not only of journalists but also of television programmers.

In order to understand how this situation came about, I want to begin this chapter by analyzing a number of issues that have had a profound impact on the serial killer's current status on television: the influence of film on the role seriality plays in television; the similarities and differences between film and television's concepts of celebrity; and the rise of tabloid television. I will then demonstrate how these issues influence the televisual representation of serial murder by focusing on the crime drama series, a television genre that draws extensively on the serial structures endemic to television and that, consequently, also pays a significant amount of attention to serial murder. Partly because of the way television celebrity operates, and partly because of the (un)suitability of television for in-depth political critique, *Twin Peaks*, *The X-Files*, *Millennium*, and *Profiler* all reflect a generalized "law-and-order" perspective on serial murder. This perspective can be seen in how these series all work to rehabilitate the FBI's reputation by depicting its valiant struggles against monstrous serial killers. Moreover, the way in which these series associate serial killers with the paranormal, the alien, and the demonic both accentuates the heroism of their FBI protagonists and suggests that serial killers are not of this world, a comforting message that has been eagerly received by their large audiences.

A Fine Romance? The Relationship between Hollywood and Television

Critics have usually presented the relationship between the established film industry and the burgeoning television industry in 1950s America as a hostile one. As the purchase of television sets and the expansion of programming both began their meteoric rise in the years after World War II, the film industry initially panicked, interpreting plummeting revenues as the final nail in the coffin of an already shaky studio system. For understandable reasons, the movie studio bosses were especially hostile toward television, and none more so than Jack Warner of Warner Brothers, who in the early 1950s even went as far as to stipulate that no televisions should be included in the set decor of Warner Brothers films (C. Anderson 2). And yet, by 1959, Warner's opinion of television had changed to the extent that he could describe it in a speech as "a very healthy influence on the motion picture industry. It's the ninth wonder of the world" (quoted in C. Anderson 5).

What happened to change the minds of Warner and the other studio bosses so radically over the course of the 1950s? During this decade, the movie studios found a way to work with rather than against television by entering into production agreements with the major television corporations. So rapid was the expansion of the television industry that these production agreements became extremely lucrative for the movie studios. In fact, by 1955, Hollywood studios had become the major source of programming for the television networks. By 1959, the initially hostile Warner Brothers found itself in the unusual position of not having a single motion picture in production, but still being extremely busy producing programming for television (C. Anderson 5). Once studio bosses realized that television could increase rather than diminish their profits, they became enthusiastic supporters of the new medium.

Although Hollywood provided a wide variety of products for the television networks, the series became a particularly important part of the industry because it provided such a stable source of income for the movie studios:

> The studios discovered that supplying television programs to the networks offered a new rationale for standardized, studio-based production. By shifting their mass production efforts into series television, a number of the major Hollywood studios were able to capitalize upon *aspects* of the studio system even as the system itself changed. Thanks to its telefilm operations, Warner Bros., for instance, maintained term contracts with actors, directors, producers, and technicians, continued regular studio operations, and guaranteed a steady supply of product that was financed, produced, and owned by Warner Bros. until the entire studio was sold in the late 1960s. (C. Anderson 7, original emphasis)

Television, far from threatening the existence of Hollywood, gave movie studios a convenient way of claiming a role within what was obviously becoming the most influential culture industry in postwar America. It is important to emphasize, however, that this period was not defined just by television's influence on film, because film also influenced television. Before studio involvement in the television industry, for example, television had not shown a marked preference for the series type of programming.

Initially, the most popular forms of programming on television tended to be anthology dramas or live comedy, forms that had been inherited from network radio, vaudeville, and theater. The rise of the series gave those working in television the opportunity not only to produce an original genre but also to increase and regularize the audience for television. As Christopher Anderson puts it, "In contrast with programming forms that traded on uniqueness [such as early experiments with the television special], weekly episodic series encouraged an experience of television viewing as something ordinary, one component of the family's household routine" (12). The ability of the series form to develop viewer loyalty to the medium made it a favorite choice of the television studios, and the series quickly became the dominant type of program on television, a position it has occupied ever since.[1] The prominence of the series in television programming is just one example of the mutually influential relationship that existed between the film and television industries in the 1950s. Just as the series format benefited both media, so did their common use of celebrities.

The Two Faces of Celebrity: Movie Stars versus Television Personalities

The relationship between movie and television fame is another story that has often been told in hostile terms. Richard Schickel, for example, has argued that it was very difficult for movie stars to make the transition into television because this move destroyed too much of the star's aura. In particular, Schickel claims, "it was not until television in general, and the talk shows in particular, began to force them into closer, often accidental, intimacy with figures of greater substantiality and substance, figures so often superior to them socially and intellectually if not in physical beauty, that the stars began to suffer by comparison" ("Stars" 15). In his classic essay on the destruction of aura in the modern era, "The Work of Art in the Age of Mechanical Reproduction," Walter Benjamin analyzes what he describes as "the social bases of the contemporary decay of the aura" (223). According to Benjamin, one of these bases is "the desire of the contemporary masses to bring things 'closer' spatially and humanly" (223). The reproduction of film stars in the medium of television represents a "humanizing" of the auratic object, which is to say, the destruction of the object's aura. To the extent that movie stars always depended on a certain degree of remoteness from their audience to guarantee their star power, Schickel's analysis of why these stars tended to fare poorly on television seems valid.

Denise Mann has taken the idea of television's hostility toward Hollywood stars even further by arguing that, during the 1950s, movie stars appeared on television programs to allow audiences to work out their ambivalent feelings toward such figures. According to Mann, the appearance of movie stars on television in the post–World War II period was welcomed because their glamour, their distance from the everyday, provided "a much needed antidote to the homogenizing tendencies of so much of the popular cultural imagery of the postwar period" (47). At the same time, however, movie stars' lack of ordinary traits, their distance from the world occupied by the average television viewer, could also lead to resentment. Accordingly, seeing the movie star on the "ordinary" medium of television would, the studios hoped, encourage more friendly feelings of identification with the movie star: "popular attitudes toward Hollywood stars were in a process of transition in postwar America. Visual representations of TV stars as ordinary individuals . . . can be seen as a compensatory gesture designed to counteract the celebrity's status as either upper class, *or* as corporate property" (51, original emphasis).[2]

Arguments such as these serve as a salutary reminder not to minimize the differences between movie and television celebrity. With that said, just as the argument about the hostility that existed between movie studios and television can be overstated, so can the argument about the differences between these two types of celebrity. Not only was there a large amount of crossover between movie stars and television during the 1940s and 1950s that was not defined (explicitly or implicitly) by hostility, but also such crossovers between movies and other media were commonplace. Network radio made extensive use of film stars such as Bob Hope and Bing Crosby, who were both under contract to Paramount, the movie studio most interested in developing contacts with the broadcasting industry during the studio system era. As Christopher Anderson has argued, "the popular success of movies and radio during the 1930s and 1940s depended at least partially on the fact that the media were not isolated from one another but were perceived as complementary experiences in which stars and stories passed easily from one medium to another" (16).

As time went by, the relationship between movie and television fame became not only closer but also two-way: if the 1940s and 1950s were characterized by movie stars moving out into the medium of television, in succeeding decades the movie industry began to take the majority of its stars from other media, predominantly television. As Dave Kehr has pointed out, "few performers arrive in film without first achieving success in some other area . . . Making it in the movies remains the most prestigious species of stardom, not because film is the most popular art . . . but because it's the last rung on the ladder, the proof that a star is a star across the board" ("Travolta" 37). Thanks to these intimate relationships between movie stardom and stardom in other fields, there is a very general sense in which movie and television stars are the same, namely, in their difference from the ordinary viewer. Despite the ways in which television "humanizes" celebrities by making them seem ordinary, the "television frame [also] marks the boundary between the ordinary social world of viewers and the extraordinary symbolic world of television" so that television stars, just like their movie counterparts, seem to occupy a different register of reality from us (McDonald, "I'm" 59). Despite the continuities between these two types of stardom, however, it remains equally important to emphasize the ways in which being a star on television is very different from film's concept of stardom.

In his groundbreaking 1981 article "Television's 'Personality System,'" John Langer asks, "What is the significance of the fact that whereas the cinema established a 'star system,' television has not?" (351). According to Langer, television has "personalities" rather than stars: "those individuals constituted more or less exclusively for and by television, who make regular appearances as news readers, moderators, hosts, compères or characters, and those individuals who exist outside of television in their own right, but are recruited *into* television at various strategic junctures as resource material—politicians, celebrities, experts" (351, original emphasis). Although Langer draws most of his examples from nonfictional television genres, he points out that the same distinction between star and personality also applies in fictional genres: "Television's traditional fiction forms—the cop show, the situation comedy, the soap opera, the mini series—are similarly structured around personalities, not 'real' personalities as in the case of actuality television, but central 'characters' through whom the narrative is generated" (353). Langer goes on to argue that audience identification is focused primarily on these characters, and not on the actors who play them, so that in *The X-Files*, for example, Mulder and Scully, rather than David Duchovny and Gillian Anderson, would be the primary focus of audience identification.

In a much more recent version of the same argument, Sara Gwenllian Jones has argued that, in the case of the series *Xena: Warrior Princess*, it is the character of Xena, rather than the actress Lucy Lawless, who is the focus of fan investment. Jones is willing to acknowledge that some fans may also be interested in Lawless but claims that "fans' interest in Lawless rarely exceeds their interest in Xena" (12). Where Jones goes beyond Langer is in arguing that fans' investment in the character rather than the star is a product of the inherent seriality of television drama: "Television's seriality intensifies the audience's imaginative engagement with the cult text and, particularly, with its characters. It effects an illusion of continuation and constancy which itself invites speculation; there is a sense in which the fictional lives of characters seem to carry on, unseen by camera or audience, between episodes" (11). Although I disagree with Langer and Jones that the vast majority of fan investment is with the character rather than the star of television drama series (one has only to visit "X-Philes" Web sites to see that Duchovny and Anderson receive at least as much attention as Mulder and Scully), there is no doubt that the lead characters in drama series do serve as "anchoring points" for the viewer (Langer 357). Even though the story of the drama series may change from week to week, we will always see the same characters, which is another way of saying that they become the most serial elements of the television drama series.

In some respects, however, the use of serial characters, rather than distinguishing television from film, is yet another point of connection between the two media. Although initially, and somewhat ironically, the film industry did not adopt the serial structure of programming that it sold so assiduously to the television networks, more recently the presence of sequels, prequels, and series of theatrical films suggests that the film industry has become more receptive to the benefits of seriality. In one sense, of course, the film industry always had serial films of a kind that tends to support the distinction between the film star and the television personality. Although one could go to the theater twenty times and see John Wayne in twenty different roles, in another sense those twenty films constituted a series—of "John Wayne films." The "star image" of John Wayne was sufficiently powerful to suggest a continuity between roles as different as a cowboy and Genghis Khan. To some extent, this "star image" version of seriality is still a feature of film consumption today, with many people going to see any and every film featuring stars like Denzel Washington, Julia Roberts, or Jim Carrey.

More recently, however, seriality has appeared in film in a way that not only makes film at least as concentrated on character rather than actor as television is but also is expressive of an interesting point of continuity and difference between how the two media represent serial murder. The existence of the long-running and extremely lucrative movie series featuring Jason (*Friday the 13th*), Freddy Krueger (*Nightmare on Elm Street*), Michael Moore (*Halloween*), and Hannibal Lecter (*The Silence of the Lambs, Hannibal, Red Dragon*) suggests two things: that seriality in film finds its purest and most durable expression in films about serial murder, and that the serial heroes of these narratives are neither law enforcement figures, nor the actors who play the killers (with the possible exception of Anthony Hopkins), but the killer characters themselves.

Television drama series like *Twin Peaks, The X-Files, Millennium*, and *Profiler* are also focused on their lead characters, but this is also the biggest difference between the films and the television dramas, for the lead characters of those dramas are not killers but representatives of law enforcement—the FBI, to be precise. As we will see later, this fact plays a major role in generating audience support for the law enforcement perspective on serial murder in these drama series. For the moment, I want to return our attention to what the films and the television series have in common, namely, seriality. In particular, I want to reiterate that the frequency with which the serial killer appears on television, and the popularity of television drama series, are just two examples among many others of the profound importance of seriality in television.

Seriality in/and Television

The ability of the Hollywood movie studios to sell the idea of the series to the medium of television is not primarily due to Hollywood's persuasive powers but rather reflects the place of seriality as one of the defining features of television. In the context of arguing for the importance of the concept of the "schedule" for television studies, Nick Browne also describes the importance of seriality:

> One of the central axes around which the form of the television schedule turns, from beginning to present, is the balance between freestanding, individual programs and the various forms of sequencing that we might call television *seriality*. Seriality in its various versions orders and regulates television programming—from daily news and talk shows through the typical weekly sequencing of primetime entertainment programs. Indeed, serial form is the paradigmatic form of television programming. (72–73, original emphasis)

Seriality has acquired this paradigmatic status in television for various reasons. At the time when serial structures were first becoming important to the medium of television, for example, seriality had certain institutional and industrial advantages. As Browne explains, in the 1950s the television industry desired both standardization and increased production capacity. The serial television drama allowed for both of these factors, as well as having more specific advantages over competing forms such as live television, including "flexibility of scheduling across time zones, and the existence of texts which could generate an after-market through syndication" (Browne 73). Seriality also encouraged certain viewing habits in those who watched television. According to Raymond Williams, in an article entitled "Most Doctors Recommend," "a series is more than a convenience, filling what are now characteristically called slots. It is a sort of late version of character training: encouraging regular habits in the viewers; directing them into the right channels at certain decisive moments in their evening lives" (81). Williams's analysis of how a series trains television viewers is paradigmatic of his more general argument concerning how those viewers are "subjected" to the experience of watching television, an experience Williams summarizes through the immensely influential concept of "flow."

Williams argues that any given night of television programming is still organized as a sequence of discrete units or shows. In practice, however, "there has been a significant shift from the concept of sequence as *programming* to the concept of sequence as *flow*" (*Television* 89, original emphasis). Consequently, Williams goes on to argue, it is no longer adequate to analyze a single program; one must also understand that program's placement within an evening's television viewing that should be regarded as a single unit: "It is evident that what is now called 'an evening's viewing' is in some ways planned, by providers and then by viewers, *as a whole*; that it is in any event planned in discernible sequences which in this sense override particular programme units. Whenever there is competition between television channels, this becomes a matter of conscious concern: to get viewers in at the beginning of a flow" (*Television* 93, original emphasis). Seriality thus becomes not only a feature of individual programs but also a defining characteristic of the experience of watching television.

Williams's ideas have been subjected to much criticism since their appearance (see Corner, chap. 6, for an example), particularly for the way they imply a rather passive television viewer. Although it may be true to say that a series directs the viewer's attention in ways that are then maintained by a flow of programming, this does not necessarily mean that the viewer is passively manipulated by this flow. A series could not direct viewers successfully if it did not provide them with certain benefits that are a result of the viewer's active engagement with the television show. Williams mentions the comfort derived from seeing familiar characters and feeling connected to their lives. This type of comfort suggests, of course, the most classic example of seriality on television, the soap opera, and Sonia Livingstone has suggested some other reasons for the popularity of the serial soap opera, such as its role in the viewer's life, entertainment, realism, emotional experience, relationship with the characters, problem solving, and escapism (56–57). This list suggests a possibility that I will explore in more detail later: that there is an analogy between the soap opera and the television crime drama; in other words, that the crime drama series can be regarded as a nighttime soap opera.

Livingstone's final category, "escapism," also reminds us that many of the reasons critics have adduced for the popularity of serial forms in television have also been used to denigrate those forms. Even critics generally sympathetic to popular culture are frequently harsh when it comes to serial forms of popular culture, as the following quote from Umberto Eco suggests: "With a series one believes one is enjoying the novelty of the story (which is always the same) while in fact one is enjoying it because of the recurrence of a narrative scheme that remains constant. The series in this sense responds to the infantile need of always hearing the same story, of being consoled by the 'return of the Identical,' superficially disguised" (86).

Although Eco's evocation of the infantile consumer of serial narratives may seem patronizing and unduly cynical, a measure of cynicism might be necessary in understanding the pecuniary appeal of seriality to advertisers and program makers. Browne has commented that "television's serial forms serve to continue the subject along the itinerary of habituated consumption" (74), and Robert Allen gives us a more detailed sense of how the television series achieves this highly desirable outcome for the sponsors of television programs:

> In order for the prospective consumer to remember a product at the purchase point, the name and superior qualities of a product must be continuously reinforced. And in order for this to occur, the viewer must be available to the advertiser on a regular and predictable basis. Thus, beginning with network radio and culminating in network television, the regularizing of viewer attention has been an axiom of programming policy. The viewer must be encouraged not just to tune in for a single program but to submit to the "flow" of programming throughout an entire evening. (47)

Obviously, some types of programming are able to meet these requirements better than others. A serial drama that involves its viewers in the lives of its lead characters stands a good chance of bringing those viewers back week after week. A succession of such dramas scheduled for the same evening stands a good chance of keeping the audience in front of the television for the entire evening, thus maximizing the advertisers' chance of reinforcing the name and qualities of their product.

Critics of television have found numerous ways of analyzing the impact of serial structures in the medium. As Charlotte Brunsdon (620–22) has usefully remarked, the field of television studies has tended to conceptualize its object of study in "impure" ways, that is, focusing not on a single program as the unit of analysis but rather on the "flow" of programming (Raymond Williams), a "segment" of television (John Ellis), the "super-text" of television (Nick Browne), or a "viewing strip" of televisual images, as determined by the viewer's use of the remote control (H. Newcomb and P. Hirsch). Brunsdon goes on to argue that this impure focus in television studies come from the fact that "this possible 'drifting' though an evening's viewing . . . has come to seem, to many commentators, one of the unique features of television watching, and hence something that must be attended to in any account of the television text" (620).

The "drifting" quality of television viewing that Brunsdon mentions, a "drifting" that asserts/creates continuities between apparently discrete elements of television product, has led many television critics to minimize the importance of breaks between different types of programs. Raymond Williams, for example, argues that the concept of an "interruption" between discrete programming units, while it "still has some residual force from an older model, has become inadequate" (*Television* 90). To the extent that such break elements exist at all, Larry Gross claims, they are negligible next to the elements that constitute television programming as flow: "we should not take too seriously the presumed differences between the various categories of media messages—particularly in the case of television. News, drama, quiz shows, sports, and commercials share underlying similarities of theme, emphasis, and value" ("Out" 131). In a similar vein, Sarah Kozloff has argued that television texts have long adapted themselves to the need to accommodate interruptions, either by "tailor[ing] their discourse to fit 'naturally' around the commercial breaks, so that, for instance, the exposition fits before the first break and the coda after the last," or by building "their stories to a high point of interest before each break to ensure that the audience will stay tuned" (90). Some programs, according to Kozloff, even have commercial breaks coincide with temporal breaks in their narratives, so that commercials are used as opportunities to advance the story by hours or even days (90).[3]

While such comments about how flow tends to dominate gaps in television texts are accurate as far as they go, they tend to miss the fact that flow never occurs in a pure form in television. Consequently, it remains important to emphasize the significance of the gaps in television programming. As Stephen Heath and Gillian Skirrow have argued, the daily or weekly reappearance of certain programs introduces a pattern of regularity into television viewing that is both a form of continuity and an interruption at the same time: "the 'central fact of television experience' is much less flow than *flow and regularity*; the anachronistic succession is also a constant repetition" (15, original emphasis). On a similar note, John Fiske does not so much disagree with the concept of flow as argue that it is a somewhat misleading term: "Flow, with its connotations of a languid river, is perhaps an unfortunate metaphor: the movement of the television text is discontinuous, interrupted, and segmented. Its attempts at closure, at a unitary meaning, or a unified viewing subject, are constantly subjected to fracturing forces" (105).

Some examples of the discontinuity that Fiske speaks of would be the commercial breaks within an episode of the series, or the break between episodes, or the break between seasons of the series, or even breaks or disjunctions within the series itself. For example, the continual postponement of the solution to a continuing story arc is a common feature of all of these drama series—whether it be Laura Palmer's murder in *Twin Peaks*, the mystery of what happened to Mulder's sister in *The X-Files*, the homicidal photographer stalking Frank Black's family in *Millennium*, or the identity of the serial killer "Jack of All Trades" in *Profiler*.[4]

The various kinds of postponement enacted in these series can be best summed up by referring to Roland Barthes's concept of the "hermeneutic code." According to Barthes, the hermeneutic code sets up "*delays . . . in the flow of the discourse*" in order to draw out the distance between question and answer through the use of what Barthes describes as "dilatory morphemes," such as the "snare" (a kind of deliberate evasion of truth), the "equivocation" (a mixture of truth and snare that frequently, while focusing on the enigma, helps to thicken it), the "partial answer" (which only exacerbates the expectation of the truth), the "suspended answer" (an aphasic stoppage of the disclosure), and "jamming" (acknowledgment of insolubility) (see Barthes 118–19).[5]

One can find examples of all these techniques in *Twin Peaks*, *The X-Files*, *Millennium*, and *Profiler*. In *Twin Peaks*, Agent Cooper gives a partial answer to the mystery when he announces that he knows who killed Laura Palmer and then does not give the name. Similarly, the opening of the third season of *Profiler* sets a snare for the viewer when it seems to resolve the "Jack of All Trades" story arc when Jack is arrested, but it later turns out that the real Jack is still at large. Despite the presence of such "dilatory morphemes," these uses of the hermeneutic code do not compromise the centrality of the serial structure itself; rather, their aim is to maximize the drama's use of that serial structure, to emphasize the seriality of the drama as much as possible. In this sense, whether we choose to emphasize the smoothness of flow in television programming, or the discontinuities created by the breaks, in both instances seriality remains an equally foundational part of the television medium.

As my increasing concentration on television drama in the last few pages suggests, one of the major consequences of the dominance of seriality in television is that the genres that lend themselves best to serialization tend to assume an equally dominant status in the medium. The television drama has proved itself particularly well suited to seriality, and that is part of the reason I am concentrating in this chapter on the drama series rather than on one of the many other television genres that feature serial murder prominently. Moreover, although it would be interesting to study the representation of serial murder in such supposedly objective televisual genres as news broadcasts and news magazines such as *Dateline* and *60 Minutes*, the license allowed by the fictional status of drama series makes for a particularly loaded look at what is at stake in representing serial killers on television.

To make an obvious point, however, the television dramas I am focusing on in this chapter all have one element in common, an element that they share with many other television drama series: crime. *Twin Peaks*, *The X-Files*, *Millennium*, and *Profiler* constitute a very small percentage of the dozens of crime-related television dramas that have flooded television since the mid-1980s. And those dramas in turn constitute a small part of the mountain of crime-related programming of every kind that has become a, if not the, dominant feature of contemporary American television. Analyzing the tabloidization of television can help us understand both the preoccupation with crime on American television and why crime is particularly well suited to being represented televisually in serial form.

The Tabloidization of Television

Although much has been written about the rise of tabloid television over the past few years, the definitive book on the subject is undoubtedly Kevin Glynn's *Tabloid Culture*. Glynn is aware of the difficulty of defining a phenomenon as complex as tabloid television, but he does offer a tentative list of some of its defining qualities that is worth quoting at length:

> It prefers heightened emotionality and often emphasizes the melodramatic. It sometimes makes heavy use of campy irony, parody, and broad humor. It relies on an often volatile mix of realistic and antirealist representational conventions. It resists "objectivity," detachment, and critical distance. It is highly multidiscursive. It

incorporates voices frequently excluded from "serious" news and often centers on those that are typically marginalized in mainstream media discourse. The "bizarre" and the "deviant" are central to its image repertoire . . . It frequently violates dominant institutional standards and procedures for the production and validation of "truth." It thrives on the grotesque, the scandalous, and the "abnormal" . . . It dwells on social and moral disorder. Among its favorite themes are the ubiquity of victimization and the loss of control over the outcomes of events, and of one's fate. Also typical are stories involving gender disturbances and ambiguities, troubled domestic and familial relationships, and paranormal phenomena that apparently outstrip the explanatory power of scientific rationalism. (7)

Although the dramas I am discussing in this chapter do not draw on as many elements of the list as shows like *The Jerry Springer Show* or *Hard Copy*, there is still a significant degree of overlap. As I will demonstrate in the second half of this chapter, *Twin Peaks*, *The X-Files*, *Millennium*, and *Profiler* all contain examples of a number of the features that Glynn lists, including the use of irony and parody; a mixture of realism and fantasy; the representation of marginalized perspectives; a concentration on the bizarre and the deviant, disorder, and the grotesque; a focus on the paranormal; and the questioning of dominant concepts of truth. Part of the reason these dramas use so many tabloid elements is their preoccupation with crime, and Glynn's list also helps us understand why the tabloidization of television has been accompanied by a greater number and variety of crime-related shows. Crime tends to activate every defining characteristic of tabloid television—especially its preoccupation with the abnormal and the ubiquity of victimization. Small wonder, then, that crime-related shows have become a dominant feature of contemporary television.

Although the number of television crime shows has undoubtedly increased sharply in recent years, television's preoccupation with crime goes back a long way, certainly to before the tabloidization of the medium began. Ray Surette reminds us that crime-related programming was not a prominent feature of network radio but that television developed very differently. From the 1950s on, crime has played a very important role in television programming, to the extent that "about one-fourth of all prime time shows from the 1960s into the 1990s have directly focused on crime or law enforcement" (*Media* 35). The rise of tabloid culture has definitely contributed to this increased focus, but television crime dramas do not necessarily participate in the immediate rough and tumble around real crimes that Glynn claims defines the tabloid media: "Actual crimes, their journalistic renditions, their docu-dramatic fictionalizations, the trials of suspects involved, and secondary journalistic accounts and fictionalizations of all these events now often occur with virtual coextensivity and with mutual reference to one another" (46). Crime dramas, rather than having this kind of immediate relationship with actual crimes, instead occupy part of a broader representational space made possible by tabloid culture.

The somewhat marginal position of crime dramas within tabloid culture helps to explain why they can use a lot of tabloid elements without being thought of and consequently dismissed as tabloid shows. According to Glynn, shows like *The X-Files* are in a category of programs that "specialize particularly in stories about phenomena considered 'mysterious' or 'inexplicable' from the perspectives of socially dominant knowledge systems" (165). In other words, *The X-Files* and shows like it explore tabloid subjects from an ideologically "approved" point of view, in the sense that they legitimate an interest in tabloid culture by making such an interest part of a more comprehensive, though still tightly controlled, critique of powerful forces within American society. The other reason shows like *The X-Files* are able to use tabloid elements is that tabloid culture has become increasingly mainstream and therefore increasingly respectable. As Fox and Van Sickel have pointed out, "The distinguishing feature of the present media culture is the alarming regularity with which *mainstream* media sources now focus on these same personalized crime stories. Material formerly regulated to the tabloid press now pervades the mainstream press as well" (54, original emphasis).

The rise of tabloid culture, along with an increasing preoccupation with crime, explains why crime-related drama series should be particularly numerous in today's media culture, but can these same features explain the preoccupation of these dramas with serial murder? One can argue, I think, that tabloid culture has only accentuated aspects of the medium's representation of crime that were already present. To the extent that representations of crime on television, in whatever genre, tend to overemphasize violent crimes (especially murder), excessively individualize the causes and forms of crime, concentrate on psychopaths as representative criminals, portray crime as an oversimplified struggle between the evil criminal and the good crime fighter, isolate crime from other social problems, and suggest that the most appropriate response to crime is overwhelming force, the serial killer as constructed in American popular culture is the logical criminal for television to focus upon (Surette, *Media* 39–41, 47–50).[6]

Indeed, serial murder plays such a prominent role in crime-related television programming of every genre, partly because of the way the medium represents crime, and partly because of the importance of seriality to the medium, that one may be inclined to minimize the differences between television drama and other television genres, preferring instead to emphasize what they have in common. In some respects it is becoming increasingly difficult to tell fictional and nonfictional crime-related television programs apart. Many critics have pointed out that "reality" crime shows frequently use fictional techniques: "'Cops' has the simple, unambiguous narrative structure, pumped-up action, heroic police protagonists, high arrest rate, and illusion of police certainty characteristic of much fictional crime drama" (Aaron Doyle 109). Conversely, television crime dramas increasingly draw on the codes of referential realism: "The context of *X-Files'* episodes is grounded in a TV drama referential realism. Locations, dates and times are typically inventoried in titles and voice-overs, in the tradition of Realist specificities. The episode *Space*, for example, is located at a NASA rocket-launching pad. News footage lends authenticity to the events" (R. Nelson 153).

Bearing these points in mind, it makes perfect sense that *The X-Files* should eventually draw attention to these generic similarities by filming an episode in its seventh season entitled "X-Cops," shot entirely in the style of an episode of *Cops*. Even more suggestively, the makers of *The X-Files* received enthusiastic cooperation from the makers of *Cops* to the extent that the producers of *Cops* invited *X-Files* director Vince Gilligan "along on an actual *Cops* shoot in the wilds of Compton, California, so that he could get a sense of the rhythms of the show. The show supplied some stock footage and readily agreed to license the rights to use their 'Bad Boys' theme song. *Cops* cameramen and sound men were brought in to supervise the taping and, in a final bit of realism, *Cops* cameraman Daniel Emmett and sound man John Michael Vaughn were enlisted to play themselves in front of the camera in the episode's final act. 'X-Cops' director Michael Watkins had long had a good relationship with the Los Angeles law enforcement community and was able to call in quite a few favors, including the use of real sheriff's deputies as extras" (Shapiro 152). Such detailed collaboration speaks volumes about the extent to which these two shows, apparently so very different, both represent crime within the terms set by the interpretive world of tabloid culture. Although *The X-Files'* interest in crime is supposedly more serious and critical than that of the frankly sensationalist *Cops*, both shows trade on tabloid clichés of crime and criminals as bizarre, deviant, and otherworldly.

In spite of these similarities, however, we also need to bear in mind Glynn's caveat that tabloid television is difficult to define because it is so hybrid. Although tabloid television, Glynn argues, is currently "embodied in a set of identifiable textual forms," "tabloidism" can be best understood as "a tendency or a collection of interrelated transgeneric tendencies, sensibilities, and orientations that have long and well-established histories" (3). Although shows such as *The X-Files* and *Twin Peaks* can technically be classified as television dramas, perhaps their success depends upon their unusually thoroughgoing formal, generic, and possibly ideological hybridity, a hybridity that is a defining feature of what Glynn calls "tabloidism." I want to suggest that these drama series combine elements of "open" and "closed" television texts in order both to highlight the differences and similarities between these dramas and other television dramas and to suggest exactly what it is about these series that makes them so popular.

As I indicated earlier, the soap opera is a relevant point of contrast with the crime drama because it is the television genre in which open elements of serial structures are most important and also because crime dramas can perhaps be thought of as types of soap opera (a comparison playfully suggested by the role of the soap "Invitation to Love" within *Twin Peaks*). Robert Allen has argued that the soap opera is defined by its "lack of narrative closure" (14). Because the soap opera has no telos, it can potentially continue forever, never coming to the end of its open-endedness.

At first glance, a drama series like *The X-Files* that runs for many years without a necessary end in sight might seem to share the same open-endedness as the soap opera, but there are also important differences between the two examples, differences that Christine Geraghty has summarized by comparing a series (such as *Millennium*) with a "continuous serial" (such as *All My Children*). According to Geraghty, one of the most important features of the continuous serial is its regular appearance at predetermined times of the week. Unlike the series, it does not periodically disappear "until the autumn" or "until the next series," but rather appears each and every day or week. The regularity of the serial, along with its continually postponed resolution, its potential endlessness (as compared with the predictable, limited number of episodes in a series), gives the two forms different temporalities. Whereas the continuous serial is predominantly future-oriented, the series is concentrated on resolving its story within the confines of a one-hour episode (10–11).

Although, as Geraghty states, the temporality of the series and that of the continuous serial are undoubtedly different, could it be a difference of degree rather than kind? Without dismissing the differences between the two forms, it might also be worth emphasizing their similarities because "by excluding so many distant relatives of the daytime soap . . . [you] are unable to stress the pervasive influence of serial form and multiple plot structure upon *all* of American television" (Feuer 5, original emphasis). Kozloff has argued that the distinction between the series and the continuous serial has never been particularly reliable: "Even in a 'classic' series like *I Love Lucy*, some storylines—such as Lucy's pregnancy—necessarily carried over week to week. And many series have always evinced nonreversible changes over the years: within a given season, each episode of *M*A*S*H* may be freestanding and all episodes may be watched in any order, but the shows dating from the years after Colonel Blake's departure necessarily represent narrative development over those made before he left" (92). Rather than a sharp distinction between serial and series, Kozloff suggests that we think of the difference between them as a continuum, partly because this concept reflects the extent to which television has become increasingly defined by "its blurring of the distinction between series and serials, or, to be more precise, its increased tendency toward serialization" (92).

Kozloff's suggestion of a continuum between serial and series provides a useful way to understand the critical and popular success of *Twin Peaks*, *The X-Files*, *Millennium*, and *Profiler* as a consequence of their formal hybridity. These dramas combine both open and closed formal elements, and *The X-Files* is a good example of this combination of traits. On the one hand, *The X-Files* is a significantly open-ended text. Story elements such as the government/alien conspiracy remain perpetually unsolved because we never receive that final clue, that final piece of information that will enable us to make sense of the whole thing. This leads to a situation where, as Peter Knight has said, "the show remains in epistemological free fall, permanently floating between revealing everything and coming up with nothing" (223). On the other hand, the show also contains some markedly "closed" elements. Most episodes do contain a formal plot/resolution structure that ensures that episode's particular enigma is resolved.[7]

Just as these dramas are formally hybrid, they also tend to be generically hybrid, thus enabling a variety of satisfactions for a variety of viewers, as described by Robin Nelson: "*X-Files* has developed into a hybrid crime thriller/horror series/serial narrative form with a dash of soap romance, offering both the pleasure of closure and the hook of continuity, but avoiding flexi-narrative fragmentation by focusing on a single story in each episode with space for the Scully/Mulder relationship slowly to develop" (152–53). The undeniable formal and generic hybridity of these series, however, is purchased at the price of their singularly unhybrid ideology.

Despite the formal and generic hybridity of *Twin Peaks*, *The X-Files*, *Millennium*, and *Profiler*, these drama series are remarkably uniform in their ideological message, coming down overwhelmingly on the side of law and order by encouraging identification with their FBI protagonists. There is nothing unusual in these dramas' having a law-and-order perspective because, as Richard Sparks has argued, "the vast majority of television crime drama emphasizes 'justice' in its outcomes" (93). In the world of the television crime drama, "justice" almost always means the criminal is dealt with by law enforcement, either by being arrested, tried, and sentenced, or by being killed. Consequently, according to Sparks, "although crime drama programmes do include a high incidence of violent and transgressive action they are viewed in the expectation that order will be restored" (93).

This "order" is embodied by the FBI protagonists, and audience identification with them is facilitated by several techniques. First, these shows portray the FBI agents as the victims rather than the perpetrators of violence and persecution. Second, they use the paranormal to restage questions of corruption and the misuse of power at a safe distance from the "real world" misdeeds of the FBI. Third, these series use "supernaturalized" serial killers to reinforce the idea that the Bureau protagonists are victims. And fourth, the apparently edgy and subversive nature of these series, which seem critical of the politics of government in general and the FBI in particular, also works to encourage audience identification with the beleaguered protagonists of these shows. In fact, as I shall demonstrate, these series partake in an entirely decaffeinated form of subversion. At their heart lies a conservative political vision that has made them extremely effective defenders of faith in the FBI. In short, these series provide a textbook example of how popular cultural images of serial killers can be used for politically conservative ends that are remarkably consistent with the aims of the FBI as described in chapter 2. In both cases, defining the FBI as a heroic but threatened source of expertise on serial murder is the key.

"I Want to Believe...in the FBI"

Today, it may seem redundant to discuss how popular culture contributes to an atmosphere of public respect for law enforcement organizations like the Federal Bureau of Investigation. After all, the belief that the FBI is a thoroughly corrupt and inefficient organization is probably more widespread today than at any time since J. Edgar Hoover's death, and yet the Bureau continues to become more and more powerful, thanks to pieces of legislation like the Patriot Act of 2001. And yet we should hesitate before assuming that popular culture has nothing to do with the disconnect that has grown up between criticism of the FBI and the fortunes of the FBI.[8]

The biggest reason for the development of this disconnect is the events of September 11, 2001, a context I will explore fully in the epilogue. In this chapter, I want to focus on the contribution of recent television crime drama in constructing a positive popular cultural image of the FBI. Despite the prestige and power that the FBI has been enjoying in the wake of 9/11, the reputation of the Bureau was in crisis until quite recently. In the mid- to late 1990s, when the actual FBI was reeling from one public relations disaster to another, shows like *Twin Peaks*, *The X-Files*, *Millennium*, and *Profiler* were preserving the reputation of the Bureau by peopling it with a large number of hip, principled, unconventional, and sexy special agents. In this way, these shows enabled the FBI to weather the storm of negative publicity until the events of 9/11 made any public relations assistance from popular culture for the Bureau irrelevant.

The first step taken by these drama series in (re)constructing a positive image of the FBI is to create a protagonist who is an employee of the Bureau, who personifies some of the characteristics traditionally associated with the FBI, but who is still a sympathetic figure.[9] Although choosing a starting point for these developments is always something of a random process, there is no doubt that David Lynch's groundbreaking television series *Twin Peaks* was a turning point in the popular cultural representation of the Bureau. In particular, the character of FBI Special Agent Dale Cooper, played by Kyle MacLachlan, set the mold for the FBI protagonists who would follow in other series. Cooper combines traits that had never been seen before in an FBI character. In some respects, he is a typical by-the-book agent. In other respects, he is wildly unconventional. He is a traditional male hero, being masculine, decisive, and brave, but he also has more unusual traits, such as vulnerability, introspection, and hesitation. Crucially, rather than being the perpetrator of violence and persecution, which was probably the most widespread image of the FBI agent in the post-Hoover era, Cooper is himself the focus of violent persecution.

This composite image of the character of Cooper evolved slowly during the two seasons *Twin Peaks* was on the air. Cooper starts out as a much more traditional character. In the pilot episode, he has "a slightly sadistic method of questioning, aiming to destabilise people," and an obsessiveness about his work that borders on madness (Chion 110). The fact that Lynch worked in an open-ended, improvisatory manner with his actors allowed Kyle MacLachlan's character to develop in a very different direction. The early obsessiveness drops away and is replaced by a character who becomes "increasingly simple and archetypal, even angelic" (Chion 110).

This gradual change in Cooper's character is also reflected by a change in the methods he uses to solve crime. When he first arrives in the sleepy Pacific Northwest lumber town of Twin Peaks, Cooper is presented as a rather urbane figure from the big city, and his attention to correct Bureau procedures and protocol, along with his determination to unlock the secrets hidden by the town's residents, emphasizes his similarity to characters from classic mystery and detective fiction. We first see evidence of the change in Cooper when his investigative methods become more unconventional, depending just as much on arcane Tibetan rituals and dream divination as on conventional, Bureau-approved techniques.

The change in Cooper's methods is just one way in which he becomes gradually disenchanted with the FBI, although he remains associated with law enforcement. As Cooper becomes more and more closely integrated into the world of Twin Peaks, a community he has felt a strong connection with from his arrival there, he moves further and further away from the FBI, a process that culminates in his initiation into the Bookhouse Boys, an extralegal vigilante organization based in Twin Peaks. Ultimately, Cooper's involvement with the Bookhouse Boys leads to his suspension from the FBI, thus establishing a trope that will be taken up by the other series: the truly honorable person is one who leaves (or seriously considers leaving) the Bureau.

The development of Cooper's character and his related growing alienation from the FBI are thrown into sharper relief by the other FBI characters in *Twin Peaks*, who represent more traditional (although still highly distinctive) stereotypes associated with the Bureau. Cooper's colleague, Albert Rosenfield, for example, represents much more closely the popular cultural stereotype of the FBI agent as the aggressive, superior, and obnoxious outsider with absolutely no sensitivity toward the feelings of the local townspeople. When his appalling rudeness earns Rosenfield a well-deserved punch from Sheriff Truman, it is Cooper who blocks Rosenfield's attempts to have the sheriff punished by emphasizing the essential decency of Twin Peaks, a decency that Rosenfield has failed to respect. In this way, Lynch both accentuates the extent to which Cooper has changed since arriving in Twin Peaks and gives the audience, in the character of Rosenfield, a more negative FBI stereotype to define the increasingly benign Cooper against.

The distance between the transformed Cooper and other members of the FBI receives its clearest and most extended treatment when Cooper's former FBI mentor, Windom Earle, joins the series. In part, the character of Earle was introduced into *Twin Peaks* in order to send the series in a new direction once the mystery of who killed Laura Palmer, the mystery that had propelled the series up to that point, had been solved. But Earle's obsessive pursuit of Cooper, which is partly due to Cooper's having had an affair with Caroline, Earle's ex-wife (whom Earle subsequently murdered), also takes audience sympathy with Cooper to another level by making Cooper the persecuted figure. As Catherine Nickerson has pointed out, in the first season of *Twin Peaks*, Cooper was a relatively straightforward character who investigated others rather than being the focus of investigation. The second season, however, "offers a fundamental readjustment of that depiction of Cooper . . . having more or less solved the murder of Laura Palmer, the show must find a new object of investigation. At least one of those objects . . . will be Cooper himself" (272–73). The exploration of Cooper's past is another factor that turns him into a likable and sympathetic character. As we learn details about Cooper's background, his difficult emotional life, and the origin of his feud with Windom Earle, the audience feels more inclined to identify with and root for Cooper as he struggles to protect the new life he has made for himself in the town of Twin Peaks.

As we will see in more detail later, the introduction of Windom Earle into the series also reflects the sharp supernaturalization of *Twin Peaks* that took place in its second season, a process also represented by the revelation that a supernatural being named BOB was responsible for the death of Laura Palmer. What I want to emphasize at the moment is how *Twin Peaks* constructs its FBI protagonist as a thoroughly sympathetic figure. I insist upon describing Cooper as an FBI protagonist because, even though he has been suspended from the Bureau, he is still a law enforcement figure (he becomes a sheriff's deputy in Twin Peaks) and clearly wants to rejoin the Bureau if he can. Moreover, the fact that Cooper is being persecuted by a former member of the FBI implies strongly that Cooper personifies the honorable version of the Bureau that the audience hopes will win out in the end. For these reasons, although the distance between Cooper and the FBI widens over the course of the series, I do not believe Cooper's alienation from his former employer reaches the point that *Twin Peaks* critiques the Bureau in any substantive fashion.[10] By stopping short of having Cooper break from the Bureau irrevocably, *Twin Peaks* upholds the FBI's image as a bastion of core American values: it is still an institution associated with the creative and successful investigation of crime.

The X-Files also offers a critique of the Bureau that is wide-ranging in some ways but that ultimately works to maintain the audience's respect for the organization. Even though the series has been widely praised by critics for its progressive and protracted attention to the corruption of the FBI in particular, and of the United States federal government in general, I do not believe that the series as a whole offers a sustained critique of the Bureau's practices and dominant ideologies, precisely because the viewer's attention remains so firmly focused on the series' heroic and victimized FBI protagonists, Fox Mulder and Dana Scully.[11]

It is undoubtedly true that during the course of the government/alien conspiracy story arc that unfolds in bewildering detail over the first seven seasons of *The X-Files*, the audience receives many negative impressions of the ways in which federal law enforcement organizations and the United States government operate. In their unflagging search for the truth, Mulder and Scully not only are lied to, misdirected, and impeded in their effort to collect facts but also frequently come under physical attack. Right from the beginning of the show, Mulder is portrayed as a marginal, if brilliant, figure within the Bureau ("the FBI's Most Unwanted," as Mulder refers to himself in the pilot episode), and Scully's developing loyalty to Mulder and to the "X-Files" they investigate gradually assigns her to the same marginal fate.

Despite this marginality, however, Mulder and Scully are still part of the Bureau. When one considers the extremity of their travails, it is truly extraordinary how infrequently either of them considers even for a moment the possibility of leaving the FBI. Their dedication to the truth comes to seem more and more identified with an idealist vision of the FBI in particular and government in general. Mulder and Scully, in other words, come to personify what law enforcement could be, if given the chance. When they are persecuted, therefore, the audience feels for them as individuals and also as embodiments of classically American values—truth, perseverance, honesty, honor, and bravery. Hal Schuster has described the characters of Mulder and Scully as "honest, hardworking, straightforward, dedicated, clean individuals" (23). This list of adjectives emphasizes the extent to which Mulder and Scully reflect well on the FBI, precisely because of their persecution by the Bureau.

To the extent that the success of *The X-Files* depends upon its offering a hidden, insider knowledge of the machinations of government, its protagonists *have* to be FBI agents, as Douglas Kellner implies: "The show deals with the pleasures of seeing and knowing as the Federal Bureau of Investigation agents, Scully and Mulder, discover and perceive novelties, bizarre and paranormal phenomena, and the secret and villainous machinations of government" (210). From this point of view, one might argue that not too much should be made of Mulder and Scully's FBI affiliation, both because it is simply an unavoidable part of the show's raison d'être and because these characters are after all thoroughly alienated from the Bureau.

The tendency to downplay the degree of Scully and Mulder's continued identification with the Bureau is representative of a broader critical reluctance to criticize the show's protagonists. Instead, many critics have tended to act as apologists for Mulder and Scully by emphasizing their victimization by a corrupt FBI rather than their status as representatives of law and order. There is no doubt that *The X-Files'* protagonists are alienated from the FBI, but this fact is less significant than their continued identity as federal law enforcement agents. Michele Malach has argued that *The X-Files* has played a major role in the rehabilitation of the image of the FBI agent, but argues that "the image of the institution remains ambiguous at best" (72). I believe, however, that one cannot separate the characters of Mulder and Scully from the organization they represent. Like Cooper, Mulder and Scully are meant to personify the best aspects of the FBI, its core values that will it is hoped become dominant once again thanks to the series' valiant and victimized heroes.

The same essentially affirmative message about the Bureau can even be found in shows such as *Profiler* and *Millennium*, which begin with their protagonists outside of the FBI. In both cases, the series' protagonists have left the Bureau not because of any disagreement with the methods or ideologies of their former employer but because they and their loved ones are threatened, thus establishing the theme of the victimized FBI agent as one of the founding premises of these shows. *Profiler*'s Samantha (aka Sam) Waters left the FBI because a serial killer named "Jack of All Trades," who has formed an obsessive attachment to her, murdered her husband. Having gone into hiding with the remainder of her family, Sam is persuaded to come back and resume her work with the Bureau in order to fight Jack and other killers like him.

Waters's reintroduction into the FBI is accomplished in the very first episode of the series; *Millennium*'s Frank Black takes a little longer to come round. A revered psychological profiler, Frank has just succeeded in capturing another serial killer when he starts receiving photographs of his family taken by a homicidal maniac, nicknamed "The Polaroid Man," with a grudge against Frank who is stalking him and his loved ones. Just like Sam Waters, Frank goes into hiding and is persuaded to return to the FBI only once he has fought and killed the mysterious photographer. Rather than representing the end of Frank's victimization, however, the photographer's death initiates another stage of that victimization. Frank's wife witnesses his killing of the photographer, and horrified by the violence she saw in Frank, she insists upon a separation. Just when it looks as if that separation might be over, Frank's wife is killed in a mysterious plague, his hair turns white overnight, and he subsequently returns almost thankfully to the Bureau as if it were a sanctuary for him and his young daughter.

These series are willing to go to melodramatic lengths in order to establish their protagonists as victim-heroes deserving of the audience's sympathy. The other major technique these shows use to garner that sympathy is to emphasize the extremity of the forces these protagonists are battling. This is where the supernatural elements of these dramas become important, and in particular the use they make of supernaturalized serial killers. By exaggerating the evil of the antagonists they face, these shows emphasize both the bravery and the practically angelic innocence of their Bureau protagonists.

Serial Killers and Their Supernatural Others

All of the crime dramas I am discussing rely on supernatural elements. In the case of *Twin Peaks*, the development of Agent Cooper's character is analogically related to the increasing use of supernatural elements in the series, so that Cooper and *Twin Peaks* become supernaturalized together. As Scott

Pollard has pointed out, conventional methods of investigation are of very little use to Cooper in the town of Twin Peaks, and this is why he turns to more unusual, explicitly paranormal, techniques. As a result, says Pollard, "Cooper is blessed by a divine touch that elevates him to quasi-supernatural status, and he becomes an unbeatable combination of visionary and sleuth" (300). The other reason that Cooper's unorthodox techniques are successful, of course, is that Laura Palmer's killer turns out to be a supernatural force named BOB, who possessed Laura's father, Leland Palmer, and forced him to kill his own daughter. Although some critics have developed nonsupernatural explanations for BOB's existence (such as the theory that he is a figment of Leland's imagination), these explanations are not persuasive because they ignore how Lynch uses BOB as a way to move between and then resolve the two major story arcs in *Twin Peaks*: the mystery of who killed Laura Palmer and the threat of Windom Earle.

Earle's introduction into the series not only introduces a much more explicit supernatural vein into *Twin Peaks* (Earle is looking for a mysterious and very powerful ancient source of evil named "The Black Lodge," which is hidden somewhere in the woods that surround the town of Twin Peaks) but is also the first sustained example of how these series make use of supernaturalized serial killers. BOB himself, technically speaking, is a serial killer. He has existed for many hundreds of years and during that time has been indirectly or directly responsible for many deaths. Windom Earle, however, is a serial killer in a much more recognizable and more threatening sense, as Nickerson explains: "Windom Earle is so disruptive because he—even more than BOB—is a radically *serial* killer. His murders don't remain in a retrievable or recuperative past because they are only understandable as part of a chain of events that stretch into the future as well as into the past" (274, original emphasis). This orientation toward the future eventually leads, in the final episode of the series, to a confrontation in "The Black Lodge" between Cooper, Earle, and BOB, which ends with Earle being destroyed by BOB, having radically underestimated the power of the evil he thought he could harness and use for his own ends. This is a suitably mystical and supernatural end to the series, but even before this (melo)dramatic conclusion, Earle had established himself as a thoroughly supernatural phenomenon through his inhuman level of intelligence and his preternatural ability to avoid capture. Like his close generic relative Hannibal Lecter, Earle is a technically human serial killer who seems to have an abundance of supernatural powers. These powers make Cooper's quixotic struggle against Earle all the more admirable to the viewer of *Twin Peaks*. The fact that the closing scene of the series implies that Cooper himself is now possessed by BOB lends Cooper's struggle against the forces of darkness a tragic dimension that further accentuates Cooper's status as a noble victim.

Although I feel that the series' supernatural conclusion was perfectly consistent with its portrayal of serial killers as paranormal and Dale Cooper as a victimized hero throughout its short existence, other critics were unhappy with the way Lynch relied upon the mystical. Mark Altman, for example, has argued: "The magic and the mumbo jumbo which helped make *Twin Peaks* proved to be the source of its undoing . . . the finale fell strongly on the side of the supernatural dispelling any doubts that perhaps all of the crazy Tibetan fantasies of Cooper were just part of an extremely overactive imagination . . . when the mystical is mistaken for an adequate way to answer a legitimate detective saga, it's a misstep" (131, original emphasis). Perhaps it was in response to such criticisms that producer Mark Frost defended the show in terms of its realism, claiming, "What we're trying to talk about in *Twin Peaks* is that violence is real and has real consequences and is awful and is pervasive and true about our lives and it is something we don't look at very often" (quoted in Altman 18). Frost's comment represents the start of a trend in which the people involved with these series have all, for some reason, tended to deny their very obvious use of supernatural elements.

Even if one were inclined to deny the presence of supernatural elements in *The X-Files*, it would be impossible to do so. As befits a show influenced by *Kolchak: The Night Stalker* (Schuster 4), *The X-Files* has explored a bewildering variety of bizarre phenomena. As Jan Delasara explains:

> The *X-Files* world is indeed surrounded by mystery. There are stories devoted to various paranormal powers: prophetic dreaming, shape-shifting, precognition, control of lightning and of fire, invisibility, distance seeing, mind reading, and psychokinetic abilities, as well as various kinds of demonic forces and possession . . . There are stories featuring monsters from the tradition of supernatural horror and plots which involve paranormal abilities that suggest an extension beyond the ordinary limits of mind and body . . . And there are mutant or beast humans ("bigfoot" women and fluke men), scientifically altered humans, humans with paranormal powers, ghosts of humans, evil children, demonic bosses, cancer eaters, fat-sucking parasites, terrorists, serial killers and escalating death fetishists. (61)

In the midst of such bizarre company, the anchoring role played by the series' protagonists is probably more important for *The X-Files* than for any of the series under discussion. No matter how strange or arduous the journey, the audience always has Mulder and Scully to sympathize with and root for. It makes perfect sense that the show's producers, bearing this in mind, would want to play up the dangers faced by their heroic FBI agents as much as possible, while always staying within what Chris Carter once described as the "realm of extreme possibility" (Lowry, *Truth* 33). By accentuating the severity of the threats they face, the show throws Mulder and Scully's bravery and heroism into sharp relief.

Given the range of phenomena that Chris Carter and the other people responsible for the making of *The X-Files* can accommodate within the range of "extreme possibility," we would not expect the show's makers or critics to deny its use of the supernatural, and yet that is exactly what they do. Revealingly, however, rather than denying that the show uses supernatural elements at all (which would be absurd), they rest their claim for the show's realism on its representation of serial killers, who are interpreted by both the makers and critics of *The X-Files* as a quintessentially human rather than paranormal phenomenon. This is a point of view with which I agree wholeheartedly, and yet it is absolutely not the way in which *The X-Files* generally portrays serial killers. Instead of stressing their humanity, *The X-Files* presents serial killers as supernatural, monstrous, and even demonic, both to emphasize the challenges faced by their heroic FBI agents and because, like so much American popular culture, *The X-Files* cannot handle the possibility that serial killers might actually be ordinarily human.

These issues come into focus when critics discuss what aspects of *The X-Files* are most responsible for its success. Jane Goldman has argued that the episodes that fans find most unsettling are "those which see the Agents pitting their wits not against aliens, mutants or spirits, but against the sheer force of evil which can exist in human beings" (59). After stressing the humanity of the serial killer characters who have appeared on the series, such as B. J. Morrow (in the episode "Aubrey"), Donnie Pfaster ("Irresistible" and "Orison"), and John Mostow and Bill Patterson (both in "Grotesque"), Goldman elaborates on this theme by quoting Chris Carter's thoughts on "Irresistible," the first episode featuring the "death fetishist" Donnie Pfaster:

> I wanted to do an episode that dealt with what really scared Scully . . . And I thought that what really scares Scully is not the paranormal, but something that is actually quite banal and normal, tangible: the idea that the man standing next to you in the supermarket line or at the post office is as frightening as anything. There's a line in *Irresistible* that I think is quite telling: that people would rather believe in aliens than in the idea that these things really exist. That was interesting to me, too. (Quoted in Goldman 59)

Although "Irresistible" certainly begins by emphasizing Donnie Pfaster's very ordinary physical appearance and understated personality, one would never guess from Carter's description of the episode that the emphasis shifts quickly to highlighting Pfaster's demonic attributes rather than his ordinariness and that it does so in a very literal way. In scenes whose impact is highlighted by conventional means of heightening suspense, such as ominous background music and backlighting, both Scully and the director of a funeral home where Pfaster works catch glimpses of Pfaster looking not like a human but like a devil, an image that dispenses very quickly with the idea that the viewer is meant to be struck by Pfaster's ordinariness. Moreover, the fact that both Scully and the funeral director glimpse Pfaster's demonic appearance, and that they do so in different scenes, contradicts the argument of many critics that the image of Pfaster as a demon is a metaphorical representation of Scully's fear of him. There is no doubt that Scully is terrified by Pfaster, but there is also no doubt that we are meant to think of Pfaster as a very literal, rather than metaphorical, embodiment of evil.

In view of the episode's use of demonic imagery, it is absurd to claim, as Goldman does, that "Irresistible was a landmark episode for *The X-Files*, the first to present the Agents with a case utterly devoid of any supernatural, paranormal or science-fiction element" (74). Contrary to what Goldman argues, supernatural elements play an absolutely central role in "Irresistible," just as they do in many other episodes of *The X-Files*. In fact, demonic visual imagery is consistently used to represent serial killers in *The X-Files*, and it plays an even larger role in the next episode featuring Donnie Pfaster, "Orison." Ironically, at the start of the episode, Scully asserts that "there's nothing supernatural about this man . . . Donnie Pfaster is just plain evil" (quoted in Shapiro 84), but the rest of the episode does its best to undermine that assertion. The visual representation of Pfaster as a demon comes in the middle of a conversation between Pfaster and Orison, the preacher who got Pfaster out of jail in order to kill him:

> "My violence is always waiting," says Pfaster. "For an instant. For when his back is turned. You can see it now." The reverend asks, "Are you crying for your sins or for yourself?" Pfaster stops crying. "No, Reverend, I cry for you. Because you cannot kill me." He raises his head. Orison's eyes go wide with fear—for he is now staring into the face of the Devil. (Quoted in Shapiro 89)

Such imagery is consistent with producer John Shiban's claim that one of the key decisions he made in putting this episode together was "to turn [Pfaster] into this totally demonic character, essentially evil as an entity" (quoted in Shapiro 92). Once again, Pfaster is clearly meant to signify demonic evil in a very literal, rather than metaphorical, sense in order to accentuate the threat to Scully when Pfaster attacks her later in the episode.

Significantly, in a series usually characterized by a notable degree of open-endedness, "Orison" contains one of the more emphatic examples of closure when Scully shoots and kills Pfaster, even though she had the option of arresting him. This reflects another important aspect of how *The X-Files* tends to make use of its serial killers; they frequently represent moments where Mulder and Scully are vulnerable to victimization in a particularly profound and personal way, thus combining two of the major features that make these series such effective cheerleaders for the FBI: the use of extreme, supernaturalized villains emphasizes the extent to which FBI agents are victimized, heroic figures. Pfaster gets to Scully like no one else she encounters in the entire series, but Mulder is equally vulnerable to serial killers, as we see in the episode "Grotesque."

"Grotesque" is a particularly interesting episode because it develops several FBI and serial killer themes in great detail. Mulder and Scully become involved in a serial killer case being investigated by Mulder's old mentor from the FBI's Behavioral Science Unit, Bill Patterson. The killer, John Mostow, has an obsession with devilish gargoyles, and when he is arrested he claims that he has been possessed by the devil and, as the saying goes, "The Devil made him do it." Even after Mostow's imprisonment, however, the murders continue, and in order to find the (real? second?) murderer, Mulder must himself descend into the killer's madness, risking his own sanity in the process. Eventually, Mulder realizes that the killer is Bill Patterson, who has been driven mad by staring into the abyss of serial killer insanity for too long. In a manner reminiscent of "Irresistible" and "Orison," the closing shot is of an imprisoned Bill Patterson, screaming insanely that he didn't do it, as his face morphs from human to devil and back again. "Grotesque" not only provides another example of how *The X-Files* uses demonic imagery to distance the serial killer from the category of the human but also manages to generate an enormous amount of sympathy for those heroic FBI profilers—Patterson as well as Mulder—who, in their brave efforts to trap serial killers, find themselves, in Mulder's closing words, "left alone staring into the abyss, into the laughing face of madness."

Although *The X-Files* committed itself to a thoroughly supernaturalized version of serial murder in order to accentuate the bravery and heroism of its FBI protagonists, *Millennium*, Chris Carter's spin-off series, initially seemed to be more promising in this regard. Indeed, comments from Carter while he was developing the series suggest that he saw *Millennium* as being very different from *The X-Files*, with less concentration on aliens and monsters and more on the dark side of human behavior. According to Carter, there were "certain stories I felt I couldn't do in *The X-Files*, which had to do with psychological terror, the real world with real criminals and truly human monsters" (Lowry, *Trust* 69). The differences between *The X-Files* and *Millennium* were certainly what struck most critics about the show when it first aired, with *Science Fiction Weekly*, for example, saying that "while *The X-Files* is steeped in unexplained phenomena, *Millennium* comes from a much more real place. There are terrible people out there who do terrible things to other people" (quoted in Schuster 41). Ironically, this undeniable difference between the two shows was seen by other critics as the main problem with *Millennium*. Jeff Jarvis, for example, argued in *TV Guide* that "in *The X-Files*, Carter gets to grapple with conspiracies on an astronomical scale, and he does it with a hip sense of humor . . . and somehow makes it sexy. But in *Millennium*, all he has to work with is murder. Somebody gets offed in a particularly disgusting manner—buried alive, decapitated (with fingers chopped off, just for good measure) or roasted in a giant microwave oven . . . In the end, all that ties the two shows together are the intriguing performances of the stars. [Lead *Millennium* actor Lance] Henriksen's a keeper. He just needs a few fun aliens to hang around with" (11).

Jarvis was quite right to point to the predominance of murder in *Millennium*. Most of the episodes in the first season focused on serial killers, to the extent that the series was criticized for falling into a banal "serial killer of the week" format. Apart from *Millennium*'s (over)reliance on serial killers, perhaps what viewers such as Jarvis also felt was missing from the show was the sense that the protagonist was being personally threatened by these killers. In the first few shows, at least, *Millennium*'s serial killers certainly challenged the abilities of the police and of Frank Black and undeniably put them in very dangerous situations. Although the killers in *Millennium* were more unusual and extreme than in any other television crime drama, however, the kind of challenge and danger they posed to Frank Black and his colleagues was familiar from many other shows. *Millennium*'s protagonist was certainly in danger, but it was the kind of danger that came with the job, as it were, and did not involve undue amounts of personal victimization.

A change in the quality of danger represented by serial killers, and an increasing emphasis on Frank Black's victimization, were both the result of the introduction of more explicit supernatural elements in later episodes of the show. In one sense, it could be argued that the supernatural was an element of the series from the very start, making its first appearance in the pilot episode with the following description of Frank Black's mysterious ability to visualize details of murders: "I see what the killer sees . . . I put myself in his head. I become the thing we fear the most . . . I become capability. I become the horror—what we know we can become only in our heart of darkness. It's my gift. It's my curse. That's why I retired." One might also argue that victimization was the other element that was established early in the series in the form of the threat to Frank's family from the mysterious "Polaroid Man." What changed as the series progressed, however, was that the themes of the supernatural and of victimization started to work together more closely and became a more prominent part of *Millennium*. Not surprisingly, the catalyst that enabled this change in the series was serial murder, and the beginning of the change can be located very specifically in the episode "Lamentation," in which a serial killer doctor by the name of Ephraim Fabricant, whom Frank had helped capture several years before, is kidnapped from a hospital where he was recovering after having donated a kidney to his sister. It transpires that Fabricant was kidnapped by a pen pal of his, a woman named Lucy Butler, who removes Fabricant's other kidney and places it in the fridge in Frank's house. At the climax of the episode, with Frank and his family apparently under siege by demonic forces, Lucy Butler is seen walking down a flight of stairs in Frank's house, flashes of lightning illuminating her face, which sometimes looks human and sometimes demonic.

The demon Lucy Butler went on to be a recurring character in *Millennium*, especially in the second season, when the turn toward supernatural themes became even more pronounced: the main continuing story arc concerned a pitched battle between devils and angels for the control of Earth. The increasing supernaturalization of *Millennium* was not popular with many of its fans, who blamed Chris Carter for handing over control of the show to producers Glen Morgan and James Wong. But bearing in mind that the episode "Lamentation," which really began the accelerated use of supernatural themes and images in the show, was written by Chris Carter, it seems likely that *Millennium*'s increasingly supernatural orientation had Carter's blessing. Although Carter began *Millennium* determined to concentrate on the human, one might speculate that human serial killers, no matter how unusual they might be, did not emphasize the threat to Frank Black's family and Frank's consequent heroism intensely enough. By making the serial killers more supernaturally monstrous, Carter repeated in *Millennium* a technique he had used with great success in *The X-Files*. Frank's heroism, his bravery in the face of intense victimization, can be shown to much greater effect when he does battle with devils rather than mere humans.

Although it was designed to compete with *The X-Files*, the NBC show *Profiler* bears some uncanny resemblances to *Millennium*, which was being developed by Chris Carter during the same period. Like Frank Black, *Profiler*'s protagonist, Sam Waters, and her family are being stalked by a serial killer. Like *Millennium*, *Profiler* presents profiling more as a magic act or psychic episode than a technique. Sam's insights into crimes come, much as they do for

Frank, in the form of brief flashes of images and sounds, almost on an intuitive level, from which she somehow builds up a sense of who the perpetrator of the crime is. The groundwork for any other supernatural elements in the show, in other words, is prepared by having Sam's "gift" play a prominent role in the series.[12]

As with the other series I have discussed, serial murder also plays a central role in *Profiler*. Indeed, in many respects, the serial killer figure known as "Jack of All Trades" is more important to *Profiler* than serial killers in any of the other series, precisely because he is a serial, recurring character. It is the cat-and-mouse game between Sam and Jack that constitutes the serial thread in *Profiler*, thus providing an equivalent to the "What happened to Mulder's sister?" thread in *The X-Files*, the "Who killed Laura Palmer?" thread in *Twin Peaks*, and the "Who is threatening Frank's family?" thread in *Millennium*. Even though the makers of *Profiler* did their best to give this story arc as much variety as they could, so that it could last as long as possible (including a frankly absurd subplot in which Jack trains a female counterpart named—can you guess?—Jill), ultimately the Jack of All Trades story arc became a burden to the series, threatening to turn *Profiler* into a single-issue show.

The "Jack of All Trades" character illustrates that the shock and thrill associated with the use of serial killers in television crime drama can subside, not only because serial killers become an expected and thus banal feature of such dramas but also because, in sharp contrast to the serial killers in *Twin Peaks*, *The X-Files*, and *Millennium*, Jack was markedly not supernatural. Ironically, although *Profiler*'s creators came to feel that the biggest problem with Jack was his lack of explicitly supernatural abilities, originally they made the decision to present Jack in relatively human terms partly because, like the other series, they were looking for the most effective way to emphasize their protagonist's victimization by a serial killer. The main emphasis of the Jack story arc was on how his stalking came to dominate Sam's life. As executive producer Ian Sander commented in a 1997 NBC.com online chat, "The idea that a lead character is both the hunter and the hunted while not completely unique is very different for a network television show. And it gives us an opportunity to explore her character in a psychological sense and in an action sense, and the writers really enjoy making this organic to the show and it emotionally works for the show" ("Transcript"). In this sense, *Profiler* probably develops the theme of the FBI agent as victim more than any of the other series.

Perhaps recognizing that a nonsupernatural serial killer just did not intensify their protagonist's victimization as much as they wanted, the show's makers had to give Jack some unusual attributes as *Profiler* went on. In order to generate suspense and to keep the story arc going, Jack had to be given preternatural abilities to repeatedly evade complex security arrangements so he could get tantalizingly close to Sam and then escape capture, abilities familiar to viewers from such characters as Windom Earle and Hannibal Lecter. At the same time, however, Jack's preternatural aspects risked making his opponents look foolish as their inability to catch him became more and more pronounced. This fact was not lost on those involved in the series, and when the decision was finally made to capture and imprison Jack, no one was more delighted than Ally Walker, the actress who played Sam Waters: "It's like, here's this crack team and everything, and they can't catch one guy who can get into the building. It's like, 'OK, I'm an idiot'" (O'Hare).

The use of supernatural elements has both advantages and disadvantages for all the shows I have discussed, not just for *Profiler*. On the one hand, using supernatural traits introduces an element of undecidability and variety into a serial format that is so familiar to television viewers that it risks becoming boring. On the other hand, such traits can also contradict the claims of these shows to be anchored in the real or, at least, in the possible. If supernatural serial killers inject an element of unreality into these series, however, the price is apparently worth it because of the way these killers throw the heroism of the FBI protagonists of these series into stark relief. The viewer is not only impressed by how brave and heroic Agent Cooper, Mulder and Scully, Frank Black, and Sam Waters are but also disinclined to associate any of these FBI protagonists with illegality, persecution, or the misuse of power. These series are absolutely unambiguous in their insistence that the FBI are the victims, not the perpetrators, of persecution and violence. Given these advantages, why would the people associated with these shows deny their use of supernatural elements?

To a greater or lesser extent, all of these shows debuted during a time when reality programming was becoming one of the dominant genres in network television. When Chris Carter was trying to pitch *The X-Files* to the Fox network, for example, nervous executives wondered whether anyone would want to watch a drama series rather than shows like *Cops, Unsolved Mysteries*, and *America's Most Wanted*. According to Carter, "No one could understand why someone would want to watch a show if it weren't true" (Lowry, *Truth* 13). The runaway success of *The X-Files*, which went on to become the most valuable show on network television (see Goldblatt), and of the other series I have discussed should have addressed such concerns for good, but I think it possible that a lingering sense that referential television is more worthwhile explains some of the disavowal of the paranormal.

There is, however, a far more compelling reason for caution about the supernatural elements used in *Twin Peaks, The X-Files, Millennium*, and *Profiler*.

In the concluding section of this chapter, I want to argue that these series' use of the supernatural, along with their intimate working relationships with the FBI, is what prevents them from being the effective critiques of law enforcement and governmental ideologies that so many critics have taken them to be.

Cheerleading for the FBI

The drama series I have discussed in this chapter claim to be anchored in the real in order to bolster the sense that they are all, to one degree or another, edgy, subversive shows that provide a genuinely critical perspective on the machinations of federal law enforcement agencies. This is obviously an appealing fantasy for the makers, fans, and critics of these shows, and there has been a remarkable unanimity of critical opinion about the political import of these dramas. When *Twin Peaks* first aired, there was a frenzy of activity among critics who desperately tried to outdo each other in singing hymns of praise to the show's formal radicalism.[13] Ironically, it was David Lynch himself who sounded one of the few contrary notes when he said, "To me, it's a regular tv show" (quoted in Leonard 237).

This comment could be just one more example of that sly postmodern irony Lynch has become so well known for, but I also think it is possible that Lynch might have been telling the truth. There is indeed something very traditional about the serial format of *Twin Peaks*, and even if the show's formal structure is complicated in exciting ways by experimental additions, we should not confuse formal with political radicalism, as Mark Altman reminds us: "As hip and progressive as the series is in form, it's [*sic*] philosophy is conservative, perfectly suited to the evolving America of the '90s in which traditional values have resurfaced. The townsfolk of *Twin Peaks* who have been most fortunate and free of tragedy include the doctor, Will Hayward, whose vocation heralds back to an earlier time and place. He has a beautiful and responsible daughter, Donna, and despite having a wife confined to a wheelchair, is relatively happy and content" (91–92). As strange as it may seem for a show that revolves around a father's murder of his daughter, *Twin Peaks* actually valorizes the traditional family by presenting the Hayward family as an ideal. This emphasis on the family is even more prominent in *Millennium* and *Profiler*, both of which, according to Gina Bellafante, are dedicated to answering the same question: "How do we keep home, hearth and the middle-class dream from eroding in a world ravaged by crime, drugs and sexual confusion?"

Even more extravagant claims have been made for the progressive impact of *The X-Files*, and the majority of these claims have concentrated on the show's political, rather than formal, radicalism. Douglas Kellner has argued that "no previous television series had presented such critical visions of the U.S. government as *The X-Files*" (213). Ruth Rosen makes a similar point, but she also goes on to remind us that such criticism of the government makes *The X-Files* profoundly American: "In the world of 'The X-Files,' the FBI agents who explore paranormal and unexplained homicides are the heroes. But they are constantly thwarted by mysterious cabals of government officials and civilian villains who specialize in the art of the cover-up and, if necessary, the act of assassination. This portrayal of the government makes 'The X-Files' profoundly American. Disbelief and distrust—especially of centralized government—are part of the national psyche" (B7). Rosen is quite right to assert that there is nothing intrinsically progressive about criticisms of big government. Indeed, in some ways, such criticisms have become the special preserve of the extreme right in the United States today.

Of more importance than the question of whether or not shows such as *The X-Files* are critical of federal law enforcement and governmental organizations is why they choose to express such criticisms through story lines concerning aliens, monsters, devils, and serial killers. Kellner sometimes has an unfortunate tendency to take refuge in what he calls the "undecidability" of *The X-Files'* politics, arguing that it is unclear whether the show "ultimately upholds the deepest values and ideologies of the existing society or puts them into question" (223). At other points in his argument, however, he recognizes that "the use of the occult and paranormal may promote irrationalism and deflect critical attention away from the actual events, structures, and personalities of history, substituting populist paranoia and conspiracy for the real crimes carried out by ruling elites and reducing history to the production of conspiratorial cartoon-like figures" (226).

While *Twin Peaks*, *The X-Files*, *Millennium*, and *Profiler* were all enjoying successful runs, the FBI was embroiled in one scandal after another, ranging from Ruby Ridge to Waco, and from problems in its forensic laboratory to accusations that it manufactured evidence against suspects. But despite having a wealth of real-world material to draw on, these series gave no hint that the FBI was involved in serious violations of civil liberties in the mundane, ordinary, here-and-now real world. The characters in these series were too busy battling aliens, devils, or monstrous serial killers to pay attention to such a trivial issue as the Bureau's misuse of its increasingly substantial powers. Through their melodramatic focus, in other words, these series quietly turned their backs on whatever subversive potential they had and in doing so became part of the problem rather than part of the solution.

It is possible that the inability of these drama series to offer a sustained political critique that accurately reflects the corruption of organizations such as the FBI may stem from a limitation of the televisual medium itself. Scheuer has argued that television "has a deep structural bias toward appearances and *concreteness*—immediacy in time and space—and against generality and abstraction" (73, original emphasis). Consequently, according to Scheuer, "television excels at depicting clear, discrete, highly localized events, and especially brief or dramatic ones that catch the eye, rupturing the ordinary flow of occurrences: crime or visible pollution, highway accidents, the effects of a hurricane, the NATO bombing of Belgrade, or a refugee camp. It is less adept at, and hence less disposed to consider, questions that range over broader expanses of time and space . . . root causes and long-term effects, context and environmental factors, abstract ideas or arguments, generalities" (73–74). While Scheuer's comments may apply to a network newscast, a genre infamous for oversimplifying complex issues, the more leisurely pace of a television drama series that might run for years should provide more than enough space to articulate the kind of critique Scheuer speaks of. Rather than reflecting the limits of the medium, the overwhelmingly sympathetic and positive image of the FBI offered by shows such as *The X-Files* is a result of these shows' close cooperation with members of the Bureau, particularly those with responsibility for apprehending serial killers.

According to Chris Carter, when he began working on *The X-Files*, the FBI was initially wary of cooperating with him, but then he started to be approached by FBI agents who were big fans of the show, and as a result the cast of the show was given an exclusive tour of FBI headquarters. Carter was sufficiently impressed by the visit to offer the following pearl of wisdom: "You go there and you realize that these people are protectors of the world" (Schuster 33). Carter and his associates were especially interested in the work done on serial killers by the Behavioral Science Investigative Support Unit, and the unit plays a prominent role in the series. Fox Mulder began his career at the unit, where he worked as an extremely successful profiler before becoming interested in the "X-Files." In addition, the character of Bill Patterson, Mulder's mentor who appears in the episode "Grotesque," was based on John Douglas, a former profiler with the FBI whose career I discuss in chapter 2.[14]

Not surprisingly, *Profiler*, a show even less critical of the FBI than *The X-Files*, has an even closer working relationship with the Bureau. Former special agents Jim Greenleaf and Robert Ressler are technical advisers to the show, and *Profiler*'s lead actors have worked closely with FBI personnel in preparing their roles. According to actor Robert Davi, who plays the character of Bailey Malone, the commitment of the FBI is "astonishing . . . They are the most prestigious law enforcement agency in the world and they are astounding in all areas" (Richardson). While Davi was visiting Bureau headquarters at

Quantico, Virginia, two agents approached him in the cafeteria and said, "'Hey, Robert Davi—you're the reason why we're here'...I thought they meant *Profiler* in the first season, but it wasn't that, it was *Die Hard* [in which he played a gung-ho FBI agent]. That felt good, so I could imagine that men and women might take up a career in law enforcement because of what we're doing on the show. This is one of the most reality based FBI shows. The guys in Washington in the computer unit are crazy about it" (Richardson). No incident can better summarize the self-congratulatory feedback loop that has been established between popular culture and federal law enforcement agencies in the contemporary United States.

The mutually beneficial relationship between popular culture and law enforcement has a long history. As we saw in chapter 2, the FBI has become extremely skilled at cooperating with a variety of popular cultural media in order to present a positive public image of the Bureau to the American public. In some respects, the television crime dramas I have discussed in this chapter are continuous with the pulp magazines and "G-man" films of the 1940s and 1950s in acting as positive publicity for the FBI. Even though *The X-Files* and *Twin Peaks* appear to be more politically progressive than representations of the Bureau from an earlier era, I have demonstrated that these dramas contain a generally positive image of the FBI that perhaps even J. Edgar Hoover would not have been too upset by. Indeed, I would argue that contemporary representations of the FBI are in some ways even more conservative than those produced during the Hoover era.

As we saw in J. Edgar Hoover's persecution of Melvin Purvis, Hoover did not tolerate individualism in the FBI, both because it threatened the cult of personality organized around Hoover himself, and because it misrepresented the institutional nature of the Bureau. The "G-man," in other words, was a depersonalized image of a Bureau employee, someone whose individuality was practically eliminated by his intense identification with the organization that employed him. Consequently, the "G-man" era of FBI representations would never have portrayed the individual FBI agent as a persecuted victim. Although no one would claim that the "G-man" image was an accurate representation of how the FBI worked, it at least had the virtue of not denying the enormous amount of institutional (fire)power the FBI wielded in the fight against crime. Indeed, the "G-man" image made a fetish of such power.

By contrast, television crime dramas such as *Twin Peaks*, *The X-Files*, *Millennium*, and *Profiler* are intent on disavowing the power of the FBI, both by making the power structure of the Bureau shadowy to the point of invisibility and by focusing instead on victimized, vulnerable, highly individualized FBI agents. Not content with failing to honestly confront the egregious misuse of power by the FBI during the modern era, these dramas go as far as to implicitly deny the existence of such power by turning their Bureau protagonists into victims. Serial killers play a crucial role in this pernicious disavowal of reality. Their supernatural otherworldliness ensures that violent confrontation takes place at a comfortable distance from the real world, while their viciousness is a productive source of the embattled, wounded, traumatized bravery of the FBI heroes of these dramas.

CHAPTER FIVE

Next Door Monsters:
The Dialectic of Normality
and Monstrosity in
True-Crime Narratives

The Persistence of True Crime

True crime is the phoenix of popular cultural genres. Ever since the genre assumed its modern form with the publication of Truman Capote's *In Cold Blood* in 1965, its demise has been predicted at regular intervals. Although true crime has been through periods of boom, it has never experienced a bust both because it has always found a way to adapt and identify new markets and because certain types of true crime have been reliable sellers decade after decade. Sometimes the genre has adapted by building synergistic relationships with other media that might otherwise have been damaging sources of competition. Publishers of true crime, for example, responded to the rise of tabloid television by aggressively placing the authors and subjects of their books on talk shows and television news magazines or by undertaking joint ventures with cable television stations, as when Kensington Publishing announced in 1999 that it had teamed up with Court TV to develop a series of true-crime books based on the cable channel's series *Crime Stories* ("Kensington").[1]

A more reliable and influential reason for true crime's longevity, however, has been the existence of perennially popular forms of true-crime books. In 1993, *Publisher's Weekly* conducted an informal survey among eight independent booksellers to find out which backlist true-crime titles were always in demand: "The consensus was that no title on Jack the Ripper ever gathers much dust . . . According to their observations, the hottest backlist titles now, in the true crime genre, deal with serial killers—the more gruesome and grotesque the better. Readers of these sorts of books are addicted to luridness; murders for political reasons don't sell in sizable quantities" (Weyr 39). Paul Dinas, executive editor for the Zebra true-crime book series (and editor of books on Jeffrey Dahmer and Richard Ramirez, among others), confirmed the importance of serial murder to true crime by saying, "Crime committed for money or revenge without sex is much less commercial, so I look for the sex angle, for murder, adjudicated killers, and increasingly for multiple bodies. The manner of death has to be very violent, very visceral" (quoted in Weyr 40). Ironically, Dinas has also commented that if *In Cold Blood* were to come across his desk today, he doubts that he would publish it because "it's not intense enough, bloody enough, or lurid enough to meet the public's demand" (Byrnes 254–55).

If the success of Capote's book was the precondition for the boom in true crime that began in the mid-1960s, serial murder has maintained that boom at a level and for a length of time practically unprecedented in the publishing industry. The status of serial murder in the modern true-crime publishing industry reflects what an enormous role the genre has played in turning serial killers into celebrities. Although aficionados of true crime might have been aware of the names of individual serial killers before the 1970s, since then the protracted boom in true crime is a large part of the reason so many serial killers have become household names.

If industry insiders like Paul Dinas feel that providing true-crime books about vicious and bloody serial killings is giving the public what they want, the question remains: why do they want it? This question leads in turn to a more general question: how can we explain the popularity of true crime as a whole, a genre that has proved to be remarkably resilient in a cultural field dominated by fads and fashions? The publishing industry itself and commentators on that industry are unlikely to be of much help in answering these questions. As the *Publisher's Weekly* article suggests, "addiction to luridness" is considered an adequate explanation for the popularity of true crime about serial murder, and the contrast of this type of true crime with books about "murders for political reasons" implies that the publishing industry sees serial murder as a crime without political dimensions. Instead, as I will demonstrate, serial killers are generally depicted in true crime as individualized monstrous psychopaths, whose crimes tell us little or nothing about the societies in which they live. True-crime narratives disconnect these individuals from the social fabric in order to present them as aberrations and freaks.

In this chapter and in the one that follows, I will argue that the popularity of true crime in general and of true-crime work on serial murder in particular can be explained by a feature of true-crime narratives that goes back to the Puritan era, namely, a preoccupation with the representativeness of the criminal; that is, whether the criminal is more appropriately placed inside or outside the community. I will demonstrate that Puritan America expended much effort to (re)integrate the criminal into the community (if not literally, at least ideologically). Over time, however, this emphasis on integration shifted so that criminals tended to be portrayed more as nonrepresentative outsiders, as sources of pollution and/or monstrosity in the body politic that needed to be excluded from the community.

Rather than the replacement of integration by expulsion in a neat and linear fashion, however, I will show that true crime manifests an unstable and deeply ambivalent oscillation between the two alternatives. It is this oscillation that makes it so difficult to control the meaning of true-crime narratives, then as now. Even during the Puritan period, when the ideological control of crime narratives was at its most explicit, there was always the danger that the criminal could inspire sentiments of pity, sympathy, admiration, or fascination in the audience that were at odds with the messages the Puritans wanted crime narratives to communicate. I will argue that over time, this danger became more pronounced as criminals became the heroes of the narratives they starred in. The mixture of moral/religious condemnation and guilty fascination is a feature shared by both early and contemporary forms of true-crime narrative. The complex forms of identification and disavowal this combination enables help to explain the popularity of true crime in general, and of serial-killer-related true crime in particular, where the tensions between horrified expulsion and ambivalent fascination with the criminal are likely to be particularly intense because of the extremity of the serial killer's actions.

I want to emphasize, however, that contemporary serial killer true-crime narratives not only continue and intensify the problematic of representativeness that characterizes early forms of true-crime narrative but also give that problematic a different form. The dilemma posed by serial killers for true crime is that despite the rhetoric of gothic monstrosity that has been constructed around them, serial killers tend to look very ordinary when they are apprehended. This ordinariness quickly becomes problematic because it makes it difficult to distinguish serial killers from "normal" men, and consequently the categories of normal and abnormal start to blur. True-crime narratives therefore have to accentuate the aberrance of serial killers by searching for the earliest (frequently childhood) signs of the killer's deviance, a search that frequently involves looking back at perfectly ordinary events and recasting them as sinister premonitions of what is to come. In this way, true-crime narratives imply that the apparent ordinariness of serial killers is,

paradoxically, the most convincing sign of their evil, recasting their ordinariness as a "mask of sanity" that hides the awful truth.

Although this chapter will be mostly concerned with how the dialectic between normality and monstrosity is created and maintained in the true-crime
genre, the next chapter will focus on how the serial killer's representativeness
in true-crime narratives is complicated even further by a desire to exonerate
certain groups by distancing them from any possible association with serial
murder. Just as true-crime narratives of Jack the Ripper attempted to distance
the Ripper from an implicitly nonviolent definition of Englishness, contemporary true-crime narratives about serial killers enact a similar gesture, but
with respect to sexuality. I will argue that the apparent ordinariness of a figure such as Ted Bundy, a young Republican and law school student, raises
the dangerous possibility of an association between violence and heterosexuality. In order to deny this association, not only must true-crime narratives
make Bundy as deviant as possible, but his tendency to blur violence and sexuality must be presented as entirely unrepresentative of heterosexuality. In
other words, by presenting Bundy as an aberrational rather than normative
straight man, true-crime narratives seek to relieve straight men of any guilt
by association with Bundy and others of his ilk.

The presumption of the mutual exclusivity of heterosexuality and violence is of course problematic in and of itself, but even more troubling is the
connection in true-crime narratives between this presumption and another,
even more pernicious one: that there is an intrinsic link between violence
and homosexuality. I will demonstrate how this link is asserted in true crime
by looking at the cases of Jeffrey Dahmer and Aileen Wuornos. Whereas the
violent actions of a Ted Bundy are believed to tell us nothing about heterosexuality in general, true-crime narratives imply that the violence of Dahmer and
Wuornos tells "us" (the implicitly straight reader of true crime) everything
we need to know about homosexuality. I will also emphasize how, once again,
it is the issue of representativeness that structures representations of serial
murder, but in a manner quite different from how it structured the true-crime
narratives of Jack the Ripper I discussed in chapter 1. I argued in that chapter that to assert the cultural/social representativeness of the serial killer is a
potentially radical act because it stresses the links between "them" and "us."
True-crime narratives about Dahmer and Wuornos, however, demonstrate
that there is nothing intrinsically progressive about asserting the representativeness of serial killers. Indeed, in this case, representativeness is thoroughly
conservative, enabling a straight "us" to generalize about a queer "them"
and to disavow any connection between those two groups. In this instance,
I will argue, representativeness aids and abets the construction of monstrosity,

rather than resisting it. In their linked analyses of normality and monstrosity and of the ways in which celebrity serial killers are used to reinforce heteronormative ideologies of sexual identity, these two chapters will reconstruct the history of how true-crime narratives have always aimed to define the boundaries of community in exclusionary ways.

In her study of true-crime stories, Anita Biressi has noted the importance of the antecedents of modern true crime, arguing that such antecedents are "evidence that modern true crime . . . consists of codes and conventions whose appearance is explicable, not only in terms of current knowledges and practices, but also in terms of the traces they bear of earlier knowledges and practices" (41). In particular, Biressi claims, true crime "contributes to the discursive production of criminal subjects and moral subjects, positing complex relations between them" (42). With these points in mind, I want to examine three examples of written discourse about crime in the United States—Puritan crime narratives, nineteenth-century journalistic coverage of crime, and true-crime narratives in the early decades of the twentieth century—in order to reconstruct the evolution of a complex framework for interpreting how the criminal and U.S. society are connected. This framework, I will argue, continues to resonate powerfully in modern true-crime narratives about serial murder.

The Beginnings of True Crime

There is a striking degree of consensus among scholars of early American crime narratives about the Puritan view of the criminal. Public hangings aroused tremendous popular interest during the Puritan period, and, not surprisingly, Puritan ministers seized the opportunity to instruct the crowds attending these events about the proper way to view the criminal's demise. Clergymen typically delivered sermons on capital cases on the Sunday before the sentence was to be carried out, or very often on the day of the execution itself (D. A. Cohen 3). By all accounts, these sermons were as well attended as the executions themselves, and their subsequent publication and distribution made them extremely influential and well-known documents. Karen Halttunen has argued that the doctrine of original sin played a profoundly important role in determining Puritan attitudes toward the criminal, and the influence of this doctrine can be detected in execution sermons: "The effect of the execution sermon's treatment of criminal causality was to establish a strong moral identification between the assembled congregation and the condemned murderer. For the doctrine that the root of crime was innate depravity undercut any notion of the murderer's moral peculiarity, with all humankind bound in that original sin committed by the first parents of the race" (*Murder* 14). Puritan crime narratives present the criminal as a representative member of his/her community, precisely because she or he has sinned. In fact, one could argue that criminals were model citizens of the Puritan community because by sinning, confessing that sin, and then asking for God's forgiveness they dramatized the process of conversion and redemption (Halttunen, *Murder* 18–19). Consequently, the criminal was as much an object of sympathy and compassion as of revulsion and punishment. By emphasizing the dangerously thin line that separated the criminal from the spectator, Puritan ministers sought to reassert their cultural, spiritual, and political authority through execution sermons. By arguing that every member of the community was subject to the withdrawal of God's grace at a moment's notice, clergymen had a powerful argument for why their congregations should let themselves be guided by the Puritan ministerial elite. This control turned out to be inherently unstable, however, precisely because it required generating a certain amount of public sympathy for the criminal.

It could be argued that there is something intrinsic in true-crime narratives that generates sympathy for the criminal. There is certainly a very obvious sense in which the true-crime narrative is always about the criminal in a way that it is not about the victim. Up to a point, this feature of crime narratives served the purposes of the Puritans well because a certain degree of identification with the criminal was necessary for the ideological message of the execution sermons to be effective. As Kristin Boudreau has demonstrated, however, even when Puritan control of crime narratives seemed absolute, there was concern about an inappropriate kind or degree of public sympathy: "The sermons of both Adams and Shurtleff underscore simultaneously how crucial audience sympathy was to the public denunciation of sin and how dangerous it could be to the authority of those who decried and punished capital crimes . . . Adams understood that sympathy, once awakened, could have disastrous consequences, and so he devoted much of his sermon to the topic of appropriate and inappropriate expressions of fellow-feeling" (255). As long as the Puritans maintained strict control over the production of crime narratives, the dangers of sympathy could be contained. As Puritan influence over American society began to weaken in the late seventeenth century, however, other forms of crime narrative began to appear that both exemplified and exacerbated that weakening. Significantly, these new forms of crime narrative all gave the criminal the opportunity to present his or her side of the story, in his or her own voice.

Over the course of the eighteenth century, it became more and more common to hear the criminal's point of view in crime narratives, first in reports of the criminal's dying words, and then later in the form of full-fledged biographies. As the social and religious background of criminals changed, and as it became less and less likely for criminals to have been born and raised as Puritans, these criminal narratives became increasingly secular. As the decline in Puritan authority accelerated, more and more crime narratives were written in the style of realism, including detailed attention to the events leading up to the murder, and information about the private lives of the protagonists (Halttunen, *Murder* 37–38). These changes contributed to the development of a celebrity culture organized around the criminal that culminated in "rogues' biographies," where criminality was seen almost as an admirable expression of unbridled personality.

Daniel Williams has noted that these changes in crime narratives were influenced by the development of Enlightenment concepts of freedom, concepts that gradually replaced the doctrine of original sin. Especially after the American Revolution, Williams has argued, "self-determination, self-reliance and self-initiative became socially celebrated ideals. Defiance of authority became pervasive, almost institutionalized" (13). But although these new understandings of the relation between self and community affected the content and character of eighteenth-century crime narratives, the celebration of criminality had very definite limits. Without the doctrine of original sin, it suddenly became much more difficult to explain the actions of criminals, especially when they seemed to violate what the Enlightenment saw as the innate goodness and rationality of humans.

Karen Halttunen has argued that, faced with this conundrum, Americans struggled to come up with an explanation for criminality that was as intellectually satisfying as the concept of innate depravity (*Murder* 44). This problem, Halttunen explains, was especially acute for those types of crime that could not adequately be explained by environmental influence, motive, or uncontrolled passion:

> A significant number of murder narratives printed between 1750 and 1820 demonstrated the inadequacy of all these attempts to explain the crime, as some men and women murdered against character, or from an inexplicable compulsion to kill, or in cold-blooded insensibility. These crimes challenged the prevailing rational view of human nature, with its attention to character as a developmental product of environmental influences, its emphasis on the powers of human reason, and its reliance on sentiment, the inner moral sense, as the ultimate guarantor of virtue. (*Murder* 46)

The answer to the dilemma posed by these inexplicable and mysterious crimes was to make a virtue out of necessity and heighten the air of mystery by resorting to the language of gothic fiction to narrate them. In particular, the notion of monstrosity assumed a prominent role in crime narratives. As

Halttunen explains, the "image of the murderer as monster expressed the incomprehensibility of murder within the rational Enlightenment social order" (*Murder* 48).

The rhetoric of monstrosity also aimed to place the criminal definitively outside the boundaries of community. The criminal was now viewed as a distinctly asocial creature; by the early decades of the nineteenth century, we have traveled a very long way from the Puritan notion of the criminal as a representative member of the community. I want to emphasize, however, that the concept of monstrosity did not simply replace the concept of representativeness as an explanation of criminality. Rather, monstrosity and representativeness coexisted in an ambivalent, dialectical relationship that became the defining feature of true-crime narratives from the early nineteenth century onward. Moreover, it is precisely the intuition that the criminal indeed represents his/her community that requires the attribution of monstrosity to stabilize the uncomfortable blurring of normal and abnormal that fascination with the criminal inspires. Journalistic coverage of crime in nineteenth-century America, a more direct influence on modern true-crime narratives, provides additional evidence of the unstable combination of attraction and repulsion that structures such narratives.

True Crime and the Press

Although America had been awash in crime narratives since colonial times, journalistic coverage of crime was a fairly late arrival on the scene. Newspapers had traditionally paid very little attention to crime, not only because they did not want to waste precious space reporting on events that most people would already have heard about through other media, but also because they were constrained by a sense of delicacy and civic responsibility (Tucher 9–10). By the 1820s and 1830s, American newspapers were beginning to feature crime reporting, but its presence remained sporadic until the explosion of the penny press in the mid-1830s. As Tucher explains, for the New York penny papers, "crime news became an immediate and natural staple: it was easy and inexpensive to gather; it was pleasant and familiar to readers already conversant with street literature; it provided New Yorkers with useful and important information about the way their city worked; and it would meet no serious competition from the established press" (11). Crime reporting in American journalism during this period was also stimulated by the occurrence of highly marketable crimes such as the murders of prostitute Helen Jewett in 1836 and shopgirl Mary Rogers (the inspiration for Edgar Allan Poe's story "The Mystery of Marie Roget") in 1841. In her study of the latter case, Amy Gilman Srebnick has commented that were it not for the newly developed concept

of public news, and the recent emergence of a reading public craving sensation from the penny press, "the story and the mystery of Mary Rogers would
probably have gone almost unnoticed. But Rogers' life and death occurred
at the very moment that a new urban and commercial written culture was
taking shape. The newspaper, the dime novel, the sensational pamphlet, and
the magazine with its serialized stories were the places where the Rogers story
was both created and popularized" (xvi). As a result, Srebnick argues, the
murder of Mary Rogers not only became an "emblematic crime" in the way it
linked female death, sexuality, and a peculiarly urban sense of mystery but also
ensured that crime reporting became a major aspect of popular journalism in
America (70).

The ability of crime stories to act as a bridge between vernacular forms
of street literature and the legitimate press during the early decades of the
nineteenth century suggests substantial continuities in how crime was represented in these media (Srebnick 70). In particular, the rhetoric of monstrosity
that was first developed in the eighteenth century continued to be a popular
way of describing criminals, whether in street ballads or in mass circulation
newspapers. Although there were some attempts, as Srebnick might put it, to
think of crimes as "emblematic," that is, as exemplifying current social and
cultural trends, it was far more tempting and ideologically satisfying to think of
criminals as examples of gothic horror. David Papke has described the way in
which crime pamphlets, which significantly tended to concentrate on murderers, presented the perpetrators: "In each case the relevant pamphlet stressed
the manner in which the criminal was overwhelmed by rage; the pamphlet
cast him as berserk, violent, evil—in a word, as a fiend" (28). The imposition
of monstrosity was an inherently unstable gesture, however, not least because
the sheer number of these narratives tended to give the lie to the claim that
these criminals were truly extraordinary and rare. Moreover, the danger that
the monster could collapse back into the ordinary man was exacerbated by the
volatile combination of morality and entertainment represented by crime
narratives.

As the influence of Puritan ideology faded further and further into the
past, it had become more acceptable to think of crime narratives as a form of
entertainment, but it remained important to also articulate a moral justification
for reading such material. For example, the preface to a bound collection of
crime narratives published in 1812 under the title *The Criminal Recorder; or, An
Awful Beacon to the Rising Generation of Both Sexes* illustrates this combination
of morality and entertainment. The preface begins by recommending the
narratives as suitably cautionary tales of guilt and punishment, adding that
adults would find them useful in steering their children away from crime.

However, perhaps concerned that this impeccably moral reason for purchasing the collection made it sound too dull, the preface then goes on to say, "Let it not be hastily supposed by the gay and youthful, that this volume is a dull or canting lecture upon religion and morals" (quoted in Papke 22). Such a comment suggests that the target audience for nineteenth-century true-crime narratives was quite diverse.

As the nineteenth century progressed, crime narratives not only became a staple feature of journalism and American popular culture in general but also tended to get more and more gory and sensational. Consequently, the claim that these narratives combined moral instruction with entertainment became increasingly necessary but also less persuasive, as the effort to articulate a moral justification for reading such material became ritualized to the point of meaninglessness. In order for true-crime narratives to become a legitimate, respectable genre, it was necessary to rearticulate a rationale for their consumption that avoided the problematic combination of morality and entertainment. This was a tall order indeed, but beginning in the 1920s Edmund Pearson seemed to succeed almost single-handedly in raising true-crime narratives to the level of literary art.

The Criminal Aesthetics of Edmund Pearson

Significantly, Edmund Pearson came to true crime not as a minister or a journalist but rather as a bibliophile and aesthete. Pearson was a librarian by trade; his early publications were mostly about books and book collecting, an interest that was facilitated by his position as editor of publications at the New York Public Library, a post he held from 1914 to 1927. Roger Lane has pointed out that a shift in the direction of Pearson's career can be detected in the final chapter of his 1923 book *Books in Black or Red*. Entitled "With Acknowledgments to Thomas De Quincey," Lane describes the chapter as "a rumination on that nineteenth-century author's famous essay entitled 'Murder Considered as One of the Fine Arts'" (xii). The influence of De Quincey on Pearson's true-crime narratives cannot be overstated. Pearson saw in De Quincey a way to have a legitimate, meaning nonsensationalist, interest in crime, as he explained in a 1928 essay, "From Sudden Death":

> De Quincey, writing a hundred years ago, is completely and delightfully modern in his method, and his work exploded a number of old superstitions. After he wrote it was never again necessary for any of his followers to assure their readers that murder is "an improper line of conduct." They could assume that they were writing for adults. He disposed of the stupid notion that any murder is interesting if it is gory enough. And he clearly stated the point (so often ignored by many of the writers

of detective stories) that the interest in a murder is enormously diminished if it is established that the victim was an evil person who deserved his fate. (226)

Using the blueprint established by De Quincey, Pearson published a series of hugely successful true-crime books beginning with *Studies in Murder* in 1924 and concluding with *More Studies in Murder* in 1936. The success of Pearson's work enabled him to leave his job at the New York Public Library in 1927 and become a full-time writer, but it also gave true-crime narratives a status they had never before possessed. Rather than being associated with the penny press or cheap forms of street literature, Pearson's true-crime narratives typically appeared in high-class magazines such as the *Forum*, *Liberty*, the *New Yorker*, and *Vanity Fair* before being published in book form. It is quite possible that the upper classes had always enjoyed true-crime narratives, of course, but previously such enjoyment had remained a secret, guilty pleasure. Pearson made it possible for true crime to come out into the open and take its place with other legitimate genres.

Several features of Pearson's work helped to make it legitimate. Again showing De Quincey's influence, Pearson presented himself as a connoisseur of crime, interested only in what he called in his 1923 essay on De Quincey the "pure murder." When he went on to define the pure murder, Pearson did so negatively, by excluding certain types of murder from consideration:

> First, it is necessary to eliminate, to exclude, to state what kind of killings are not *pure murders*. The rule against the murder of public characters is sound, as everyone will agree. The political assassination has too many other aspects aside from the destruction of the individual; the whole matter is confused, hopelessly, with issues which have nothing to do with the problem of murder. Next, and this is an extremely important, although difficult, point, the *crime passionnel* is, generally speaking, to be ruled out. The jealous lover, the forsaken maiden, the injured husband, the discarded mistress, the vengeful wife,—these stock characters in the melodrama of life are forever killing somebody or other, but there is in their deeds an extraneous and even sensational interest, which detracts from its value in the eyes of the austere amateur of murder. Their crimes are, with rare exceptions, so excessively cheap,—the stuff for the Sunday supplement in the yellow press. The folk who dote upon them,—vulgarians and riff-raff. ("With" 199–200, original emphasis)

I have quoted Pearson at such length to illustrate both his strictures against "sensational interest" as a criterion for selecting crimes and the class snobbery that underlies those strictures. Pearson wanted to make crime narratives safe for respectable members of society, and that meant rejecting the sensational, including serial killers, whom Pearson described as those murderers for whom "murder is not a master-stroke, to have its one—or in extreme cases, two exhibitions,—but with whom it has become a settled habit, an addiction" (206). Pearson admitted that "there will be objections to this, and some brilliant names will be cited in disproof"; Pearson mentioned H. H. Holmes as one of these "brilliant names," but he insisted that such killers did not represent a pure murder (206).

Given all the crimes Pearson excluded, what was left to constitute a pure murder? Pearson addressed this issue in an essay entitled, with disarming candor, "What Makes a Good Murder?":

> The amateur collector of murders is a much more discriminating person than the chance observer understands. He is often a determined antiquarian and reactionary; when any new murder comes out he bends his attention toward an old one... disgusted by the blatant taste of the Chicago school of murderers, he returns to the first murder of all, that Cain-Abel affair. He prefers his murderers to be mellowed by time; to possess the rich bloom of age. (3)

Pearson was publishing his true crime narratives during the era of Prohibition, when mobsters such as Al Capone came to dominate the criminal landscape of America. With his aesthetic sensibilities offended by the brutality of the "Chicago school of murderers," Pearson turned back eagerly to a more civilized age, and consequently the vast majority of his essays dealt with nineteenth-century crimes. Miriam Allen DeFord has argued that Pearson saw murder as "fundamentally a puzzle to be solved by the use of a sharp mind and all the available printed material" (xvi). Consequently, DeFord continues, his work was characterized by "the patient piling up of evidence, the search for a logical solution, the ambient play of dry humor" (xviii). None of the qualities that DeFord describes in Pearson's writing necessitated an engagement with the gory details of a crime. Instead of blood and guts, Pearson was attracted to certain moments in the crimes he wrote about that to him were especially dramatic and meaningful. For example, in "Murder at Smutty Nose; or, The Crime of Louis Wagner," Pearson focused on the moment immediately before the murders began: "He had only one house to consider; he knew that all the others were empty. There was no light in it. As for the helpless women asleep within, no philosophy or faith yet invented have been able to explain why such as they should be deserted by earth and heaven at this moment" (24). The philosophical and aesthetic questions raised by murder were of much more interest to Pearson than a blow-by-blow account of the murders themselves.

Pearson's imagination was particularly fired by the contrast between appearance and reality, or more particularly, between middle-class respectability and murderous deceit. The fact that gunmen and gangsters were so obviously dangerous was precisely what made them uninteresting to Pearson. He was far more engaged by the possibility that an individual whom, as he put it in "Nineteen Dandelions," "the neighbors respect is, as a matter of fact, as dangerous as a rattlesnake. That while he is talking to you, he may be deciding that you will be the next on his list. That if he offers you a cup of tea or if he invites you to dinner you will accept at your peril" (86). Many of the cases that Pearson wrote about possessed this combination of respectability and treachery, and together they formed for Pearson a kind of canon of crime, the existence of which is yet more evidence of De Quincey's influence on Pearson's aesthetic approach to murder. The following passage from "Two Victorian Ladies" illustrates both Pearson's concentration on particularly loaded moments and his arrangement of those moments in a tableau of canonical images:

> In the histories of extraordinary murders there are occasionally moments strongly impressive, tragic, and endowed with the ability to haunt the reader for ever: Burke and Hare carrying their sack through the streets; Professor Webster alone and in terror in his laboratory as he tries to dispose of his victim . . . With such moments belongs that terrible scene when Constance Kent leaned over her dead brother, as the candle flickered, dimmed, and went out, leaving them both in darkness. (262)

Although Pearson wrote about a large number of different crimes during his career, he kept returning to one case that in his opinion had a unique status as the purest murder ever committed: the case of Lizzie Borden, accused and acquitted of killing her father and stepmother in Fall River, Massachusetts, in 1892. In *Studies in Murder*, Pearson claimed that the "Borden case is without parallel in the criminal history of America. It is the most interesting, and perhaps the most puzzling murder which has occurred in this country" (3).

The Borden case had everything that Pearson looked for in a good murder: the middle-class respectability of both the victims and the accused killer was in dreadful contrast with the brutal way in which the victims were hacked to death with an ax. The case was complex enough for Pearson to show off his powers of deduction and his narrative skills in recreating his version of events. But perhaps most importantly, there remained something insoluble about the Borden case, and this enduring residue of mystery made the murders at the Borden House, as Pearson put it in "The Bordens: A Postscript," "the most fascinating of all puzzles. Neither detectives, lawyers, nor criminologists can solve the questions which they present, for they lie deep in that mysterious region, the human heart" (302).

Such sentiments, along with Pearson's determined refusal to engage with the crimes that dominated his own time, may suggest that he wanted to elevate the genre of true crime out of history altogether, turning it into a disinterested object of aesthetic contemplation. In spite of De Quincey's profound influence on Pearson's work, however, there was one important way in which Pearson differed from his mentor. Unlike De Quincey's "murder-fancier," who remained relatively unconcerned about such issues as the criminal's punishment, Pearson engaged vigorously with contemporaneous debates about criminal responsibility, the insanity defense, the death penalty, and the causes of crime. Although the mixture of antiquarianism and contemporaneity that defined Pearson's true-crime writing seems an unlikely one, it was probably the single most important reason for Pearson's success. Pearson's habit of concentrating on old cases helped to give true-crime writing an air of respectability, while his involvement in the hot-button legal issues of the day gave true-crime work a social utility that made reading it almost a civic duty, rather than evidence of the reader's prurience.

It also helped, of course, that Pearson's views on law and order were decidedly conservative. Writing against a background of widespread police corruption and mobster lawlessness, as well as the popularization of the insanity defense, as used in the high-profile case of Leopold and Loeb in 1924 (the year Pearson's first true-crime book appeared), Pearson was a determined reactionary on the subject of criminal responsibility.[2] On the subject of causation he could be devastatingly caustic, as in this commentary on the claim that dime novels cause crime: "It was the most useful explanation for crime, and the easiest excuse for the offender, until its place was taken by the cigarette, and then by the moving pictures. Finally, we achieved the psychosis, the inhibition, the slave phantasy, the fixation and the pituitary gland, and at last think there are no more evil-doers" (*Dime* 93). Not surprisingly, Pearson felt that the insanity defense was a related evasion of criminal responsibility: "You frequently hear it said that all murderers are insane. If not raving lunatics, they are insane at the moment of the crime, and that is why it is useless to punish them. This assertion represents thought at its lowest ebb" ("What Does" 26). Pearson believed that the appropriate fate for a convicted murderer was execution; indeed, if Pearson had a problem with the death penalty at all, it was not with its use but with the fact that it was not used enough. Nothing puzzled Pearson more than the belief that "throngs of innocents [were] hounded to the gallows or the electric chair by brutal police, hectoring district attorneys and corrupt judges" ("Man" 198). Instead, Pearson argued, in a time awash with what he regarded as baseless reasons not to hold criminals responsible for their actions, it was a major achievement even to convict a criminal, let alone execute him.

One might assume that Pearson's vigorous defense of the death penalty and his attacks on the insanity defense in his true-crime work were based on the belief that criminals are a class apart, so to speak, set definitively outside the community of law-abiding citizens. And yet, just as so much of Pearson's true-crime writing refused to take the appearance of middle-class respectability for granted, his support of the concept of criminal responsibility was dictated by his determination not to view criminals as monsters, separate from ordinary people: "Most of the folk who have committed murder are not insane; they are 'nastily like ourselves,' and their dreadful deed only represents something which, under certain circumstances, we might have done. The plea of insanity may be raised to save a guilty man, or it may be only a cry of horror to prove that there is a wide difference between the wicked murderers and ourselves,— virtuous folk that we are!" (*Instigation* 26–27).

Pearson's analysis of how the insanity defense can be used to construct the criminal as a comfortably distant monster is perceptive indeed; Pearson forced his reader to face the uncomfortable fact that the difference between him/her and the criminal was one of degree, rather than kind. He insisted on this point not to exonerate the criminal, but rather to encourage a clear-eyed attitude toward society's responsibility to punish the criminal. In this respect, the Puritans can be said to have had as much influence on Pearson as Thomas De Quincey had, and it is this peculiar mixture of Puritanism and aestheticism that gives Pearson's work its distinctive flavor and makes it decidedly different from the type of contemporary true crime exemplified by the work of Ann Rule.[3]

There is no doubt that Pearson gave a new respectability to true-crime narratives, and the next generation of true-crime writers worked hard to maintain this status, often by distinguishing their work from less respectable forms of true crime. For example, Anthony Boucher, in his 1958 introduction to Edgar Lustgarten's *The Murder and the Trial*, argues that "Fact-crime writing—as distinguished from the sensational journalism of most 'true-crime' magazines —demands four qualities from its maker: *literacy . . . scholarship* and dogged research . . . *insight* into human character and motives . . . [and] a feeling of *irony*, of relish" (x, original emphasis). Boucher asserts the legitimacy of nonsensational true crime by giving it generic properties, thus allowing it to inhabit the same plane of respectability as other middlebrow genres.

But for all of Pearson's and Boucher's efforts, they were fighting a losing battle. As much as Pearson desired to eschew sensationalism and ignore contemporary crime, he was unable to resist entirely the encroachment of modern crime and the modern world. By the time Pearson published his last book, *More Studies in Murder*, in 1936, he had to admit that the market in true crime was getting so crowded that it was more difficult for him to find suitable cases to write about. Although he still invoked De Quincey in arguing for the rarity of a murder like "an almost flawless gem" (10), the presence of chapters such as "The Corpse on the Speak-Easy Floor" (about an accidental death in a Harlem speak-easy) underlines how far Pearson had traveled from his earlier concept of the "pure murder" and how much he had to change in order to accommodate the tastes of his audience.[4]

In retrospect, Pearson's career represents the last flowering of the detached, ironic, aesthetic approach to murder inaugurated by Thomas De Quincey. By the 1930s, the industry of true-crime writing had simply become too large to need the veneer of respectability; instead, it was quite content to churn out gory and sensationalistic narratives for an eager public. However, what Pearson and Boucher could not have known was that another sea change for true crime was to take place. Ironically, although the book that would revolutionize the genre, Truman Capote's *In Cold Blood*, seemed to have the same combination of detachment and engagement that characterized Pearson's work, Capote's understanding of what it meant for the author of true crime to be detached and engaged was very different from that of Pearson. *In Cold Blood* inaugurated a period of unprecedented authorial intimacy with the subjects of true-crime narratives, to the point where the authors as well as the subjects of these narratives could become famous.

The Absent Presence of Truman Capote

Every study of true-crime narratives acknowledges the fundamental importance of *In Cold Blood* to the genre. In a 1990 *Publisher's Weekly* article detailing the healthy state of true crime, Rosemary Herbert quotes Neil Nyren, vice-president and publisher at Putnam, as saying that "there may already have been some true crime books, but Capote's marked a watershed. It was the first one to make the genre really respectable" (33). As I have shown, Edmund Pearson should be given the credit for making the genre respectable; it would be more accurate to say that Capote made true crime controversial and at the same time, not coincidentally, enormously profitable. Although a writer of Capote's stature had never written true crime before, this was not the most controversial aspect of *In Cold Blood*. Far more controversial was Capote's loud and oft-repeated claim that his study of the murder of the Clutter family in their farmhouse in Holcomb, Kansas, in 1959 constituted a new genre: the nonfiction novel. This claim provoked heated debate among a wide range of critics and was largely responsible for the book's huge sales and the enormous amount of publicity that surrounded its publication.[5]

Capote's claim that *In Cold Blood* was the first example of a new genre focuses attention on what exactly was new, if anything, about Capote's text compared with earlier true-crime narratives. As we have seen, Pearson attempted to remove sensationalism from true crime by cultivating a pose of ironic authorial detachment from the murder. However, one should not infer from this pose that Pearson was absent from his work. As we have seen, Pearson was a very strong presence in his work, constantly commenting on a range of issues in a concerted effort to steer the reader's opinion in the desired direction, so much so that when Pearson included the phrase "if I may venture an opinion" in one of his last true-crime essays ("Wicked" 64), he was clearly commenting ironically on the fact that his true-crime work as a whole could be described accurately as a "ventured opinion."

As engaged as Pearson was with the issues raised by his essays, however, he remained detached from the individuals he wrote about. Although one can detect a note of admiration in Pearson's work for such individuals as Constance Kent and Lizzie Borden, that admiration was so rigorously controlled that it was never in danger of becoming identification with the criminal. One might argue that it was easy for Pearson to distance himself from his subjects because he normally wrote about cases far in the past, but even when he wrote about contemporaneous cases, he still maintained the same careful distance. Capote, on the other hand, was much more engaged with the subjects of his narrative than Pearson. Bruce Bawer has described Capote's relationship with the two convicted murderers who are the subject of *In Cold Blood*, Perry Smith and Richard Hickock: "Capote developed a warm friendship with the murderers during his years of research; at the end, he accompanied them to the scaffold, wept for days over their deaths, and even paid for their grave markers" (42). It is hard to imagine Pearson entering into such a relationship with convicted murderers, and few true-crime writers have followed Capote in this respect.[6] A far more influential feature of *In Cold Blood* was the fact that, although Capote spoke at length about his relationship with Smith and Hickock in interviews, the formal structure of *In Cold Blood* itself hides this engagement. By inventing the "nonfiction novel," scrupulously removing every trace of his presence from the text, Capote claimed to have written a completely objective account of the case.

Not surprisingly, this inflated claim attracted a lot of critical attention, most of it negative, but the sympathetic interviewer George Plimpton gave Capote a chance to explain his decision to leave himself out of *In Cold Blood*: "My feeling is that for the non-fiction novel form to be entirely successful, the author should not appear in the work. Ideally. Once the author does appear, he has to appear throughout, all the way down the line, and the I-I-I intrudes when it really shouldn't. I think the single most difficult thing in my book, technically, was to write it without ever appearing myself, and yet, at the same time, create total credibility" (38). Even though Capote spent nearly six years gathering information on, researching, and living with the case, he appears nowhere in the book, and the word *I* is never used. Although Capote supposedly made this decision in the interests of objectivity, an objectivity that he believed was crucial if the book was to be successful, many critics felt that it was precisely Capote's decision to remove himself from the text that accounted for the failure of *In Cold Blood*. Hilton Kramer, for instance, writing in the *New Leader* not long after the book's publication, complained that "so successful has the author been in keeping himself 'out' of the tale that one closes the book mentally searching him out, suspecting at last that there is a far more revealing story to be told in his own involvement with the characters and events whose fate is so icily recounted" (quoted in Malin 68). This remark encourages us to consider what role Pearson's definite presence in his writing played in his success. Although Capote assumed that the audience wanted the writer to hide in a true-crime narrative, perhaps it wanted the writer to be visible, actively discussing, speculating, and judging.

Far more serious than such complaints about Capote's absence, however, were the repeated aspersions cast on the supposed factuality of the book; critics pointed to numerous examples of dialogue between characters that Capote could not possibility have known about to argue that there was a good deal more fiction in Capote's book than he admitted. Perhaps the most egregious example of this aspect of the book is its closing episode, which consists of a conversation between Alvin Dewey, the local FBI agent who supervised the murder investigation, and Sue Kidwell, a friend of Nancy Clutter, one of the murder victims. This conversation takes place some four years after the main events of the book, and there is no indication of how Capote could have reproduced this conversation in such detail. Capote indicates, in a cursory preface to *In Cold Blood*, that all conversations he did not hear personally were verified for him by reliable sources. Not surprisingly, this assurance was regarded as inadequate by many of Capote's readers, especially as the final paragraph of the book suggests that Capote was doing something other than giving the reader an objective account of events:

> "And nice to have seen you, Sue. Good luck," he called after her as she disappeared down the path, a pretty girl in a hurry, her smooth hair swinging, shining—just such a young woman as Nancy might have been. Then, starting home, he walked toward the trees, and under them, leaving behind him the big sky, the whisper of wind voice in the wind-bent wheat. (410)

It is hard to see how this beautifully written paragraph, with its poetic evocations of poignant loss and the possibility of regeneration, can be said to be "nonfiction" in any meaningful sense. Although Capote vehemently denied inventing any of the information in *In Cold Blood*, in his interview with George Plimpton Capote did comment on the fact that keeping himself out of his narrative did not necessarily mean that he gave up all control over how to present the events: "I make my own comment by what I choose to tell and how I choose to tell it. It is true that an author is more in control of fictional characters because he can do anything he wants with them as long as they stay credible. But in the nonfiction novel one can also manipulate: if I put something in which I don't agree about I can always set it in a context of qualification without having to step into the story myself to set the reader straight" (38). One can see just why Capote was so excited about his "invention" of the nonfiction novel; the form allowed him to claim objectivity and authorial invisibility while at the same time relinquishing none of his control over the shaping and presenting of events. The pretense of objectivity was necessary to make one's interest in crime respectably nonsensationalist, but the ability of the author to manipulate the facts, often in frankly fictional ways, allowed for the construction of an exciting, dramatic, and yes, sensationalist narrative.

Interestingly, the aspect of *In Cold Blood* that attracted the most criticism upon its initial appearance has had a profound influence on the subsequent development of the true-crime genre. Although critics objected vehemently to the concept of the "invisible" author in Capote's work, such invisibility has now become a standard feature of true-crime narratives, allowing a writer such as Ann Rule an enormous amount of leeway in how she presents her facts. I am not suggesting that Ann Rule distorts the facts, but she is able to enhance those facts with passages that read as if they come from popular fictional genres, such as the romance novel: "As 1981 arrived and the crowd whooped and whistled, Janis Miranda was already half in love. Inwardly she marveled at that; she was the woman who didn't trust men. She had been bruised in the wars of love too many times. But this man was different. Somehow special. When Randy Roth asked if he might call her, she agreed enthusiastically" (*Rose* 10). Although Rule could not possibly know the exact thoughts that went through Miranda's head at this moment, the contemporary true-crime reader does not care; the incident and the way it is recounted ring true and that is what matters.

The fact that contemporary true-crime writers such as Rule do not need to apologize for the presence of fictional elements or to defend the veracity of their narratives suggests that the true-crime reader of today has a very different understanding of what the "true" in "true crime" means than the reader of Edmund Pearson's day. In Pearson's time, "true" crime meant sticking to the facts as closely as possible, struggling to write what Pearson once referred to as "painfully veracious histories" ("Scenery" 300). Now the truth of true crime means getting to the heart of the matter; emotional truth is prized far more than literal truth, and it is this emotional truth that writers such as Ann Rule give their readers. Moreover, the contemporary true-crime reader never thinks to protest about the invisible author of true-crime narratives because, thanks to Truman Capote, the author of contemporary true-crime narratives is not really invisible at all.

In the midst of the avalanche of success enjoyed by *In Cold Blood*, no one seemed to notice the absurdity of Capote's boasting, on the one hand, about how scrupulous he had been about keeping himself out of his account and yet, on the other hand, being more than happy to ride the tidal wave of publicity generated by the book. Rather than an inconsistency, however, this bizarre combination of invisibility and relentless self-publicizing is probably *In Cold Blood*'s most profound influence on contemporary true-crime narratives. Capote showed true-crime writers how to participate in the culture of celebrity that had grown up around criminals; indeed, in many ways Capote set the stage for writers of true-crime narratives to become even more famous than their subjects, demonstrating that part of the reason celebrity criminals have become so common in recent decades is that the groups who come into contact with those criminals—lawyers, law enforcement officers, FBI agents, and true-crime writers—can now become famous in their own right.

Despite the runaway success of *In Cold Blood*, Capote did not write any more true crime, perhaps because he eventually grew tired of the controversy his book inspired. What at first appeared to be his other substantial excursion into the genre, a long essay entitled "Handcarved Coffins," was in fact an act of revenge on those critics who had questioned the veracity of *In Cold Blood*. Capote initially claimed that "Handcarved Coffins" was nonfiction (even his publisher, Random House, listed it under the category of reportage), but he later admitted that it was fiction. The exact combination of "reportage" and "fiction" in *In Cold Blood* remains a matter of debate. Curiously, the only reference I have found to Capote's desire to write a true-crime narrative after *In Cold Blood* can be found in a collection of the selected correspondence of Chicago serial killer John Wayne Gacy. In a letter dated June 5, 1980, Capote told Gacy that he was "well acquainted with your case" and that he "would be interested in doing an interview with you . . . Let me know if this possible" (McClelland n.p.). No record exists of Gacy's reply. There is a certain logic in Capote's being drawn to serial killers such as Gacy, for the combination of objectivity and engagement that constitutes *In Cold Blood* would prove to be particularly useful to contemporary true-crime narratives about serial murder.

Although *In Cold Blood* has had a profound influence on contemporary true crime, there is one important aspect of Capote's work that has generally not been adopted by later writers in the genre. A significant part of Capote's intimate relationship with Perry Smith and Richard Hickock was an attempt to generate public sympathy for them by arguing that they may not have been legally responsible for their crimes because they were suffering from temporary insanity. Capote spends a significant part of *In Cold Blood* discussing what he sees as the shortcomings of the McNaghten rules for determining criminal insanity, and he even includes a detailed discussion of a 1960 article published in the *American Journal of Psychiatry* on "murder without apparent motive" to support his claim that the death penalty may not have been merited in this case.[7] Capote's sympathy for the criminals, his attempt to argue that they were also victimized by their crimes, was another feature of *In Cold Blood* that was heavily criticized on the book's publication.[8] More recently, those true-crime writers who acknowledge Capote's influence on their work usually politely ignore his sympathy for Smith and Hickock, largely because that sympathy is now completely absent from contemporary true crime, a fact that illustrates the complicated relationship between earlier forms of discourse about crime and contemporary true-crime narratives.

In some respects, the absence of sympathy for the criminal in contemporary true-crime narratives recalls the Puritan view of sympathy as a dangerously unstable emotion. In other words, inasmuch as sympathy for the criminal implies a recognition of the criminal's humanity, a humanity shared by both the criminal and the reader, contemporary true-crime writers eschew sympathy altogether, preferring instead to present their readers with the comforting thought that the monsters they write about have nothing to do with them. In this respect, contemporary true crime departs sharply from both Puritan crime narratives and the work of Edmund Pearson. Even though the Puritans recognized the dangers of sympathy, they still saw it as a necessary part of crime narratives because of the role they wanted those narratives to play in the ideological reintegration of the criminal into the community. Pearson was much more openly hostile to the idea of feeling sympathy with criminals, but he would definitely have resisted turning criminals into asocial monsters with no visible connection to the reader of true crime. Given these dissonances between contemporary true-crime narratives and earlier traditions, it comes as no surprise that contemporary true crime is dominated by a figure that the Puritans regarded as incomprehensible and that Pearson explicitly excluded from the category of the "good" murder: the serial killer. The prevalence of the serial killer in contemporary true crime also reminds us that the closest affinity between today's version of the genre and earlier discourse about crime can be found in the nineteenth-century "yellow" press. The "fiend" who dominated the sensationalistic journalistic coverage of violent crime in antebellum crime narratives is the most direct antecedent for the serial killer that stalks through today's true-crime narratives. Both the fiend and the serial killer lend themselves easily to presentation as monstrous outsiders, soothingly different from the genre's implicitly normal readers.

The Stranger Beside Ann Rule

No contemporary true-crime writer exemplifies the complex inheritance of earlier forms of true-crime narrative and the genre's recent preoccupation with serial killers better than Ann Rule. The fact that Rule has also been the biggest-selling author in the genre for many years reflects just how comforting the image of the monstrous serial killer is to the reading public. Rule has stated that "I was very impressed by Capote's *In Cold Blood* in 1964 [*sic*] and used to wish that I could someday, somehow, get into a killer's mind and write about it" (pers. comm., 1 Oct. 1996). Although Rule would eventually get her wish, her route to publishing true crime was very different from that of Capote's. After graduating from the University of Washington with a degree in creative writing in 1954, Rule trained to be a cop with the Seattle police department until she was dropped from the force after the discovery of her severe nearsightedness. Although she never worked as a police officer, Rule formed a number of friendships that would serve her well as information sources when she began writing true crime in 1968. More importantly, her time with the Seattle police inclined Rule to look at the criminal world from the point of view of law enforcement. Although this distinguished Rule sharply from her model, Capote, it proved to be an extremely popular aspect of her work and has since become a general feature of contemporary true crime, for reasons and with consequences that I will discuss in the next chapter.

Although Rule began trying to sell true-crime work in 1963, she did not get her break until 1968 when Al Govoni, editor of the national publication *True Detective Magazine*, offered Rule the position of northwest stringer for the magazine. Govoni liked Rule's work but told her she would have to use a male pseudonym because the magazine's readers would not believe that a woman knew anything about murder ("Ann" 6).[9] Over the next ten years, Rule wrote literally hundreds of true-crime articles, soon breaking out of the true-crime magazine ghetto and publishing with magazines such as *Cosmopolitan, Ladies' Home Journal, Redbook,* and *Good Housekeeping.* Rule was by now an established figure in true crime, but the publication of her first book, *The Stranger Beside Me,* in 1980 took her career and the genre of true crime to a new level.[10]

The subject of *The Stranger Beside Me* was a figure who would become, for many, the personification of serial murder: Ted Bundy. The success of *Stranger* was a watershed for the genre of true crime in several ways. It established the fact that books about serial killers could be bestsellers. Although the market quickly became flooded by a tidal wave of books about famous and would-be-famous serial killers of the past and present, Rule's book maintained its place at the head of the pack, having gone through thirty printings by 1994. In the process, *Stranger* was instrumental in turning Ted Bundy into the world's best-known serial killer, ensuring Bundy a definitional status in the pantheon of serial killers only rivaled by that of Jack the Ripper. Moreover, the success of *Stranger* established that true-crime writers themselves could become celebrities, albeit second-order celebrities, whose fame in some sense depended upon the fame of their criminal subjects.[11] Although her fame has been enormously beneficial to Rule in financial terms, it has also made her, like many other celebrities, subject to stalking and harassment. A 1990 *San Francisco Chronicle* newspaper article sums up the mixture of fear and money Rule's success has brought her:

> Her book led to a flood of late-night calls and unannounced visitors. An elderly woman showed up hysterical on Ms. Rule's doorstep and claimed Mr. Bundy had been stealing her underwear for years. A man afraid he himself might become a serial killer got on a bus bound for Seattle and brought his diary to get the author's opinion. A decade after the book's publication, and even after Mr. Bundy's execution, Ms. Rule still can't shake her subject; a young woman calls regularly claiming to be Mr. Bundy's daughter. If such feedback isn't gratifying, the money is. Ms. Rule is already a millionaire. She lives in a sun-filled triple-tiered house on Puget Sound. For her next two books, she is getting total advances of $3.2 million. (Cox 3)

An even more significant consequence of *Stranger*'s success is that Rule was able to parlay her reputation as a true-crime writer into expert status as an authority on serial murder. Not only does Rule frequently conduct seminars for law enforcement personnel on the psychology of serial killers but she also, as I mentioned in chapter 2, testified before the 1983 Senate committee that was so instrumental in shaping the federal response to serial murder. No incident could better illustrate the imbrication of true crime and official law enforcement discourses about serial killers; both discourses have a vested interest in exaggerating the scale of the serial murder problem and maximizing public panic over this issue.

The critical response to the boom in true crime enabled by Rule's success has been complex. As I mentioned at the start of this chapter, one reaction has been to regularly prophesy the end of the boom, but one gets the impression that this prophecy is as much a product of wishful thinking as it is an accurate assessment of the state of the industry. In a 1991 *New York Times Book Review* article, journalist Marilyn Stasio quoted Liz Perl, chief publicist for Avon books, on this issue: "Publishers are always saying that true crime has peaked, because, let's face it, these books do not represent the industry's shining hour" (46). Although it is true that sales have declined somewhat in recent years from their peak in the 1980s, largely because the market became glutted, in general true crime continues to sell very well, and this has led many commentators to worry about the consequences of the genre's success.

In a 1986 article in the *New York Times Magazine*, Richard Levine argued that although many states have devised victim compensation laws in response to the lucrative film and publishing deals signed by serial killers after their arrest, "these laws hardly eliminate the confusion of entertainment and jour-nalistic values in books about murders. After his arrest, John Wayne Gacy, short and heavyset, let it be known that he wanted Rod Steiger to play him in any movie version of his story . . . Last May, Mark Harmon, who had been dubbed 'the sexiest man alive' on the cover of *People* magazine, played Ted Bundy in an NBC-TV series about the serial killer" (132). Such observations about the interpenetration of Hollywood fame and criminal fame are accurate as far as they go, but they restrict themselves to describing the phenomenon rather than explaining it. The level of success enjoyed by Rule and the genre of true crime, along with the various consequences of that success, is by now such an established fact that simply bemoaning it is beside the point. A more productive aim would be to explain the reasons for that success and, in par-ticular, to analyze to what extent this success is dependent upon the dialectic between the criminal-as-monster and the criminal-as-representative that has been a structuring presence in so many forms of true-crime narrative.

A large part of Rule's success is due to a feature of her work that recalls both Pearson and Capote, albeit in different ways. Rule gives true-crime narratives an ethical dimension and also stresses their social utility. Rule's ethical take on the genre comes through in the way her work frequently articulates a "pro-woman" emphasis, an emphasis that takes several forms, including Rule's habit of dedicating her books to the victims of crime. The preface to her 1993 book *A Rose for Her Grave* is typical:

> This book is dedicated to women, to the friends I cherish and to the friends I will never know. Too many times I have to write about the tragedies that befall my sisters. *A Rose for Her Grave* is no exception. I am continually amazed at the strength women have shown in the face of catastrophe, particularly the survivors who pick up their lives and go on after losing a child to a conscienceless killer. I

salute all women who have had dreams, for themselves, for their children and for those they love. (N.p.)

By emphasizing the fact that women are overwhelmingly the victims in the cases she writes about, Rule makes a seemingly obvious point, and yet it is a point rarely mentioned by other true-crime writers. In some instances, Rule even implies that all women share a bond with female victims that joins them together in their opposition to the criminal: "So many women would remember Randy Woodfield, remember dates and places and things he'd said. In the end, it would be women who would help to trap him, women who could place him in areas where it was dangerous for him to have been remembered" (*I-5* 116).

In a similar vein, Rule frequently writes about her work with victims' rights groups, claiming that these groups keep her focused on the victim rather than the criminal. Finally, Rule has often argued that true-crime narratives have educational value and that the duty of the true-crime writer to educate the reader means the writer should eschew sensationalism: "I have always believed that true crime writing should not only absorb its readers but also educate them. There is no need to embroider spectacular cases; human behavior is in and of itself more fascinating than anything found in fiction. Those who have read my work before know that I do not stress blood and gore and grotesque details; I focus my research on the *whys* of murder more than on the *how*" (*Rose* xi, original emphasis). It is easy to dismiss this presentation of true crime as an ethical and utilitarian genre as a cynically self-serving attempt to distract our attention from its exploitative elements. We must also acknowledge, however, that Rule's claims are, by and large, accurate descriptions of her work. Like Pearson, Rule is relatively uninterested in the physical details of homicide, preferring instead to concentrate on what these acts of violence tell us about the complexities of the human heart. What Rule says about Randy Roth, the subject of one of her true-crime narratives, could be applied to Rule herself: "He had learned that he could make more money with roses and sweet talk and promises he never intended to keep than he ever could with a knife and a mask" (*Rose* 267). That one could win a wider audience for true-crime work by not using gore did not occur to Rule at the start of her career. Rather, it was the product of the later stage of her career, when she made a conscious and deliberate effort to diversify her true-crime product by ceasing to write about serial killers.

In some ways, this was a decision that was forced upon Rule by the success of the early part of her career. *The Stranger Beside Me*, her book about Ted Bundy, and what she has referred to as her "serial killer trilogy," *The I-5 Killer, Lust*

Killer, and *The Want-Ad Killer* (all written under the pseudonym of "Andy Stack"), made Rule's reputation as a true-crime writer and enabled her to receive multimillion dollar advances for her future books. These early books were more graphic and gory than Rule's later work, but it was not necessarily the gore that led to Rule's decision to write about different kinds of cases. The deciding factor was the level of fame achieved by serial killers. Obviously, this was a phenomenon Rule had done much to contribute to, but it presented her with a problem as a true-crime writer. Because many more serial killer cases now received blanket coverage from the moment of the suspect's arrest, there was little incentive to do a book about a case that everyone already knew about. Consequently, Rule was practically forced into looking for relatively unknown cases to write about, a decision that to all intents and purposes made it impossible for Rule to write about serial killers even if she had wanted to.

Fortunately, a decision that may not have been entirely voluntary on Rule's part turned out to be extremely successful. After having conquered the lower, more gory end of the true-crime market, Rule was now able to colonize the higher end of the market as well. In the process, she not only achieved even greater personal career success but also moved true crime even further into the mainstream. Part of the reason she was able to do these things is that she had established a solid fan base that she turned to in the search for unknown cases to write about. Using the forum of the self-published "Ann Rule's Newsletter," Rule let her readers know that she was not interested in writing about cases that had received saturation media coverage, such as O. J. Simpson and Jon-Benet Ramsey. Instead, Rule explained, she wanted her readers to "Find me a 'sleeper' . . . one that has little publicity outside your own town or city" ("Ann" 2). Dramatic evidence of the success of this strategy can be found in one of Rule's more recent books, *Every Breath You Take*, which details the murder of a mother by her millionaire ex-husband. In an extraordinary twist, Rule learned about the case because the victim told her sister that if anything ever happened to her, she should ask Rule to tell her story. If the fame of serial killers necessitated a change in direction for Rule's work, this change was facilitated by Rule's own fame (which was a corollary of the fame of serial killers, of course), which meant that her subjects now sought her out.

Normality, Monstrosity, and the Gothic in True Crime

Even if Ann Rule has left serial killers behind in her more recent work, the first part of her career still provides us with many examples of true crime's most representative ways of characterizing serial killers. Indeed, Ann Rule is never more representative of modern true-crime writers than when she describes the serial killers she writes about as monsters, as in *Lust Killer*, her book about

Jerome Brudos: "In the convoluted medicalese of the psychiatrist, Jerome Henry Brudos was quite sane, and eminently dangerous. In the language of the man on the street, he was a monster, He [*sic*] would always be a monster" (166). Typically, in presenting the serial killer as a monster, Rule defines herself against "expert" discourse, which is dismissed for being disconnected from reality. The perception of the killer's monstrosity, on the other hand, is offered as eminently commonsensical, an obvious fact about the killer that any sensible, objective person can see.

Such representative moments in Rule's work bring us back to two persistent questions we are still trying to answer: why serial killers continue to be one of the most prominent and readily salable parts of the true-crime genre, and why serial killers are so often described as monsters. Given both the extent and the overdetermined nature of the presence of famous serial killer monsters in true crime, it might seem somewhat irrelevant to enter objections to such a figure. It is precisely because this figure is such a prominent part of the true-crime genre, however, that we must understand the cultural work it does, critique that work, and suggest some alternatives. We might begin by pointing out the impossibility of distinguishing the normal from the monstrous as neatly as the figure of the monstrous serial killer seems to do. In his landmark work *The Normal and the Pathological*, philosopher Georges Canguilhem argues that "there is no fact which is normal or pathological in itself. An anomaly or a mutation is not in itself pathological. These two express other possible norms of life" (144). Consequently, Canguilhem goes on to claim, "if the normal does not have the rigidity of a fact of collective constraint but rather the flexibility of a norm which is transformed in its relation to individual conditions, it is clear that the boundary between the normal and the pathological becomes imprecise" (182). Although Canguilhem's emphasis on the flexibility of the category of "normal" is a useful corrective to the rigidity with which true-crime writers use the term, it does nothing to explain the appeal of referring to "normality" and "monstrosity" as if they were mutually exclusive terms, or why this mutual exclusivity is such an extraordinarily widespread and enduring feature of modern true-crime narratives. To shed some light on these issues, we must turn to other sources.

In his 1978 lecture "The Dangerous Individual," Canguilhem's one-time student Michel Foucault studies what he calls the "psychiatrization of criminal danger" (128) by recounting how the historical coincidence of the development of psychiatry and the rise of the notion of the "dangerous criminal" in the nineteenth century worked together to produce the "great monster" of popular lore: "The individual in whom insanity and criminality met in such a way as to cause specialists to raise the question of their relationship, was not

the man of the little everyday disorder, the pale silhouette moving about on
the edges of law and normality, but rather the great monster. Criminal psychiatry first proclaimed itself a pathology of the monstrous" (131). Criminal
psychiatry, then, was attracted toward apparently motiveless, brutal crimes,
the crimes for which the concept of the dangerous criminal, the great monster,
was needed most urgently. Monstrosity was not an objective feature of such
cases; rather, it was something constructed by both official and popular criminal narratives to serve certain ideological ends, as Foucault demonstrates in
I, Pierre Rivière, his study of a nineteenth-century French murderer. Foucault
argues that Rivière's remarkable confessional narrative about his murder of his
family was regarded as threatening because it presented Rivière as an individual thoroughly integrated into his community. The response to this threat was
to subsume Rivière's narrative "under a vast number of narratives which at
that period formed a kind of popular memoir of crime" (203–4). The purpose
of this act of subsumption, Foucault claims, was to "alter the scale, to enlarge
the proportions" of Rivière's story in order to emphasize that the details of the
story, "however commonplace and monotonous they may be, appeared 'singular,' 'curious,' 'extraordinary,' unique, or very nearly so, in the memory of man.
In this way such narratives could make the transition from the familiar to the
remarkable, the everyday to the historical" (204). By analyzing the tendency
of discourse about crime to transform the mundane into the extraordinary,
Foucault shows us the social function of monstrosity: by calling the serial killer
a monster, true crime distances the killer from the everyday and relocates him
in the transhistorical (or, to be more precise, ahistorical) pantheon of serial
killers through the ages.

Philosopher Sylvère Lotringer has commented that "our society desperately needs monsters to reclaim our moral virginity" (quoted in S. Moore 5),
and there are many reasons to resist the attempts to distance "monstrous"
serial killers from the rest of us. While not diminishing the horrors of what
serial killers do, and while acknowledging that the vast majority of people
are genuinely sickened by and afraid of serial killers, we must resist the ways
in which true-crime narratives seek to overstate the gap between them and
us because we thus miss the opportunity to make connections between more
"mundane" forms of violence and serial murder. In an article about the British
serial killer Fred West, Suzanne Moore laments the consequences of the media
coverage of the case: "The vicarious identification with which some sections
of the population have lapped up each grisly detail will go unquestioned. It
will be easier to turn West into another monster, different from other men,
than to ask how he might be the same as them" (5). The fact that West's wife,
Rosemary West, eventually turned out to have been an equal participant in

the murders suggests that Moore's point needs to be expanded even further: monstrosity forecloses the complicated relationship both women and men can have with violence.

Quite apart from these ethical issues, however, it is also important to resist the automatic imputation of monstrosity to serial killers because of evidence that suggests this imputation can obstruct murder investigations. Journalist Duncan Campbell, for example, in an article entitled "Maniac Theory Hid Violent Pattern of 'Domestic' Murder," discusses the case of British murderer Michael Shorey, sentenced to life in prison for the murders of Elaine Forsyth and Patricia Morrison in 1991. Although investigators eventually realized that Shorey, who knew both the victims, was responsible for their deaths, they were initially misled by the assumption that the murders were the work of a "maniac" serial killer with no connection to the victims. This case illustrates that serial killers can enable the public to forget the fact that around 85 percent of murders are committed by people who know each other and that incidents of serial murder, thankfully, continue to be extremely rare.

Even in cases involving serial murder, however, conventional ways of thinking about the crime can obstruct the investigation. In the case of Peter Sutcliffe, better known as the "Yorkshire Ripper," responsible for the murders of some thirteen women in the north of England in the 1970s and 1980s, the police and the media decided early on that Jack the Ripper, that most famous of celebrity serial killers, was the most appropriate template with which to interpret Sutcliffe's crimes, as his nickname implies. The assumption that Sutcliffe killed only prostitutes meant that his murders of nonprostitutes were not connected with the series until after his arrest, substantially hampering the investigation. The appeal of thinking of Sutcliffe as a modern-day reincarnation of Jack the Ripper proved to be so strong that it created myopia among the police and the media. Detective Robert Keppel, who has investigated both the Ted Bundy and the Green River Killer murders, has argued that police investigations are sometimes better focused if they concentrate on the ordinary rather than the extraordinary. He points out that when canvassing a neighborhood in which a murder has recently taken place, police often ask, "Did you see anything unusual?" Keppel suggests a better question: "Keeping in mind that serial killers are not seen running down the street with a bloody knife in their teeth, which *would* be something unusual, the more appropriate question that police might want to ask when tracking a serial killer is 'What did you see that was usual?'" (*Riverman* 455, original emphasis).

Keppel's emphasis on the "usual" aspects of serial killers receives bizarre confirmation from the killers themselves. Ted Bundy, for example, once explained that serial killing played just a small role in his life: "Well, this particular activity is just a small, small portion of what was predominantly a normal existence ... which *continued* to be a normal existence, not only at the will or whim of this antisocial pathological mental condition. It was just a *different* part" (Michaud and Aynesworth, *Conversations* 115, original emphasis). In the same vein, Florida serial killer David Gore has reflected that it was precisely his normality that made him so dangerous:

> It is my belief that the reason I never came under suspicion is because I was so normal in every aspect of my life. People couldnt [*sic*] believe someone like me was committing such horrible crimes. I did NOT look or act like a serial killer. One of my victims was a 19 year old girl who I had known all my life. When I abducted her, & took her to my trailer she was in shock, she couldnt believe IT WAS ME. At first she thought I was joking. (Furio 206, original emphasis)

It seems ironic that serial killers themselves recognize something that true-crime narratives about them assiduously disavow, namely, their combination of ordinary and monstrous traits. The self-perception of serial killers is just one more reason why we should resist the automatic labeling of serial killers as monsters by true-crime narratives. But no matter how compelling the reasons to acknowledge the ordinariness of serial killers may be, such acknowledgments by themselves will never change the situation. This is because from the point of view of true-crime writers, drawing attention to the ordinariness of serial killers actually necessitates the use of monstrosity. This necessity is not ethical but practical: how does one build a compelling narrative around such a dull and ordinary individual as the average serial killer? Monsters are the answer.

True-crime writers solve the problem of the killer's ordinariness by drawing upon gothic conventions in their narratives; that is, by turning serial killers into monsters: "gothic paradigms allow for the creation of a compelling narrative and, consequently, the generation of character and plot out of 'bland ordinariness' and incomprehensible randomness" (Nixon 226). Although serial killers may resist being turned into monsters, their objections are usually ignored, and they are not strong enough to overturn the gothic trend in true-crime narratives about serial killers because that trend serves a number of other purposes apart from allowing for the construction of an exciting narrative. Not only are readers encouraged to define their "ordinary" selves against the "monstrous" killers, but the gothic, Nixon argues, also allows for the production of a "friend" who tells the story of his or her friendship with the monster (as in Ann Rule's *The Stranger Beside Me*) or a "heroic counterpredator" such as the police or the FBI. In other words, cops become heroes in true-crime narratives because they are counterparts to the gothic figure of the serial killer and as such add order and closure (through the narrative of the legal system, for example) to a chaotic narrative.[12] Readers prefer these somewhat fantastic narratives to more mimetic narratives that could not offer the same types of consolations or resolutions.

The presumption of the serial killer's monstrosity also dictates some more specific features of true-crime narratives, many of which are driven by a desire to explain (or disavow) the killer's apparent ordinariness. One of the most common images in true-crime narratives about serial killers is that of the "mask of sanity."[13] In some respects, we see an early version of this concept in the work of Edmund Pearson, where it takes the form of not being able to trust an individual's outwardly respectable and trustworthy appearance. Pearson's concern about what we might term unreadable respectability, however, has much closer connections to the type of the confidence man that I discuss with reference to H. H. Holmes in chapter 1. The "mask of sanity," in contrast to Pearson's concerns, is a much more pathological concept. This concept turns the killer's apparent ordinariness into the most compelling sign of his evil by depicting that ordinariness as a facade hiding the "truth" of the serial killer's identity. Donald Sears, for example, comments that "perhaps the most frightening characteristic of the serial killer is that he usually presents to the public the image of the all-American boy, the nice man next door, or the shy, quiet neighbor down the street" (x). Sears goes on to reassure his reader that the killer's apparent normality is false: "underneath his benevolent appearance lies a driven killer who stalks his prey with determined fervor" (x).

But although the presumption of monstrosity in true-crime narratives is necessary in order to distance serial killers from ordinary men, this presumption immediately creates a dilemma: how do we tell the difference between the mask of sanity and a real face? If serial killers appear to be ordinary men, how can we distinguish between "apparently" ordinary men who are "actually" serial killers and "really" ordinary men? The intractability of these questions means that the mask of sanity as a diagnosis and sign of monstrosity is never enough; it always has to be bolstered by a second common feature of true-crime narratives about serial killers: the search for the origins of deviance.

Little Monsters

One way in which true-crime narratives can undermine and demonize the serial killer's apparent normality is to conduct a search for the origins of the killer's deviance by going back to his childhood. This is a distinctively recent innovation in true crime. There is nothing in Pearson's work that comments upon the influence of an individual's childhood on an adult's actions. Nevertheless, I think it reasonable to surmise, based on his frequent withering comments about psychology and psychoanalysis, that Pearson would have felt this influence to be just one more in a long line of "mitigating" factors designed to erode the concept of criminal responsibility and would have resisted its importance vigorously.

Capote was much more sympathetic to the idea that childhood trauma can explain adult actions; indeed, this is part of the reason Capote believed Perry Smith in particular deserved to be treated mercifully. But although Capote and the contemporary true-crime writer may both believe in the cliché "The child is father to the man," this phrase has a very different resonance in recent true-crime narratives. Rather than going back to the killer's childhood to look for mitigating circumstances, modern true-crime writers go looking for details in the killer's childhood that will allow them to claim that the seeds of monstrosity have been lurking, though cunningly disguised, in the killer since childhood. In the next chapter, when we study the case of Ted Bundy in detail, we will see that Ann Rule's work on Bundy contains this feature, but then so does the vast majority of true-crime work on serial killers as a whole. The detail most often alluded to in Ted Bundy's childhood is described by ex-FBI agent John Douglas:

> Though the family photos of Ted with tricycle and red wagon or sled and snowman, building sand castles at the beach, or trimming the Christmas tree seem typically idyllic and middle American, there were other warnings that things were not all okay with the youngster. When Louise's [Bundy's mother] sister, Julia, was fifteen, she awoke on more than one occasion to find her three-year-old nephew placing kitchen knives in the bed next to her. Ted, she said, "just stood there and grinned." (*Obsession* 299)

Douglas draws a rather heavy-handed contrast between the Norman Rockwell episodes from Bundy's life and a scene straight out of a slasher movie in order to emphasize that Bundy's monstrous qualities were practically innate. The conjunction of Bundy and knives obviously lends itself well to the retrospective construction of deviance, but if no suitably deviant episode exists, one can be constructed by going back to seemingly innocuous childhood incidents and reinterpreting them in the light of later events.

The most sustained example of what I call the "Had I but known" school of true crime narratives is *A Father's Story*, Lionel Dahmer's memoir about his infamous son, which is filled with examples of the ordinary turned into the ominous: "When we went fishing, and he seemed captivated by the gutted fish, staring intently at the brightly colored entrails, was that a child's natural curiosity, or was it a harbinger of the horror that was later to be found in Apartment 213?" (54). All such questions are clearly meant to be rhetorical.

In the world of the true-crime narrative, the lives of serial killers are bound by an inexorable logic that leads them to their crimes. Wendy Lesser has described the important role played by determinisms of various kinds in the formal structure of true-crime narratives:

> Part of the point about these works about real-life killers like Bundy or Gary Gilmore is that their reputation precedes them. So, as with Oedipus, the story is actually closed before it even opens. The killer thinks he's a free agent, but *we* know exactly where he's headed . . . In some works about murder, this sense of genre determinism conspires with other shaping factors, such as sociological or psychological determinism, to make the murderer's fate, and hence that of his victim, seem unavoidable. (20, original emphasis)

The reader of true crime takes great comfort in the deterministic logic that binds these children to their evil fate from their very earliest days. No matter how absurd this determinism may be, it has the advantage of making that apparently ordinary life as deviant as possible from its very beginning. To suggest any other possibility would risk having the ordinary be simply, well, ordinary.

Not only do the dark childhoods of serial killers allow us to distance them as products of "bad families," unlike our "good families," but the focus on the family background of the killers also works to individualize the phenomenon of serial murder, making sure that society at large is not implicated in the actions of the serial killer. Most frequently, this individualizing takes the form of narratives of individual psychological development, and Richard Tithecott has described how these narratives aim to reconstruct the "origins of the story of *his* violence, origins which we figure as belonging solely to the individual, to *a* life" (34, original emphasis). Although it may seem that discussing the serial killer's family background might contradict the focus on individualism, in fact, as Tithecott goes on to explain, it complements it: "If the crimes of a serial killer cannot be neatly and completely figured as originating in the criminal's individual identity, his family can function by mopping up the remaining meaning, leaving the rest of us untainted" (40).

I have described in this chapter the significant points of continuity and difference in the ways contemporary true-crime narratives and earlier examples of the genre manage the tensions involved in deciding whether criminals in general and serial killers in particular should be located inside the community or outside, whether they should be seen as representative subjects or monstrous outsiders. Although the emphasis is overwhelmingly on the need to cast the serial killer out of the social, I have demonstrated that this move can never be performed cleanly or conclusively in contemporary American culture because that culture has such a complex and ambivalent relationship with the serial killer. As we will see in the next chapter, this same tension between expulsion and engagement is still at play when the tension between the normal and the monstrous is cast in a way quite specific to recent true-crime narratives, namely, as a matter of sexual orientation.

CHAPTER SIX

The Unbearable Straightness of Violence: Queering Serial Murder in True Crime

The other man was none other than the arch-fiend, the monster
of monsters himself.
—H. H. Holmes, *Holmes the Arch-Fiend*

The "monster" may sleep, but he only slumbers—waiting for his
chance to roam free once more.
—Ann Rule, *Lust Killer*

The frequency and durability of the term "monster" in true-crime narratives suggest that it is an undifferentiated category, effective precisely for its ability to convey many shades of meaning without having to articulate them explicitly. In practice, however, "monstrosity" proves to be an internally diverse category in true-crime discourse. Although it is true that true-crime narratives characteristically use the terms "normality" and "monstrosity" as if their meaning was clear, just as often those narratives give these terms a particular inflection in order to respond to a particular dilemma. When we consider the fact, for example, that the vast majority of serial killers are straight men and the vast majority of their victims are women, it becomes clear that it is not just a gender- or sexuality-neutral "us" that is threatened by an association with the apparently normal serial killer, but more specifically heterosexual men. Consequently, there is a compelling reason for true-crime narratives to assert the "innocence" of straight men by disavowing the implicit link between heterosexual maleness and violence that is suggested by serial killers. One way of doing this, as I described in the previous chapter, is to accentuate the abnormality of the apparently normal serial killer as much as possible by giving him a thoroughly deviant childhood. Another way is to map the terms "normality" and "monstrosity" onto "heterosexuality" and "homosexuality," thus demonizing homosexuality by arguing that it is intimately connected (indeed, almost identical) with violence. In other words, true-crime narratives illustrate the supposed lack of connection between heterosexuality and violence by emphasizing just how closely homosexuality and violence are related.

True crime's focus on the violence of homosexuality exemplifies the very selective attention the genre pays to the sexual dimensions of serial murder. In fact, one might argue that such narratives normally ignore sexuality altogether because they want to avoid acknowledging the existence of what Gloria Steinem has described as "supremacy crimes." Writing about mass murder as well as serial murder in a 1999 post to the *Ms. Magazine* Web site, Steinem argues that "these 'senseless' killings begin to seem less mysterious when you consider that they were committed disproportionately by white, non-poor males, the group most likely to become hooked on the drug of superiority. It's a drug pushed by a male-dominant culture that presents dominance as a natural right; a racist hierarchy that falsely elevates whiteness . . . and a homophobic one that empowers only one form of sexuality." And yet, as Steinem points out, there is no acknowledgment of the existence of supremacy crimes in media representations of mass and serial murder. In the context of discussing the Columbine High School killings, Steinem suggests that the links between sexuality and murder become an issue only when the killer and/or the victims are gay: "What if these two young murderers, who were called 'fags' by some of the jocks at Columbine High School actually had been gay? . . . What if they had been lovers? . . . Would we hear as little about their sexuality as we now do?" Steinem's series of rhetorical questions emphasizes the fact that the silence surrounding heterosexuality and violence is purchased at the price of demonizing other sexualities.

Some true-crime writers have denied that the genre is preoccupied by homosexual rather than heterosexual serial killers. Dennis McDougal, for example, in his book on California serial killer Randy Kraft, argues that homosexual serial killers actually get less attention than their heterosexual counterparts because the former are too horrible to contemplate. According to McDougal, "that men could do such things to other men was so far removed from the consciousness of mainstream America that the news media and, by extension, most middle-class Americans chose to ignore it altogether" (362). Ironically, the very existence of McDougal's book contradicts his claim and suggests instead the presence of a definite market for popular cultural representations of homosexual serial killers. Indeed, it would be far more accurate to say that the attention "mainstream America" pays to homosexual serial killers is obsessive. As David Hirsch suggests in summarizing the message of "serial-killer-of-the-week TV movies," this attention is so obsessive precisely because it is always combined with the covert aim of rallying support for heterosexuality: "Isn't it always the same story: missionary style only with your legally exogamous, intraracial, intergendered spouse; and woman (fags, dykes, and other transsexuals included), please stay quietly in your domestic closet" (443–44). I will demonstrate in this chapter that true-crime narratives about Ted Bundy, Jeffrey Dahmer, and Aileen Wuornos demonstrate exactly how these messages about hetero/homosexuality are articulated. In Bundy's case, the challenge of removing the implication of violence from heterosexuality is especially acute because Bundy was not only apparently normal but, in many ways, mainstream society's golden boy.

The Straight and Narrow: Ted Bundy

A discussion of Ted Bundy has become a standard feature of almost every popular and academic book about serial murder, and that is precisely why I must add to the countless retellings of his case. As Ann Rule has said, the term serial murder "seemed to have been coined for Ted Bundy" (*Stranger* 435), and there is no doubt that Bundy remains the exemplary American serial killer, the individual most likely to come to mind when the term "serial murder" is used. Bundy maintains his status as America's most famous serial killer partly because his exemplarity can be phrased in a variety of ways. For Robert Keppel, one of the investigators into the original "Ted" killings in Seattle in the mid-1970s, Bundy is an exemplary figure for law enforcement: "For police investigative purposes, his case is prototypical. There is no question that it remains the exemplar of what works, and what does not work, when local law-enforcement agencies are faced with the fact that some unknown subject, almost certainly a male, has begun to periodically murder people, usually women and children" (*Signature* v). For feminist critic Jane Caputi, Bundy is an exemplary figure in a very different way: "Just as Jack the Ripper seemed to personify the underside of Victorian England, so too Ted Bundy epitomized his society, presenting a persona of the superficially ideal, all-American boy" ("New" 4). In addition to Bundy's usefulness for law enforcement and his signifying "all-Americanness," there are two additional factors that give Bundy an exemplary role in my own discussion.

The first factor is Bundy's response to his celebrity status. Although he was initially resentful and disturbed by the intense media scrutiny given to his case, there are many signs that Bundy soon came to enjoy the attention. His refusal to consider a plea bargain in his Florida capital murder trial that could have saved his life, for example, along with his decision to represent himself in that trial can be read as a desire to take center stage in a drama in which he was the undisputed star. After his conviction, Bundy became even more conscious of his celebrity status, reportedly boasting to psychologist Dorothy Otnow Lewis, "Do you realize I am the most celebrated inmate on death row?" (quoted in Leiby 1). Bearing these points in mind, one cannot help but agree with Joyce Carol Oates when she imagines Bundy taking pride in all the books that have been written about him and "smiling as he reads, on the back of the paperback, that a reviewer for the *New York Times* has called him 'the most fascinating killer in modern American history'" (56).[1] Bundy's self-importance is bizarrely mirrored by the media's emphasis on how accomplished he was in his peculiar field. The unstable combining of admiration and condemnation that characterizes so much of the popular cultural response to Bundy is symptomatic of his second exemplary feature: Bundy presents the puzzling relationship between normality and abnormality in serial killers in a particularly concentrated form because of the apparent extreme contrast between his successful, ambitious, handsome, white, straight, Republican, male, middle-class exterior, and the "monster within."

This so-called contradiction in Bundy was a feature in writing about the case from its very earliest stages. In a December 1978 article in the *New York Times Magazine*, Jon Nordheimer emphasized how Bundy differed from the stereotype of mass killers:

> The stereotype of mass killers—with minds bedeviled by tumors or hallucinations —is all too familiar to the American public. They were the drifters, the malcontents, the failures and the resenters. Ted Bundy, for all appearances, in no way resembled any of them. He had all the personal resources that are prized in America, that guarantee success and respect. He loved children, read poetry, showed courage by chasing down and capturing a purse snatcher on the streets of Seattle, rescued a child from drowning, loved the outdoors, respected his parents, was a college honor student, worked with desperate people at a crisis center and, in the words of one admirer, "Ted could be with any woman he wanted—he was so magnetic!" (111)

The problem for true-crime writers became how to reconcile Bundy's all-American appearance with the fact that he was accused of the brutal murder of dozens of young women in a four-year, cross-country murder binge. As the remark of Ted's "admirer" indicates, the problem was exacerbated by the fact that Bundy was handsome and attractive to women. All through his trials, and even after he was sentenced to death, Bundy was a magnet for women who became known as "Ted groupies," who gave him both moral and financial support, and who claimed undying love for their hero. In other words, it was precisely the extent to which Bundy appeared to be a poster boy for dashing heterosexuality that necessitated a vigorous effort to prove that he was no such thing. His apparent heteronormativity would, paradoxically, become the defining feature of Bundy's deviance.

Normalizing Deviance/Deviating Normality

Ted Bundy had a complex relationship to the issue of his "normality." Part of him understood that his normality could be a useful disguise in the context of a large-scale murder investigation involving many suspects: "Which one do they pick? Do they pick the law student with no criminal background, who was probably even known by some of the prosecutors working the case? Or are they going to go after the types . . . you know, the guys in the files . . . the real weirdos?" (quoted in Michaud and Aynesworth, *Ted* 137). Although this anecdote suggests that normality is a facade hiding the reality of deviance, Bundy objected strenuously to juridical attempts to describe him in just this way: apparently normal but really deviant. Commenting on a psychological profile drawn up on him while in prison that described him as defensive, inse-cure, passive-aggressive, and dependent on women, Bundy argued that "there are probably tens of thousands of people in the city walking around . . . more or less like me. And as you told me, these characteristics are not predicted by anyone necessarily, because many people have them and are never violent, and there are many people who are violent who never have those character-istics" (quoted in Winn and Merrill 168). In emphasizing the relative nature of the concepts of "normality" and "deviance," Bundy hoped to avoid being classified by such terms.

Nevertheless, the longer Bundy remained in prison, the more resigned he became to being portrayed as superlatively deviant: "Because of my associa-tion with all these crimes, the experts refuse to perceive me as being, uh, even remotely—you know, anything that approaches being normal" (quoted in Michaud and Aynesworth, *Ted* 258). Although such comments demonstrate that Bundy was perceptive, to some extent at least, in identifying how the judi-cial system constructed him as a deviant subject, he apparently did not realize that the production of such deviance was based not on denying his normality, but rather on exaggerating that normality to the point where nothing could seem more deviant. What we might call the hyperbolizing of Bundy's normal-ity was necessary because he appeared to be so ordinary; his ordinariness had to be turned into the most compelling evidence of his difference from "really" ordinary men. I discussed in the previous chapter the techniques true-crime narratives have developed to turn the ordinary into the monstrous, and these are exactly the techniques used in true-crime work on Bundy. The "mask of sanity" image, for example, is omnipresent in writing about the Bundy case, as in this example from Myra McPherson: "Most serial killers are white, male, above average in intelligence, and adroit at wearing a mask of charm and sanity . . . Bundy wore the mask even better than most" (273).

Similarly, the strategy of searching for an originary sign of deviance in the serial killer's childhood can also be found in work on Bundy, where such signs establish the "fact" that the combination of a "surface" normality with a "real" deviance was Bundy's ultimate defining feature. In McPherson's work, the originary incident consisted of the three-year-old Bundy's slipping knives into his aunt's bed, an anecdote that I discussed in the previous chapter. When McPherson quotes the reaction of Dr. Dorothy Otnow Lewis when she heard this anecdote, we can see how valuable such an incident is to the effort of making Bundy unambiguously, always-already, deviant: "I was astonished that someone finally revealed how disturbed he'd been. We had been looking and looking for signs of pathology. I mean, you don't get this way by accident" (276). Although not all true-crime writers on Bundy zero in on a particular incident from his childhood, they all assume that the secret to Bundy is to be found in his earliest years.

For Ann Rule, the answer to the mystery represented by Bundy can be found by emphasizing how unusual and unstable his childhood was. Bundy was born out of wedlock to a mother who moved frequently, pretended to be his older sister, and had changed her son's name by both deed poll and her marriage before he was five years old. Rule argues that such a background contributed to what Bundy would become. According to Michaud and Aynesworth, by the time Bundy was a small child the die was already cast. Although Bundy "looked and acted like" other children, in fact "he was haunted by something else: a fear, a doubt . . . that inhabited his mind with the subtlety of a cat. He felt it for years and years, but he didn't recognize it for what it was until much later. By then this flaw, the rip in his psyche, had become the locus of a cold homicidal rage" (*Only* 47). When Michaud and Aynesworth go on to argue that Bundy's "critical challenge from his teen years onward was the perfection and maintenance of a credible public persona, his mask of sanity" (57), we see how the various strategies true-crime narratives use to make normality the best evidence of deviance work together to achieve this end. Although references to a knife-wielding three-year-old and a "mask of sanity" might seem to connote nothing but deviance, in fact these references work together to produce a powerful, albeit paradoxical, image of deviance that is defined by its appearance of normality.

One might feel that the "smoking gun" in Bundy's childhood that apparently explains his subsequent pathology is so vague in these true-crime narratives as to be practically nonexistent, but as Michaud and Aynesworth admit in a moment of unusual honesty in one of their two books about Bundy, *The Only Living Witness*, if no evidence of Bundy's monstrosity existed, true-crime writers simply would have to invent it. At one point in their account,

Michaud and Aynesworth quote Bob Dekle, the Florida assistant state's attorney who prosecuted Bundy for the murder of twelve-year-old Kimberly Leach, as saying, "People . . . think a criminal is a hunchbacked, cross-eyed little monster slithering through the dark, leaving a trail of slime. They're human beings" (*Only* 6). Michaud and Aynesworth attempt to undermine Dekle's assertion of Bundy's humanity by arguing that "within Ted Bundy, human being, that slithering hunchback lives . . . In Ted, the cross-eyed creature lurks on a different plane of existence and can only be seen by means of a tautology; its presence must be inferred before it can be found" (6). Michaud and Aynesworth's remarks are typical of true-crime accounts of Bundy in that the only way they can get around the problem of Bundy's ordinariness is to assume the presence of the extraordinary, of the monstrous, and then go looking for it, comforted by the thought that Bundy's apparent normality is just that, an apparition, with no stability next to the reliable solidity of the monster.[2]

The insistence on Bundy's monstrosity in true-crime narratives about his case has the same function as the carnivalesque atmosphere that surrounded his execution in January 1989. As the scheduled time for the execution approached, a large crowd gathered outside the prison, laughing, cheering, and waving banners bearing slogans such as "Bundy BBQ," "I like my Ted well done," and "Fry, Bundy, Fry." Jane Caputi has explained the intensity of the hatred directed toward Bundy as a consequence of his doing "the supremely unmanly thing of confessing to his crimes and manifesting fear of death" ("New" 5), but I find Joseph Grixti's interpretation of the celebratory crowd more persuasive: "The crowd, echoing as it did some of the symbolic functions performed by the torch-waving crowds that so frequently rose to destroy the monster at the climax of horror movies in the 1930s, partly reflected a firm determination not to lose sight of the murderer as outsider—an unnatural growth that society had finally recognized for what it was and was now dealing with accordingly" (89). Bundy is the contemporary equivalent of Frankenstein's monster: something we have made that has to be destroyed to protect ourselves from the knowledge of our own involvement in the creation of monsters.

Although it is important to emphasize the ways in which Bundy was vilified, the public and true-crime reaction to Ted Bundy was not exclusively condemnatory. Indeed, when we look at the ways in which the public expressed its admiration for Bundy, we will see much more clearly why his apparent normality seemed to have particularly troubling implications for normative heterosexuality, for the public often perceived Bundy as an especially roguish example of that classic straight stereotype: the ladies' man. For example, when Bundy escaped from jail in Aspen, Colorado, in 1977, where he was awaiting trial for a series of murders, having already been convicted of attempted kidnapping in Utah, "T-shirts appeared reading: 'Ted Bundy is a One Night Stand.' Radio KSNO programmed a Ted Bundy Request Hour, playing songs like 'Ain't No Way to Treat a Lady.' A local restaurant offered a 'Bundyburger' consisting of nothing more than a plain roll. 'Open it and see the meat has fled,' explained a sign" (Caputi, *Age* 50–51). These reactions illustrate how many were tempted to identify with Bundy's outlaw-like exploits, or at least to make light of them. Given the extent to which Bundy was being identified as a representative (that is, hypersexual, irresponsible, exploitative in his relationships with women, contemptuous of the law) straight man, it became imperative for true-crime narratives to compensate for the public reaction by proving that he was no such thing, and to emphasize instead that Ted Bundy was an aberration that told us nothing about heterosexuality at all.

Expertise and/in Serial Killing

Not all examples of admiration for Bundy were as direct as those seen in Colorado. A more indirect and much more frequent type of admiration is a common feature of true-crime narratives about the case, namely, the tendency to regard Bundy as a, perhaps the, expert on serial murder. There is evidence that Bundy thought of himself in this way from an early stage of his protracted journey through the legal system. Nordheimer, in his 1978 article, quotes from a letter written by Bundy in which he says, "Prosecutors, policemen, journalists, old girlfriends, friends and family of 'the victims,' psychologists, psychiatrists, ex-roommates, former teachers and defense attorneys have all ventured opinions, observations and assorted drivel about this mysterious creature. I think it's my turn. I am, after all, the ultimate Bundy expert" (111). At this point, Bundy was a self-appointed expert and little more, but by the time he reached the end of his capital trial in Florida, he was already in the process of being rehabilitated, in a manner of speaking, by the representatives of law and order. Immediately after sentencing him to death, Judge Edward Cowart addressed the following extraordinary remarks to Bundy: "You're a bright young man. You'd have made a good lawyer, and I'd have loved to have you practice in front of me—but you went another way, partner. Take care of yourself. I don't have any animosity to you. I want you to know that" (quoted in Rule, *Stranger* 394). Despite the fact that he had just sentenced Bundy to death for the brutal murders he committed in the Chi Omega Sorority House, and despite the fact that Bundy had been a conspicuous failure as a law student and had made errors during his trial that undoubtedly damaged his defense, Cowart could not resist the temptation to do a little male bonding before Bundy was taken to death row. In particular, Cowart's comment about Bundy's promise as a lawyer was just the first sign of the authority that Bundy would arrogate to himself and be given by others while he waited to be executed.

Appropriately, true-crime writers played a central role in bestowing expert status upon Bundy. This expert status existed in a mutually supportive relationship with Bundy's fame. In other words, Bundy's fame was another contributing factor in his acquisition of expert status, and his status as an expert increased his fame even more. What role did true-crime narratives play in creating this pernicious dialectic? In their 1989 book *Ted Bundy: Conversations with a Killer*, Michaud and Aynesworth describe how they came up with the idea of having Bundy talk about his crimes in the third person, in an attempt to get him to be more forthcoming about those crimes. Michaud and Aynesworth hoped that by enabling him to distance himself from his acts, this grammatical sleight of hand would encourage Bundy to open up to them. But Michaud and Aynesworth were also aware that their plan pandered to Bundy's inflated sense of self-importance, and this is exactly what they used as a selling point for the idea when they explained it to Bundy: "You're the expert, Ted. You know the cases. You know the investigations. You're the suspect. Who else is in a better position to pull this all together?" (59). Not surprisingly, the idea appealed to Bundy, and although some might argue that allowing Bundy to assume the role of expert was a small price to pay for the information he shared about his crimes, others might argue that granting someone like Bundy expert status licenses him to take pride in his grisly "accomplishments."

Thanks partly to such arrangements, in the twelve years he spent on death row before his execution in 1989, Bundy "enjoyed his assumed status as the world's foremost authority on serial murder. It flattered his outsized ego that so many psychiatrists, reporters, and writers were interested in interviewing him" (*Serial* 42). How can we explain this intense interest in Bundy's thoughts about serial murder and his elevation to a position of authority about the subject? In his lecture on the "dangerous individual," Michel Foucault describes the necessity for the dangerous criminal to produce a certain kind of discourse about himself: "Beyond admission, there must be confession, self-examination, explanation of oneself, revelation of what one is ... The magistrates and the jurors, the lawyers too, and the department of the public prosecutor, cannot really play their role unless they are provided with another type of discourse, the one given by the accused about himself, or the one which he makes possible for others, through his confessions, memories, intimate disclosures, etc." (126–27). From this perspective, we could argue that an individual such as Bundy is encouraged to produce discourse about himself and others of his kind both to increase public knowledge about the issue of serial murder and to emphasize how necessary it is to punish such a dangerous criminal. Allowing Bundy to become an expert, in other words, functions as an indirect way of producing justifications of why he must be put to death. It is certainly true that Bundy's expert status did not always work in his favor. Robert Keppel, for example, has described how he was able to use Bundy's arrogance about his supreme status among serial killers to extract valuable information from him, both about his own murders and about other ongoing cases, such as the Green River murders (*Riverman* 216, 225). In a similar vein, Polly Nelson, Bundy's death penalty appeal lawyer, has claimed that her attempts to defend Bundy were hampered by his cooperation with the FBI (159ff.). Clearly, Bundy was seduced by the notion that the FBI would come to him for help, and he agreed to work with them even though it hurt his case.

Although it is tempting to argue that Bundy was encouraged to consider himself an expert on serial murder in order to create situations where he might confess unambiguously to his crimes (something he never did), I think it far more accurate to claim that Bundy's authoritative status expressed the indirect admiration of law enforcement personnel, true-crime writers, and many of their readers for an individual who occupied a superlative place in the pantheon of serial killers. Indeed, this veiled admiration for serial killers is a feature not just of true-crime narratives about Ted Bundy but of true-crime narratives about serial murder in general, many examples of which feature an emphasis on the superlative aspects of a killer's crimes.[3] In many instances, this emphasis on superlativeness, on individual serial killers as the best or greatest of their kind, extends even to homosexual serial killers, in the process often canceling out the genre's generally condemnatory attitude toward homosexuality. In *Angel of Darkness*, for example, Dennis McDougal is at pains to emphasize that Randy Kraft killed so many men that he deserves the title of the most prolific, and therefore the worst, serial killer ever. Similarly, Joel Norris has argued that Jeffrey Dahmer is much worse than other serial killers, almost as if serial murder was a competition. With this said, it must also be emphasized that gay and lesbian serial killers are never allowed to have the same expert status as someone like Bundy, or, to put it another way, gay and lesbian serial killers are not allowed the same kind of fame as straight serial killers like Bundy.

This claim can be demonstrated by a brief discussion of Andrew Cunanan, whose murder of fashion designer Gianni Versace in 1997 made headlines around the world and set off an avalanche of media coverage. With so much attention paid to the manhunt for Cunanan, which came to an end when he was found dead in a houseboat in Miami, he could not help but become a star, but a star of a very particular kind. As with Jeffrey Dahmer, as we will see in more detail later, the vast majority of media coverage of Cunanan was framed by an assumed connection between homosexuality and violence. Matthew Soar explains: "Common references to Cunanan as the 'gay serial killer' . . . and even a 'homicidal homosexual' . . . were emblematic of a slew of claims that articulated Cunanan's sexuality with his violent actions, often through conspicuous references to sadomasochistic sex" (50). We should certainly not be surprised by this feature of media coverage about the case, but the coverage of Gianni Versace was much more complex. As Soar puts it, "the *murderer's* gayness was treated as uniformly and overwhelmingly problematic, *the* core factor in his descent," whereas "one victim's gayness, when articulated to wealth, would be seen as thoroughly innocuous, if not innocent" (49, original emphasis). The fact that Versace was already famous when he was murdered protected him from being blamed, like so many other gay murder victims, for contributing to his own death. As a consequence, not only was Cunanan's fame diminished, becoming something much more akin to notoriety (as Gary Indiana has put it, media coverage of the case tended to follow the pattern established by the Kennedy assassination, "world's most important person slain by world's least important person" [241]), but also Cunanan's other victims tended to be ignored, their deaths seen as relatively unimportant next to that of Versace. In this way, "the narrative made it clear that only celebrities have real lives" (Indiana 242).

But although Versace's wealth and fame saved him from condemnation as a gay murder victim, this does not mean that his gayness survived unscathed. Rebecca Farley explains that, in order for Versace to signify as an "innocent" victim, his gayness had to be eliminated: "In life, Versace's (gay) body was transgressive; in death it was mutilated. By leaving the (transgressive, dead) body out altogether, Versace's narrative became a prosocial tale of capitalist success, a handsome, benign family man destroyed by the 'evil' of a perverted gay lifestyle" (2). In this way, the association between gayness and perverted violence could be reinforced. At the same time, and to the extent that, as I argued in the introduction, celebrity and transgression are always connected, Cunanan's murder of Versace sent the comforting message that "such violent deaths do not occur in our everyday reality, but rather can safely be relegated to a realm beyond the normal—to the world of fashion rock stars and celebrity killers" (Bronfen, "Celebrating" 178). Fame thus maintains its complexly ambivalent status as both desirable goal and social dysfunction in contemporary American culture.

These efforts to demonize Cunanan and exonerate Versace were greatly facilitated by Cunanan's suicide, and the same might be said of Dahmer's murder in prison in November 1994. Even before his death, however, it must be emphasized that Dahmer's fame was qualitatively different from Bundy's. The collective unwillingness to turn Dahmer into an expert on serial murder meant that, like Cunanan, Dahmer was more notorious than famous, and this explains the widespread perception that poetic justice, at least, had been served when Dahmer was killed. Perhaps we will not allow killers like Dahmer to become experts on serial murder because we do not want to hear what they have to tell us, or perhaps it is because we assume that whatever they have to say would pertain only to queerness and thus have no relevance to an implicitly straight "us." The corollary to this assumption, of course, is that Bundy is allowed to be famous and to be an expert because we assume that what he says applies not to heterosexuality in general but rather only to the thoroughly aberrant, individualized mutation of heterosexuality personified by Bundy. And so, by a somewhat circuitous route, we have come back to the necessity for asserting the mutual exclusivity of heterosexuality and violence in true-crime narratives about serial murder.

The assertion of this mutual exclusivity can take a number of forms. One is a denial of the hatred of women as a motive for serial murder, because admitting the existence of such a motive would make it more difficult to distinguish serial killers from other groups of men who commit crimes of violence against women.[4] In *To Kill Again*, for example, Donald Sears claims that "it is somewhat misleading . . . to say that serial killers commit their crimes because of a hatred of women" (72). In a similar vein, Kathy McCarthy quotes psychologist Helen Morrison in the course of arguing that "the killer's motive—and an internal motive exists—is 'highly irrational, highly disorganized,' never so simple as 'I hate women' or 'I hate prostitutes'" (24). In developing a more "accurate" sense of a straight serial killer's motive, true-crime writers do not necessarily come up with something excessively outré; rather, their inclination is to choose ordinary motives that can be safely individualized. In accounts of Ted Bundy, for example, the motives most often adduced as explanations for his behavior are resentment at being illegitimate and being rejected by a woman he was in love with. The accuracy of these motives is, in a sense, beside the point; what is most germane about them from the true-crime writer's point of view is that they apply only to Ted Bundy's individual life circumstances and thus cannot be applied to all heterosexual men. In the process, any suggestion that Bundy might represent a "type," that is, heterosexual men, is rigorously removed from the discourse of true crime. In true-crime narratives, Bundy never represents anyone other than himself—only in this way can he be rendered safe for consumption by the straight male reader.

If "ordinary" heterosexual men appear at all in true crime, it is in the guise of the police. Their horrified reactions to serial murder allow them to stand in for "normal" heterosexual men, thereby further distancing serial killers from that norm. In *Lust Killer*, for example, Ann Rule argues that "what had happened to Linda Salee enraged normal men. Especially police officers. If they could not have saved her, they would now find her killer and hand him over to the judicial system" (90). At such moments in true-crime narratives, the police are figured as men with a properly chivalrous and protective attitude toward women. It is also important to establish a relationship between the victim and the police because, as Richard Tithecott has argued, "when, as in the case of Ted Bundy, the victims and killer are assumed to be heterosexual, our tendency is not to group victim and killer together and exclude them from us, but to figure the victim as representative of our world, our civilization, and to figure the killer as a senseless monster from without or below" (73). The police therefore do double duty in true-crime accounts of straight serial killers: they represent ordinary men and they also rescue the victim from any imputation that she facilitated her own murder (except, of course, if the victim is a prostitute, in which case, male attitudes toward the victim are markedly less chivalrous).

Although the true-crime techniques I have discussed thus far are important ones in asserting the mutual exclusivity of heterosexuality and violence, by far the most successful technique is simply not mentioning heterosexuality at all. It is truly extraordinary that the heterosexuality of straight serial killers is never commented on by true-crime writers. Instead, as Tithecott argues, although the actions of "'straight killers' are considered to arise from an inability to control themselves sexually . . . because heterosexuality is naturalized, it is the (individual) killer's inability to control himself which is condemned, not his sexuality and not the 'lifestyles' which are considered as essential to that sexuality. The heterosexuality of a 'heterosexual killer' mostly *goes without saying*" (73, original emphasis). The true-crime treatment of Jeffrey Dahmer presents a very different situation. In Dahmer's case, as with other "gay killers," it is precisely his sexuality and the "gay lifestyle" that are condemned for contributing to and in many ways being practically identical with serial murder.[5]

Queerness and/as Violence

Richard Tithecott has neatly summarized the appeal of the Dahmer case to a heteronormative culture: "For a heterosexual culture, the Dahmer case represents an opportunity to explain acts of savagery by referring to his putative homosexuality, to confuse homicidal with homosexual tendencies, confuse 'sexual homicide' with homo sex" (73). True crime is one of the most influential media in which this association of homosexuality with violence takes place in contemporary American society, but obviously it did not inaugurate this association. True crime is just the latest instance of a long and ignoble history of equating homosexuality and violence, and I want to reconstruct some of the main points of this history before going on to demonstrate how true-crime coverage of the Dahmer case represents a continuation of this history.

In *Death, Desire, and Loss in Western Culture*, Jonathan Dollimore comments that "notions of death have been at the heart of nearly every historical construction of same-sex desire" (329–30). Although the association between homosexuality, violence, and death is ancient, it is possible to distinguish forces that have been particularly influential in developing this association in modern America. One such force is psychoanalysis, which developed a sharp, moralistic disapproval of homosexuality, particularly after 1945. As Henry Abelove has noted, Freud's position on homosexuality was in many ways quite liberal. He did not believe it was an illness; he did not think homosexuals should be prosecuted or that homosexuality should be regarded as a disgrace, and he argued that "no homosexual needed to be treated psychoanalytically unless he also, and quite incidentally, happened to be neurotic" (59–60). Although Freud's opinions about homosexuality were not adopted enthusiastically by any of his followers, it was in America that opposition was most intense: "From the very beginning of the transplantation of psychoanalysis onto these shores, American analysts have tended to view homosexuality with disapproval and have actually wanted to get rid of it altogether" (Abelove 62).

Most frequently, American psychoanalysts express this disapproval by finding a variety of ways to associate homosexuality with violence, whether it is by noting aggressive behavior in passive effeminate boys (MacDonald), by finding a "natural" association between homosexuality and crime (McHenry), by viewing homosexuality as a form of psychic masochism or welcoming of aggression (Bergler), or by claiming that the homosexual has a "natural" propensity toward violence, as in this comment from Charles Berg and Clifford Allen's 1958 book *The Problem of Homosexuality*: "The homosexual, by the very nature of his psychological make-up, his unresolved Oedipus complex and so on, has a great deal of aggression which is normally repressed but which, given suitable circumstances, will burst out into unexpected violence" (59). But as Abelove explains, by far the most detailed American psychoanalytic demonization of homosexuality can be found in the work of Charles Socarides:

> He argued, in a series of pieces published mostly in the 1960s, that homosexuality was in fact a severe illness, accompanied often by such psychotic manifestations as schizophrenia or manic-depressive mood swings. While heterosexual pairings could make for "cooperation, solace, stimulation, enrichment, healthy challenge and fulfillment," homosexual pairings could bring only "destruction, mutual defeat,

exploitation of the partner and the self, oral-sadistic incorporation, aggressive on-slaughts, attempts to alleviate anxiety, and a pseudo-solution to the aggressive and libidinal urges which dominate and torture the individual." (67)[6]

Such views influenced American opinion about homosexuality well outside the narrow circles of psychoanalytic practitioners. For example, in a 1951 ex-posé entitled *Terror in the Streets*, designed to maximize public panic about an epidemic of violent crime in American cities, Howard Whitman describes the problem of the "homosexual prowler": "he is, if you will, the sex-deviated version of what we colloquially call the 'wolf.' Instead of going on the prowl for females, he goes on the prowl for boys and men. He accosts and inveigles them in the cheap movie houses; he makes a flagrant display of himself in the public lavatories; he infests the most beautiful public parks, making them repugnant and fearsome to decent citizens. Police know that such men are dangerous—that when trapped, they may kill" (147–48). Although Whitman later dis-tinguishes the prowlers from the "many thousands of homosexuals who lead their own, private, unaggressive lives" (163), it is reasonable to assume that it is the vivid picture of the vampiric, wolflike, altogether monstrous prowler that will stick in the straight reader's mind as a representative homosexual.[7]

Although psychoanalytic discourse about homosexuality is one influence on the tendency of true crime to link homosexuality and violence, a more recent and more virulent (in every sense) influence is the AIDS epidemic, which has provided writers with a potent metaphor for the lethality of gay men, enabling the linking together of homosexuality, AIDS, and violence in an associative chain.[8] Part of the power of this chain and part of the reason that it came together so quickly is the fact that, as Simon Watney has put it, "Aids has been mobilised to a prior agenda of issues concerning the kind of society we wish to inhabit" (*Policing* 3). To the extent that gay men are always-already abject in a heterosexual culture, linking them with death seemed the natural thing to do. In this sense, representations of deadly gay AIDS carriers, while appearing to be novel, are in fact nothing of the kind. As Ellis Hanson explains, a peculiarly late-Victorian conception of vampirism drives many of the representations of gay men with AIDS: "I am talking about essentialist representations of gay men as vampiric: as sexually exotic, alien, unnatural, oral, anal, compulsive, violent, protean, polymorphic, polysemous, invisible, soulless, transient, superhumanly mobile, infectious, murderous, suicidal, and a threat to wife, children, home, and phallus" (325). In short, as Leo Bersani has argued, "Nothing has made gay men more visible than AIDS" (19), a pathologized visibility that has cast gay men in heterosexual culture as sick, infected, wasted bodies, the object of a fascinated and horrified straight gaze.[9]

Dahmer's Closet

The straight gaze that assumes a correlation between homosexuality and violence takes many forms in true-crime narratives about Jeffrey Dahmer, some more subtle than others. For example, the assumption appears in a description of Dahmer's apartment where the physical proximity between evidence of his sexual preference and evidence of his murders is taken to stand for the proximity of homosexuality and violence: "In the bathroom, where, Dahmer confessed, he had dismembered many of his victims, a picture of a nude male was taped next to the mirror. In the bedroom, on top of a dresser, were a television, a beer can, and a pornographic male homosexual videotape. The top dresser drawer contained about thirty Polaroid photos taken by Dahmer at various stages of his victims' deaths" (A. Schwartz 9). This juxtaposition of homosexuality and violence can be found in other accounts of serial murderers of men, as in Jack Olsen's description of the 1973 Dean Corll–Elmer Wayne Henley murders in Houston, Texas. At one point, Olsen reports a conversation between Lieutenant Breck Porter and Dorothy Hilligeist, in which Porter tells Hilligeist that her son David has been found buried along with many other victims, "'Well, what's *happening* out there?' the shocked woman asked. 'It looks like a homosexual thing,' Lieutenant Porter said. 'We haven't even figured it out ourself yet, but it looks like these clowns were molestin' young boys and then killin' 'em'" (118, original emphasis). It is fair to assume that if the police had found the bodies of young women, they would not have referred to the murders as a "heterosexual thing."

Part of the reason for this linking of homosexuality and violence in true crime is that true-crime writers often adopt a law enforcement perspective when discussing queer lifestyles and cultures. Richard Tithecott has described this perspective as "anthropological" (67), and the term is apt because it captures the fact that the audience for true crime is assumed to be both straight and receptive to a presentation of gay culture as outlandishly different.[10] For an example of the law enforcement perspective, consider Anne Schwartz's account of one of the most infamous incidents surrounding the Dahmer case, namely, the police's inadvertent return of one of Dahmer's victims, a Laotian boy named Konerak Sinthasomphone, to Dahmer. Sinthasomphone had escaped from Dahmer's apartment when Dahmer went out to get some beer, and neighbors saw Sinthasomphone running down the street, naked and bleeding. The police were called and they arrived at about the same time that Dahmer returned with his beer. After talking with Dahmer (Sinthasomphone was too incoherent to speak, because Dahmer had drugged him), the officers concluded that this was nothing more than a gay lovers' tiff, and they returned Sinthasomphone to Dahmer, who murdered him later that night.

When this incident was made public, community activists charged that it typified the inferior quality of police service given to the minority and queer populations of Milwaukee. In discussing this incident, Schwartz (who, perhaps not incidentally, is married to a Milwaukee police officer) argues that the officers did nothing wrong and that there was no reason to suspect any foul play on Dahmer's part. Schwartz explains the notorious radio message, "My partner's gonna get deloused at the station," sent by one of the police officers to the precinct station after Sinthasomphone had been returned to Dahmer, as being literally true, explaining that police officers often do need to get cleaned up and even deloused during a shift (93–94). Because of her uncritical adoption of the law enforcement point of view, Schwartz neither accepts that the remark could possibly have been motivated by racism and homophobia nor challenges the view that a drugged and bleeding adolescent is a common and unexceptionable part of a "gay lovers' tiff."

The assumption that extreme violence is a normal part of homosexuality can also be found in true-crime accounts of serial killers other than Dahmer. For example, in their book *Murder in Mind*, Clark and Morley describe approvingly the unwillingness of a police officer investigating accusations against Kansas City serial killer Robert Berdella to assume foul play, even though there was abundant evidence to do so: "Cole admitted that he was not sure at the time whether they were not simply looking at a homosexual lovers' quarrel that had gone too far. The scars to the man's body indicated torture, but he may have consented to that torture as part of a sado-masochistic relationship, or he might even have been paid for it as a prostitute. This functional detective would not believe anything, unless it was proved to him beyond a shadow of a doubt" (254–55). Incredibly, Clark and Morley go on to describe how this "functional detective" realized the seriousness of the case only when they dug up a human skull in the backyard: "I thought, yeah, there probably is something more to this than just a lovers' quarrel" (256). Such remarks speak volumes about the level of violence that is assumed to be an ordinary part of homosexuality.

Such perspectives on homosexuality, although disturbing, can seem positively benign compared with moments in true-crime work when homosexuality and homosexuals are explicitly demonized and vilified, both as murderers and as victims. The assumed link between homosexuality and violence is often invoked to explain why male-on-male murders are so much worse than "regular" murders of women by men.[11] In his book on Randy Kraft, McDougal explains that heterosexual murderers "beat up on each other, shot each other, stabbed and strangled and slapped each other. But they rarely went in for torture or dismemberment," qualities that McDougal claims define gay murders (81). But worse than this, according to McDougal, is the fact that, in gay murders, the dividing line between sexual activity and murder is so fragile: "Heterosexuals did it too, of course: tying each other up and going through crazy rituals of submission and punishment . . . But when it came to body dumps of nude young males, raped and maimed at the hands of another, it could generally be traced back to a lover whose anger or ecstasy—or both— got out of hand" (81).[12]

This argument that not only is there a link between homosexuality and violence but homosexual sexual activity is *by definition* either closely related to, or actually is, violence is encapsulated by one of the most controversial aspects of the Dahmer case—the use of the term "homosexual overkill" to describe Dahmer's murders. This term, originally coined by Milwaukee County medical examiner Jeffrey M. Jentzen in 1990 to describe another local murder case, was supposedly meant to indicate the "objective" fact that Dahmer used more force than was necessary to kill his victims, but it is clear that the term says more about social attitudes toward homosexuality than about Dahmer's killing methods. In fact, Dahmer's characteristic method of first drugging his victims into unconsciousness, then strangling and dismembering them is relatively humane compared with the extreme sexual sadism that characterizes many serial murderers of women. Moreover, it is in fact more accurate to use the term "homosexual overkill" to describe murders of gay men or lesbians that are motivated by homophobia. Gary David Comstock notes that homicides with homosexual victims often show "evidence of overkill and excessive mutilation. In a study of autopsy findings by physicians, one psychiatrist stated that 'multiple and extensive wounds are not uncommon in the fury of' anti-homosexual murder" (47).[13] These points indicate how inconsistently the term "overkill" is applied. As the National Gay and Lesbian Task Force asked, in a statement issued a week after Dahmer's arrest, "When, for example, has the term 'heterosexual overkill' been used to describe the serial killing of women by a male perpetrator?" (quoted in A. Schwartz 174).

The Guilty Victims

The demonization of queerness in true-crime work on male-on-male murders is not limited to the perpetrators but also extends to the victims of these crimes. Blaming the victim is a time-honored tradition in true-crime work about the serial murder of women, especially where the victims are prostitutes, working-class, poor women and/or women of color, and this tradition has carried over to discussions of the male victims of male serial murderers. For example, Anne Schwartz argues that "all of Jeffrey Dahmer's victims facilitated him in some way" and that "their life-styles and unnecessary risk-taking contributed to their deaths." Schwartz, rather than feeling some compassion for the victims or understanding of the social milieu they inhabited, states that "the youths who left gay bars with men they didn't know were leading lives full of risks and, in the end, were killed as a result of their own negligence and recklessness. They were looking for nameless, faceless sex" (115). One could not find a clearer example of the relative exoneration of the murderer and the placing of responsibility on the shoulders of the victims for their own deaths.

The issue of how the victims of male-on-male serial murders are represented, however, is more complicated than Schwartz's remarks suggest. Even though we find true-crime writers blaming Dahmer's victims, homosexuality is apparently thought to be so bad, to be such a stigma on one's character, that we also find these same writers attempting to relieve some of the victims from the taint of homosexuality. For example, Ed Baumann in his account of the Dahmer case, *Step into My Parlor*, describes one of Dahmer's victims, Oliver Lacy, as being "all boy," an ambiguous phrase under the circumstances (65). At another point, Baumann is assured by the girlfriend of another victim, David Thomas, that Thomas was not homosexual, "'No way,' she insisted. 'That's not David'" (162). A corollary of this attitude is that a male-on-male serial murder case becomes more serious when there are heterosexual victims. For example, when McDougal discusses Randy Kraft's murder of Ronnie Wiebe, who was "definitely not a homosexual," he claims that Wiebe's death "took the entire investigation out of the realm of gays killing gays and put it into a more general arena: anybody who happened to be male, young, and naive enough to get sucked into whatever scam these killers were laying on their prey was susceptible" (83). These kinds of attitudes are no improvement over blaming the victim. Writers such as Baumann and McDougal would probably still find gay victims culpable, while at the same time exonerating heterosexual victims.

The problem with the way that homosexuality and violence are represented in true-crime work is that such work rarely gives more positive representations of gay lifestyles and cultures. The closest that many true-crime accounts of Dahmer come to presenting a more sympathetic perspective on homosexuality is when they discuss the impact of Dahmer's murders on Milwaukee's gay community.[14] However, even if true crime does occasionally elucidate the climate of prejudice that exists in Milwaukee toward queer communities, there is still a tendency for this work to divorce Dahmer himself from these social dynamics and instead to present him as essentially mysterious. Dvorchak and Holewa, in a chapter of their book *Milwaukee Massacre* revealingly entitled "Mystery Man," claim that "no one may ever know how a man who worked and mingled among the masses could script his own real-life *Silence of the Lambs* and do things that might startle the fictional Hannibal the Cannibal" (28). Similarly, Joel Norris writes that "the mystery that Jeffrey Dahmer embodied when he was arrested the previous year would still remain a mystery as Dahmer was escorted out of the courtroom by the officers" (8).

This emphasis on mystery is clearly designed to foreclose the possibility of putting forward an interpretation of serial murder that focuses on how our understanding of it is produced by complex interactions of institutional and discursive social practices that together make up the overdetermined phenomenon of serial murder. Instead, the emphasis on mystery encourages a view of serial murder as the individualized expression of an aberrant personality. What is especially interesting in Dahmer's case (and in the cases of other serial murderers of men) is that it is his homosexuality, and the precise relation of his homosexuality to his murders, that is left a mystery by true-crime writers. For example, it is notable that in a discussion that is distinguished by a high degree of detail about such areas of Dahmer's life as his childhood, Norris is curiously reticent about Dahmer's homosexuality and his deep ambivalence about it. According to the reports of his probation officer and Brother John Paul Ranieri, who at the time Dahmer was arrested ran an informal counseling service for gay people in a bar called the Wreck Room in Milwaukee, Dahmer was deeply conflicted about his sexual preference and agonized about whether or not he was really gay (J. Norris 241). One might argue that by mentioning this point Norris acknowledges, albeit implicitly, the role of internalized homophobia in the Dahmer case, but he does so in an extremely limited sense. Even if true-crime writers identify Dahmer's guilt about his homosexuality as a motive for the murders, they do so in a way that is appealing to a homophobic audience. The unspoken argument is that to be homosexual is so disgusting and traumatic that of course one would murder again and again in order to assuage one's guilt about being gay.

A more productive, and less homophobic, aim for true crime would be to explain why Dahmer felt ambivalent about his homosexuality or why he hated other homosexuals. Examination of these issues in true crime has the potential to correct some of the biases of the genre, but rarely does, simply because gay self-hatred can be acknowledged but never analyzed in detail. Instead, true-crime writers such as Norris present Dahmer's conflicted sense of gayness as a fait accompli and imply that it therefore requires no comment. The reason for this silence is that to explore the sources of Dahmer's conflicted homosexuality would involve acknowledging both the familial (Dahmer's father was virulently homophobic) and social context of widespread homophobia. If anything, true-crime narratives imply that self-loathing is a perfectly understandable feeling in a homosexual (indeed, this feeling is the closest many true-crime writers come to empathizing with their subjects). Thus, the treatment of gay self-hatred in true crime contributes to the genre's tendency to place the killer's homosexuality at the very center of why they kill, whereas heterosexuality is never implicated in the same way.

These failings in true crime are even more serious given the fact that there is evidence to suggest that many "gay serial killers" share both Dahmer's ambivalence about being homosexual and his growing up in a homophobic environment. John Wayne Gacy's insistence on being bisexual, not homosexual, for instance, may have something to do with the fact that "when Gacy was arrested for the murders, his mother told the police that if her husband had known that his son had sex with men he would have killed him" (Wilkinson 61). Similarly, in *Freed to Kill*, her book about Larry Eyler, a serial killer active in the mid-1980s, Gera-Lind Kolarik describes how, upon his initial arrest in 1983, Eyler was far more willing to talk about murder than about his homosexuality (96, 98). David Bergman has pointed out that "within the patriarchy, violence between men is more acceptable than affection between them" (143), and this seems to be an attitude many "gay serial killers" have internalized.

Reading between the lines, one can infer from Kolarik's account that the police interviewing Eyler also felt more comfortable discussing his violence than his sexual orientation. Despite the many differences in how true crime represents "straight" and "gay" male serial killers, there is a common thread, a further unspoken assumption: a violent man occasions no surprise in our culture. Although the explanations for that violence vary according to the man's sexual orientation, true-crime narratives take for granted the fact that men have the potential to be violent in much the same way that they take the heterosexuality of straight serial killers for granted. If we now turn to a discussion of Aileen Wuornos, we will see that part of the intensely negative reaction to Wuornos (a reaction that continued right up until her execution in October 2002) can be explained by another example of an assumed mutual exclusivity, not between heterosexuality and violence, but between femininity and violence.

Aileen Wuornos Is Not a Woman

Thanks to the assumption that women and violence are mutually exclusive, when women do act violently, they are often rhetorically excluded from womanhood, especially when they murder (their own) children. Similarly, to the extent that hegemonic definitions of womanhood are heterosexual, a lesbian also violates the code of womanhood, and consequently a violent lesbian violates that code even more seriously. Bearing these points of mind, we can begin to see how overdetermined the popular and true-crime response to the crimes of Aileen Wuornos was, but this is just part of the story, because even among the relatively small population of violent (lesbian) women, Wuornos was highly unusual.

In general, violent women have attracted nothing but punishment in American culture, and very often disproportionate punishment. L. Kay Gillespie has described how capital punishment for women in the United States dates back to executions of women aboard ships bound for the colonies in the 1600s. Although executions usually involved hanging, women, as a rule, were not hanged. Rather, Gillespie explains, "boiling, garroting, burning, and other means were believed to be far better methods of execution for women since it was believed women were less sensitive to pain and required something more drastic" (1). For many years, lesbians were not singled out for especially vicious treatment simply because the category of lesbianism did not exist. With that said, there is abundant evidence to suggest that, just as with the association of homosexuality and violence, the assertion of a correlation between lesbianism and violence has a long history.

In *Sapphic Slashers*, her study of the murder of Freda Ward by her lover, Alice Mitchell, in Memphis, Tennessee, in 1892, Lisa Duggan demonstrates how the case, even though it featured "neither clearly 'lesbian' characters nor explicitly sexual relations between women," was still "sold" as a "lesbian love murder story" (153). According to Duggan, the Mitchell case "marked the emergence of a new recognizably American type—the mannish lesbian or invert" (154). The Mitchell case lent itself well to sensationalist treatment, partly because of the brutality of the crime (Mitchell slashed Ward's throat in broad daylight in downtown Memphis), partly because prominent families were involved, but mostly because of the involvement of two women, a phenomenon that "presented an astonishing and confusing twist that confounded the gendered roles of villain and victim" (46). The fact that the press was able to find and resurrect similar cases from the past lent even more credence to the idea that Mitchell represented a type, rather than being an aberrational individual, and when Lizzie Borden was arrested and charged with the murder of her father and stepmother on the day Mitchell left for the Tennessee state asylum, it was the final ingredient that assured widespread dissemination of news about the Mitchell case and intense speculation about what had caused the sudden outbreak of violent women.

Alice Mitchell represents an example of the earliest stages of the conflation of lesbianism and violence. Estelle Freedman provides us with a more recent example taken, not coincidentally, from the 1950s, a decade of acute concern about the fragility of traditional gender roles for women. Freedman describes how the image of the aggressive female homosexual was initially associated with African American women, but after World War II the image was extended to include white working-class prisoners. Particularly influential during this period was a series of Hollywood-produced women's prison films (such as *Caged* [1950]) that depicted "a dangerously aggressive lesbian criminal" who "threatened the innocence of young women" (404). Freedman argues that the "association of lesbianism and criminality may have served as a warning to women who might be tempted to acknowledge their homosexual desires. To do so meant, in part, to become part of a criminal underworld, to lose both class, and, for white women, race privilege" (415). The image of a dangerously aggressive lesbian criminal certainly comes close to describing how Wuornos signifies in true-crime narratives, but it is unclear how much class or race privilege Wuornos as a poor, working-class white woman ever had to lose. Perhaps a more relevant context in which to situate Wuornos is the history of American female murderers. As we will see, even in this group, Wuornos stands out as unusual.

One of the most common features in true-crime narratives about Wuornos is the description of her as the "first female serial killer." A cursory glance at a reference book such as Kerry Segrave's *Women Serial and Mass Murderers* will confirm that, technically speaking, this is a nonsensical claim, as there were many women before Wuornos who killed serially.[15] However, when Segrave describes some of the significant differences between male and female serial murderers, Wuornos's "originary" status becomes a little more plausible:

> Only a handful of the women profiled employed more typically "male" methods of aggressive murder; the few women who worked with men in some fashion tended to use "male" methods. It is only among these that we can find examples of women who murdered at a place other than their residence, the victim's residence, or their place of employment. Still, there are no female murderers like Richard Speck, Ted Bundy, the sniper who killed from the Texas tower, or the man who killed in the McDonalds near San Diego. There are no female counterparts to a Bundy or a Gacy, to whom sex or sexual violence is part of the murder pattern. (4–5)

Wuornos was unusual compared with other female serial killers in that Wuornos seemed to kill "like a man": she killed outdoors rather than at home; she used a gun rather than poison; she killed strangers rather than friends or family members; whatever her motive was, it was definitely not financial. Not surprisingly, these are the elements of the Wuornos case that true-crime narratives focus on, but, as I will demonstrate, their reasons for doing so are suspect. Rather than attempting to establish an objective account of what Wuornos did and why, true-crime narratives about her instead emphasize her difference from other female serial killers in order to demonize lesbianism, to turn Wuornos into a bloodthirsty monster, to exonerate her victims, and to gain a competitive advantage in the extraordinary media feeding frenzy that erupted around Wuornos, of which true-crime narratives were one small part.

Because Wuornos acted alone,[16] she cannot be located in other roles frequently reserved for women in true-crime narratives about serial murder. Frequently, true-crime narratives blame women for murders committed by men. These women are either the "seductive" victims or "emasculating" mothers or wives of the murderer.[17] Women also appear as the "helpmates" of serial murderers, and this role can take a variety of forms. Rule notes that Ted Bundy "would always have at least one woman entranced with him" in the years leading up to his eventual execution (*Stranger* 170). In *The Phantom Prince*, Bundy's longtime lover, Elizabeth Kendall, speaks of her willingness to act as a "cover" for Bundy in order to "counteract the image of 'freak' he had been given by the press" and says that she was "willing to play whatever game it was if I could stay by his side" (121). Sheila Isenberg has described the phenomenon of women who form relationships with and often marry convicted murderers *after* their conviction, noting that serial murderers appear to be especially attractive to these women. In fact, "Hillside Strangler" Kenneth Bianchi was able to persuade Veronica Lynn Compton to attempt to commit a murder in the manner of the "Strangler" on his behalf, in order to fool the police into thinking that the real "Hillside Strangler" was still at large (Isenberg 57–58).

The case of Veronica Compton indicates that women can also appear in true-crime discourse about serial murder as accomplices to male murderers. Women involved in serial murder with a man are seen either as the passive victim and abused partner of their male accomplice or as the dominant and far more deviant partner, with the narrative emphasis of most true-crime accounts falling on the latter alternative. In the case of Carol Bundy, convicted with her partner, Douglas Clark, of serial killings in California in the 1980s, the emphasis is on passivity: "If they were caught, Doug promised to take the rap and Carol would get off. Her defense would be that she was that Los Angeles stereotype: the dumb, station-wagon-driving housewife. A housewife mesmerized by Douglas Clark's charm" (L. Farr 108). Because Wuornos did not rely on these stereotypes of femininity in order to explain the murders she committed, her case does not resemble that of Carol Bundy, but is more closely related to that of Judith Ann Neeley, sentenced to death in Tennessee in 1988 for the murder of several children. In Neeley's case, we see the same dialectic between passive victim/dominant partner as in the Bundy/Clark case, only this time it is Judith Ann Neeley who is represented as the evil, dominant partner, while her husband, Alvin, is portrayed as a wimp. Interestingly, the qualities that are resented in Judith Neeley (and, by extension, in Wuornos) are the same qualities that are admired in men—dominance, independence, aggressiveness, and sexual self-confidence. This indicates that a murdering woman is often perceived as a threat to the predominant sex/gender system.

The threat that the woman who murders represents becomes even more acute when the murderer does not accept that she has done wrong but instead justifies what she has done. Wuornos's version of events was that her victims were all men who picked her up from where she was standing by the side of freeways, with the intent of having sex with her.[18] Wuornos claimed that after the financial arrangements had been made, sexual intercourse started, which is when the men became violent and abusive. Eventually, Wuornos said, she was forced to kill these men to protect herself: "I killed 'em because they got violent with me and I decided to defend myself. I wasn't gonna let 'em beat the shit outta me or kill me, either" (D. Kennedy 62). Far from apologizing for what she did, Wuornos claimed that "what I did is what anybody else had a right to do" and that she felt "like a hero. 'Cause I've done some good. I'm a killer of rapists" (Reynolds 235–36).

Murder as Resistance

Wuornos's assertion of her right to defend herself as a prostitute being attacked by abusive clients raises the question of whether her actions could be better understood by being placed in a tradition of women's resistance to male violence. This tradition must be acknowledged alongside the recognition of how often women appear in legal discourse as the victims or sidekicks of male serial murderers. Women's resistance to male violence can take many forms. It can involve organized feminist actions protesting the media's coverage of the Hillside Strangler case, such as Suzanne Lacy's performance piece "In Mourning and in Rage" (Delacoste and Newman 278). It can involve the work of the US PROStitutes Collective in forming the Black Coalition Fighting Black Serial Murders to protest the lack of attention given to the "Southside Slayings," the deaths of at least seventeen black women over a three-year period in South Central Los Angeles (Delacoste and Alexander 284–89). It can involve drawing attention to the lack of concern about and/or attention to the victims of serial murderers when those victims are working-class women, lesbians, women of color, or prostitutes (see the Combahee River Collective's "Twelve Black Women: Why Did They Die?" in Delacoste and Newman 68–70). It can involve direct action against those institutions that encourage violence against women (see "Actions Against *Hustler*" by The Preying Mantis Women's Brigade, in Delacoste and Newman 264–65).

Perhaps the most significant act of resistance is recognizing women's own capacity for violence: "Those who at first thought seem 'deviant' ('violent women') may be numerous enough to redefine 'the norm.' When we find many of us doing something only men are supposed to do; and nearly all of us expressing in some form what is supposed to be male behavior, maybe we need to enlarge our notion of who *we* are" (Uccella and Kaye 321, original emphasis). In *When She Was Bad*, Patricia Pearson discusses why feminists have often been reluctant to face up to the existence of violent women, and she describes the consequences "of our refusal to concede female contributions to violence":

> It affects our capacity to promote ourselves as autonomous and responsible beings. It affects our ability to develop a literature about ourselves that encompasses the full array of human emotion and experience. It demeans the right our victims have to be valued. And it radically impedes our ability to recognize dimensions of power that have nothing to do with formal structures of patriarchy. Perhaps above all, the denial of women's aggression profoundly undermines our attempt as a culture to understand violence, to trace its causes and to quell them. (243)

Being honest about Wuornos's status as a violent woman and locating Wuornos's murders within a tradition of resistance to violence against women open up a consideration of her murders as a political act, as an act of protest.[19] Not surprisingly, both true-crime work on the case and the judicial system in general have proved to be extremely resistant to such an interpretation of Wuornos's crimes. The attitude of Wuornos's arresting officers to her argument of self-defense was disbelief, and this disbelief is never seriously challenged by true-crime accounts of the case, which tend merely to reflect the law enforcement perspective. Such disbelief is conditioned by certain narrow attitudes and points of view that characterize discussion of the case. For example, at several points it is suggested that Wuornos's claim that she killed the men as a way of defending herself from attempted rapes must be false, because it is not possible to rape prostitutes.[20] In Michael Reynolds's book about the case, *Dead Ends*, Wuornos's account of the attack she suffered at the hands of her first victim, Richard Mallory, brings the following response (it is not clear whether this response comes from Reynolds, or whether it is his transcription of the reaction of the police officers interviewing Wuornos): "Lee sounded more like an offended deb on prom night than the 'professional prostitute' she claimed to be" (201–2).

This assumption that a prostitute cannot be raped or mistreated at the hands of a client is also encouraged by a persistent habit of viewing the situations that Wuornos described from a "male" point of view and judging

Wuornos's actions on that basis. For example, during Wuornos's interrogation, one of the investigating officers asked Wuornos why, once she had trained her gun on her victim, she did not escape, as she was "in control" of the situation. Wuornos pointed out that she and her attacker were normally in an extremely isolated area and that she was usually completely nude. The investigating officer's response to this was still to insist that she could have got dressed while keeping the gun on the man and then run off to safety (Reynolds 222–23). The law enforcement perspective on Wuornos exhibits not only a failure to understand the situation that Wuornos claimed she was in, but also an inability or unwillingness to appreciate that a woman's assessment of the degree of danger in a particular situation may be very different from that of a man.

Because of the unwillingness of police and true-crime work on the case to accept Wuornos's explanation of self-defense, other motives and explanations must perforce be found. This search is complicated by the fact that, as I have explained, Wuornos differed from other female serial killers in the type of weapon she used, the location of the crimes, the type of victim, and above all motive. The vast majority of female serial killers murder for economic reasons, usually to collect insurance money on family members. Ann Jones has even gone so far as to suggest that murder for these women, particularly those who lived in the early decades of the twentieth century, was actually a form of entrepreneurship in a society that offered very few opportunities for women to practice and excel in the cutthroat tactics of the business world (136–37, 146). Although Wuornos did take money and possessions from her victims, it is clear that robbery was not her primary motive for the murders. However, to describe Wuornos, as police did after her arrest, as a "killer who robs, not a robber who kills" (Reynolds 232) is also wide of the mark. This description of Wuornos, rather than being simply mistaken, however, is a crucial element in how true-crime accounts of Wuornos respond to her anomalous status among female serial killers. This response can be summed up by the police's confident pronouncement after Wuornos's arrest that she "pretty much meets the guidelines of a serial killer"; that is, Wuornos killed like a man (Reynolds 232).

In order to demonstrate that Wuornos was not an "ordinary" female multiple murderer, quietly poisoning family members, but something far more dangerous and threatening, a female serial murderer, true-crime accounts of the case must demonstrate that Wuornos not only killed the seven men but enjoyed doing so:

A pattern was emerging—not a pattern of robbery, but of killing. Stranger-on-stranger homicide. No apparent motive; the robberies seemed to be merely opportunistic. Following the killing, the murderer just took the money. The crimes had occurred almost monthly, with a "cooling off" period between them. They seem calculated, enjoyed. Not content with one shot or two, the killer had lavished four, six, nine rounds on the torsos. This most recent one, Humphreys, had a new wrinkle, the shot to the head. There was a definite escalation to the killing. And Humphreys' shot close to the heart suggested an intimacy. Enjoyment, humiliation, control. All the red flags that mark a serial killer. (Reynolds 90)

Although Reynolds claims that the state of her victims' bodies showed how much Wuornos enjoyed killing, in fact her crime scenes were relatively mild compared with those of many serial killers. The murders committed by Ted Bundy, the Hillside Stranglers, and many other male serial murderers, for example, were characterized by extreme degrees of sexual sadism, including violent sexual assault, torture, and both pre- and postmortem mutilation of the victims' bodies, bodies that were then often posed publicly in humiliating and degrading positions. Nothing of this kind was found to have taken place with Wuornos's victims, and this is consistent with the claim that "there are no female counterparts to a Bundy or a Gacy, to whom sex or sexual violence is part of a murder pattern" (Segrave 4). The absence of persuasive evidence regarding Wuornos's "enjoyment" of her murders is an example of the double standard that emerges when male and female murderers are compared. Even though the murdering methods of the women may be relatively mild compared with those of their male counterparts, the women are still much more likely to be described as vicious sadists, while the men are rarely described as such. It is clear that descriptions of women in this context, and of Wuornos as enjoying her crimes, are "projections of a sexual double standard, which judges women not by 'objective' criteria but by an idealized stereotype of feminine gentleness" (Cameron and Frazer 23).

These questions of enjoyment and sexual sadism are important because these elements are seen as integral characteristics of a serial murderer. Even though true-crime work never seriously challenges the description of Wuornos as a vicious serial murderer, it does represent those who disagree with this description. Alexander Schauss, a forensic researcher from Seattle, claims that if Wuornos was a serial murderer, she would have killed more victims, being unable to resist the compulsion that drove her to kill. Wuornos's attorney, Tricia Jenkins, defines serial murder as being committed for pleasure, and says that this crucial element was missing in Wuornos's case. Former FBI agent Robert Ressler argues that "if Wuornos is said to be a serial killer . . . we have to rewrite the rules" (quoted in D. Kennedy 66, 67).

Despite such caveats to the description of Wuornos as a serial murderer, this is still the label that law enforcement and true-crime writers adhere to, even in the face of evidence that would give credence to Wuornos's claim of self-defense, evidence that at least one of her victims was a heavy consumer of pornography and had a history of violence against women (Reynolds 18; D. Kennedy 4, 129). Far from accepting Wuornos's claims that her victims attacked her, however, true-crime narratives about her unproblematically reflect and reinforce the positive image of Wuornos's victims given by the law enforcement system. In marked contrast to the victims in the other cases we have discussed, who are characteristically blamed and criticized, Wuornos's victims, all middle-aged white men, are treated solicitously. For example, during the search for the body of one of Wuornos's victims, Peter Siems, a national police teletype described the missing man as "a devout Christian and family man [who] has no history of mental instability" (Reynolds 60). The implication is clear—such a man could not bear any responsibility for his disappearance. Instead, he must have been victimized by the suspects, whom the teletype described as "two W/Fs [white females] who appeared to be lesbians" (60). In order to bolster the image of Wuornos as a "predatory prostitute" (D. Kennedy 140) who victimized her clients, even the suggestion that the victims picked up Wuornos with the intention of having sex with her must be resisted. As one police officer said when confronted with this theory, "I hate to say it because you've had too many family people who've been killed and their wives are mourning enough already" (Schmich 19–20). It is hard to imagine the families of Jeffrey Dahmer's victims being treated with such consideration.

Lesbian Man Haters

While the evidence that supports Wuornos's claim of self-defense is inconclusive and subjective at best, we might still well ask why the reaction to Wuornos has been so intense and why most true-crime writers are so certain that she was in fact a serial murderer who enjoyed killing men. In her analysis of the links between masculinity and violence, *Boys Will Be Boys*, Myriam Miedzian asks us to imagine a reversal of the current situation where 90 percent of violent crimes are committed by men:

> Imagine the reaction if close to 90 per cent of all violent crimes were committed by women! If tabloid headlines carried stories, with some regularity, of man-hating women leaving behind them cross-country trails of murdered men's bodies; of ex-wives, driven by fits of jealousy, killing their former husbands and their children; of groups of women killing each other in rival gang fights. Imagine the scorn that would be heaped on women for killing *each other* off at such high rates! How quickly such behavior would be perceived as an aberration, a deviation from the norm of male behavior, a "women's problem" to be dealt with urgently! (11–12)

Wuornos's murders raise precisely the specter of this "aberration" among law enforcement personnel and true-crime writers, the specter of a man-hating woman cutting a swathe across Florida and leaving "respectable" family men in her wake. Curiously, hatred of men is accepted in true-crime accounts of Wuornos as a sufficient motive for women to become murderers (see Segrave 4), while it is precisely this relation between men and hatred of women that is denied in the case of a serial murderer like Ted Bundy. This says something revealing about deeply rooted male insecurities and guilt about their relations with and treatment of women.

Even more suggestive is the fact that Wuornos's lesbianism is used by true-crime narratives about her to confirm the link between man hating and female murderers. Just as true-crime narratives assume a relationship between Dahmer's homosexuality and his homicidal violence, they also automatically equate lesbianism with hating men and wishing violence against them. For example, when police set up a computer program to coordinate leads resulting from the release of composite sketches of the two female suspects in the series of murders, "in the middle of December 1990, leads no. 5, 243, 297 and 361 identified the sketches as two women, lesbian man-haters, capable of violence" (D. Kennedy 35–36). Some writers even lean on the authority of the FBI to establish their point about lesbianism. In an article written for *Glamour* magazine, Susan Edmiston quotes Robert Ressler as saying, "There may be an intrinsic hatred of males here, as well as an identification with male violence which helped push her across the line into what has been considered a 'male' crime" (325). In stark contrast to the complex motives attributed to male serial murderers, and the evocation of those male murderers as essentially unsolvable mysteries, Wuornos's motives are presented with absolute clarity: she is a lesbian; *therefore* she hates men and *therefore* she killed them.

This understanding of Wuornos's lesbianism as a sufficient motive for her murders explains both the intensity of the reaction of a predominantly male judicial system to her, and the persistence of belief both in her guilt and in her enjoyment of the murders. Wuornos knew, even before she was arrested, that she would be dismissed as a man hater, in spite of her argument about what really happened immediately preceding the murders she committed: "One night in September [1990] they [Tyria Moore and Wuornos] had been watching Roseanne doing a comedy special on the TV. Roseanne was a hoot. She was doing this routine about serial killers, about how they were always men who were psychos; but if one of them turned out to be a woman, everybody would just call her a man-hater, and Lee had just burst out, 'That's me she's talking about!'" (Reynolds 95). The question remains, what impact did

Wuornos's portrayal as a violent, man-hating lesbian have on her treatment by the judicial system? Did the prejudicial image of her in the media contribute to her being given the death penalty?

Legal scholars seem to agree that a defendant's lesbianism is not a mitigating circumstance in capital cases, but they remain split on whether it could be an aggravating circumstance (see Robson; Streib). After her conviction, an appeal on Wuornos's behalf was launched by the National Center for Lesbian Rights on the grounds that homophobia had denied her a fair trial; the state of Florida objected, saying that lesbianism was irrelevant (Robson 194). Bearing in mind that the majority of women on death row in the United States are lesbian or bisexual (see Brownworth), Wuornos's lesbianism is certainly not irrelevant. With that said, her sexual preference was just one of a number of circumstances that made the death penalty verdict practically inevitable in Wuornos's case. Those circumstances are described succinctly by Gillespie:

> It could be argued that a woman found guilty of criminal homicide and eligible for the death penalty has a greater likelihood of execution if she is perceived to have an extensive criminal history . . . if she fails to portray the expected societal gender role of a woman (crying, remorse, emotional outbursts, "natural" motherly affection, etc.); if she has an accomplice who is willing to testify against her; if her case has been widely publicized by the press and if the press has given her a derogatory nickname. (99)

Almost all of these circumstances apply to Wuornos, and they illustrate the fact that her lesbianism was just one of the "inappropriate" gender traits she possessed that stacked the deck against her.

The poor quality of Wuornos's legal representation also played a major role, according to Phyllis Chesler, who invites us to compare the treatment given to Wuornos with that given to another serial killer tried by the state of Florida, Ted Bundy. Because Wuornos was indigent she was assigned a public defender who had twelve other ongoing capital cases in addition to Wuornos's and so could not possibly represent her adequately. By contrast, Chesler explains:

> Several lawyers offered to defend Bundy pro bono, an expert advised him on jury selection pro bono; at one point, no fewer than five public defenders assisted Bundy, who insisted on representing himself. (Several lawyers would have defended Wuornos pro bono in the first of five trials, but only if at least $50,000 in expenses could be raised. I became ill and could not raise the funds.) Even more interesting: the State of Florida offered Bundy a life sentence without parole, under the

circumstances a sweetheart deal for him; he refused the plea bargain. Wuornos's lawyer tried to set up a similar arrangement for her but one county prosecutor thought she deserved to die and refused to agree to a plea bargain. (122)

Not surprisingly, true-crime narratives about Wuornos do not discuss these issues. Dominated by the perspective of law enforcement, such narratives are complicit in the decision of the judicial process to hold Wuornos to a different standard than either Bundy or Dahmer. The existence of the differential standard can be partly explained by the fact that, in some respects, Dahmer had simply done what was expected of someone like him by being a murderous queer. Although what he had done was horrific, he had not violated any heteronormative assumptions about queerness. Wuornos, on the other hand, although she had apparently confirmed the stereotype of the violent lesbian, was still not exempt from the restrictive codes of womanhood that are applied to all women, regardless of their sexual orientation. Her failure to show remorse and her aggressive defiance in the courtroom made Wuornos a far more controversial and monstrous figure than Dahmer.

Wuornos's refusal to behave in an approved female manner not only increased public hostility toward her but also meant that there were remarkably few individuals or groups fighting for her life once she had declared her determination to be executed. As Sharon Krum has pointed out, even with a murderer as reviled as Timothy McVeigh, "anti-capital punishment groups were campaigning for a stay of execution, petitioning for clemency, holding candlelight vigils, anything to save the man responsible for 156 deaths from the gurney and the needle." In Wuornos's case, "the death penalty protesters were conspicuous by their absence. Not one was in or outside the court demanding that the state save her life." In the morality play that is a capital murder case, there is no mercy for a woman who is seen as refusing her femininity. Indeed, right up to her execution, Wuornos refused to play the role expected of her, and it should come as no surprise that while on death row she changed her story and claimed to have committed the murders not in self-defense but in cold blood: "I want the world to know I killed these men, as cold as ice. I've hated humans for a long time. I am a serial killer. I killed them in cold blood, real nasty" (Burkeman). Wuornos's almost parodically vicious assertion of her extreme, inhuman deviance represents her attempt to seize control of the narratives about her and to become their author, rather than their subject.

Differentiating Monsters and the Difference It Makes

The futility of Wuornos's attempt to seize control of her own story is suggested by the fact that in November 2002, just one month after her execution, it was announced that a "biopic" was to be filmed based on Wuornos's life. *Monster*, released in December 2003, was writer/director Patty Jenkins's first feature and starred the glamorous Charlize Theron as Wuornos and Christina Ricci as Wuornos's lesbian lover. *Monster* is the latest in a long line of artistic products inspired by Aileen Wuornos. In some cases, these products self-consciously examine media representations of Wuornos from a feminist and/or queer standpoint, such as Millie Wilson's 1994 installation *Not a Serial Killer*, Tammy Rae Carland's 1995 video *Lady Outlaws and Faggot Wannabes* (see Basilio), and Carla Lucero's 2001 opera *Wuornos* (see *Wuornos*). In other instances, as in the well-known documentaries by Nick Broomfield, *Aileen Wuornos: The Selling of a Serial Killer* (1992) and *Aileen: Life and Death of a Serial Killer* (2003), Wuornos-related products associate themselves with the tradition of muckraking, determined to get to the "truth" of the case by exposing the shoddy motives of those who tried to exploit Wuornos for their own ends.

Inevitably, there is no guarantee that even such impeccably progressive and well-meaning critiques of the exploitative use of Wuornos may not be exploitative themselves, but at least these products had the virtue of concentrating their attention on Wuornos herself. What was so disturbing about the critical reaction to *Monster*, a reaction that those associated with the film were happy to go along with, was how rapidly attention became focused on Charlize Theron rather than Aileen Wuornos. Not only did reviewers concentrate on outdoing each other in making increasingly hyperbolic claims about Theron's acting abilities (Roger Ebert won this competition hands down by describing Theron's performance as "one of the greatest performances in the history of the cinema"), but also the focus on Theron produced nuggets of information whose grotesque inappropriateness would have been obvious if Wuornos had been on anyone's mind at all, as when Theron announced that her boyfriend "was more than pleased with the weight I gained [to play the role]. Because with everything else that grew, so did my boobs" (Sardis 8).

Ironically, when Wuornos was first contacted, shortly after her arrest, by a Hollywood producer interested in making a film about her, Wuornos pleaded with the producer to "Please don't make me a monster" (MacNamara, "Kiss" 101). Although there has been much debate about whether Jenkins's film demonizes Wuornos, in my opinion the film's title and content are symptomatic not only of the fact that Wuornos's plea to Hollywood fell on deaf ears but also that the category of monstrosity remains the most prevalent and persuasive way of selling serial killers to the American public.

True-crime narratives occupy a relatively small space in the huge market for serial killer popular culture, but as I have demonstrated in this chapter, the genre plays an important role in influencing the public's response to serial killers. In the interests of educating their readers about the relation of serial murder to heterosexuality and queerness, true-crime narratives not only diversify the seemingly monolithic concept of "monstrosity" but also perform the related gesture of diversifying the equally monolithic concept of celebrity. A close reading of true-crime narratives about serial killers demonstrates that while Ted Bundy, Jeffrey Dahmer, and Aileen Wuornos are all celebrities, only Bundy can be regarded as "famous" in anything close to the conventional sense of that word. Although, as I explain in the introduction to this study, fame in its ancient merit-based sense is now almost entirely dead, it continues to have a strange, shadowy existence as the appropriate way to describe the celebrity enjoyed by a safely individualized heterosexual serial killer such as Ted Bundy. In a similar fashion, to the extent that the concept of "notoriety" still has any meaning at all, it aptly describes the celebrity personified by Jeffrey Dahmer and Aileen Wuornos, both of whom are representative of the equally notorious types of the homicidal homosexual and the man-hating lesbian.

The major role played by heterosexuality and homosexuality in true-crime narratives of serial murder is consistent with what Eve Kosofsky Sedgwick has argued about the centrality of the homo-/heterosexual definition in twentieth-century Western culture: "An understanding of virtually any aspect of modern Western culture must be, not merely incomplete, but damaged in its central substance to the degree that it does not incorporate a critical analysis of modern homo/heterosexual definition" (1). I have attempted in this chapter to contribute to the "critical analysis" Sedgwick speaks of, but my attempt would be incomplete if I did not discuss the crucial issue of whether these representations succeed in their goal. In other words, do true-crime narratives succeed in safely quarantining Ted Bundy from heterosexuality? Moreover, do these narratives succeed in separating heterosexuality and homosexuality from one another, so that heterosexuality may be protected from any contaminating association with an always-already "queered" violence?

There can be no definitive answers to these questions because the answers consist of readers' responses to these true-crime narratives, responses that are extremely difficult to reconstruct or tabulate with any degree of accuracy. I believe there is cautious room for optimism, however, if we remind ourselves that a mutually constitutive relationship exists between heterosexuality and homosexuality, a relationship that means that, no matter what true crime narratives might attempt, they cannot be separated. Diana Fuss has explained how, despite the fact that heterosexuality tries to place homosexuality outside a putatively straight definitional space (on the other side of the virgule separating hetero/homo), such attempts are doomed to fail: "Borders are notoriously unstable, and sexual identities rarely secure. Heterosexuality can never fully ignore the close proximity of its terrifying (homo)sexual other, any more than homosexuality can entirely escape the equally insistent social pressures of (hetero)sexual conformity. Each is haunted by the other" ("Inside" 3).

The heterosexual fear of the homosexual "other," Fuss goes on to argue, results in an ambivalent fascination with "the specter of abjection, a certain preoccupation with the figure of the homosexual as specter and phantom, as spirit and revenant, as abject and undead" ("Inside" 3). This tendency of heterosexuality to think of "the homosexual as the abject" ("Inside" 3) is perfectly realized in true-crime narratives about queer serial killers. Indeed, one can argue that this is precisely why such killers are so fascinating to the true-crime genre: they seem to exemplify the homosexual abject to a heterosexual order obsessed by fear of contamination from the other. Although mainstream heterosexist culture would assume that the straight fascination with abject queerness is noncontaminating, I think it much more likely that that fascination creates permeable, rather than absolute, boundaries.

Serial Killing in America after 9/11

In the war on terror, the handwringers see all sorts of difficulties
with an attack on Iraq. But when a psychologist studies Saddam
Hussein, he or she sees something very different. The very
definition of terror is to have weapons of mass destruction in the
hands of this sociopathic serial killer.
—Curtis Schmidt, "The Psychopathology of Saddam"

What business do your governments have to ally themselves with
the gang of criminality in the White House against Muslims?
Don't your governments know that the White House gang is the
biggest serial killers in this age?
—From a November 2002 audiotape purporting to feature the
voice of Osama bin Laden

And so, if we are to be judged by the wishes in our unconscious,
we are, like primitive man, simply a gang of murderers.
—Sigmund Freud, "Thoughts for the Times on War and Death"

It has become the ultimate truism to say that everything changed on September
11, 2001. Without wanting to minimize the impact of the awful events that
took place on that day, I think it is possible to overestimate the extent to which
the United States has changed since 9/11. To claim, for example, that the
country was profoundly altered by the eruption of an act of violence the like
of which had never been seen in the United States before is simultaneously to
be accurate and not to tell the whole story. The mainland United States had
certainly never been subjected to violent attacks of such magnitude before
9/11, and yet to imply that prior to the attacks America existed in a state of
unsullied innocence is to ignore both the participation of the United States in
similar acts of violence in other countries (either by sponsoring such acts or
by committing them outright) and the defining role that violence has played
in the foundation and continued development of the country. Despite the
temptation to treat 9/11 as some kind of epistemic break, in other words, it is
important to insist on the continuities that exist between "before" and "after";
only by studying the continuities can we understand fully the impact of 9/11
on American culture.[1]

In the context of reflecting upon the event of 9/11, Jacques Derrida has
argued that "terror is always, or always becomes, at least in part, 'interior.'
And terrorism always has something 'domestic,' if not national, about it. The
worst, most effective 'terrorism,' even if it seems external and 'international,'

244

is the one that installs or recalls an interior threat, *at home* . . . and recalls that
the enemy is *also always* lodged on the inside of the system it violates and
terrorizes" ("Autoimmunity" 188, original emphasis). Derrida's comments
remind us of the fact that the 9/11 attackers lived and trained inside the
United States. This fact alone complicates the construction of the terrorist as
a foreign outsider, but there are also other ways in which terrorism is part of the
domestic scene of the United States. Not surprisingly, one of the continuities
that are suppressed by hegemonic accounts of the meaning of 9/11 is the
long history of acts of terrorism within the United States. In his recent book
America's Culture of Terrorism, Jeffory Clymer discusses a number of such
acts, including the 1886 Haymarket bombing in Chicago, the 1910 bombing
of the *Los Angeles Times* building, the 1920 explosion on Wall Street, and,
more recently, the 1993 World Trade Center attack and the 1995 Oklahoma
City bombing. Clymer argues that the United States "has had a long and
pervasive amnesia about different acts and forms of terrorism in its history"
(211), and according to Clymer this amnesia has intensified in the wake of
the 9/11 terrorist attacks, which, he argues, have "become something like
a hyperterrorist event that has occluded . . . other, more 'mundane' forms of
terrorism that were occurring before 9/11 and that are still occurring now"
(212). As an example of the "mundane" terrorism Clymer speaks of, we might
consider the December 2003 conviction of Clayton Waagner, self-described
terrorist and member of the Army of God, on charges of threatening the use
of weapons of mass destruction. Although the hundreds of envelopes stuffed
with white powder (that he claimed was anthrax) and threatening letters that
Waagner mailed to abortion clinics and reproductive rights organizations
constituted a campaign of terror that should have attracted widespread media
coverage, there was virtually no media attention given to Waagner's conviction
(Clarkson). In a similar vein, the May 2003 arrest of William Krar and Judith
Bruey in Noonday, Texas, exposed the existence of a highly organized and
heavily armed right-wing conspiracy that was in the process of selecting targets
for its stockpile of five hundred thousand rounds of ammunition, more than
sixty pipe bombs, dozens of machine guns, silencers, pistols, mines, explosives,
and even a chemical cyanide bomb capable of killing thousands if detonated
in a shopping mall or subway (P. Harris 21).

Critics who point to such incidents as evidence that the Bush administration, in its obsession with Islamic terrorists, is ignoring the increasingly
powerful and deadly assortment of domestic extremists are missing the point
somewhat, for this selective attention has the support of the majority of the
American public. As I will explain later, part of the reason that 9/11 is so
often thought of, with amnesiac insistence, as a break, a discontinuity, rather

than as a continuation of a previously established history of terrorism in the United States is that such amnesia is necessary to maintain the existence and utility of a series of binaries that include inside/outside, innocence/guilt, and domestic/foreign. My focus in this epilogue will be on the role that serial murder plays in this complex drama of (re)memory and willful forgetting. Serial murder is the exception to the rule of seeing 9/11 as an epistemic break, in that it constitutes a principle of continuity between pre- and post-9/11 America. It must be acknowledged, however, that serial murder also seems to provide another tempting opportunity to draw a clear line of demarcation between the United States before and after the traumatic event. Despite the long-standing iconic status of the serial killer in American culture before 9/11, in the immediate aftermath of the attacks it seemed reasonable to suppose that the serial killer would be quickly replaced by the terrorist as the personification of criminal evil.[2] What actually happened, however, turns out to be considerably more complicated. I will argue that the figure of the serial killer plays an even more central role in post-9/11 America than it did before the attacks. Its omnipresence as an icon of evil enabled the serial killer to become the lingua franca of both sides of the "war against terror." Consequently, the terrorist did not replace the serial killer; rather, the two categories overlapped. The serial killer provided a way to present the figure of the terrorist to the American public in a way that was both familiar enough to keep public fear and paranoia at manageable levels and deviant enough to mobilize the necessary level of public support for the systematic dismantling of civil liberties in the United States and for the invasions of Afghanistan and Iraq. Moreover, and quite paradoxically, the reassertion of the quintessential "Americanness" of the serial killer facilitated the reinforcement of the terrorist as a foreign "other" and allowed the majority of Americans to maintain an image of both themselves and their country as paragons of innocence that had been violated by terrorism.

Business As Usual

Although I will demonstrate how intimately the serial killer and the terrorist have become entwined with each other in the aftermath of 9/11, it is also important to emphasize that the serial killer industry that existed in the United States before the attacks has continued to flourish and has done so in many instances without any reference to terrorism at all. Indeed, if anything, this industry is experiencing a boom. For example, the following are just a few of the serial-killer-related movies that have been released since 2001: *Dahmer* (David Jacobson, 2002); *Bundy* (Matthew Bright, 2002); *Speck* (Keith Walley, 2002); *Murder by Numbers* (a documentary on the appeal of serial killer films that premiered on the Independent Film Channel as part of their "Serial Killer Cinema Weekend" in February 2002); *Red Dragon* (Brett Ratner, 2002), the latest installment in one of the longest-running serial killer movie franchises ever; and, of course, *Monster* (Patty Jenkins, 2003), featuring Charlize Theron's Oscar-winning performance as Aileen Wuornos. What strikes one immediately about this list is how many of these films are based on actual serial killers. Could it be that American audiences in post-9/11 America find a perverse comfort in consuming representations of familiar serial killers rather than having to grapple with the fears raised by the terrorist?

Movie studios certainly seem confident that the American public will continue to have a sharp appetite for serial killers, as we can see from the following partial list of projects that at the time of this writing are under development or scheduled to be released: *Suspect Zero* (E. Elias Merhige, 2004) stars Ben Kingsley as an avenging former FBI agent who has dedicated himself to tracking down serial killers, including the most dangerous of them all, "Suspect Zero"; *Mindhunters* (Renny Harlin, 2004) will feature well-known actors such as Val Kilmer and Christian Slater as part of a group of FBI agents who are training to join the elite psychological profilers program. When one of the group turns out to be a serial killer, the others must figure out who the killer is before they are all murdered; famed director Ridley Scott is developing a film version of Patrick Süskind's revered serial killer novel, *Perfume*; Arnold Entertainment has acquired the rights to *The Night Stalker*, Philip Carlo's true-crime book on Richard Ramirez, and is considering Benicio del Toro for the title role; the *Starz!* film network is doing a made-for-cable film version of *The Riverman*, Robert Keppel's true-crime book on Ted Bundy and the Green River Killer. To make an obvious point, this list contains in compressed form examples of many of the subjects I have touched on in this study: the celebrity status of serial killers, the willingness of film stars to be associated with serial killer projects, and the continued salience of those figures and institutions that have traditionally been used to sell serial murder to the American public, namely, Ted Bundy and the FBI.

What explains the continued American public interest in serial killer popular culture? Sigmund Freud's still-relevant 1915 essay "Thoughts for the Times on War and Death" suggests a variety of answers to this question, including some that will enable us to begin demonstrating how serial murder in post-9/11 America is imbricated with discourses on terrorism and war. Writing in the context of World War I, Freud defines the modern attitude toward death as an unwillingness to face the possibility of our own death: "Our own death is indeed unimaginable, and whenever we make the attempt to imagine it we can perceive that we really survive as spectators. Hence the psychoanalytic school could venture on the assertion that at bottom no one believes in his own death, or to put the same thing in another way, in the unconscious every one of us is convinced of his own immortality" (304–5). According to Freud, our "tendency to exclude death from our calculations" (306) draws us toward fictional representations of death: "It is an inevitable result of all this that we should seek in the world of fiction, of general literature and of the theatre compensation for the impoverishment of life. There we still find people who know how to die, indeed, who are even capable of killing someone else. There alone too we can enjoy the condition which makes it possible for us to reconcile ourselves with death—namely, that beyond all the vicissitudes of life we preserve our existence intact . . . In the realm of fiction we discover that plurality of lives for which we crave. We die in the person of a given hero, yet we survive him, and are ready to die again with the next hero just as safely" (306–7). Fictional representations of death allow us to maintain our attitude of disavowal toward the possibility of our own death.

Although the modern disavowal of death can be maintained in times of peace, Freud argues that war "is bound to sweep away this conventional treatment of death. Death will no longer be denied; we are forced to believe in him. People really are dying, and now not one by one, but many at a time, often ten thousand in a single day" (307). Despite our commitment to the idea that we have become more civilized than primitive man, war "strips us of the later accretions of civilization, and lays bare the primal man in each of us . . . it stamps the alien as the enemy, whose death is to be brought about or desired" (316). The figure of the terrorist exposes us to a similarly unadorned confrontation with our primal selves, that "gang of murderers" Freud mentions in one of the epigraphs to this epilogue. As Samuel Weber presciently argued in 1997, there is an intimate connection between war and terrorism: "The spectacle of war is increasingly supplemented by that of 'terrorism'—which, as its name indicates, defines itself less through institutional acts than through emotional effects: the production of terror . . . The isolated act of terrorism becomes the pretext for a war against it, in which cause and perpetrator tend to converge in the shadowy figure of the elusive enemy" (102). Serial murder plays several roles in the complex relationship that exists between war, terrorism, and our own potential for violence. On the one hand, as the continued health of the serial killer popular culture industry indicates, serial killers provide an ambivalent place of refuge: they are familiar and therefore in many ways less threatening than the terrorist. More important, they allow us to maintain a pleasing image of ourselves as civilized and nonviolent; it is they who are violent, not us. On the other hand, the multiaccentuality of serial murder that I have emphasized throughout this study also allows the American public to stage the destabilizing possibility that serial murder and terrorism are related, not mutually exclusive, categories.

The Terror of Serial Killing/Terrorism as Serial Killing

The slippage between the categories of serial murder and terrorism takes various forms and to some extent depends on whether one classifies the terrorist attacks of 9/11 as a crime or as an act of war. As Caleb Carr points out, "Over the past forty years, American and other world leaders have generally identified international terrorism . . . as a type of crime, in an effort to rally global indignation against the agents of such mayhem and deny them the more respected status of actual soldiers" (*Lessons* 7).[3] The immediate response of the United States government to the 9/11 attacks was to call them a crime, but the terminology shifted very quickly to the language of warfare. The 9/11 attacks were then described as an "act of war" whose closest parallel was the Japanese attack on Pearl Harbor in 1941. Just as that act precipitated American entry into World War II, so 9/11 would be presented as forcing America into the "war on terror."

Rather than being motivated by a desire for terminological accuracy, however, the change of interpretive frame from crime to war was more a matter of political expediency. As Carr argues, seeing terrorists as criminals "generally limits to reactive and defensive measures the range of responses that the American and other governments can employ" in their fight against terrorism (*Lessons* 8). Implicitly, therefore, seeing terrorism as an act of war enables the American government to go on the offensive against terrorism, and this is exactly what it has done, as the citizens of Afghanistan and Iraq can testify. Seeing terrorists as war enemies also has profound consequences on the home front. Some of the most controversial provisions of legislation such as the Patriot Act (passed in 2001) and the rumored "Patriot Act II" have involved attacks on American civil liberties justified by the country's being at war with terrorism. The establishment of military tribunals to try individuals suspected of committing or supporting acts of terrorism; the indefinite detention of such individuals (including American citizens) with no requirement to either file charges against them or provide them with legal representation; the enormous expansion of federal information-gathering activities (including wiretapping and the monitoring of Internet use), activities which in many cases no longer require a warrant—these are all features of the contemporary United States that would have been more or less inconceivable before 9/11.

The rigor with which official U.S. government sources have disallowed the discourse of crime as an explanatory framework for the 9/11 attacks should have been another factor influencing the replacement of the serial killer with the terrorist. The figure of the serial killer has proved to be stubbornly persistent, however, precisely because he gives both sides of the war against terrorism a convenient way of describing the post-9/11 world. In the context of the demonization of Saddam Hussein that led up to the invasion of Iraq, for example, Curtis Schmidt (a psychologist and former Jesuit chaplain at the U.S. Army's European headquarters in Heidelberg, Germany), in a guest column in the *Denver Post*, described Hussein in the following terms: "Despite the fact that he is not presenting at a clinic, we can, by his words, actions and history, assess his mental state with considerable clarity. As a serial murderer, he has demonstrated, for any nation willing to look, the utter lack of empathy and concern for people's humanity that is so characteristic of the sociopath" (B7). Such a description of Saddam Hussein is representative of a larger tendency among the Western media to describe (Arab) terrorism in psychological terms. By making terrorism the product of a sick psyche, one disallows the possibility that there might be legitimate political reasons for anger against the United States.

Given that Schmidt is an American, writing in an American newspaper, for a predominantly American audience, we should not be surprised that he makes use of the familiar figure of the serial killer as a way to translate the deviance of Saddam Hussein into terms familiar to his audience. Much more surprising, however, is evidence that radical Islamists themselves make very similar use of the serial killer. In November 2002, the Arab television network Al Jazeera was given an audiotape that their contact claimed contained a message from Osama bin Laden. With American intelligence analysts vouching for the tape's authenticity, the American media publicized a government-translated version of the message, which included the following section addressed to the people of Britain, France, Italy, Canada, Germany, Australia, and Israel, all countries taken to be allies of the United States: "What business do your governments have to ally themselves with the gang of criminality in the White House against Muslims? Don't your governments know that the White House gang is the biggest serial killers in this age?" ("Bin Laden"). The most pertinent detail here is that this section of the tape was explicitly addressed to Westerners. Whether or not the speaker was actually bin Laden, it made sense to him to use a figure whom all the listeners would recognize as a shorthand for extreme violence to vilify the U.S. government. What more logical choice than a serial killer?

In their analysis of how the U.S. government has attempted to turn the terrorist into a monstrous figure, Jasbir K. Puar and Amit S. Rai have argued that representations of "terrorist-monsters" work by a logic of "absolute morality [that] separates good from a 'shadowy evil.' As if caught up in its own shadow dance with the anti-Western rhetoric of radical Islam, this discourse marks off a figure, Osama bin Laden, or a government, the Taliban, as the opposite of all that is just, human, and good" (118). The serial killer gets used by both sides because they share a similarly absolutist discourse about their respective enemies. But although the serial killer accomplishes the demonization of the enemy in an economical and effective way, it is a figure, as we have seen before, that signifies in multiple ways. If in some instances the serial killer person-ifies absolute evil, in other instances the same figure proves to be a morass of definitional instability, making it much more difficult to think through the relationship of serial murder and terrorism with any degree of certainty.

What Are the D.C. Snipers?

When James D. Martin, a fifty-five-year-old program analyst at the Na-tional Oceanic Atmospheric Administration, was shot and killed outside the Shoppers Food Warehouse in Wheaton, Maryland, on October 2, 2002, no one could have known that it was the beginning of a twenty-three-day killing spree that would eventually claim ten lives and leave three people wounded. During the three-week period the killers were at large, the American public was convulsed as it tried to understand the motivation behind the seemingly random attacks. From the beginning, two explanations were especially popu-lar: one, that this was a serial killer; two, that this was a terrorist act, possibly committed by one of the many Al Qaeda cells rumored to exist inside the United States. Although these two theories quickly emerged as the leading contenders, however, it was difficult to find any consensus about which theory was more persuasive.

Some held firmly to the conviction that the shootings were the work of a serial killer. One participant in a Web log debate on the subject, for example, insisted that "we really need to work on our termanology here . . . Next thing you know the next guy to rob a 7–11 will be a 'terrorist.' Jesus christ, this is just getting rediculous. He is a SERIAL KILLER . . . SERIAL KILLER . . . SERIAL KILLER" ("Fear," original emphasis). Others were just as insistent that the killer should be thought of as a terrorist. In a *Washington Post* article, for example, Caleb Carr, after explaining why the killings did not match the profiles of a serial killer or a spree killer, claimed that "a terrorist (or the members of a terrorist cell) could be expected to conduct himself exactly as the Washington sniper has" ("Just" A21). Still others argued that it did not really matter whether it was a serial killer or a terrorist committing the murders, both because the murders were terrorizing the community (regardless of who was committing them) and because, as William Safire argued, no matter who the murders were being committed by, they would most likely inspire terrorists: "If these weekday murders are the acts of a homicidal maniac and not part of a terrorist conspiracy, then surely the plotters of last year's devastating strikes . . . are saying: What a perfect follow-up, cheap and simple and maddening. Why didn't we think of that?" (A9).

What these diverse reactions have in common is an intense anxiety about our inability to distinguish a serial killer from a terrorist. The D.C. Sniper case demonstrated that our use of the serial killer as a way to translate the terrorist into familiar terms is unstable; in this instance the serial killer and the terrorist threaten to collapse into each other in a way reminiscent of Jean Baudrillard's comments about the 9/11 hijackers: "They have even—and this is the height of cunning—used the banality of American everyday life as cover and camouflage. Sleeping in their suburbs, reading and studying with their families, before activating themselves suddenly like time bombs. The faultless mastery of this clandestine style of operation is almost as terroristic as the spectacular act of September 11, since it casts suspicion on any and every individual. Might not any inoffensive person be a potential terrorist?" (19–20). Baudrillard's description can be applied almost word for word to the iconic image of the serial killer as a harmless next-door neighbor, an image personified by Jeffrey Dahmer. Given the choice, many Americans might prefer the more familiar figure of the serial killer to that of the terrorist, but if we cannot distinguish between them, that choice is taken away from us, leaving us disoriented and threatened.

To some extent, the arrests of John Allen Muhammad and John Lee Malvo addressed these feelings of disorientation. As Sara L. Knox has argued, the blanket television coverage of the arrests consoled the audience by making the sniper shootings "definite, assessable, *televisable*. They could finally see for themselves the search for evidence, the houses the accused had lived in: no more conjectured bullet trajectories, and possible escape routes" (original emphasis). In other ways, however, the threatening confusion between serial killer and terrorist in the sniper case was not really resolved by the arrests. On the one hand, those who had believed all along that a serial killer was responsible could take some comfort from the fact that, technically speaking, Muhammad and Malvo were not members of any terrorist group. On the other hand, as the media reiterated again and again, they bore very little resemblance to any other serial killers. As journalists N. R. Kleinfield and Erica Goode argue in an article revealingly titled "Serial Killing's Squarest Pegs: Not Solo, White, Psychosexual or Picky": "As criminologists and academicians try to find the proper context for the sniper suspects—which of the notorious killers of yesteryear to align them with—they have been struck by how unconventional the pair appears to be. In so many ways, based on the still sketchy information known about them, they seem to defy the broad connections that have been drawn among their criminal predecessors." If we read between the lines, the problem seems to be that Muhammad and Malvo disturb the logic that organizes the pantheon of celebrity serial killers by refusing close kinship with any of the "notorious killers of yesteryear." To use a literary analogy, the D.C. Sniper case seems to be a canonical text that explodes the idea of the canon.

. If Muhammad and Malvo troubled both self-proclaimed and official experts on serial murder by reminding them of how elusive such an apparently familiar category remained, those who feared that the sniper killings were committed by terrorists could take only limited comfort from the arrests. Even though Muhammad and Malvo were not members of any terrorist group, Muhammad's approval of the 9/11 attacks, along with his recent conversion to Islam, was widely reported, and such details made it very difficult to separate the D.C. snipers definitively from the category of "terrorist," as journalist Mark Steyn's heavily ironic commentary indicates: "It turned out police were looking for a Muslim convert. A Muslim convert who last year had discarded the name 'Williams' and adopted a new identity as 'Muhammad.' A Muslim convert called Muhammad who in the wake of Sept. 11 had expressed anti-American sentiments. Could even the most expert psychological profiler make sense of such confusing, contradictory clues? Apparently not" (37). In response to the definitional quagmire opened up by the D.C. Sniper case, some reacted by trying to (re)locate the perpetrators firmly in a recognized category. One USA Today reader, for example, suggested that Muhammad and Malvo should be tried under the "domestic terrorist" standard that was used in the prosecution of Timothy McVeigh.[4]

Ironically, prosecutors seemed to take this reader's advice. After Attorney General John Ashcroft took the sniper case away from Maryland prosecutors and instead moved Muhammad and Malvo to Virginia to be tried (mostly because Virginia has a much "better" record on capital punishment, in that it hands out and carries through many more death penalties than Maryland), Virginia prosecutors decided to prosecute Muhammad under the state's anti-terrorism law, which had been passed in the wake of 9/11, and which stipulated the death penalty for anyone found guilty of ordering killings as part of an effort to intimidate communities or influence governments. According to the prosecutors, this decision was appropriate in view of Muhammad's attempt to extort $10 million from local governments in return for ending the shootings, but it is clear that the decision to prosecute Muhammad as a terrorist was also strategic. Because the prosecution had no direct evidence that Muhammad actually pulled the trigger in any of the shootings, prosecution under the antiterrorism statute provided the prosecutors with the best chance of having Muhammad sentenced to death. The strategy worked, despite defense objections that it misused a statute intended to apply to hierarchical organizations rather than individuals, but it could not disguise the fact that Muhammad was described as a serial killer in court proceedings and in media coverage of the case far more often than he was described as a terrorist. Owing to the persistence of such definitional instability, after Muhammad's conviction the vast majority of people were content to heave a huge sigh of relief and move on to other cases whose demonology was much more familiar and much simpler.[5]

Back to the Future

Given the complexities of the D.C. Sniper case, it is worth reiterating that part of the appeal of the serial killer popular culture industry I discussed at the start of this epilogue is its familiarity. Whether a film is based on Ted Bundy, Jeffrey Dahmer, or Aileen Wuornos, the pantheon of familiar names allows the viewer to return to pre-9/11 days, when evil had a comfortingly American face and one did not have to concern oneself with the bothersome question of why anyone would hate America enough to want to destroy the World Trade Center. In other words, we have yet more evidence of serial murder's multiaccentuality and what an important role that multiaccentuality has played in giving serial murder its iconic status. Serial murder is able to both translate the frightening realities of post-9/11 America into comprehensible terms and serve as a perversely positive nostalgic oasis. This combination of qualities comes into focus more clearly if we examine a final example of the place of serial murder in post-9/11 American culture.

On September 24, 2001, while the United States was still convulsed by the aftermath of the September 11 attacks, an unknown perpetrator murdered Gina Wilson Green in her home in Baton Rouge, Louisiana. The same individual went on to kill at least four other women in and around the Baton Rouge area: Charlotte Murray Pace, Trineisha Dene Colomb, Pam Kinamore, and Carrie Lynn Yoder. Initially, the case was overlooked by the national media because of the preoccupation with the fallout from 9/11. As time passed, however, the number of victims, the length of time the killer was at large (the last murder took place in March 2003 and Derrick Todd Lee was not arrested and charged with the crimes until May 2003), and the paucity of information about the suspect all ensured that a significant amount of media attention was eventually paid to the case. Thus, the killings in Baton Rouge give us a way of examining how a "classic" serial murder case gets represented by the media in a post-9/11 world.

To some extent, the marks of 9/11 and its aftermath are visible everywhere in reporting about the case.[6] Columnist C. T. Rossi, for example, begins his article on the case with the following words: "While the juggernaut of the federal government is attempting to redirect its full weight toward using law enforcement as a counter-terrorism force, one local community is already wrapped in the grasp of a terrorist. No dirty bombs or hijacked planes. Neither is this terror accompanied by the call for jihad or suicide bombers. The terrorist acts that have covered Baton Rouge, Louisiana, in a cloak of communal fear come from the hands of a serial killer." Such an angle on a serial murder case illustrates the extent to which terrorism has become part of the available lexicon in writing about serial murder, a development that ironically brings mainstream discourse about serial murder much closer to radical feminist writing about "terroristic" sexual violence that was previously dismissed as extremist.[7]

The context of 9/11 also intrudes into the Baton Rouge serial murder case in more practical ways. Not only has the FBI gained much more power in the post-9/11 era, it has also undergone a major reorientation in its responsibilities. According to some commentators, much of the impetus for this change came from Attorney General John Ashcroft, who immediately after 9/11 ordered the Bureau to shift from evidence gathering on the terror suspects to protection against and prevention of future terrorist attacks (Brill 15, 37). This reorientation has gone so far that some people are beginning to question how much interest the FBI has in investigating criminal cases (Locy 10A). Responding to such concerns at a March 18, 2003, press conference on the Baton Rouge case, Special Agent-in-Charge Kenneth Kaiser emphasized the Bureau's commitment to investigating the case properly: "I want to assure the public that even with the looming war and the war on terrorism, that the FBI has resources committed on a full-time basis to the task force . . . I have been in contact with and have briefed the director of the FBI several times and he's asked me if the FBI in Louisiana is fully engaged in the task force, and we are" ("Yoder"). When one considers what a fundamentally important role the investigation of serial murder has played in the FBI for the past twenty-five years, the fact that it was thought necessary to make such a statement in such a high-profile case is truly staggering.

Apart from such examples where the shadow of 9/11 can be detected, however, the striking feature of the vast majority of reporting about the Baton Rouge case is just how rare such examples were. For the most part, the Baton Rouge case seems to have followed a very typical, even time-honored pattern: a mysterious killer, a frightened community, a puzzled police force, and an almost overwhelming sense of déjà vu. As Rossi puts it, "Prior to the advent of thousands dying in fiery skyscraper bombings, the serial killer was the most provocative news event that reporters could have come across their desks...Now the crime story that was once the ringmaster of all media circuses has returned to town." It is hard not to detect in Rossi's words a note of relief that things had returned to normal. Next to the horrific, unparalleled spectacle of the destruction of the World Trade Center, the events unfolding in Baton Rouge had a reassuringly familiar, even ritualistic quality.[8]

I have demonstrated in this epilogue that serial murder plays a number of different, sometimes complementary, and sometimes conflicting roles in post-9/11 America. I am not at all sure whether any one role is dominant, but I do believe that the role that comes closest to being dominant is the one evoked by Rossi: serial murder as Americana. In his essay "Welcome to the Desert of the Real!" cultural critic Slavoj Žižek explains the impact of the 9/11 attacks in the following words: "The safe sphere in which Americans live is experienced as under threat from the Outside of terrorist attackers who are ruthlessly self-sacrificing *and* cowards, cunningly intelligent *and* primitive barbarians. Whenever we encounter such a purely evil Outside, we should gather the courage to endorse the Hegelian lesson: in this pure Outside, we should recognize the distilled version of our own essence" (387, original emphasis). One's immediate reaction to Žižek's comments is to say that post-9/11 America has not endorsed Hegel in the way he describes and has instead sought ways to strengthen the gap between inside and outside. Žižek goes on to explain the choice facing America after the attacks: "Either America will persist in, strengthen even, the attitude, 'Why should this happen to us? Things like this don't happen *here*!'—leading to more aggression toward the threatening Outside, in short: a paranoiac acting out—or America will finally risk stepping through the fantasmatic screen separating it from the Outside World, accepting its arrival into the Real world, making its long-overdue move from 'Things like this should not happen *here*!' to 'Things like this should not happen *anywhere*!'" (389, original emphasis). The invasions of Afghanistan and Iraq can, of course, be interpreted as instances of "aggression toward the threatening Outside," but what I want to emphasize is the role of serial murder in the choice Žižek describes.

At first glance, it might seem as if American culture's renewed and intensified engagement with serial murder since 9/11 contributes solely to the "paranoiac acting out" of which Žižek speaks. Thinking of Saddam Hussein as a serial killer, for example, only demonizes him further and thus contributes to the atmosphere of tub-thumping patriotism that dominates public discourse in the contemporary United States. American culture's continued engagement with the figure of the serial killer, however, is also an example of a much more positive impulse (even if that impulse has not had positive consequences), namely, what Žižek describes as recognizing "the distilled version of our own essence." In other words, in the wake of 9/11, America has indeed looked inward at its own distilled essence, and what it sees there is the serial killer. The significance of this moment should not be underestimated. As I have documented throughout this study, although American culture's response to the serial killer has always been composed of both attraction and repulsion, by and large the attraction has been disavowed, and repulsion has been allowed to construct the image of the serial killer as monstrous outsider.

Thanks to 9/11, American culture is now more inclined to think of the serial killer as a quintessentially American figure; indeed, as a piece of "Americana," with all that term implies about folksiness and even a perverse kind of nostalgic fondness. Ironically, however, this new relationship with the serial killer, a relationship that I would describe as more honest, has emphatically not led to a thoroughgoing reinterpretation of America as a space absolutely defined by, rather than empty of, violence. Instead, it seems to me that the serial killer's presumed Americanness actually reinforces the trio of matched binaries serial killer/terrorist, inside/outside, America/the rest of the world and in doing so further reifies the distance between Inside and Outside. In this sense, the presence of the serial killer enables a misrecognition of "our own essence" that Žižek speaks of, a misrecognition that in turn enables the continued understanding of violence as a characteristic of the Outside, and the renewal of a highly paradoxical notion of American innocence. America has finally recognized that "Serial Killers Are Us," but only in a way that reinforces the gap between Us and Them.

NOTES

INTRODUCTION

1. Some might think that making action figures of serial killers is tasteless, but Johnson hastens to assure the potential consumer that he does have standards: "I wouldn't do Osama bin Laden. I watched that happen on TV . . . I have some personal qualms about that" (Robinson).

2. In an attempt to defend his making of serial killer action figures, David Johnson makes an accurate, albeit self-serving, point: "I didn't make these guys famous . . . These guys were famous long before I got here. If the interest wasn't there, I wouldn't be here" (Robinson).

3. A message from "serialkillersshouldnotprofit@aol.com," for example, stated that "you will rot in hell with these killers," while "Smithpi@hotmail.com" had a more elaborate critique: "You should pull your site off the net. I just watched the John Walsh show and your a fucking idiot. I hope your never a victim, because if you do then you would understand what all those people were trying to tell you. You a dumb shit."

4. Some commentators continue to maintain that a "benign" interest in serial murder is possible. Criminologist Jack Levin, for example, in an ABC News online Web chat, argues: "Many people who read true crime books or are fascinated by serial killer docudramas are actually escaping psychologically from the mundane all-too-real problems of everyday life—like how do I pay my bills, how do I avoid the mugger on the next block. What I'm trying to say is that for most Americans the fascination with serial killers is quite benign" ("Jack"). While I agree that the consumption of serial-killer-related popular culture can potentially serve escapist ends (although even this claim remains to be confirmed or contradicted

by comprehensive audience research into who uses such popular culture and for what purposes), I do not share Levin's confidence that one can easily distinguish a "benign" from a "malevolent" fascination with serial killers. Indeed, I find such terminology unhelpful because it is normally used either to deny that one's own interest in serial murder is malign or to condemn everyone else's interest in the subject as malign. Neither position helps us understand the phenomenon of serial killer celebrity.

5. I take the term "multiaccentuality" from V. N. Voloshinov's book *Marxism and the Philosophy of Language*. In the context of discussing how the linguistic sign "becomes an arena of the class struggle," Voloshinov argues that "various different classes will use one and the same language. As a result, differently oriented accents intersect in every ideological sign" (23). It is this intersecting of accents that Voloshinov describes as "multiaccentuality," and according to Voloshinov, "it is thanks to this intersecting of accents that a sign maintains its vitality and dynamism and the capacity for further development" (23). Strictly speaking, therefore, to describe the ideological sign of "serial murder" as multiaccentual is redundant because multiaccentuality is a characteristic of ideological signs per se. Nevertheless, the term "multiaccentuality" remains a useful way of emphasizing the diversity of ideological meanings given to the concept of serial murder, as well as the continued ability of that concept to evolve and develop new meanings.

6. Warren Susman has described this change from merit to visibility as a shift from a culture of character to a culture of personality. According to Susman, this shift involves a concentration on spectacle, on getting attention, rather than on embodying morality or ethics (277).

7. See also Neal Gabler's study of "the conversion of life into an entertainment medium," in which he comments on how broadly celebrity can be distributed in contemporary America: "Though stardom in any form automatically confers celebrity, it is just as likely now to be granted to diet gurus, fashion designers and their so-called super-models, lawyers, political pundits, hairdressers, intellectuals, businessmen, journalists, criminals—anyone who happens to appear, however fleetingly, on the radar of the traditional media and is thus sprung from the anonymous mass. The only prerequisite is publicity" (7).

8. As Gabler notes, "Judged by traditional values, criminals are objects of reproach and scorn. But judged by the values of entertainment, which is how the media now judged everything, the perpetrator of a major, or even a minor but dramatic, crime, was as much a celebrity as any other human entertainer" (181). After discussing Timothy McVeigh's attempts to control who interviewed him after his arrest for the Oklahoma City bombing, Gabler concludes that "at the time, McVeigh clearly didn't see himself as an indicted suspect in a heinous crime. He saw himself as a celebrity promoting a new movie" (182).

9. As the influence of merit declines and that of notoriety rises, economics also becomes an increasingly important defining factor in fame. The point of fame is no longer whether something is ethical but whether it sells. As in so many other instances, the domination of the market economy in fame signals the end of ethics and the triumph of the point of view described by Joshua Gamson: "Celebrity itself is thus commodified; notoriety becomes a type of capital . . . In the context of the celebrity industry, the word 'name' aptly summarizes the relevant commercial characteristic: recognition by consumers as a brand, familiarity in

itself. The perceived ability to attract attention, regardless of what the attention is for, can be literally cashed in" (62). Gamson's description of celebrity as a primarily economic category is confirmed by Irving Rein, Philip Kotler, and Martin Stoller's book *High Visibility: The Making and Marketing of Professionals into Celebrities.* The authors define the core essence of celebrity as its commercial value (14) and consequently emphasize that "celebrity has married business—information and entertainment channels can now transmit images at a rate and capacity never before known or understood—resulting in opportunities for aspirants who want to use their name as a brand and as a marketing tool" (2). One could hardly find a better example of how merit has ceased to be an operative principle in defining fame. For an alternative point of view, which discusses an example of how celebrity can be a means of escape from (rather than a capitulation to) market relations, see Margolis.

10. Interestingly, in comparison to my earlier comments on fame as an economic category, Tyler Cowen's economic approach to fame gives him a more positive attitude about its "decline": "Despite the considerable imperfections of a market in renown, my view of commercialized fame is largely an optimistic one. Markets increase the supply of star performances and the supply of fame with remarkable facility. The offer of praise is a relatively inexpensive means of payment; fame is a 'cheap date' for the fans. We use fame to reward and control stars, thus drawing forth a dazzling array of diverse and creative performances. Fame mobilizes the human propensity to talk in support of great achievements" (11). Charles L. Ponce de Leon sounds a similar note in his study of the emergence of human interest journalism when he argues: "The culture of celebrity is not some grotesque mutation afflicting an otherwise healthy organism, but one of its central features, a condition arising directly from the encouragement that modern societies provide for social mobility and self-invention" (4).

11. The technologically dependent nature of fame is described rather neatly by Cowen: "Fame-seeking, celebrity, and fandom are deeply rooted psychological phenomena, existing in most societies, but they are amplified and facilitated by commercial market economies and modern technologies. The modern American notions of fame and celebrity date from the 1920s and 1930s, when radio, the recording industry, and motion pictures gave stars an unparalleled ability to reach wide audiences. Today, television, the compact disk, and the Internet give fans further assistance in finding, following, and enjoying their stars from a distance. Fame has become the ideological and intellectual fabric of modern capitalism. Ours is an economy of fame. Our culture is about the commodification of the individual and the individual image" (8).

12. On a related note, Daniel A. Cohen, in his study of early American crime narratives, draws a connection between the spread of printed text and the rise of fictionality, a fictionality that could facilitate the development of the "new" kind of fame Braudy describes: "An inevitable result of [criminal narratives' transcendence of regional boundaries] was a gradual loosening of the link between crime literature and social reality. New England's earlier gallows literature had consisted largely of local, ephemeral publications. The readers of such works often already knew of the events being described, either through newspapers, word-of-mouth, or personal observation. Indeed, many of the readers of execution sermons, criminal confessions, and gallows poetry undoubtedly attended the executions

of their subjects . . . However, when crime pamphlets described events that were both geographically and temporally remote from their readers, journalistic inhibitions concerning factual accuracy were sometimes significantly weakened. In such cases, the line between truth and fiction could easily blur. For example, when a fictional story about a man falsely accused of murder was reprinted in America during the late eighteenth century, it was repeatedly presented to readers as a factual account. By the first half of the nineteenth century, such journalistic fictions were commonplace" (29–30). The rise of fictionality in reporting is symptomatic of the shift in fame I have been discussing; concerns about accuracy become less relevant when attention-seeking notoriety, rather than merit, is the defining factor in fame.

13. P. David Marshall has argued that the etymological roots of the word *celebrity* suggest the inherently democratic nature of the concept: "celebrity status involves the message of possibility of a democratic age. The restrictions of a former hierarchy are no longer valid in the new order that is determined by merit and/or the acquisition of wealth. This democratic sense of the term is drawn from the original Latin *celebrem*, which had not only the connotation of famous but also that of 'thronged.' The celebrity, in this sense, is not distant but attainable—touchable by the multitude" (6). While I would agree with Marshall that "celebrity" is, at least potentially, a democratizing concept, in my opinion it has nothing to do with merit.

14. It is important to emphasize not only the existence of criminals-as-celebrities but also celebrities-as-criminals. Caryn James has argued that in "this era of ever faster and more relentless media, the famous morph from one kind of celebrity to another in a flash . . . O. J. Simpson's résumé is a catalogue of how fluid celebrity is: football hero and star of television commercials, accused murderer and star of his own endlessly televised trial. However dimmed his star, his fame will not go away" ("Humbling" 23). In some respects, the "ascent" of serial killers into the sphere of celebrity has been accompanied by the increasing devaluation/criminalization of existing members of that sphere, heightening the similarities between the two groups.

15. See Taylor and Thaler for confirmation and extension of the argument that the Simpson case permanently altered the ways in which the American mass media represent crime.

16. It is important to note that just as fame is differentially distributed among criminals (so that serial killers have a much greater chance of becoming famous than burglars), fame is also differentially distributed among serial killers themselves. Philip Jenkins has argued that the distribution of fame among serial killers has a racial dimension, with white serial killers attracting more media attention than their black counterparts because the former group are closer to the prevailing stereotype of serial killers (see "African-Americans" 27).

17. Although Panzram's book never appeared in the form he envisioned, his optimism about public interest in his writings has been amply confirmed. In 1970, Thomas E. Gaddis and James O. Long produced a version of Panzram's journals under the title of *Killer: A Journal of Murder*. A film version of Gaddis and Long's book, bearing the same title, was released in 1995, with James Woods in the role of Panzram. Finally, selections from Panzram's writings appear in Brian King's book *Lustmord: The Writings and Artifacts of Murderers*.

18. For discussions of the relationship between David Berkowitz and the media, see Caputi (*Age* 39–40); Harden; and "Talk." Cintra Wilson discusses Berkowitz in the context of demonstrating the lengths to which some people will go to exploit a murderer's fame: "Even the Christians are embracing the power of murder-porn to get their point across. I was recently exposed to a religious-cum-educational videotape for 'teens at risk' that has been distributed to various prisons and schools: *The Choice Is Yours—with David Berkowitz*. This video was a hardsell of harried, pro-life Christian propaganda built around an interview with America's original postal-worker-turned-psychopath, 'Son of Sam' serial killer David Berkowitz, who has loudly undergone a . . . conversion while serving a life sentence with no possibility of parole in the Sullivan Correctional Facility, a maximum-security prison . . . What I couldn't stop thinking about was, What kind of Christian organization would stoop to *using the celebrity of a serial killer to promote teen interest in Christianity?* Roll over, Jesus" (202–3, original emphasis).

19. Richard Schickel points out that Bundy could have avoided the death penalty if he had plea-bargained. According to Schickel, however, "that did not fit his scenario. He wanted to have a full trial in which, acting as his own lawyer, he could play big scenes, which turned out to be dramatically satisfying . . . but which, in the end, led him to death row" (*Intimate* 10).

20. On a related note, Harold Schechter has argued that the serial killer is a product of Western culture's transformation of death from something familiar and ordinary to something shameful and forbidden. According to Schechter, the serial killer reminds us that "our bodies are, finally, just so much dead meat" ("Skin" 23).

21. For a detailed examination of the social utility of criminals, see David E. Ruth's illuminating discussion of the American gangster.

22. When Jeffrey Dahmer was murdered in prison in 1994, the families of his victims were delighted, but his death also presented them with something of a problem. Throughout the short time Dahmer was in prison, there had been persistent rumors that he was in negotiations with both publishers and movie studios about selling his story. If such a deal had ever been struck, legal restrictions would have prevented Dahmer from receiving any of the money; instead, it would have been distributed among his victims' families. Dahmer's murder obviously ended this possibility, so the families explored another option: auctioning off Dahmer's property, including such banal items as his toothbrush, but also many items he had used in commission of the murders, such as a saw, a hammer, the fifty-five-gallon vat he used to decompose the bodies, and the refrigerator where he stored the hearts of his victims. Although the families' motives for suggesting this auction may have been noble, they could not avoid participating in what Mark Pizzato has described as "the prior fetishization of such props and the consumption of [Dahmer's] cannibal drama by a mass audience" (91). When the logic of consumerism dominates, is anyone truly innocent, or are there just varying degrees of guilt, of implication?

CHAPTER ONE

1. Childs's set included realistic plaster casts of the victims' mutilated bodies which, rumor has it, were subsequently purchased as souvenirs by Marilyn Manson. See J. Smith.

2. Depp researched the role of Abberline by visiting London, where he was given an exclusive tour of the East End by Donald Rumbelow, ex-police officer and author of several well-known books on the Ripper case. The tour ended with a visit to the Ten Bells Pub, where one of the Ripper's victims used to drink. A spokesman for the Ten Bells said of Depp: "He was a really nice bloke, very friendly. He had a couple of halves of lager and talked about the Ripper. He knew his stuff" ("Depp on").

3. Indeed, the Hughes brothers' Ripper is, in a sense, doubly British. He is part of the British establishment, being a Freemason who is killing on behalf of Queen Victoria, and he is also, in the midst of a host of American actors, played by the respected British actor Ian Holm.

4. One way of measuring just how unusual the Ripper murders were is to give a more representative example of death in the East End during this period. In his book *East End 1888*, historian William Fishman describes how in January 1888, a few months before the murders began, Wynne Baxter, the coroner who was to preside over the inquests into the deaths of several of the Ripper's victims, heard evidence concerning the death of James Butler, a forty-three-year-old dock worker. Butler was found dying in the street by William Jones, a car man. Jones and others managed to get Butler to a hospital, but he was dead on arrival. Baxter ruled the cause of death as heart failure, but it is abundantly clear from what we know of Butler's life that he was basically worked to death (Fishman 16). This incident not only illustrates a far more common type of death in the East End but also reminds us of the kinds of social conditions in which the murders took place. More recently, Fishman has argued for the continued salience of the Ripper murders in understanding contemporary social conditions in the East End of London because, in some respects, not much has changed since 1888. See Gould.

5. For more information on James Greenacre's murder of Hannah Brown, see Curtis 67–68. Greenacre was sentenced to death for the murder in May 1837, while Sarah Gale, his lover and accomplice, was transported for life.

6. According to Joan Smith, these walking tours have become increasingly unpopular with local people. Tourists have had stones thrown at them, and one was even shot with a pellet from an air rifle.

7. William G. Eckert provides an interesting description of a collection of these letters held by the Public Record Office in London: "Some letters include drawings of knives, swords, satanic figures, and victims. Some letters are written in neat handwriting while others are scribbled, and the material used ranges from bonded paper to the backs of a daily newspaper. The content in some instances is easily discernible, but difficult to understand in others. Some exhibit red spotting, which is meant to simulate bloodstains" ("Ripper" 165). Eckert's description suggests the amount of forethought and labor that went into some of these letters.

8. Mark Seltzer argues that the mystery of the Ripper's identity is the secret to his success: "The absence of any knowledge of the identity of the killer has made Jack the Ripper the prototype of the serial killer: the blank surface that reflects back the commonplace anxieties and crises of his culture" (126).

9. Perhaps the most egregious example of this association of foreignness and criminality in Doyle comes in his second novel, *The Sign of Four* (1890), where Holmes concludes on the basis of "diminutive footmarks, toes never fettered by boots, naked feet, stone-headed wooden mace, great agility, small poisoned darts" (161) that the murderer is an aborigine from the Andaman Islands. Watson's description of the "savage," Tonga, toward the end of the novel makes the chain of association between foreignness, criminality, and degeneration even more explicit: "Never have I seen features so deeply marked with all bestiality and cruelty. His small eyes glowed and burned with a sombre light, and his thick lips were writhed back from his teeth, which grinned and chattered at us with half animal fury" (177–78).

10. We should add photography to criminal anthropology and fingerprinting as an influential technology facilitating the production of the criminal body during this period. Allan Sekula has argued that the mid-nineteenth-century disciplines of physiognomy and phrenology "shared the belief that the surface of the body, and especially the face and head, bore the outward signs of inner character" (11). This belief, Sekula argues, helps to explain the popularity of a genre such as the photographic portrait: "We understand the culture of the photographic portrait only dimly if we fail to recognize the enormous prestige and popularity of a general physiognomic paradigm in the 1840s and 1850s. Especially in the United States, the proliferation of photography and that of phrenology were quite coincident" (12). But the interaction between photography and phrenology was not confined to the parlors of the American middle class. Sekula goes on to claim that the two technologies also met in the field of criminal jurisprudence, providing researchers into the biological dimensions of criminality with "an opportunity to lend a new organic facticity to the already established medical and psychiatric genre of the case study" (13).

Apart from the Whitechapel killings, the year 1888 also saw the Eastman Dry Plate and Film Company unveil "The Kodak," "the world's first self-contained hand camera" (R. Jenkins 5). Despite such a suggestive coincidence, at first glance photography seems to have little relevance to the Ripper case because, for obvious reasons, no photos of the Ripper exist. And yet the connections between photography and the visualization of criminality remind us that visualization played a vital role in the media and public response to the Whitechapel murders. A large part of the reason why the mystery of the Ripper's identity (in other words, our inability to visualize the Ripper) continues to be productive rather than frustrating is that other aspects of the case (possible suspects, including artists' impressions of the Ripper, the victims, the crime scenes, and so on) were intensely visualized by the press, both through vivid description and through numerous illustrations, thus providing a crucial visual dimension to reporting on the case. Many people at the time of the murders would have felt the appropriateness of documenting evidence of the Ripper's crimes through photography because, according to Bill Jay in his essay "The Photographer As Aggressor," by 1888 camera enthusiasts were frequently portrayed by the press as intrusive, even to the point of committing "constructive assaults on modest women" (quoted in R. Jenkins 5). Photography and criminality were thus connected not least by a potential relationship of equivalence.

11. See Friedland for further information about the Lipski case. The case was particularly controversial because of rumors that Lipski had sexually assaulted Angel before killing her, rumors that were never explicitly confirmed or denied by a reticent courtroom and press. The case became so notorious that "Lipski" became a widely used term of antiSemitic abuse.

12. The text of the letter was as follows: "25 Sept: 1888. Dear Boss, I keep on hearing that the police have caught me but they wont fix me just yet. I have laughed when they look so clever and talk about being on the *right* track. That joke about Leather Apron gave me real fits. I am down on whores and I shant quit ripping them till I do get buckled. Grand work the last job was. I gave the lady no time to squeal. How can they catch me now. I love my work and want to start again. You will soon hear of me with my funny little games. I saved some of the proper *red* stuff in a ginger beer bottle over the last job to write with but it went thick like glue and I can't use it. Red ink is fit enough I hope *ha. ha*. The next job I do I shall clip the lady's ears off and send to the police officers just for jolly wouldn't you. Keep this letter back till I do a bit more work then give it out straight. My knife's so nice and sharp I want to get to work right away if I get a chance. Good luck. Yours truly, Jack the Ripper. Dont mind me giving the trade name" (quoted in Sugden 260–61, original emphasis).

13. If the "Dear Boss" letter was indeed written by journalists, their use of American idiomatic expressions might be taken as further evidence of how firmly established the theory of an American Ripper had already become.

14. A particularly bizarre example of Ripper-related popular culture takes its inspiration from these letters. In 1997, entrepreneur Stuart S. Shapiro formed an Internet company called "Killer Fonts," where customers can download fonts based on the actual handwriting of criminals such as Jeffrey Dahmer, Billy the Kid, and John Dillinger. One of the first fonts Shapiro produced was based on Jack the Ripper's handwriting in the "Dear Boss" letter because his wife had just been fired and she wanted to write a nasty letter to her ex-boss. See Warrick.

15. The *National Police Gazette* provided much less coverage of the Whitechapel Murders than one might anticipate. In the issue of December 1, 1888, Fox acknowledged this fact but explained it by saying that the murders had been covered in such exhaustive detail elsewhere that any further coverage was unnecessary. Fox clearly felt that there was a market for further coverage, however, because two weeks later, in the issue of December 15, Fox advertised the availability of *The Whitechapel Murders* pamphlet at the price of 25 cents and then continued to run the ad for the next few issues.

16. There is also evidence to suggest that some parts of the American media were more reluctant to accept the Texas murders as distinctively American and were genuinely surprised to see such violence break out in London. An article dated October 10, 1888, in the *Austin Statesman* quotes the *Fort Worth Gazette* as saying, "When the mysterious murders occurred in Austin a few years ago people were greatly shocked, but it was 'Texas, you know,' and anything might be expected in that horribly wild place. Now they are duplicated in the most populous city in the world" (*Austin Statesman*). Americans were accustomed to the extremes of frontier violence, but such violence seemed incongruous on the streets of London. As we will see, the association of serial murder and frontier violence would also be a factor in the case of H. H. Holmes.

17. Although the tendency to assume the foreignness of the Ripper was less common in America than in England, it did exist. The November 20, 1888, issue of the Washington, D.C., newspaper *Evening Star* carried an article entitled "Is the Ripper a Malay Cook?" that described a Malay suspect who was living in Austin during the murders in 1884: "He was strongly suspected and was shadowed by detectives for two or three days, when he suddenly disappeared and has not been heard of since. Detectives here think it is possible he has drifted to Europe and is the Ripper" ("Is").

18. Although the prosecution had wanted a conviction for first-degree murder, the jury found Ali guilty of murder in the second degree, perhaps indicating their dissatisfaction with the evidence. Upon his release from prison in 1902, the French government arranged for Ali's return to Algeria.

19. British writers on the case who are sympathetic to Americans sometimes adopt a related procedure; they admit that the Ripper was probably an American but then let Anglo-Saxon Americans off the hook by "othering" the American Ripper. Thus, in his 1928 book, Guy Logan, despite having argued that murder has no nationality, eventually concluded that the Ripper "had come from the States in the first place, and that he was an American Jew" (27).

20. To put it another way, xenophobia and Englishness are involved in an intimate, mutually constitutive relationship, as Werner Hamacher has suggested: "The hatred of the foreign is a part of self-hatred, a part of the hatred triggered by the compulsion to be oneself. Xenophobia derives from the fear of oneself, the fear of the violence required for becoming and remaining oneself—an other, something inassimilable and foreign to the point of invisibility and impalpability" (291). Thus, although xenophobia begins as an attempt to disavow the possibility of an English Ripper, it comes as no surprise that xenophobia eventually leads, by a circuitous route, precisely to the discussion of that possibility.

21. One of the most popular recent suspects in the Whitechapel murders is an American doctor, Francis Tumblety. See Evans and Gainey for an exhaustive analysis of this ultimately unconvincing candidate.

22. In "The Master of Murder Castle: A Classic of Chicago Crime," a 1943 article published in *Harper's Magazine*, John Bartlow Martin explains why H. H. Holmes merits our attention: "He deserves to rank with the great criminals of history. Crime writers reserve the word 'monster' for top-notch murderers. A monster ranks above such lesser criminals as fiends, beasts, and phantoms. He must meet certain rigid requirements. His victims, killed over a period of years and not for money alone, must be numerous and preferably female, and he must do unusual things with their bodies; he must inhabit a gloomy, forbidding dwelling, and he should be of a scientific bent. The master of murder castle possessed all these qualifications and more" (76).

In a similar vein, William Brannon in a 1962 essay entitled "The Anatomical Practice of Dr. H. H. Holmes," describes Holmes as "a colossus in the annals of American crime" (66). Finis Farr, in his 1973 history of Chicago, is even more explicit in his defense of Holmes's significance, describing him as "a Chicagoan who has been neglected, and denied his place in the history of American crime. For Mudgett was the most heartless and monstrous killer of human beings about whom we have any record. It will be granted that Mudgett cannot be

268 NOTES TO PAGES 52–55

compared as a killer with military men; what we have here is a free-lance murderer, working on his own, but in that line Mudgett stood supreme" (217).

These examples illustrate how quickly supposedly objective assessment can become not-so-veiled admiration. Indeed, in some cases the admiration is not veiled at all. In his introductory comments to Brannon's essay, Anthony Boucher, the well-known true-crime writer and editor, explains that he sometimes uses the pseudonym of H. H. Holmes "out of pure admiration for a man who was, within his chosen field, superb both as an artist and as a craftsman" (*Quality* 66). Such expressions of admiration, which cannot be found in the work of female true-crime writers, illustrate both a male identification with what is taken to be a strong and assertive man, and the reasons why so many true-crime writers urge an aesthetic approach to crime. Such an approach is used to license expressions of admiration for killers by removing tiresome considerations of morality and ethics.

23. Bloch is a key modern mythographer of serial murder, the author not only of one of the best-known pieces of Jack the Ripper fiction, "Yours Truly, Jack the Ripper," but also of *Psycho*, based on the crimes of Wisconsin serial killer Ed Gein and subsequently the basis for the Alfred Hitchcock movie of the same name.

24. The *Chicago Daily News* of July 26, 1895, noted: "The police are so overwhelmed with evidence of Holmes' various crimes that they hardly know which clews to follow first . . . If only a small portion of them pan out Holmes will hold a record of which Jack the Ripper would be proud" ("Wealth" 1). The fact that Chicago journalists did not pursue the subject of possible similarities between Holmes and the Ripper is curious in view of the existence of the Whitechapel Club in Chicago. The Whitechapel Club, named after the area of London in which Jack the Ripper committed his murders, was founded by Chicago journalists in 1889 and was designed to be a social (that is, drinking) club with a restricted membership. The most striking feature of the club was its headquarters, decorated with human skulls and a large number of weapons used in various Chicago murders. Although the club had folded by the time of Holmes's arrest in 1894, its existence indicates that the city's journalists were extremely familiar with the Ripper case. See Larson 31–33 and Lorenz for more information.

25. All reviews quoted are from the inside cover of the Pocket Star edition of *Depraved*.

26. The rise of the life insurance industry was offered as an explanatory context for Holmes's actions by Cesare Lombroso, the famous criminologist, in an influential 1898 article published in the *North American Review* on why homicide was on the rise in the United States: "Even some of the greatest and most important of the economical associations of America, as for example that of life insurance, furnish to heartless speculators in human life incentives for assassination . . . as witness the case of Holmes, to whom poison served as the means and life insurance the motive for the commission of his nefarious deeds" (4). The phrase "speculator in human life" summarizes the combination of killer and businessman that I am arguing defines Holmes.

27. Seltzer argues that Holmes's awareness of himself as a product, and his desire to control the distribution of that product, extended to his manner of burial. Immediately after his execution, in accordance with his instructions, Holmes's body was placed in a coffin

that was then filled with cement. That coffin was then lowered into the ground, and several tons of concrete filled the grave. Thus, Holmes made it impossible for anyone to use his body for research and/or pecuniary purposes. Holmes retained the copyright on Holmes. See Seltzer 233-34.

28. When confronted by the obvious falsehoods in his confession, Holmes was quite forthright in admitting that it was a fabrication, produced for a particular audience for a handsome fee: "Of course, it is not true, but the newspapers wanted a sensation and they got it" (quoted in Geyer 504). Holmes was both aware of how he was being constructed as a celebrity and happy to participate in that process.

29. The full text of the letter is as follows: "Dear Sir: My ideas are that you should get from the New York *Herald* and the Philadelphia *Press* all the cuts they have and turn those we want over to the printer, to have them electroplated at his expense. Use the large cut with full beard published August 25 in the *Herald* for my picture on page opposite the opening chapter, having the autographs of my two names (Holmes and Mudgett) engraved and electroplated at the same time, to go under the picture . . . As soon as the book is published, get it onto the Philadelphia and New York newsstands. Then get reliable canvassers who will work afternoons here in Philadelphia. Take one good street at a time, leave the book, then return about half an hour later for the money. No use to do this in the forenoon, when people are busy. I canvassed when a student this way, and found the method successful. Then, if you have any liking for the road, go over the ground covered by the book, spending a few days in Chicago, Detroit, and Indianapolis. Give copies to the newspapers in these cities to comment upon, it will assist the sale" (quoted in Schechter, *Depraved* 316-17). Holmes's incredible eye for detail at a time when his life was hanging in the balance speaks volumes about both his mental state and his tendency to view murder in strictly financial terms.

30. Corbitt's reporting of the Holmes case shared the economic motive that he attributed to Holmes. At the end of his book was an advertisement for a company that we can surmise had sponsored Corbitt: "Just one-half block East from the Holmes Castle at No. 628 W. 63rd Street is the establishment of THE CO-OPERATIVE TAILORS, who are doing first-class work for little money. You had better try them" (127). Perhaps the reason so few writers on the Holmes case are willing to argue for a mutually informing relationship between his business schemes and his murders is that it raises the potentially uncomfortable issue of profiting from death, an issue writers about crime cannot easily divorce themselves from.

31. Kohl and Middleton also ran dime museums in New York City, Milwaukee, Cincinnati, Louisville, St. Paul, Minneapolis, and Cleveland (Bogdan 37).

32. If one reads Barnum's famous speech "The Art of Money Getting," reprinted in the multiple editions of his autobiography, *Struggles and Triumphs*, that appeared between 1869 and 1889, it becomes even more clear what an inspiration Barnum would have been to someone like Holmes. Barnum taught his bourgeois audience in this speech to "treat their employees as expendable bodies" (B. Adams 36), and that is exactly what Holmes proceeded to do, literalizing Barnum's cutthroat business metaphor.

33. Holmes was also an archetypal confidence man, of course, because of his urban location. Part of the reason the figure of the confidence man became the focus of so much

concern in nineteenth-century America is that he provided a convenient way to articulate anxieties about the consequences of industrialization and urbanization for American society. In his influential 1899 book *The Growth of Cities in the Nineteenth Century*, Adna Ferrin Weber never mentions Holmes by name, but his description of the dangerous potentialities enabled by the city could have been written with Holmes in mind: "The mediocrity of the country is transformed by the city into the highest talent or the lowest criminal" (442). Holmes was unavoidably an urban phenomenon, and this was another disquieting thought at a time when the United States was becoming defined more and more by its cities.

CHAPTER TWO

1. When he was arrested, Fish had in his possession a number of newspaper clippings about the case of Fritz Haarmann. Haarmann was a German serial killer active in post–World War I Hanover who may have been responsible for the deaths of as many as fifty youths. In his discussion of Foucault, Weeks comments that another consequence of the invention of a "type" is that it opens up "the possibility of new modes of self-articulation" (102). Once the type of "mass murderer" exists, in other words, it allows individuals who commit such acts to think of themselves as mass murderers and to compare themselves to other examples of the same type, as suggested by Fish's interest in Haarmann.

2. Dickson's term does surface occasionally in the literature, as when John Godwin refers to "multicide" approvingly in his 1978 book *Murder U.S.A.: The Ways We Kill Each Other*.

3. Currently, the FBI's relationship with popular culture is characterized by a policy of "openness," which involves pursuing a proactive relationship with media sources, a relationship typified by the television program *America's Most Wanted*, co-produced by a regular production team and the FBI's Public Affairs Office. Although the FBI remains cautious about the possible negatives of being associated with the sensationalism of such shows, on the whole the Bureau recognizes that "weekly 'crime-time' television shows have resulted in the apprehension of fugitives, the solution of difficult cases, and positive publicity for the law-enforcement agencies involved" (S. A. Nelson 2).

4. Earlier complaints about America's crime-ridden state had stopped short of calling for a national police force but still provided a good sense of which way the wind was blowing. In an article entitled "Our Permanent Crime Wave" that appeared in *Harper's Magazine* in 1927, Edward Hale Bierstadt lamented that "in Europe, one finds a national organization, built for permanency; in America, one finds a local organization, constructed to meet the exigencies of the political administration" (65). Bierstadt went on to argue that "as the prevention and detection of crime are national rather than local problems, it will be more efficient if we consider them from a national rather than from a local point of view" (65). With such views, Bierstadt would probably have greeted the formation of the Bureau with great enthusiasm.

5. The list of G-man-related films provided by Kim Newman illustrates both the intensity of the popular cultural response to this figure and the length of time the FBI was able to capitalize upon the image: *Trapped by G-Men* (1937), *Federal Bullets* (1937), *Border G-Men* (1938), *When G-Men Step In* (1938), *Federal Manhunt* (1939), *Federal Fugitives* (1941),

Parole, Inc. (1949), *Federal Man* (1950), *Federal Agents at Large* (1950), *I Was a Communist for the FBI* (1951), *FBI Girl* (1951), and *FBI Code 98* (1964) (Newman 128).

6. Not everyone approved of using the gangster to construct a mutually beneficial relationship between popular culture and law enforcement. In a 1931 article in *Scribner's Magazine*, journalist Malcolm Logan punctured the myth of the "supercriminal" gangster, arguing that the reality of these gangsters was far more mundane: "there are few of these arch-criminals who can survive a painstaking inquiry into their records" (43). Nevertheless, Logan concluded, the media would continue to glorify the gangster because the image of the supercriminal sold newspapers and allowed the police to pose as geniuses whenever a gangster was arrested.

7. P. Jenkins, "Serial" 386–87, argues that even if one does acknowledge the presence of the mobile serial killer, there is still no justification for the claim that such a killer requires new federal institutions to control him. Jenkins notes that there were mobile serial murderers in the United States in the 1920s, and local police departments were quite capable of networking with police departments in other jurisdictions in order to track and capture such killers.

8. Although the institutional benefits of the concept of serial murder for the FBI were quickly apparent, the term itself took a little while to catch on. Throughout the 1980s, one can find examples of "mass murder" being used either interchangeably with "serial murder" or as an umbrella term including the smaller categories of "serial murder" and "simultaneous murder." The most stubborn adherents to this terminology were Jack Levin and James Alan Fox in their popular and influential book *Mass Murder: America's Growing Menace*. By the 1990s, however, even Levin and Fox had capitulated to the FBI use of "serial murder," thus concluding the gradual ascent of this term, an ascent that began some ninety years before.

9. John Douglas, in a book written after his retirement from the FBI, is refreshingly honest about having seen the Bureau's work on serial murder as an opportunity to expand his sphere of influence: "Once the profiling program was well-established and respected for helping to solve violent crimes such as murder, rape, and kidnapping . . . I wanted to expand outward and start bringing other investigative agencies like Secret Service and ATF into our orbit" (Douglas and Olshaker, *Anatomy* 50).

10. The place of psychological profiling in the FBI's response to serial murder may seem to contradict what I said earlier about the hostility of law enforcement to psychological perspectives on crime. According to its defenders, however, what differentiates profiling from idle speculation about a murderer's unconscious motivations is its strict focus on crime scene evidence. Any psychological speculations are firmly anchored in such evidence. This crime scene focus, law enforcement agencies argue, makes psychological profiling both more reliable and more objective than conventional psychological perspectives on murder.

11. The film's presentation of the human face of the FBI has both major and minor dimensions. One of the main ways in which Demme's film humanizes the Bureau is through the extraordinary number of long close-ups of Clarice Starling's face as she does battle with the world around her. Jodie Foster's ability to make her face into a canvas for her emotions highlights this aspect of the film even more.

12. Although someone with Demme's self-professed radical politics might be expected to be uncomfortable about lionizing the FBI, in an interview after the release of the film Demme drew a distinction between the FBI as a whole and the work of the BSU: "I feel great about the Behavioral Science Unit . . . [they] are the pioneers, not only in looking for ways to catch [serial killers], but to prevent them from being produced" (Taubin, "Demme's" 77). Demme's understanding of the aims and effectiveness of the BSU is questionable at best.

13. Despite these criticisms, even today it is relatively easy to find unqualified praise of the FBI's expertise in profiling and serial murder. Ann Rule, for example, in her foreword to former FBI profiler Russell Vorpagel's book, claims that "in the hands of those FBI agents and superior detectives who employ profiling, it is an almost mystic process" (10).

14. Two other aspects of Douglas's post-Bureau career should be acknowledged. One began in 1998 with the publication of *John Douglas's Guide to Careers in the FBI*, a book published in association with Kaplan Educational Centers. Since then, Douglas has published several other guides with Kaplan, using his celebrity to sell these books. Not surprisingly, these Kaplan books all contain advertisements for Douglas and Olshaker's true-crime books. The other aspect began in 1999, with the publication of an absolutely terrible thriller, *Broken Wings*, again co-authored with Olshaker. The novel takes its title from a slang term for a disgraced FBI agent, a group of whom have formed a loose confederation under the leadership of John Donovan, a painfully obvious stand-in for Douglas himself. As awful as this book is, it clearly did well enough to spawn a sequel, *Man Down*, published in 2002.

15. Lindsay was eventually allowed to retire from the Bureau. Since then, he has published several more novels featuring his maverick FBI protagonist, Mike Devlin. Revealingly, Lindsay's jaundiced picture of his former employer seems to have softened over the years. His 1997 novel *Freedom to Kill*, for example, ends with the FBI director (who is clearly based on Louis Freeh) offering Devlin the opportunity to serve the FBI as a permanent maverick, perhaps signaling Lindsay's own rapprochement with the Bureau.

16. The serial killer's utility for the FBI was underlined by the media's response to a 1999 serial murder case involving Rafael Resendez-Ramirez, who was riding on freight trains throughout the southwestern United States to evade capture. The case came in the midst of a torrent of criticism aimed at the FBI about a variety of subjects; the media's generally positive and respectful coverage of the Bureau's investigation of the case emphasized why the FBI enjoyed and needed the serial killer so much: he gave them unquestioned authority (Klaidman and Zarembo).

17. Interestingly, J. Edgar Hoover was also against the federalization of crime investigation in many instances. In 1964, when turning down requests for the FBI to become responsible for drug-related crimes, Hoover said, "I am against, and have been for years, the growth of the FBI. I think we are entirely too big today, bigger than we should be. I would have liked to see the FBI remain small; but that has been impossible because Congress has yearly enacted legislation expanding the investigative jurisdiction of the Bureau" (quoted in Powers, *Secrecy* 403). It should be noted, however, that Hoover's qualms about the excessive size of the Bureau came not from ethical objections to overfederalization but from a fear that the organization might become too big for him to control.

CHAPTER THREE

1. For a comprehensive list of serial killer movies, go to the Internet Movie Database Web site: http://us.imdb.com/List?tv=on&&keywords=serial-killer. As one might expect, the number of these films has increased enormously over the years. According to Eric Hickey, between the 1960s and the 1990s, the average number of "multiple-homicide films in which serial killing is the primary agenda" increased from an average of twelve a year in the 1960s to fifty-four a year in the 1990s (4). In part, of course, this increase is due to an expansion of the industry in those years, but it undoubtedly also reflects increased public interest in and demand for films on the subject of serial murder.

2. In a similar vein, Stephen Prince has noted that characteristic cinematic techniques tend to distance the viewer from representations of violence: "Changing camera positions, controlled lighting, montage editing, music, and special effects create significant aesthetic pleasure and emotional distance for viewers, who can use these cues as a means of insulating themselves from the depicted violence" (*Screening* 28). Prince's argument has a surface plausibility, but there is no intrinsic reason why the techniques he describes should distance the viewer from representations of violence (even if we assume, as Prince does, that the viewer will perceive these techniques as "cues"). Indeed, such techniques are just as likely to draw the viewer further into the artifice.

3. One of the notable features of *Red Dragon* was the reappearance of screenwriter Ted Tally, who won an Oscar for his screenplay for *The Silence of the Lambs* but was one of the many who declined to participate in the making of *Hannibal* because he was disturbed by the tone of Harris's novel. By the time *Red Dragon* came around, Tally had not only overcome such qualms but also presumably overcome the beliefs he held when he wrote the play *Coming Attractions* in 1986. As Tally described it, *Coming Attractions*, a critique of the celebrity culture that was growing up around serial killers, came out of his "indignation and . . . a kind of despair" at the fact that "in the rapacious, all-pervasive glare of television, infamy and entertainment shine with the same light" (275). Leaving aside the accuracy of such an observation, we might note the irony in the fact that the moral high ground was taken by someone who was to make such an instrumental contribution to serial killer celebrity culture just a few years later.

4. My reason for choosing military metaphors will become clear later in the chapter when I discuss the distinction between "strong" and "weak" violence in relation to serial killer films.

5. To some extent, the decision about how to market *Seven* was forced upon New Line. Although Chris Pula recognized that both Morgan Freeman and Brad Pitt "shared tremendous celebrity . . . their fan bases were not consistent with audiences who want a psychological thriller and certainly not one of this ilk, this darkness" (Matzer S13). In this case, having big stars was a marketing problem rather than a marketing solution.

6. The reader will notice that my discussion of *NBK* focuses on the film's director in a way that my discussions of the other films do not. The reason for this emphasis is Oliver Stone's eagerness to be identified as an auteur with a serious, even profound, message. Stone's overblown claims for *NBK* require a director-centered approach from the critic.

7. According to Leong, Sell, and Thomas, *Natural Born Killers* has been linked to more copycat killings than any other film (70).

8. Jane Hamsher, one of the film's producers, notes that it was the coincidental occurrence of the Nicole Brown Simpson murder just as *NBK* was ready for release that persuaded Warner Brothers that the film might be a hit and should therefore be promoted properly (215).

9. Interestingly, according to Hamsher, Quentin Tarantino was inspired to write the screenplay that became the basis for *Natural Born Killers* by an example of tabloid television: an episode of *A Current Affair* that profiled the trial of the Night Stalker, Richard Ramirez, and the presence of female "groupies" at the trial (25–26).

10. Stone chose this ending over an alternative ending he filmed. In the alternate ending, Mickey and Mallory are killed while trying to escape from the prison by Owen, another convict. David Courtwright quotes Stone as saying that he stuck with the original ending because it "had more juice" (35). If Stone had chosen the alternative ending, there would still have been the danger of conveying a trite moral: "Crime does not pay," "Those who live by the sword die by the sword," and so on, but at least Stone would have avoided his egregious capitulation to the celebrity culture organized around serial killers. Clearly, the "juice" was too sweet for Stone to resist.

11. Herzfeld's choice of non-American villains gives an American audience the opportunity to mock Slovak and Razgul's (outdated/naive) belief in a Hollywood version of America (where fame is the ultimate value) while also indulging their own residual belief in such a fantasy.

12. Unless otherwise indicated, all reviews of *15 Minutes* are taken from the online movie review site "Rotten Tomatoes," which can be found at the following address: http://www.rottentomatoes.com/m/15_minutes/.

13. Stars can also help films in other ways. As Laurent Bouzereau has argued, in the context of comparing *The Silence of the Lambs* with the far more controversial *Henry, Portrait of a Serial Killer*, the presence of the well-known Anthony Hopkins in the former film makes it more accessible to a mainstream audience: "It's okay to like Hannibal, because he is, after all, Anthony Hopkins, and that's Hollywood. But Henry is another story" (197).

14. The audience's inability to distance itself from what it sees in *MBD* and the film's emphasis on the ordinariness of its killer explain why Ben's death in this film does not serve the same disavowing function as Kürten's death in *Copycat*. Appropriately, given his penchant for copying, *Copycat*'s audience never finds out "Peter Kürten's" "real" identity, so that he remains (to adapt Judith Butler's phrase) "a kind of imitation for which there is no original" (313). The continued mystery about Kürten's identity, along with the fact that, like so many other serial killers, Kürten is presented as a superhuman, almost supernatural being (Epstein 71, 73), establishes a distance between audience and killer in *Copycat* that makes Kürten's death a satisfactory way for the audience to disavow any previous feelings of identification with this character. By the time of Ben's death, however, the audience has come to know him too intimately and an identificatory relationship with him has become too well established for it to feel that his death necessarily resolves anything.

15. I do not want to give the impression that McNaughton's approach to the film was entirely unconnected to budgetary constraints. Just like the filmmakers behind *Man Bites Dog*, McNaughton was to some extent forced into making decisions that turned out to be aesthetically appropriate: "I immediately thought: Here was a real-life horror. And, anyway, we had no budgets for chain saws and special effects and monsters" (quoted in Bouzereau 199).

16. McNaughton's refusal to make a slasher movie is especially notable because that is exactly the kind of film MPI wanted him to make. In fact, when MPI first saw *Henry* they were dismayed: "When the filmmakers organized a screening of *Henry* for MPI, their comments were: 'Where's the blood and where's the tits? You've made a goddamn art film. What are we going to do with this?'" (Bouzereau 201). Subsequently, MPI got behind McNaughton's film to the extent of suing the MPAA to have its X rating removed.

CHAPTER FOUR

1. The rise of seriality in television also pleased advertisers. The commercial sponsors of television programs wanted a reliable audience for their advertisements just as much as the studios wanted a reliable audience for their shows.

2. In his classic study of the "power elite," sociologist C. Wright Mills argued that celebrities function as a "screen" for the upper classes by distracting the public's attention from what the upper classes are doing: "In part, [celebrities] have stolen the show, for that is their business; in part, they have been given the show by the upper classes who have withdrawn and who have other business to accomplish" (75). With this point in mind, television appearances by film stars in the 1950s had the potential to disguise both the upper-class status of the film stars themselves and the activities of those (deliberately) less visible groups that made up the power elite.

3. Kozloff's remarks are echoed by David Lynch's explanation of how he adjusted himself to the constraints of television when making *Twin Peaks*: "You do have these breaks every 11 minutes or so . . . and so if you can make the scenes work and put a couple together, you hit a commercial and then it's a whole new ball game when you come back. You do find yourself thinking in terms of making these little 11-minute movies, and it's kinda neat" (quoted in Knickelbine 111).

4. In the context of a television drama series, an "arc" refers to a continuing story pattern that gets played out over the course of more than one episode and sometimes over more than one season. A story arc can be developed continuously until it is completed, but it is more usual for a drama series to treat a story arc discontinuously, inserting what are known as "stand-alone" episodes in the midst of a story arc and then coming back to that arc at a later point. *The X-Files'* ongoing conspiracy narrative about alien invasion of Earth, developed over several seasons, is one of the more complicated story arcs in a television drama series.

5. In *The X-Files*, it is often serial murder itself that plays the role of the hermeneutic code, interrupting the ongoing conspiracy narrative with a "stand-alone" serial killer episode that delays further revelations about the conspiracy.

6. Elayne Rapping has suggested that criminals are represented by tabloid television crime shows such as *Hard Copy* as domestic terrorists: "Like the terrorist, the tabloid

criminal is an alien, an outsider who poses a threat to social order because he does not conform to the psychological and moral norms by which we, in Western society, have learned to live peacefully together" (268). In the epilogue, I will develop Rapping's thought-provoking insight by comparing the figures of the terrorist and the serial killer.

7. In the case of *The X-Files*, at least, this combination of open and closed elements resulted partly from a demand by the network: "Fox still harbored various creative concerns, not the least of them being the issue of closure, or how completely and neatly the episodes would be resolved . . . Carter did agree to some conciliatory modifications—part of an unavoidable evolutionary process with any series—and even he says some of those changes have been for the better. The idea of a Scully voice-over while typing up her field report notes, for example, was tacked on to the first regular episode, 'Deep Throat,' to mollify Fox's desire to provide resolution to the story—'bringing closure,' as Carter puts it, 'to a non-closed case'" (Lowry, *Truth* 20).

8. I am borrowing the title of this section from Michele Malach's essay "I Want to Believe . . . in the FBI: The Special Agent and *The X-Files*" because it captures so precisely the structure of audience investment that I believe these drama series encourage.

9. These series' focus on character is not accidental but a standard feature of the televisual medium. As Jeffrey Scheuer has argued, television is especially preoccupied with individuals: "A particularly common form in which television concretizes is the human form: it *personalizes*, focusing on—and often exaggerating the importance of—individuals (heroes and villains, freaks, clowns, and celebrities)" (74–75, original emphasis).

10. The characters of Gordon Cole (Cooper's deaf FBI boss, played by David Lynch himself) and the cross-dressing DEA agent Denise/Dennis Bryson (played by David Duchovny before he hit the big time with *The X-Files*) are two more examples of the positive portrayal of federal law enforcement in *Twin Peaks*, inasmuch as their characters imply that the organizations they belong to have a strong tolerance for personal eccentricity.

11. We should not underestimate the significance of a female protagonist in explaining the success of *The X-Files*. Although Scully is there partly to suggest the existence of a more liberal Bureau in the process of reforming Hoover-era prohibitions on the hiring of female agents, what is most notable about the character of Scully is how insistently the show has resisted representing her in terms of sexist stereotypes. This resistance began with the casting of Gillian Anderson as Scully, a choice that Chris Carter insisted on over the studio's demands that a busty blonde bombshell-type be given the role (Lowry, *Truth* 15). The most notable way in which the show has not played by the conventional gender rules of crime drama has been its repeated refusal to have the characters of Mulder and Scully become romantically involved with each other, despite active lobbying by huge numbers of fans for precisely this outcome. Despite this seeming commitment to the nonsexist representation of its lead female character, however, it should be noted that although Scully's FBI career is undoubtedly stymied by her association with Mulder, *The X-Files* is careful to avoid suggesting the presence of institutional sexism within the Bureau, even though there is abundant evidence that such sexism exists (see De Long and Petrini and, in a fictional vein, the novels of Thomas Harris). In this respect, as in so many others, *The X-Files* proves to be rather protective of the Bureau's reputation.

12. Just as with the other shows, those associated with *Profiler* have been at pains to deny its use of paranormal or supernatural elements. For example, in a 1998 CNN report by Jim Moret, Ally Walker (who plays Sam Waters) said that her character's "gift" in profiling was "'not paranormal at all . . . There are actually profilers in the world who do this kind of thing, and they look at crime sites and the behavior associated with the clues that are left there. And they determine what kind of person would leave clues, leave them in that way, and you can tell what kind of person would do the crime . . . They can get really specific,' she added. 'They can get down to age, what kind of religious beliefs they would have.'" Walker's understanding of FBI procedure is sketchy, to say the least.

13. John Leonard has reprinted some of these hyperbolic initial responses to *Twin Peaks*: "'As strange and unsettling a project as any in the medium's history' (*People*). 'The first TV masterpiece of the '90s . . . *Dallas* with an IQ, *Dynasty* without all that lousy acting' (Dallas *Morning News*) . . . 'Just this side of a godsend . . . a captivating blend of the existential and the pulpy, the surreal and the neo-real, the grim and the farcical' (Washington *Post*) . . . 'Like nothing you've ever seen in prime time, or on God's earth. It may be the most hauntingly original work ever done for American TV (*Time*)'" (237).

14. Robert Ressler, the other key figure in the FBI's work on serial killers, has compared himself to Mulder and Scully in a way that indicates that they not only share methodologies but also a common language of monsters: "'What my colleagues and I have done is design a little expertise . . . looking beyond what the conventional police investigator sees,' Ressler explains. 'That's where I become a prototype for Mulder and Scully. What they're doing is stepping beyond the traditional role of the investigator and looking at things from a perspective that very few people have. Theoretically they're into aliens and monsters and cannibals and vampires. But basically, that's what I'm into. Aliens I don't know, but I'm into vampires and I'm into cannibals'" (quoted in Goldman 62).

CHAPTER FIVE

1. The blurb on the front covers of the Kensington Publishing series emphasized the advantage the books had over television: "What they couldn't tell you on TV!" More recently, network television has followed the lead of its more adventurous cable competitors in this area. In July 2001, CBS announced the broadcast of "Murder, They Wrote," a series of six episodes of its popular show *48 Hours*, each one inspired by a different true-crime book (J. Schwartz). Featuring a mixture of interviews (including an interview with the book's author) and crime reenactment, each episode compressed a true-crime title into a one-hour program. Although such synergistic relationships between different media are becoming more and more popular, they are not always possible. In an October 28, 2002, *USA Today* article on the D.C. sniper shootings, Charles Spicer, executive editor of the "True Crime Library" series at St. Martin's Press, is quoted as saying, "I don't think I'm going to do something on the sniper case . . . The reason is, it's going to be so completely covered in the media" (Donahue D1).

2. Pearson was aware of the Leopold and Loeb case but thought it insignificant and unworthy of attention. In "The Bordens: A Postscript," Pearson describes being upbraided by a reader for his obsession with the Borden case. When this reader asked Pearson whether

he thought Leopold and Loeb the equal of the Borden assassin, Pearson was unambiguous in his defense of the earlier case: "The unknown assassin of Mr. and Mrs. Borden could give the two bright youths from Chicago not only cards and spades, but a stroke a hole, half-fifteen, ten yards start, and any other handicap known to sport, and still beat them, hands down—in courage, in coolness, in resolution, in audacity, in intellectual power, and in everything that goes to make up the 'perfect murder,' which they set out to commit and so egregiously foozled" ("Bordens" 292). Once again, the Borden case inspired Pearson to conspicuous levels of eloquence.

3. Pearson often defends the Puritans in his work. For example, in his book-length study of the Borden case, Pearson claims that "the more the influence of the Puritan fades, the less his hands rest upon arts and life, the more do dramatists, novelists and critics work themselves into a fury about him. To excoriate the Puritan—the world's whipping boy— brings one such firm convictions of one's own breadth and tolerance, that even a scanty knowledge of history is thought superfluous" (*Trial* 9–10). Pearson's contempt for cant, no matter how reactionary, deserves our admiration.

4. There is evidence to suggest that Pearson even rethought his position on serial killers. According to Jane Durnell and Norman Stevens, while in Hollywood in 1934 to work on the film *The Bride of Frankenstein*, Pearson wrote a screenplay on Jack the Ripper (xxi).

5. Appropriately, given the prominence that serial murder would later have in the true-crime genre, *In Cold Blood* was first published serially in the *New Yorker* in the fall of 1965 before being released in book form in 1966.

6. The exception to this rule, perhaps, is Norman Mailer's relationship with Gary Gilmore as detailed in Mailer's monumental book *The Executioner's Song*. Mailer's text is indebted to *In Cold Blood* on many levels.

7. The article was authored by Joseph Satten, Karl Menninger, Irwin Rosen, and Martin Mayman and was entitled "Murder without Apparent Motive: A Study in Personality Disorganization."

8. Ironically, this feature of Capote's work is about as close as Capote comes to having anything in common with Edmund Pearson. Although their respective stances on criminal responsibility and the death penalty are diametrically opposed (Pearson insists upon the validity of these ideas while Capote attempts to relativize them), both writers concentrate on these issues as a way of suggesting that true-crime narratives may have social utility. For Pearson, true-crime narratives can help bring about a clear-eyed view of the need to punish criminals, while *In Cold Blood* at some points reads like a crusade against the death penalty and for the reform of legal concepts of insanity. This emphasis on the social utility of true crime as a way of making the genre respectable gets developed much more explicitly in the work of Ann Rule.

9. After a year, Govoni told Rule that she could write under her real name, but Rule decided to keep the pseudonym in order to protect herself and her family from potentially vengeful criminals.

10. The way Rule took true crime into mainstream magazines replicates, in many ways, Pearson's success in the 1920s and 1930s. The difference, however, is that Rule's work proved to be especially popular with women's magazines. This is partly because people were

beginning to acknowledge publicly a fact about the demographics of true-crime readership that had been rumored for many years: that the majority of the genre's readers were women. Rule's popularity in women's magazines is also a reflection, as we will see shortly, of the "pro-woman" emphasis in her work.

11. The most egregious example of the second-order celebrity of true-crime writers is undoubtedly Jason Moss's 2000 book *The Last Victim: A True-Life Journey into the Mind of a Serial Killer*. The book details Moss's contacts with John Wayne Gacy and a number of other high-profile serial killers. Moss describes how he wrote letters to these killers that he felt would appeal to their personalities, a tactic that culminates with Moss visiting Gacy in prison, where Gacy assaults him. Although Moss claims that he began this project for disinterested academic reasons, one is entitled to feel some skepticism when he says that he was not motivated by the desire for financial gain. Despite presenting himself as Gacy's "last victim," Moss in fact victimizes Gacy. Perhaps the most remarkable feature of Moss's book is that it achieves something seemingly impossible; he makes us feel somewhat sorry for a brutal serial killer like Gacy because Moss is so obvious about his desire to exploit Gacy's fame for his own pecuniary benefit.

12. Cops also become heroes in true-crime narratives because they come to personify "normal" men as opposed to the "abnormal" serial killer. In *Lust Killer*, for example, Ann Rule comments at one point that "what had happened to Linda Salee enraged normal men. Especially police officers. If they could not have saved her, they would now find her killer and hand her over to the judicial system" (90). The police are presented as chivalrous men who protect and revenge victimized women.

13. The concept of the "mask of sanity" was developed by psychologist Hervey Cleckley in a 1941 book that took its title from the concept. In a strikingly appropriate coincidence, Cleckley later served (along with Emmanuel Tanay) as one of the court-appointed psychiatrists who examined Bundy in 1979 to determine whether or not he was legally competent to stand trial in Florida. Both Tanay and Cleckley concluded that he was.

CHAPTER SIX

1. This review appears on the back cover of the Signet edition of Ann Rule's best-selling book about Bundy, *The Stranger Beside Me*.

2. The only exception to this rule of writing about Bundy is *The Phantom Prince*, Elizabeth Kendall's fascinating account of her long-term relationship with Bundy during his years in Seattle. Despite Kendall's doubts about Bundy, she generally emphasizes how normal Bundy was and presents their relationship as the most compelling evidence of that normality. Interestingly, Kendall also provides evidence that Bundy was quite aware of how he was being read: "He said that being Ted Bundy in public was just too hard. If he was relaxed and normal, people said he was putting up a good facade to hide his weirdness; if he got upset or irritated with the press or police, people said he was evil; if he was jovial, people said he thought the idea of murder was funny" (123). Bundy understood the public need to define him as deviant, no matter how he behaved.

3. The broader phenomenon of seeing serial killers as experts on serial killing leads to other curious consequences; for example, true-crime writers will tell the story of a crime

from the killer's point of view (as in Cahill's book on John Wayne Gacy), or in what I call the "Lecter syndrome," serial killers are consulted about other serial killers, as when Brian Masters encouraged the British serial killer Denis Nilsen to provide an analysis of Jeffrey Dahmer. Perhaps the most striking example of this trend is serial child killer Ian Brady's "textbook" on serial murder, *The Gates of Janus: Serial Killing and Its Analysis*, published in 2001 against a background of enormous controversy and, of course, huge sales. At stake here is not just the question of what point of view one tells a "true crime" story from but also the status of convicted serial killers as authoritative repositories of supposedly authentic information, a status that configures serial killing more as a vocation than as a pathology.

4. Ironically, as we will see, hatred of men is regarded as a more than adequate motive to explain Aileen Wuornos. This, of course, is a consequence of the assumed identity between lesbianism and man hating, but such explanations of Wuornos's motive cannot entirely avoid the implication that hating men is a reasonable position to take!

5. By denying any link between heterosexuality and violence, true crime is opposing itself to a large body of feminist work that explores this subject. According to many critics, however, the tendency of some radical feminist analyses to argue for a link between heterosexuality and violence that (potentially) implicates all men is as reductive as asserting no link at all. With respect to serial murder, Philip Jenkins has argued that feminist writers on the subject, such as Jane Caputi, have tended to exaggerate the scale of the problem in order to support their political analysis: "The feminist literature thus continues to circulate extraordinarily high and inaccurate estimates of serial murder activity long after they have been discredited elsewhere" (*Using* 142). In addition, argues Jenkins, the feminist construction of serial murder assumes "that the normal serial killer was a man killing women or girls for sexual pleasure, and cases involving women offenders were all but ignored" (151).

Although Jenkins's criticisms are accurate, I also want to note that the feminist analysis of serial murder, unlike many other types of analysis, recognizes both that the vast majority of violent crimes are committed by men and takes that fact seriously. There is also evidence to suggest that the feminist linking of heterosexual maleness and violence comes much closer to defining the experience of actual women than the denial of any connection enacted by true crime. In a 1991 *48 Hours* show on CBS about serial murder, a Detective Creed, who was in the middle of a serial murder investigation, was quoted as saying, "You wouldn't believe the calls from wives and girlfriends that are calling up saying that they think their husband or boyfriend is the killer" ("Serial Killer" 4). In the "real world," connecting maleness and violence is not considered a stretch at all. Myriam Miedzian has articulated a helpful middle ground on this issue by recognizing the fact that "most acts of violence are committed by men" but also insisting that "*to say that men as a group are more violent than women is by no means to assert that all men are violent, violence-prone, or accepting of violence as a way of resolving conflicts and attaining power. It means only that a significantly higher percentage of men than women exhibit these tendencies.* This in no way denies that a large percentage of men are not violent at all, that a certain percentage of women are violent, or that some women are more violent than some men" (5, original emphasis). Miedzian finds a way to avoid arguing either that heterosexuality and violence are mutually exclusive or that they are practically identical.

6. For a representative example of Charles Socarides' work, see his 1968 book *The Overt Homosexual*.

7. Whitman emphasizes the authenticity of his views about homosexuality by revealing that they come from an authoritative source—the police: "With Patrolman Jack West, a veteran of vice and clean-up squads, I toured the downtown section of Detroit. What we saw in Grand Circus Park, in Cadillac Square, in Capitol Park, was both pathetic and horrible. We saw aggravated, unabashed cases of sex deviation. We saw the prowlers and the exhibitionists, the blatant accosters looking for pickups. 'I want you to see how they operate,' Patrolman West said. It was disgusting, but he showed me" (148). This breathless, voyeuristic vision of a Dantesque queer underworld is a common feature of contemporary true-crime narratives.

8. A savage irony of the assumed link between homosexuality and violence is that, if these two things are linked at all, it is in the sense that homosexuals are the victims of violence rather than its perpetrators. Books such as Gregory M. Herek and Kevin T. Berrill's *Hate Crimes* and Barbara Perry's *In the Name of Hate* give details of the epidemic of homophobic violence against gays and lesbians, of which the high-profile murder of Matthew Shepard in 1998 is just one example. Eve Kosofsky Sedgwick has argued that such violence is socially sanctioned through the concept of homosexual panic, which is used as a "defense for a person (typically a man) accused of antigay violence [and] implies that his responsibility for the crime was diminished by a pathological psychological condition, perhaps brought on by an unwanted sexual advance from the man he then attacked" (19).

Sedgwick's argument is alarmingly confirmed by the case of Nicolo Giangrasso, accused in Texas in 1991 of beating Charlie Perez Resendez to death. Although Giangrasso confessed, he was allowed to plead guilty to the lesser charge of involuntary manslaughter rather than stand trial for murder. Having accepted Giangrasso's claim of homosexual panic as a mitigating circumstance, on August 30, 1991, San Antonio district judge Terence McDonald gave Giangrasso a ten-year suspended sentence (Lopez 60). For more on homosexual panic, see Arthur Dong's film *Licensed to Kill*, which features extensive interviews with several murderers of gay men. Homosexual panic is just one of several motives mentioned in a film that is notable for insisting on the normality of these killers by refusing to describe them as monsters.

9. One consequence of the association between homosexuality, AIDS, and death has a twisted logic all its own: HIV-infected persons are regarded as murder weapons in their own right. C. Bard Cole and Chris McManus have described several examples of such situations: "Currently, several HIV-infected persons who allegedly bit, spat at, or intentionally bled on corrections officers are facing charges of attempted murder for using their bodily fluids as deadly weapons. Two of these cases have already concluded with convictions and are now on appeal; Curtis Weeks of Texas was sentenced to 99 years to life in prison for spitting on a prison guard, while Gregory D. Smith of New Jersey received 25 years for biting a penitentiary warden" (20).

10. The film historian Richard Dyer has made a similar point about films featuring gay murders: "Films about gay murders tend to be a semi-prurient, anthropological excursion into this peculiar, other, dangerous world, with endless scenes of gay

bars . . . It's an imaginary, anonymous, fetishistic, sexually-driven and very violent world" (McKenna 3).

11. For an example of an analysis that assumes that women are the natural victims of men, as opposed to children or other men, see the concluding part of *The Man Who Killed Boys*, Clifford Linedecker's study of the Chicago-based serial murderer of young men John Wayne Gacy, where he discusses approvingly various behavior modification therapies practiced in United States correctional facilities. One of these, Linedecker explains, is an aversion therapy for child molesters that works through the administering of electric shocks: "Prisoners are alternately shown slides of children and of adult women in G-strings or provocative clothing. If the inmates hesitate too long over the slides of children before switching to pictures of adult women they are given electrical shocks" (247). The message could not be clearer. We must return these men to "normality," where women are the correct objects of sadism and abuse.

12. McDougal presents these thoughts as the opinions of a police officer, George Troup. This underlines my earlier point about the tendency of true-crime writers to internalize law enforcement perspectives. Contrary to what one might expect, however, McDougal does not lump all gay serial killers together. For example, he discusses the cases of Patrick Kearney and William Bonin not only to bolster the association between homosexuality and violence but also to make the point that the subject of his book, Randy Kraft, was worse than either of them. The impulse to see a particular serial killer as the "worst ever" that I described earlier can result in unanticipated (and probably unintended) moments of fine discrimination in true-crime narratives.

13. See Herek and Berrill 24–25 for more on this subject.

14. Even Anne Schwartz acknowledges this aspect of the case (173), but Martha Schmidt's account is far more detailed and sympathetic.

15. Amy Archer-Gilligan killed somewhere between twenty and forty people in her home for the aged in Windsor, Connecticut, between 1907 and 1916 and received a life sentence. She eventually died at a Connecticut hospital for the insane in 1962 at the age of eighty-nine. Belle Gunness is believed to have killed around sixteen to twenty-eight men (many of whom had responded to Gunness's newspaper advertisement for a husband) at her farm in La Porte, Indiana, between 1896 and 1908. Gunness disappeared after her farmhouse was destroyed by a mysterious fire. She was never seen again.

16. At one point in the investigation, Wuornos's lover, Tyria Moore, was thought to have been Wuornos's accomplice. Moore was eventually cleared of any involvement in the murders and went on to become a key witness for the prosecution, being instrumental in eliciting a confession from Wuornos.

17. Examples of this type of attitude toward women are legion in true crime. See Gaute and Odell 107–8. See also Strean and Freeman's discussion of the German serial murderer Jürgen Bartsch (188ff.).

18. The prosecution claimed that the victims were simply good Samaritans who picked Wuornos up because they wanted to help an apparently stranded woman. I will return to this issue of how Wuornos's victims are portrayed in comparison to the victims of other serial murderers.

19. Of course, things are not quite as simple as this. By castigating feminists for a tendency to cast all women as victims and to explain violent women away with one extenuating/exonerating circumstance or another, Pearson forces us to confront some hard issues. She may be right to say that too much has been made of Wuornos as a victim of child abuse, and perhaps the kind of person Wuornos was has been sugarcoated by sympathetic writers, but on the other hand there has been so much vilification of Wuornos in the media that these sympathetic defenses really are the exception that prove the rule. Moreover, Pearson does not answer some difficult questions of her own. How do we critique the inconsistent use of abuse or self-defense as a mitigating circumstance without dismissing these explanations tout court, a position Pearson seems dangerously close to? Similarly, although it is true that a phenomenon such as battering within the lesbian community has often been overlooked because of the (frequently, politically self-interested) assumption that women are nonviolent, it is also understandable why lesbians in particular might want to deny the violence that exists in their community in view of the fact that so many straights assume the existence of "predator lesbians" (see Griggers 169).

20. For an especially flagrant example of this attitude, see Wilson and Seaman's description of the "Hillside Strangler" murders (256).

EPILOGUE

1. The most generous thing one can say about the belief that 9/11 constitutes an epistemic break is that such a judgment is premature, as Jürgen Habermas has argued: "Only in retrospect will we be able to understand if the symbolically suffused collapse of the capitalistic citadels in lower Manhattan implies a break of that type or if this catastrophe merely confirms, in an inhuman and dramatic way, a long-known vulnerability of our complex civilization" (27).

2. Even Roy Lewis Norris, an incarcerated serial killer, responded to 9/11 with outrage and saw Osama bin Laden as the epitome of evil. Despite the fact that he committed a horrendous series of murders of young women with his partner, Lawrence Bittaker, in California in 1979 and 1980, Norris still felt he had the right to take the moral high ground with respect to bin Laden. With no apparent sense of irony, Norris released a statement after 9/11 arguing that, if bin Laden should ever be apprehended, he should be punished by being "surgically paralyzed from the neck down and forced to look only at the faces of his victims for the rest of his life," describing this as a "just ending for a would be martyr of HATE!" (R. Norris, original emphasis). Apart from the obvious fact that this is hypocrisy on a grand scale, Norris's response speaks volumes about how quickly and completely the terrorist in general and bin Laden in particular became evil personified in the wake of 9/11.

3. The attitude of the British government toward terrorism in the 1980s constitutes a classic example of this tendency. Margaret Thatcher insisted on describing the acts of groups such as the Irish Republican Army (IRA) as crimes, both to deny legitimacy to the group and to ensure that captured members of the IRA would not enjoy privileged status as political prisoners. See Schlesinger, Murdock, and Elliott, 4.

4. Whether or not one thinks of Muhammad and Malvo as "domestic terrorists" in the mold of McVeigh or not, such a comparison has the virtue of highlighting a significant

commonality between McVeigh and Muhammad: they are both Gulf War veterans. Although research into a possible link between mass/serial murder and military service is in its infancy, the theorizing of such a link offers the tantalizing possibility of being able to connect "domestic" and "foreign," "illegitimate" and "legitimate" forms of violence. See Castle and Hensley.

5. Although the definitional quagmire that surrounds the concepts of "terrorism," and, to a lesser extent, "serial murder," may be uncomfortable for members of the American public, those who have the power to label individuals as terrorists have a different take on the matter, as Lon Troyer explains: "Definitional ambiguity is not an unfortunate state of affairs for the discourse on terrorism—it is its tactical strength. The malleability of the term allows for its opportunistic application." The actions of the D.C. Sniper case prosecutors are opportunistic in precisely this sense.

6. There is even a connection between the D.C. sniper shootings and the Baton Rouge murders. Because John Muhammad and John Lee Malvo had reportedly been in Baton Rouge in the year before their arrest, their DNA was tested to see if it matched the DNA of the Baton Rouge killer. The results cleared Muhammad and Malvo, but the fact that the test was thought to be worth carrying out suggests that law enforcement officials saw the pair more as serial killers than as terrorists ("Muhammad").

7. I have in mind here such works as Robin Morgan's *The Demon Lover: On the Sexuality of Terrorism*, which locates terrorism in the context of patriarchal violence, Rhonda Hammer's *Antifeminism and Family Terrorism*, which seeks to rename "domestic violence" as "family terrorism" as a way to understand the seriousness and impact of such violence, Jane Caputi and Diana E. H. Russell's essay "Femicide: Sexist Terrorism against Women," and Isabel Marcus's essay "Reframing 'Domestic Violence': Terrorism in the Home."

8. The arrest of suspect Derrick Todd Lee also contained familiar elements, with friends and acquaintances expressing their disbelief that Lee could be involved ("I could not believe it when the police came and said he was wanted for killing women. None of us could believe it" ["Arrest"]). Typically, this bewilderment was accompanied by ample evidence that Lee had a history of violence against women (see NaaNes). In October 2004, Lee was found guilty of the first-degree murder of Charlotte Murray Pace.

WORKS CITED

Abelove, Henry. "Freud, Male Homosexuality, and the Americans." *Dissent*, 1986, 59–69.

Achenbach, Joel. "Serial Killers: Shattering the Myth." *Washington Post*, 14 Apr. 1991, F5–6.

Adams, Bluford. *E Pluribus Barnum: The Great Showman and the Making of U.S. Popular Culture*. Minneapolis: University of Minnesota Press, 1997.

Adams, Rachel. *Sideshow U.S.A.: Freaks and the American Cultural Imagination*. Chicago: University of Chicago Press, 2001.

Aileen: Life and Death of a Serial Killer. Dir. Nick Broomfield and Joan Churchill. Lantern Lane Entertainment, 2003.

Aileen Wuornos: The Selling of a Serial Killer. Dir. Nick Broomfield. DEJ Productions, 1992.

Allen, Robert. *Speaking of Soap Operas*. Chapel Hill: University of North Carolina Press, 1985.

Altman, Mark. *Twin Peaks: Behind the Scenes*. Las Vegas, NV: Pioneer Books, 1990.

Anderson, Benedict. *Imagined Communities*. London: Verso, 1983.

Anderson, Christopher. *HollywoodTV: The Studio System in the Fifties*. Austin: University of Texas Press, 1994.

"Ann Rule—Queen of Crime." *Real Crime Book Digest* 1, no. 5 (1993/94): 6–7.

Ansen, David. "A Fresh Meal for Dr. L." *Newsweek*, 7 Oct. 2002, 68.

"Arrest Shocks Motor Lodge Residents." *CNN.com*, 28 May 2003. http://www.cnn.com.

Ault, Richard L., Jr. "NCAVC's Research and Development Program." *FBI Law Enforcement Bulletin* 55, no. 12 (1986): 6–8.

Austin Statesman. 10 Oct. 1888. *Casebook: Jack the Ripper.* http://casebook.org/press_reports/austin_statesman/as881010.html.

Barbas, Samantha. *Movie Crazy: Fans, Stars, and the Cult of Celebrity.* New York: Palgrave, 2001.

Barthes, Roland. "Delay and the Hermeneutic Sentence." In *The Poetics of Murder: Detective Fiction and Literary Theory,* ed. Glenn W. Most and William W. Stowe, 118–21. New York: Harcourt Brace Jovanovich, 1983.

Basilio, Miriam. "Corporal Evidence: Representations of Aileen Wuornos." *Art Journal* 55 (1996): 56–61.

Baudrillard, Jean. *The Spirit of Terrorism.* London: Verso, 2002.

Baumann, Ed. *Step into My Parlor: The Chilling Story of Serial Killer Jeffrey Dahmer.* Chicago: Bonus Books, 1991.

Bawer, Bruce. "Capote's Children." *New Criterion,* Jun. 1985, 39–43.

Bellafante, Gina. "Mission: Paranormal." *Time,* 28 Oct. 1996. Available at http://www.summernight.de/Proftime.htm.

Benjamin, Walter. "Critique of Violence." In *Reflections: Essays, Aphorisms, Autobiographical Writings,* 277–300. Trans. Edmund Jepthcott. New York: Schocken Books, 1986.

———. "The Work of Art in the Age of Mechanical Reproduction." In *Illuminations: Essays and Reflections,* ed. Hannah Arendt, 217–51. New York: Schocken Books, 1969.

Berg, Charles, and Clifford Allen. *The Problem of Homosexuality.* New York: Citadel Press, 1958.

Bergler, Edmund, M.D. *One Thousand Homosexuals.* Paterson, NJ: Pageant Books, 1959.

Bergman, David. *Gaiety Transfigured: Gay Self-Representation in American Literature.* Madison: University of Wisconsin Press, 1991.

Bernstein, Jill. "Eat Drink Man Woman." *Premiere,* Feb. 2001, 59–61, 106–7.

Bersani, Leo. *Homos.* Cambridge, MA: Harvard University Press, 1995.

Bierstadt, Edward Hale. "Our Permanent Crime Wave." *Harper's Magazine,* Dec. 1927, 61–70.

"Bin Laden, Alive and Dangerous." *CBSNEWS.com,* 14 Nov. 2002. http://www.cbsnews.com/stories/2002/11/14/attack/printable529368.shtml.

Birch, Helen. "Murder Most Freudian." *Observer,* 9 Dec. 1990, 57.

Biressi, Anita. *Crime, Fear, and the Law in True Crime Stories.* New York: Palgrave, 2001.

Black, Joel. *The Aesthetics of Murder: A Study in Romantic Literature and Contemporary Culture.* Baltimore: Johns Hopkins University Press, 1991.

Blair, Sara. "Henry James, Jack the Ripper, and the Cosmopolitan Jew: Staging Authorship in *The Tragic Muse.*" *ELH* 63, no. 2 (1996): 489–512.

Bloch, Robert. *American Gothic.* New York: Simon & Schuster, 1974.

Bloom, Clive. *Cult Fiction: Popular Reading and Pulp Theory.* New York: St. Martin's Press, 1996.

Bogdan, Robert. *Freak Show: Presenting Human Oddities for Amusement and Profit.* Chicago: University of Chicago Press, 1988.

Boorstin, Daniel J. *The Image: or; What Happened to the American Dream.* New York: Atheneum, 1962.

Booth, General William. *In Darkest England and the Way Out*. New York: Funk & Wagnalls, 1890.

Borchard, Edwin M. *Convicting the Innocent: Errors of Criminal Justice*. Hamden, CT: Archon Books, 1961.

Borradori, Giovanna. *Philosophy in a Time of Terror: Dialogues with Jürgen Habermas and Jacques Derrida*. Chicago: University of Chicago Press, 2003.

Boswell, Charles, and Lewis Thompson. *The Girls in Nightmare House*. New York: Fawcett, 1955.

Boucher, Anthony. Introduction to *The Murder and the Trial*, by Edgar Lustgarten, ix–xi. New York: Charles Scribner's Sons, 1958.

————, ed. *The Quality of Murder: Three Hundred Years of True Crime Compiled by Members of the Mystery Writers of America*. New York: Dutton, 1962.

Boudreau, Kristin. "Early American Criminal Narratives and the Problem of Public Sentiments." *Early American Literature* 32, no. 3 (1997): 249–69.

Bouzereau, Laurent. *Ultraviolent Movies: From Sam Peckinpah to Quentin Tarantino*. New York: Citadel Press, 1996.

Bradshaw, Peter. "Hopkins Makes a High-Camp Meal of Hannibal." *Guardian Weekly*, 22–28 Feb. 2001, 19.

Brady, Ian. *The Gates of Janus: Serial Killing and Its Analysis*. Los Angeles: Feral House, 2001.

Brannon, William T. "The Anatomical Practice of Dr. H. H. Holmes." In *The Quality of Murder: Three Hundred Years of True Crime Compiled by Members of the Mystery Writers of America*, ed. Anthony Boucher, 66–78. New York: Dutton, 1962.

Braudy, Leo. *The Frenzy of Renown: Fame and Its History*. New York: Oxford University Press, 1986.

Brazil, John. "Murder Trials, Murder, and Twenties America." *American Quarterly* 33, no. 2 (1981): 163–84.

Brill, Steven. *After: How America Confronted the September 12 Era*. New York: Simon & Schuster, 2003.

Bronfen, Elisabeth. "Celebrating Catastrophe." *Angelaki* 7, no. 2 (2002): 175–86.

————. *Over Her Dead Body: Death, Femininity, and the Aesthetic*. New York: Routledge, 1992.

Brophy, John. *The Meaning of Murder*. New York: Thomas Y. Crowell, 1967.

Browne, Nick. "The Political Economy of the Television (Super) Text." In *American Television: New Directions in History and Theory*, ed. Nick Browne, 69–79. Langhorne, PA: Harwood Academic, 1994.

Brownworth, Victoria A. "Demons and Killers." *Curve Magazine* 13, no. 2 (2003): 48–49.

Brunsdon, Charlotte. "What Is the 'Television' of Television Studies?" In *Television: The Critical View*, ed. Horace Newcomb, 609–28. 6th ed. New York: Oxford University Press, 2000.

Burgess, Ann W., et al. "Sexual Homicide: A Motivational Model." *Journal of Interpersonal Violence* 1, no. 3 (1986): 251–72.

Burkeman, Oliver. "Florida Executes Woman Serial Killer." *Guardian*, 10 Oct. 2002. http://www.guardian.co.uk/print/0,3858,4520932-103681,00.html.

Butler, Judith. "Imitation and Gender Insubordination." In *The Lesbian and Gay Studies Reader*, ed. Henry Abelove, Michèle Aina Barale, and David M Halperin, 307–20. New York: Routledge, 1993.

Byars, Jackie. "The Prime of Miss Kim Novak: Struggling over the Feminine in the Star Image." In *The Other Fifties: Interrogating Midcentury American Icons*, ed. Joel Foreman, 197–223. Urbana: University of Illinois Press, 1997.

Byrnes, Tom. *Writing Bestselling True Crime and Suspense*. Rocklin, CA: Prima, 1997.

Cahill, Tim. *Buried Dreams: Inside the Mind of a Serial Killer*. New York: Bantam, 1986.

Cameron, Deborah. "St–i–i–i–ll Going: The Quest for Jack the Ripper." *Social Text*, fall 1994, 147–54.

———. "That's Entertainment?" *Trouble and Strife* 13 (1988): 17–19.

Cameron, Deborah, and Elizabeth Frazer. *The Lust to Kill*. London: Polity Press, 1987.

Campbell, Duncan. "Maniac Theory Hid Violent Pattern of 'Domestic' Murder." *Guardian*, 4 Jul. 1991, 6.

Canguilhem, Georges. *The Normal and the Pathological*. Trans. Carolyn R. Fawcett. New York: Zone Books, 1989.

Capote, Truman. "Handcarved Coffins: A Nonfiction Account of an American Crime." In *Music for Chameleons*, 67–146. New York: Random House, 1980.

———. *In Cold Blood: A True Account of a Multiple Murder and Its Consequences*. New York: Signet, 1965.

Caputi, Jane. *The Age of Sex Crime*. Bowling Green, OH: Bowling Green State University Popular Press, 1987.

———. "American Psychos: The Serial Killer in Contemporary Fiction." *Journal of American Culture* 16, no. 4 (1993): 101–12.

———. "The New Founding Fathers: The Lore and Lure of the Serial Killer in Contemporary Culture." *Journal of American Culture* 13, no. 3 (1990): 1–12.

Caputi, Jane, and Diana E. H. Russell. "Femicide: Sexist Terrorism against Women." In *Femicide: The Politics of Woman Killing*, ed. Jill Radford and Diana E. H. Russell, 13–21. New York: Twayne, 1992.

Carr, Caleb. "Just Suppose It's Terrorism: In the Sniper Attacks, a New Kind of Enemy Is at Work." *Washington Post*, 17 Oct. 2002, A21.

———. *The Lessons of Terror*. New York: Random House, 2002.

Castle, Tammy, and Christopher Hensley. "Serial Killers with Military Experience: Applying Learning Theory to Serial Murder." *International Journal of Offender Therapy and Comparative Criminology* 46, no. 4 (2002): 453–65.

"The Castle to Be Rebuilt." *Chicago Daily News*, 8 Aug. 1895, 1.

Cawelti, John G. *Apostles of the Self-Made Man*. Chicago: University of Chicago Press, 1965.

Chesler, Phyllis. "Who's Crazy Now? Florida Offers Serial Killer Ted Bundy a Sweetheart Deal, Railroads a 'Bad Girl' to the Chair." *Argonaut* 3 (1992): 117–25.

Chion, Michael. *David Lynch*. London: BFI, 1995.

Clark, Charles S. "The FBI under Fire." *CQ Researcher* 7, no. 13 (1997): 315–19, 321–22, 324–28, 330–31.

Clark, Steve, and Mike Morley. *Murder in Mind: Mindhunting the Serial Killers*. London: Boxtree, 1993.

Clarkson, Frederick. "The Quiet Fall of an American Terrorist." *Salon*, 10 Dec. 2003. http://archive.salon.com/news/feature/2003/12/10/waagner/.

Cleckley, Hervey M. *Mask of Sanity: An Attempt to Clarify Some Issues about the So-Called Psychopathic Personality*. St Louis, MO: C. V. Mosby, 1941.

Clover, Carol J. *Men, Women, and Chainsaws: Gender in the Modern Horror Film*. Princeton, NJ: Princeton University Press, 1992.

Clymer, Jeffory A. *America's Culture of Terrorism: Violence, Capitalism, and the Written Word*. Chapel Hill: University of North Carolina Press, 2003.

Cohan, Steven, and Ina Rae Hark, eds. *The Road Movie Book*. New York: Routledge, 1997.

Cohen, Daniel A. *Pillars of Salt, Monuments of Grace: New England Crime Literature and the Origins of American Popular Culture, 1674–1860*. New York: Oxford University Press, 1993.

Cohen, Jeffrey Jerome. "Monster Culture (Seven Theses)." In *Monster Theory: Reading Culture*, ed. Jeffrey Jerome Cohen, 3–25. Minneapolis: University of Minnesota Press, 1996.

Cohen, Paula Marantz. *Silent Film and the Triumph of the American Myth*. New York: Oxford University Press, 2001.

Cole, C. Bard, and Chris McManus. "Intent to Kill." *Christopher Street* 167 (1991): 20–23.

"Collectors: A Film by Julian P. Hobbs." Abject Films. 9 May 2003. http://www.abjectfilms.com/collectorstext.html.

Colville, Gary, and Patrick Lucanio. *Jack the Ripper: His Life and Crimes in Popular Entertainment*. Jefferson, NC: McFarland, 1999.

Comstock, Gary David. *Violence against Lesbians and Gay Men*. New York: Columbia University Press, 1991.

"Consider McVeigh Example When Punishing D.C. Area Snipers." *USA Today*, 28 Oct. 2002, A11.

Copeland, Larry, and Laura Parker. "Arrest Eases Fears of La. Women." *USA Today*, 28 May 2003, 3A.

Copycat. Dir. Jon Amiel. Warner Bros., 1995.

Corbitt, Robert L. *The Holmes Castle*. Chicago: Corbitt & Morrison, 1895.

Corner, John. *Critical Ideas in Television Studies*. Oxford: Clarendon Press, 1999.

Courtwright, David T. "Way Cooler Than Manson: *Natural Born Killers* (1994)." *Film and History* 28, nos. 3/4 (1998): 28–36.

Cowen, Tyler. *What Price Fame?* Cambridge, MA: Harvard University Press, 2000.

Cox, Meg. "The Price Crime Writers Pay: They Are Hounded by Lunatics, Lawyers, and Death Threats." *San Francisco Chronicle*, 9 Dec. 1990, 3.

Creekmur, Corey. "On the Run and on the Road: Fame and the Outlaw Couple in American Cinema." In *The Road Movie Book*, ed. Steven Cohan and Ina Rae Hark, 90–109. New York: Routledge, 1997.

Crowley, Harry. "Homicidal Homosexual." *Advocate*, 2 Sep. 1997, 24–25, 29–33.

Curtis, L. Perry, Jr. *Jack the Ripper and the London Press*. New Haven, CT: Yale University Press, 2001.

Dahmer. Dir. David Jacobson. Blockbuster Films, 2002.

Dahmer, Lionel. *A Father's Story*. New York: William Morrow, 1994.

Davids, Diana. "The Serial Murderer as Superstar." *McCall's*, Feb. 1992.

deCordova, Richard. *Picture Personalities: The Emergence of the Star System in America*. Urbana: University of Illinois Press, 1990.

DeFord, Miriam Allen. Introduction to *Masterpieces of Murder: An Edmund Pearson True Crime Reader*, ed. Gerald Gross, xv–xxi. Boston: Little, Brown, 1963.

Delacoste, Frédérique, and Priscilla Alexander, eds. *Sex Work: Writings by Women in the Sex Industry*. Minneapolis: Cleis Press, 1987.

Delacoste, Frédérique, and Felice Newman, eds. *Fight Back! Feminist Resistance to Male Violence*. Minneapolis: Cleis Press, 1981.

Delasara, Jan. *PopLit, PopCult, and "The X-Files": A Critical Exploration*. Jefferson, NC: McFarland, 2000.

DeLong, Candice, and Elisa Petrini. *Special Agent: My Life on the Front Lines as a Woman in the FBI*. New York: Hyperion, 2001.

Dennett, Andrea Stulman. *Weird and Wonderful: The Dime Museum in America*. New York: New York University Press, 1997.

Denning, Michael. *Mechanic Accents: Dime Novels and Working-Class Culture in America*. New York: Verso, 1987.

"Depp on Jack the Ripper's Trail." *BBC News*, 28 Jan. 2001. http://news.bbc.co.uk/hi/english/entertainment/newsid_1141000/1141815.stm.

"Depp Takes From Hell to Top of US Box Office." *Guardian Unlimited*, 22 Oct. 2001. http://www.guardian.co.uk/Archive/Article/0,4273,4282283,00.html.

Depue, Roger L. "An American Response to an Era of Violence." *FBI Law Enforcement Bulletin* 55, no. 12 (1986): 2–5.

Derrida, Jacques. "Autoimmunity: Real and Symbolic Suicides. A Dialogue with Jacques Derrida." In *Philosophy in a Time of Terror: Dialogues with Jürgen Habermas and Jacques Derrida*, by Giovanna Borradori, 85–136, 186–93. Chicago: University of Chicago Press, 2003.

———. "Force of Law: The 'Mystical Foundation of Authority.'" In *Deconstruction and the Possibility of Justice*, ed. Drucilla Cornell, Michel Rosenfeld, and David Gray Carlson, 3–67. New York: Routledge, 1992.

"Detectives Work at the Castle." *Chicago Daily News*, 29 Jul. 1895, 3.

De Vries, Hent, and Samuel Weber, eds. *Violence, Identity, and Self-Determination*. Stanford, CA: Stanford University Press, 1997.

Dickson, Grierson. *Murder by Numbers*. London: Robert Hale, 1958.

"Dismay in Whitechapel." *New York Times*, 1 Oct. 1888, 1.

Dixon, Wheeler Winston. *Disaster and Memory: Celebrity Culture and the Crisis of Hollywood Cinema*. New York: Columbia University Press, 1999.

Dollimore, Jonathan. *Death, Desire, and Loss in Western Culture*. New York: Routledge, 1998.

Donahue, Deirdre. "Publishers Avoid D.C. Sniper Story." *USA Today*, 28 Oct. 2002, 1D.

Douglas, Jim. "Total Movie's Top 10 Cinematic Psychos." *Total Movie* 3 (2001): 56–61.

Douglas, John E. *Anyone You Want Me to Be: A True Story of Sex and Death on the Internet.* New York: Simon & Schuster, 2004.

———. *John Douglas's Guide to Careers in the FBI.* New York: Simon & Schuster, 1998.

———. *Man Down.* New York: Atria Books, 2002.

Douglas, John E., and Alan E. Burgess. "Criminal Profiling: A Viable Investigative Tool against Violent Crime." *FBI Law Enforcement Bulletin* 55, no. 12 (1986): 9–13.

Douglas, John E., and Mark Olshaker. *The Anatomy of Motive: The FBI's Legendary Mindhunter Explores the Key to Understanding and Catching Violent Criminals.* New York: Scribner, 1999.

———. *Broken Wings.* New York: Pocket Books, 1999.

———. *The Cases That Haunt Us.* New York: Scribner, 2000.

———. *Journey into Darkness: The FBI's Premier Investigator Penetrates the Minds and Motives of the Most Terrifying Serial Killers.* New York: Pocket Books, 1997.

———. *Mindhunter: Inside the FBI's Elite Serial Crime Unit.* New York: Scribner, 1995.

———. *Obsession: The FBI's Legendary Profiler Probes the Psyches of Killers, Rapists, and Stalkers and Their Victims and Tells How to Fight Back.* New York: Scribner, 1998.

Douthwaite, L. C. *Mass Murder.* New York: Henry Holt, 1929.

Doyle, Aaron. "'Cops': Television Policing as Policing Reality." In *Entertaining Crime: Television Reality Programs*, ed. Mark Fishman and Gray Cavender, 95–116. New York: Aldine De Gruyter, 1998.

Doyle, Arthur Conan. "The Sign of Four." In *Sherlock Holmes: The Complete Novels and Stories*, 1:105–205. New York: Bantam Books, 1986.

Duggan, Lisa. *Sapphic Slashers: Sex, Violence, and American Modernity.* Durham, NC: Duke University Press, 2000.

Durnell, Jane B., and Norman D. Stevens. "Biographical Note." In *Edmund Pearson—The Librarian: Selections from the Column of That Name*, ed. Jane B. Durnell and Norman D. Stevens, xvi–xxiv. Metuchen, NJ: Scarecrow Press, 1976.

Dvorchak, Robert J., and Lisa Holewa. *Milwaukee Massacre: Jeffrey Dahmer and the Milwaukee Murders.* New York: Dell, 1991.

Dyer, Richard. *Heavenly Bodies: Film Stars and Society.* London: BFI/Macmillan, 1986.

———. "Kill and Kill Again." *Sight and Sound* 7, no. 9 (1997): 14–17.

———. *Seven.* London: BFI, 1999.

———. "*A Star Is Born* and the Construction of Authenticity." In *Stardom: Industry of Desire*, ed. Christine Gledhill, 132–40. London: Routledge, 1991.

———. *Stars.* New ed. London: BFI, 1998.

Ebert, Roger. "Monster." *Chicago Sun-Times*, 9 Jan. 2004. http://rogerebert.suntimes.com/apps/pbcs.dll/article?AID=/20040330/REVIEWS/40310032/1023.

Eckert, Allan W. *The Scarlet Mansion.* Boston: Little, Brown, 1985.

Eckert, William G. "The Ripper Project: Modern Science Solving Mysteries of History." *American Journal of Forensic Medicine and Pathology* 10, no. 2 (1989): 164–71.

————. "The Whitechapel Murders: The Case of Jack the Ripper." *American Journal of Forensic Medicine and Pathology* 2, no. 1 (1981): 53–60.

Eco, Umberto. *The Limits of Interpretation*. Bloomington: Indiana University Press, 1990.

Edelstein, David. "The Pot Calling the Kettle Bloody." *Slate*, 9 Mar. 2001. http://slate.msn.com/id/102144.

Edmiston, Susan. "The First Woman Serial Killer?" *Glamour*, Sep. 1991.

Edmundson, Mark. *Nightmare on Main Street: Angels, Sadomasochism, and the Culture of Gothic*. Cambridge, MA: Harvard University Press, 1997.

Egger, Steven A., ed. *Serial Murder: An Elusive Phenomenon*. New York: Praeger, 1990.

————. "Serial Murder: A Synthesis of Literature and Research." In Egger, *Serial* 3–34.

————. "A Working Definition of Serial Murder and the Reduction of Linkage Blindness." *Journal of Police Science and Administration* 12, no. 3 (1984): 348–57.

Ellis, John. *Visible Fictions: Cinema, Television, Video*. Rev. ed. New York: Routledge, 1992.

Epstein, Su C. "The New Mythic Monster." In *Cultural Criminology*, ed. Jeff Ferrell and Clinton R. Sanders, 66–79. Boston: Northeastern University Press, 1995.

Evans, Stewart, and Paul Gainey. *Jack the Ripper: First American Serial Killer*. New York: Kodansha International, 1996.

Evans, Stewart, and Keith Skinner. *The Ultimate Jack the Ripper Companion: An Illustrated Encyclopedia*. New York: Carroll & Graf, 2000.

Ewen, Stuart. *All Consuming Images: The Politics of Style in Contemporary Culture*. New York: Basic Books, 1988.

"The Failed FBI." *New York Times*, 14 Apr. 2004. http://www.nytimes.com/2004/04/14/opinion/14WED2.html.

Farley, Rebecca. "The Word Made Flesh: Media Coverage of Dead Celebrities." *M/C: A Journal of Media and Culture* 2, no. 3 (1999). http://www.media-culture.org.au/9905/dead.html.

Farr, Finis. *Chicago: A Personal History of America's Most American City*. New Rochelle, NY: Arlington House, 1973.

Farr, Louise. *The Sunset Murders*. New York: Pocket Books, 1992.

"Fear of the Dark." *A Small Victory*, 22 Oct. 2002. http://www.asmallvictory.net/oldshit/001514.html.

Feuer, Jane. "Melodrama, Serial Form, and Television Today." *Screen* 25, no. 1 (1984): 4–16.

15 Minutes. Dir. John Herzfeld. New Line, 2001.

Filippelli, Connie. "H. H. Holmes: Dr Death, America's First Serial Killer." *Crime Library*, 2000. http://www.crimelibrary.com/serial6/holmes/.

Fisher, Philip. "Appearing and Disappearing in Public: Social Space in Late-Nineteenth-Century Literature and Culture." In *Reconstructing American Literary History*, ed. Sacvan Bercovitch, 155–88. Cambridge, MA: Harvard University Press, 1986.

Fishman, W. J. *East End 1888: Life in a London Borough among the Laboring Poor*. Philadelphia: Temple University Press, 1988.

Fiske, John. *Television Culture*. New York: Methuen, 1987.

Foucault, Michel. "The Dangerous Individual." In *Michel Foucault: Politics Philosophy Culture; Interviews and Other Writings, 1977–1984*, ed. Lawrence D. Kritzman, trans. Alan Sheridan et al., 125–51. New York: Routledge, 1988.

———. *The History of Sexuality*. New York: Vintage Books, 1990.

———, ed. *I, Pierre Rivière, Having Slaughtered My Mother, My Sister, and My Brother...: A Case of Parricide in the Nineteenth Century*. Trans. Frank Jellinek. Lincoln: University of Nebraska Press, 1982.

Fowles, Jib. *Starstruck: Celebrity Performers and the American Public*. Washington, DC: Smithsonian Institution Press, 1992.

Fox, Richard Kyle. *The History of the Whitechapel Murders: A Full and Authentic Narrative of the Above Murders, with Sketches*. New York: R. K. Fox, 1888.

———. "The Whitechapel Murders." *National Police Gazette*, 1 Dec. 1888, 2.

Fox, Richard L., and Robert W. Van Sickel. *Tabloid Justice: Criminal Justice in an Age of Media Frenzy*. Boulder, CO: Lynne Rienner, 2001.

Franke, David. *The Torture Doctor*. New York: Hawthorn Books, 1975.

Freedman, Estelle B. "The Prison Lesbian: Race, Class, and the Construction of the Aggressive Female Homosexual, 1915–1965." *Feminist Studies* 22, no. 2 (1996): 397–423.

Freeh, Louis J. "Where the FBI Stands Today." *Vital Speeches* 60, no. 7 (1994): 194–96.

Freud, Sigmund. "Thoughts for the Times on War and Death." In *Collected Papers*, 4:288–317. London: Hogarth Press, 1953.

Friedland, Martin L. *The Trials of Israel Lipski*. London: Macmillan, 1984.

From Hell. Dir. Albert Hughes and Allen Hughes. 20th Century Fox, 2001.

Furio, Jennifer. *The Serial Killer Letters: A Penetrating Look inside the Minds of Murderers*. Philadelphia: Charles Press, 1998.

Fuss, Diana. "Inside/Out." In *Inside/Out: Lesbian Theories, Gay Theories*, ed. Diana Fuss, 1–10. New York: Routledge, 1991.

———. "Monsters of Perversion: Jeffrey Dahmer and *The Silence of the Lambs*." In *Media Spectacles*, ed. Marjorie Garber et al., 181–205. New York: Routledge, 1993.

Gabler, Neal. *Life The Movie: How Entertainment Conquered Reality*. New York: Alfred A. Knopf, 1998.

Gaddis, Thomas E., and James O. Long. *Killer: A Journal of Murder*. New York: Macmillan, 1970.

Gamson, Joshua. *Claims to Fame: Celebrity in Contemporary America*. Berkeley: University of California Press, 1994.

Gaute, J. H. H., and Robin Odell. *The Murderers' Who's Who: Outstanding International Cases from the Literature of Murder in the Last 150 Years*. New York: Methuen, 1979.

Geraghty, Christine. "The Continuous Serial—A Definition." In *Coronation Street*, ed. Richard Dyer, 9–26. London: BFI, 1981.

Geyer, Frank P. *The Holmes-Pitezel Case: A History of the Greatest Crime of the Century and of the Search for the Missing Pitezel Children*. Philadelphia: Publishers' Union, 1896.

Gibbs, Nancy. "Under the Microscope." *Time*, 28 Apr. 1997, 28–35.

Giles, David. *Illusions of Immortality: A Psychology of Fame and Celebrity*. New York: St. Martin's Press, 2000.

Gillespie, L. Kay. *Dancehall Ladies: The Crimes and Executions of America's Condemned Women*. Lanham, MD: University Press of America, 1997.

Gitlin, Todd. "The Culture of Celebrity." *Dissent*, summer 1998, 81–83.

Gledhill, Christine. Introduction. In Gledhill, *Stardom* xiii–xx.

———. "Signs of Melodrama." In Gledhill, *Stardom* 207–29.

———, ed. *Stardom: Industry of Desire*. London: Routledge, 1991.

Glynn, Kevin. *Tabloid Culture: Trash Taste, Popular Power, and the Transformation of American Television*. Durham, NC: Duke University Press, 2000.

Godwin, Grover Maurice. *Hunting Serial Predators: A Multivariate Classification Approach to Profiling Violent Behavior*. Boca Raton, FL: CRC Press, 2000.

Godwin, John. *Murder U.S.A.: The Ways We Kill Each Other*. New York: Ballantine, 1978.

Goldberg, Vicki. "Death Takes a Holiday, Sort Of." In *Why We Watch: The Attractions of Violent Entertainment*, ed. Jeffrey Goldstein, 27–52. New York: Oxford University Press, 1998.

Goldblatt, Henry. "TV's Most Lucrative Franchise: It's a Mystery." *Fortune*, 12 Jan. 1998, 114.

Goldman, Jane. *The X-Files Book of the Unexplained*. Vol. 2. New York: HarperPrism, 1996.

Goldstein, Jeffrey. "Why We Watch." In Goldstein, *Why* 212–26.

———, ed. *Why We Watch: The Attractions of Violent Entertainment*. New York: Oxford University Press, 1998.

"Gone Crazy on Holmes." *Chicago Daily News*, 27 Jul. 1895, 1.

Goodman, Mark. "Cops, Killers, and Cannibals." *People Weekly*, 1 Apr. 1991.

Gould, Mark. "Low Lives Relived in the East End." *Guardian Unlimited*, 26 Oct. 2001. http://www.guardian.co.uk/Archive/Article/0,4273,4284159,00.html.

Gourgouris, Stathis. "Enlightenment and *Paranomia*." In *Violence, Identity, and Self-Determination*, ed. Hent De Vries and Samuel Weber, 119–49, 361–65. Stanford, CA: Stanford University Press, 1997.

Griggers, Camilla. "Phantom and Reel Projections: Lesbians and the (Serial) Killing Machine." In *Posthuman Bodies*, ed. Judith Halberstam and Ira Livingston, 162–76. Bloomington: Indiana University Press, 1995.

Grixti, Joseph. "Consuming Cannibals: Psychopathic Killers as Archetypes and Cultural Icons." *Journal of American Culture* 18, no. 1 (1995): 87–96.

Gross, Gerald, ed. *Masterpieces of Murder: An Edmund Pearson True Crime Reader*. Boston: Little, Brown, 1963.

———. Preface. In Gross, *Masterpieces* xi–xiv.

Gross, Larry. "Exploding Hollywood." *Sight and Sound* 5, no. 3 (1995): 8–9.

———. "Out of the Mainstream: Sexual Minorities and the Mass Media." In *Remote Control: Television, Audiences, and Cultural Power*, ed. Ellen Seiter et al., 130–49. New York: Routledge, 1989.

Grunenberg, Christoph. "Unsolved Mysteries: Gothic Tales from Frankenstein to the Hair-Eating Doll." In *Gothic: Transmutations of Horror in Late Twentieth-Century Art*, ed. Christoph Grunenberg, 160–212. Cambridge, MA: MIT Press, 1997.

Habermas, Jürgen. "Fundamentalism and Terror: A Dialogue with Jürgen Habermas." In *Philosophy in a Time of Terror: Dialogues with Jürgen Habermas and Jacques Derrida*, by Giovanna Borradori, 25–43, 179. Chicago: University of Chicago Press, 2003.

Halberstam, Judith. "Skinflick: Posthuman Gender in Jonathan Demme's *The Silence of the Lambs*." *Camera Obscura* 27 (1991): 36–53.

———. *Skin Shows: Gothic Horror and the Technology of Monsters*. Durham, NC: Duke University Press, 1995.

Halttunen, Karen. *Confidence Men and Painted Women: A Study of Middle-Class Culture in America, 1830–1870*. New Haven, CT: Yale University Press, 1982.

———. "Early American Murder Narratives." In *The Power of Culture: Critical Essays in American History*, ed. Richard Wightman Fox and T. J. Jackson Lears, 66–101. Chicago: University of Chicago Press, 1993.

———. *Murder Most Foul: The Killer and the American Gothic Imagination*. Cambridge, MA: Harvard University Press, 1998.

Hamacher, Werner. "One 2 Many Multiculturalisms." In *Violence, Identity, and Self-Determination*, ed. Hent De Vries and Samuel Weber, 284–325. Stanford, CA: Stanford University Press, 1997.

Hammer, Rhonda. *Antifeminism and Family Terrorism: A Critical Feminist Perspective*. Lanham, MD: Rowman and Littlefield, 2002.

Hamsher, Jane. *Killer Instinct: How Two Young Producers Took on Hollywood and Made the Most Controversial Film of the Decade*. New York: Broadway Books, 1997.

Hanson, Ellis. "Undead." In *Inside/Out: Lesbian Theories, Gay Theories*, ed. Diana Fuss, 324–40. New York: Routledge, 1991.

Harden, Blaine. "Film Reawakens Painful 'Son of Sam' Memories." *New York Times*, 20 Jun. 1999, 1, 22.

Harris, Melvin. *The Ripper File*. London: W. H. Allen, 1989.

Harris, Paul. "They Seemed Normal but Plotted to Kill Thousands." *Observer*, 21 Mar. 2004, 21.

Harris, Thomas. *Hannibal*. New York: Delacorte Press, 1999.

———. *Red Dragon*. New York: Dell, 1981.

———. *The Silence of the Lambs*. New York: St. Martin's Press, 1988.

Hart, Lynda. *Fatal Women: Lesbian Sexuality and the Mark of Aggression*. Princeton, NJ: Princeton University Press, 1994.

Hazelwood, Robert, and John Douglas. "The Lust Murderer." *FBI Law Enforcement Bulletin* 49, no. 4 (1980): 18–22.

Heath, Stephen, and Gillian Skirrow. "Television: A World in Action." *Screen* 18, no. 2 (1977): 7–59.

Henry, Portrait of a Serial Killer. Dir. John MacNaughton. MPI Home Video, 1986.

Herbert, Rosemary. "Publishers Agree: True Crime Does Pay." *Publisher's Weekly*, 1 Jun. 1990, 33–36.

Herek, Gregory M., and Kevin T. Berrill, eds. *Hate Crimes: Confronting Violence against Lesbians and Gay Men*. Newbury Park, CA: Sage, 1992.

H. H. Holmes: America's First Serial Killer. Dir. John Borowski. Waterfront Productions, 2002.

Hickey, Eric. *Serial Murderers and Their Victims*. 2nd ed. Belmont, CA: Wadsworth, 1997.

Hill, Annette. "'Looks Like It Hurts': Women's Responses to Shocking Entertainment." In *Ill Effects: The Media/Violence Debate*, ed. Martin Barker and Julian Petley, 135–49. 2nd ed. London: Routledge, 1998.

Himmelfarb, Gertrude. *The Idea of Poverty: England in the Early Industrial Age*. New York: Knopf, 1984.

Hirsch, David A. H. "Dahmer's Effects: Gay Serial Killer Goes to Market." In *Disciplinarity and Dissent in Cultural Studies*, ed. Cary Nelson and Dilip Parameshwar Gaonkar, 441–72. New York: Routledge, 1996.

Holmes, the Arch-Fiend; or, A Carnival of Crime. Cincinnati, OH: Barclay, 1895.

Holmes, Ronald M., and James De Burger. *Serial Murder*. Newbury Park, CA: Sage, 1988.

Howlett, James B., Kenneth A. Hanfland, and Robert K. Ressler. "The Violent Criminal Apprehension Program." *FBI Law Enforcement Bulletin* 55, no. 12 (1986): 14–18.

Hudson, Samuel E. *"Leather Apron"; or, The Horrors of Whitechapel. London 1888*. Philadelphia: Town Printing House, 1888.

Indiana, Gary. *Three Month Fever: The Andrew Cunanan Story*. New York: Cliff Street Books, 1999.

Ingebretsen, Edward J. *At Stake: Monsters and the Rhetoric of Fear in Public Culture*. Chicago: University of Chicago Press, 2001.

Isenberg, Sheila. *Women Who Love Men Who Kill*. New York: Simon & Schuster, 1991.

"Is the Ripper a Malay Cook?" *Evening Star*, 20 Nov. 1888. *Casebook: Jack the Ripper*. http://www.casebook.org/Press,_reports/evening_star/881120.html.

"Jack Levin: Author and Criminologist on Serial Killers." *ABC News*, 24 Jun. 1999. http://abcnews.go.com/sections/us/DailyNews/chat_jacklevin.html (no longer available).

Jackson, Devon. "Serial Killers and the People Who Love Them." *Village Voice*, 22 Mar. 1994, 26–32.

Jackson, Janet L., and Debra A. Bekerian. "Does Offender Profiling Have a Role to Play?" In *Offender Profiling: Theory, Research, and Practice*, ed. Janet L. Jackson and Debra A. Bekerian, 1–7. New York: John Wiley & Sons, 1997.

James, Caryn. "The Humbling of the Megastars." *New York Times*, 27 Jun. 1999, sec. 2.

———. "Now Starring, Killers for the Chiller 90's." *New York Times*, 10 Mar. 1991, sec. 2.

———. "What We Don't Know about TV Could Kill Us." *New York Times*, 18 Sep. 1994, 13, 22.

Jarvis, Jeff. "Millennium." *TV Guide* 44, no. 46 (1996): 11.

Jeffers, H. Paul. *Who Killed Precious? How FBI Special Agents Combine High Technology and Psychology to Identify Violent Criminals*. New York: St. Martin's Press, 1992.

Jeffreys, Diarmuid. *The Bureau: Inside the Modern FBI*. Boston: Houghton Mifflin, 1995.

Jenkins, Philip. "African-Americans and Serial Homicide." In *Contemporary Perspectives on Serial Murder*, ed. Ronald M. Holmes and Stephen T. Holmes, 17–32. Thousand Oaks, CA: Sage, 1998.

————. "Myth and Murder: The Serial Killer Panic of 1983–1985." In *The Mythology of Crime and Criminal Justice*, ed. Victor E. Kappeler, Mark Blumberg, and Gary W. Potter, 53–73. Prospect Heights, IL: Waveland Press, 1993.

————. "Serial Murder in the United States, 1900–1940: A Historical Perspective." *Journal of Criminal Justice* 17 (1989): 377–92.

————. *Using Murder: The Social Construction of Serial Homicide*. New York: Aldine De Gruyter, 1994.

Jenkins, Rupert. "East of Eden: Murder as Phenomena." *Camerawork* 29, no. 2 (1992): 4–13.

The John Walsh Show. Ed. Click Active Media. 2 Jan. 2003. http://www.johnwalsh.tv/cgi-bin/topics/today/cgi?id=90 (site now discontinued). Archived at http://joe.skcentral.com/johnwalsh2.html.

Jones, Ann. *Women Who Kill*. New York: Ballantine Books, 1981.

Jones, Meg. "Gory, Gory, Gone: Web Auction Site eBay Banning Sale of Murderers' Merchandise." *JSOnline: Milwaukee Journal Sentinel*, 15 May 2001. http://www.jsonline.com/news/state/may01/ebay16051501a.asp.

Jones, Sara Gwenllian. "Starring Lucy Lawless?" *Continuum: Journal of Media and Cultural Studies* 14, no. 1 (2000): 9–22.

Kagan, Dan. "Serial Murderers." *Omni* 6 (1984): 20, 120.

Kalifornia. Dir. Dominic Sena. MGM/UA, 1993.

Kappeler, Victor E., Mark Blumberg, and Gary W. Potter. *The Mythology of Crime and Criminal Justice*. Prospect Heights, IL.: Waveland Press, 1993.

Katz, Jonathan Ned. *The Invention of Heterosexuality*. New York: Dutton, 1995.

Keeney, Belea T., and Kathleen M. Heide. "Gender Differences in Serial Murderers: A Preliminary Analysis." *Journal of Interpersonal Violence* 9, no. 3 (1994): 383–98.

Kehr, Dave. "Heartland." *Film Comment* 26, no. 3 (1990): 61–62.

————. "Travolta vs. Winkler: Transfers from Other Media." In *The National Society of Film Critics on the Movie Star*, ed. Elisabeth Weis, 34–45. New York: Penguin Books, 1981.

Kelleher, Michael D., and C. L. Kelleher. *Murder Most Rare: The Female Serial Killer*. Westport, CT: Praeger, 1998.

Kellner, Douglas. "*The X-Files* and Conspiracy: A Diagnostic Critique." In *Conspiracy Nation: the Politics of Paranoia in Postwar America*, ed. Peter Knight, 205–32. New York: New York University Press, 2002.

Kendall, Elizabeth. *The Phantom Prince: My Life with Ted Bundy*. Seattle, WA: Madrona, 1981.

Kennedy, Dolores. *On a Killing Day*. Chicago: Bonus Books, 1992.

Kennedy, Lisa. "Writers on the Lamb: Sorting Out the Sexual Politics of a Controversial Film." *Village Voice*, 5 Mar. 1991.

"Kensington in Deal with Court TV." *PublishersWeekly.com*, 30 Aug. 1999. http://publishersweekly.reviewsnews.com/index.asp?layout=articlePrint&articleID=CA167243.

Keppel, Robert D., with William J. Birnes. *The Riverman: Ted Bundy and I Hunt for the Green River Killer*. New York: Pocket Books, 1995.

———. *Signature Killers: Interpreting the Calling Cards of the Serial Murderer*. New York: Pocket Books, 1997.

Kessler, Ronald. *The FBI*. New York: Pocket Books, 1993.

Kessler, William F., M.D., and Paul B. Weston. *The Detection of Murder*. New York: Greenberg, 1953.

Kiger, Kenna. "The Darker Figure of Crime: The Serial Murder Enigma." In *Serial Murder: An Elusive Phenomenon*, ed. Steven A. Egger, 35–52. New York: Praeger, 1990.

Killer: A Journal of Murder. Dir. Tim Metcalfe. Breakheart Films, 1996.

"Killer Collectibles: Inside the World of 'Murderabilia.'" *ABC News*, 7 Nov. 2001. Archived at http://64.233.161.104/search?q=cache:IP7uB9_RWsoJ:abcnews.go.com/sections/2020/2020/2020_011107_murderabilia.html.

King, Barry. "The Star and the Commodity: Notes toward a Performance Theory of Stardom." *Cultural Studies* 1, no. 2 (1987): 145–61.

King, Brian, ed. *Lustmord: The Writings and Artifacts of Murderers*. Burbank, CA: Bloat, 1996.

Klaidman, Daniel, and Michael Isikoff. "A Fire That Won't Die." *Newsweek*, 20 Sep. 1999, 24–27.

Klaidman, Daniel, and Alan Zarembo. "The Faces of a Fugitive." *Newsweek*, 5 Jul. 1999, 20–23.

Klaprat, Cathy. "The Star as Market Strategy: Bette Davis in Another Light." In *The American Film Industry*, ed. Tino Balio, 351–76. Rev. ed. Madison: University of Wisconsin Press, 1985.

Klein, Andy. "Man Bites Dog II: The Interview." *Los Angeles Reader*, 9 Apr. 1993, 23–24.

Kleinfield, N. R., and Erica Goode. "Serial Killing's Squarest Pegs: Not Solo, White, Psychosexual, or Picky." *New York Times*, 28 Oct. 2002, A22.

Knickelbine, Scott. *Welcome to Twin Peaks: A Complete Guide to Who's Who and What's What*. Lincolnwood, IL: Publications International, 1990.

Knight, Peter. *Conspiracy Culture: From Kennedy to the X-Files*. London: Routledge, 2000.

Knox, Sara L. "Crime, Law, and Symbolic Order: The Rhetoric of Transparency." *Theory and Event* 7, no. 1 (2003). http://muse.jhu.edu/journals/theory_and_event/v007/7.1knox.html.

Kolarik, Gera-Lind, with Wayne Klatt. *Freed to Kill: The True Story of Serial Murderer Larry Eyler*. New York: Avon Books, 1992.

Kooistra, Paul. *Criminals as Heroes: Structure, Power, and Identity*. Bowling Green, OH: Bowling Green State University Popular Press, 1989.

Kozloff, Sarah. "Narrative Theory and Television." In *Channels of Discourse, Reassembled: Television and Contemporary Criticism*, ed. Robert Allen, 67–100. 2nd ed. New York: Routledge, 1992.

Krajicek, David J. *Scooped!: Media Miss Real Story on Crime While Chasing Sex, Sleaze, and Celebrities*. New York: Columbia University Press, 1998.

Kramer, Hilton. "Real Gardens with Real Toads." In *Truman Capote's "In Cold Blood": A Critical Handbook*, ed. Irving Malin, 65–68. Belmont, CA: Wadsworth, 1968.

Krum, Sharon. "Lady Killer." *Guardian*, 2 August 2001. http://www.guardian.co.uk/print/0,3858,4232311-103691,00.html.

Lane, Roger. Introduction to *Studies in Murder*, by Edmund Pearson, ix–xvi. Columbus: Ohio State University Press, 1999. First published 1924.

Langer, John. "Television's 'Personality System.'" *Media, Culture, and Society* 4 (1981): 351–65.

Larson, Erik. *The Devil in the White City: Murder, Magic, and Madness at the Fair That Changed America*. New York: Crown, 2003.

Lasch, Christopher. *The Culture of Narcissism*. New York: Warner Books, 1979.

Lawson, W. B. *Jack the Ripper in New York; or, Piping a Terrible Mystery*. New York: Street & Smith, 1891.

Leiby, Richard. "The Warped Mind or Warped Soul at the Heart of a Killer." *Washington Post*, 26 Oct. 2002, C1.

Leitch, Thomas M. "Nobody Here But Us Killers: The Disavowal of Violence in Recent American Films." *Film and Philosophy* 1 (1994). http://www.hanover.edu/philos/film/vol_01/leitch.htm (site now discontinued).

Leonard, John. *Smoke and Mirrors: Violence, Television, and Other American Cultures*. New York: New Press, 1997.

Leong, Ian, Mike Sell, and Kelly Thomas. "Mad Love, Mobile Homes, and Dysfunctional Dicks: On the Road with Bonnie and Clyde." In *The Road Movie Book*, ed. Steven Cohan and Ina Rae Hark, 70–89. New York: Routledge, 1997.

Lesser, Wendy. *Pictures at an Execution*. Cambridge, MA: Harvard University Press, 1993.

Levin, Jack, and James Alan Fox. *Mass Murder: America's Growing Menace*. New York: Berkley Books, 1985.

Levine, Richard M. "Murder, They Write." *New York Times Magazine*, 16 Nov. 1986.

Levy, Emanuel. "The Democratic Elite: America's Movie Stars." *Qualitative Sociology* 12, no. 1 (1989): 29–54.

Leyton, Elliott. *Hunting Humans: The Rise of the Modern Multiple Murderer*. London: Penguin Books, 1989.

Licensed to Kill. Dir. Arthur Dong. Deep Focus Films, 1997.

Lindberg, Gary. *The Confidence Man in American Literature*. New York: Oxford University Press, 1982.

Lindsay, Paul. *Code Name: Gentkill; A Novel of the FBI*. New York: Villard, 1995.

———. *Freedom to Kill: A Novel of the FBI*. New York: Villard, 1997.

———. *Witness to the Truth: A Novel of the FBI*. New York: Random House, 1992.

Lindsey, Robert. "Officials Cite a Rise in Killers Who Roam U.S. for Victims." *New York Times*, 21 Jan. 1984, 1, 7.

Linedecker, Clifford. *The Man Who Killed Boys*. New York: St. Martin's, 1980.

Lipsitz, George. *The Possessive Investment in Whiteness: How White People Profit from Identity Politics*. Philadelphia: Temple University Press, 1998.

Livingstone, Sonia. *Making Sense of Television: The Psychology of Audience Interpretation*. 2nd ed. New York: Routledge, 1998.

Locy, Toni. "Anti-terror Crew Chases Leads Big and Small." *USA Today*, 8 Oct. 2003, 10A.

Logan, Guy B. H. *Masters of Crime: Studies of Multiple Murders*. London: Stanley Paul, 1928.

Logan, Malcolm. "Glorifying the Criminal." *Scribner's Magazine* 90 (1931): 43–46.

Lombroso, Cesare. "Why Homicide Has Increased in the United States—II." *North American Review* 166, no. 1 (1898): 1–11.

Lopez, Nora. "Judicial Gay Bashing: A Texas Tradition?" *Advocate* 590 (1991): 60.

Lorenz, Larry. "The Whitechapel Club: Defining Chicago's Newspapermen in the 1890s." *American Journalism* 15, no. 1 (1998): 83–102.

Lowenthal, Leo. "The Triumph of Mass Idols." In *Literature, Popular Culture, and Society*, 109–40. Englewood Cliffs, NJ: Prentice-Hall, 1961.

Lowry, Brian. *Trust No One: The Official Third Season Guide to The X Files*. New York: HarperPrism, 1996.

———. *The Truth Is Out There: The Official Guide to The X Files*. New York: HarperPrism, 1995.

MacDonald, Martha Wilson, M.D. "Criminally Aggressive Behavior in Passive, Effeminate Boys." *American Journal of Orthopsychiatry* 8, no. 1 (1938): 70–78.

MacNamara, Mark. "American Psycho." *West* (*San Jose Mercury News*), 7 Apr. 1991, 14–22.

———. "Kiss and Kill." *Vanity Fair*, Sep. 1991, 91–106.

Madison, Cathy. "Robert and Me." *Utne Reader*, May–Jun. 2000, 5.

Malach, Michele. "'I Want to Believe . . . in the FBI': The Special Agent and *The X-Files*." In *"Deny All Knowledge": Reading the X Files*, ed. David Lavery et al., 63–76. Syracuse, NY: Syracuse University Press, 1996.

Malin, Irving, ed. *Truman Capote's "In Cold Blood": A Critical Handbook*. Belmont, CA: Wadsworth, 1968.

Man Bites Dog. Dir. Remy Belvaux. Roxie Releasing, 1993.

Mann, Denise. "The Spectacularization of Everyday Life: Recycling Hollywood Stars and Fans in Early Television Variety Shows." In *Private Screenings: Television and the Female Consumer*, ed. Lynn Spigel and Denise Mann, 41–69. Minneapolis: University of Minnesota Press, 1992.

Marcus, Isabel. "Reframing 'Domestic Violence': Terrorism in the Home." In *The Public Nature of Private Violence: The Discovery of Domestic Abuse*, ed. Martha Fineman and Roxanne Mykitiuk, 11–35. New York: Routledge, 1994.

Margolis, Stacey. "The Public Life: The Discourse of Privacy in the Age of Celebrity." *Arizona Quarterly* 52, no. 2 (1995): 81–101.

Marshall, P. David. *Celebrity and Power: Fame in Contemporary Culture*. Minneapolis: University of Minnesota Press, 1997.

Martin, John Bartlow. "The Master of Murder Castle: A Classic of Chicago Crime." *Harper's Magazine*, Dec. 1943, 76–85.

Martin, Robert K., and Eric Savoy, eds. *American Gothic: New Interventions in a National Narrative*. Iowa City: University of Iowa Press, 1998.

Martin, Robert K., and Eric Savoy. Introduction to Martin and Savoy, *American* vii–xii.

Matzer, Marla. "Selling 'Seven.'" *Hollywood Reporter*, 18 Jun. 1996, S13–15.

McCarthy, Kathy. "Serial Killers: Their Deadly Bent May Be Set in Cradle." *Los Angeles Times*, 10 Jun. 1984, 2, 24.

McClelland, C. Ivor, ed. *They Call Him Mr. Gacy: Selected Correspondence of John Wayne Gacy*. Brighton, CO: McClelland Associates, 1989.

McDonald, Paul. "'I'm Winning on a Star: The Extraordinary Ordinary World of *Stars in Their Eyes*." *Critical Survey* 7, no. 1 (1995): 59–66.

———. "Star Studies." In *Approaches to Popular Film*, ed. Joanne Hollows and Mark Jancovich, 79–97. New York: Manchester University Press, 1995.

McDonough, John. "Director without a Past." *American Film* 16, no. 5 (1991).

McDougal, Dennis. *Angel of Darkness: The True Story of Randy Kraft and the Most Heinous Murder Spree of the Century*. New York: Warner, 1991.

McHenry, F. A. "A Note on Homosexuality, Crime, and the Newspapers." *Journal of Criminal Psychopathology* 2 (1940): 533–48.

McKenna, Neil. "Fleet Street's Gay Film Script." *Independent on Sunday*, 20 Jun. 1993, 3.

McKinney, Devin. "Violence: The Strong and the Weak." In *Screening Violence*, ed. Stephen Prince, 99–109. New Brunswick, NJ: Rutgers University Press, 2000.

McPherson, Myra. "The Roots of Evil." *Cosmopolitan*, Sep. 1989, 272–90.

Medved, Michael. *Hollywood vs. America: Popular Culture and the War on Traditional Values*. New York: Harper Collins, 1992.

Michaud, Stephen G. "The FBI's New Psyche Squad." *New York Times Magazine*, 26 Oct. 1986.

Michaud, Stephen G., and Hugh Aynesworth. *The Only Living Witness: A True Account of Homicidal Insanity*. New York: Signet, 1983.

———. *Ted Bundy: Conversations with a Killer*. New York: Signet, 1989.

Michaud, Stephen G., with Roy Hazelwood. *The Evil That Men Do: FBI Profiler Roy Hazelwood's Journey into the Minds of Sexual Predators*. New York: St. Martin's Press, 1998.

Miedzian, Myriam. *Boys Will Be Boys: Breaking the Link between Masculinity and Violence*. New York: Doubleday, 1991.

Mills, C. Wright. *The Power Elite*. New York: Oxford University Press, 1956.

Mindhunters. Dir. Renny Harlin. Dimension Films, 2004.

Mizejewski, Linda. "Stardom and Serial Fantasies: Thomas Harris's *Hannibal*." In *Keyframes: Popular Cinema and Cultural Studies*, ed. Matthew Tinkcom and Amy Villarejo, 159–70. London: Routledge, 2001.

Monster. Dir. Patty Jenkins. MDP Worldwide, 2003.

Moore, Alan, and Eddie Campbell. *From Hell*. Paddington, Australia: Eddie Campbell Comics, 1999.

Moore, Suzanne. "Death and the Maidens." *Guardian*, 11 Mar. 1994, sec. 2, p. 5.

Moret, Jim. "Climbing into the Heads of 'Profiler' Stars." *CNN.com*, 21 Apr. 1998. http://www.cnn.com/SHOWBIZ/9804/21/the.profiler/.

Morgan, Robin. *The Demon Lover: On the Sexuality of Terrorism.* New York: Norton, 1989.

Morin, Edgar. *The Stars.* New York: Grove Press, 1960.

Moss, Jason, with Jeffrey Kottler. *The Last Victim: A True-Life Journey into the Mind of the Serial Killer.* New York: Warner Books, 1999.

"Muhammad, Malvo Cleared in Baton Rouge Serial Killings." *FOXNews.com*, 27 Nov. 2002. http://www.foxnews.com.

Murder By Numbers. Dir. Mike Hodges. IFC Original Productions, 2002.

NaaNes, Marlene. "Derrick Todd Lee: From Class Clown to Serial Killer?" *Sunday Advocate* (Baton Rouge, LA), 22 Jun. 2003. http://web.lexis-nexis.com/universe/.

Natural Born Killers. Dir. Oliver Stone. Warner Bros., 1994.

Nelson, Polly. *Defending the Devil: My Story as Ted Bundy's Last Lawyer.* New York: William Morrow, 1994.

Nelson, Robin. *TV Drama in Transition: Forms, Values, and Cultural Change.* New York: St. Martin's Press, 1997.

Nelson, Scott A. "Crime-Time Television." *FBI Law Enforcement Bulletin* 58, no. 8 (1989): 1–9.

Newcomb, Horace, and Paul M. Hirsch. "Television as a Cultural Forum." In *Television: The Critical View*, ed. Horace Newcomb, 455–70. 4th ed. New York: Oxford University Press, 1987.

Newman, Kim. "The FBI." In *The BFI Companion to Crime*, ed. Phil Hardy, 127–29. Berkeley: University of California Press, 1997.

"News of the Day Abroad." *New York Times*, 4 Sep. 1888, 1.

New York Sun. 10 Nov. 1888. *Casebook: Jack the Ripper.* http://www.casebook.org/press_reports/new_york_sun/nys881110.html

Nickerson, Catherine. "Serial Detection and Serial Killers in *Twin Peaks.*" *Literature/Film Quarterly* 21, no. 4 (1993): 271–76.

Nixon, Nicola. "Making Monsters, or Serializing Killers." In *American Gothic: New Interventions in a National Narrative*, ed. Robert K. Martin and Eric Savoy, 217–36. Iowa City: University of Iowa Press, 1998.

Nochimson, Martha. *No End to Her: Soap Opera and the Female Subject.* Berkeley: University of California Press, 1992.

Nordheimer, Jon. "All-American Boy on Trial." *New York Times Magazine*, 10 Dec. 1978.

Norganthau, Tom. "The Echoes of Ruby Ridge." *Newsweek*, 28 Aug. 1995, 24–28.

Norris, Joel. *Jeffrey Dahmer.* New York: Pinnacle, 1992.

Norris, Roy L. "Roy Lewis Norris on September 11, 2001." *Serial Killer Central.* http://www.skcentral.com/911.html.

Oates, Joyce Carol. "'I Had No Other Thrill or Happiness.'" *New York Review of Books*, 24 Mar. 1994, 52–59.

O'Brien, Daniel. *The Hannibal Files: The Unauthorised Guide to the Hannibal Lecter Trilogy.* London: Reynolds & Hearn, 2001.

O'Hare, Kate. "'Profiler' Ally Walker Ready for a Change." *TVQuest Tribune Media Service*, 3 Aug. 1998. http://profiler2.crosswinds.net/archives/press/article025.htm (site now discontinued).

"Old World News by Cable." *New York Times*, 7 Oct. 1888, 1.

Olsen, Jack. *The Man with the Candy: The Story of the Houston Mass Murders*. New York: Simon & Schuster, 1974.

Osborne, Richard. "Crime and the Media: From Media Studies to Post-Modernism." In *Crime and the Media: The Post-Modern Spectacle*, ed. David Kidd-Hewitt and Richard Osborne, 25–48. London: Pluto Press, 1995.

Paley, Bruce. *Jack the Ripper: The Simple Truth*. London: Headline, 1996.

Papke, David Ray. *Framing the Criminal: Crime, Cultural Work, and the Loss of Critical Perspective, 1830–1900*. Hamden, CT: Archon Books, 1987.

Pearson, Edmund. "The Borden Case." In *Studies in Murder*, 3–120. Garden City, NY: Garden City, 1924.

———. "The Bordens: A Postscript." In *Murder at Smutty Nose and Other Murders*, 291–302. Garden City, NY: Doubleday, Page, 1926.

———. *Dime Novels; or, Following an Old Trail in Popular Literature*. Boston: Little, Brown, 1929.

———. "From Sudden Death—I." In *Queer Books*, 214–36. Garden City, NY: Doubleday, Doran, 1928.

———. *Instigation of the Devil*. New York: Charles Scribner's Sons, 1930.

———. "Librarian Authors: Edmund Pearson." *Library Journal* 57 (1932): 992.

———. "The Man Pays—Sometimes." In *Instigation of the Devil*, 197–205. New York: Charles Scribner's Sons, 1930.

———. "Murder at Smutty Nose; or, The Crime of Louis Wagner." In *Murder at Smutty Nose and Other Murders*, 1–69. Garden City, NY: Doubleday, Page, 1926.

———. "Nineteen Dandelions." In *More Studies in Murder*, 84–97. New York: Harrison Smith and Robert Haas, 1936.

———. "Scenery by Currier & Ives." In *More Studies in Murder*, 295–300. New York: Harrison Smith and Robert Haas, 1936.

———. *Trial of Lizzie Borden: Edited, with a History of the Case*. Garden City, NY: Doubleday, Doran, 1937.

———. "Two Victorian Ladies." In *Murder at Smutty Nose and Other Murders*, 234–62. Garden City, NY: Doubleday, Page, 1926.

———. "What Does a Murderer Look Like?" In *Instigation of the Devil* 20–36.

———. "What Makes a Good Murder?" In *Instigation of the Devil* 75–85.

———. "The Wicked Hansom." In *More Studies in Murder*, 60–64. New York: Harrison Smith and Robert Haas, 1936.

———. "With Acknowledgments to Thomas De Quincey." In *Books in Black or Red*, 191–213. New York: Macmillan, 1923.

Pearson, Patricia. *When She Was Bad: Violent Women and the Myth of Innocence*. New York: Viking, 1997.

Pence, Jeffrey S. "Terror Incognito: Representation, Repetition, Experience in *Henry: Portrait of a Serial Killer*." *Public Culture* 6 (1994): 525–45.

Perry, Barbara. *In the Name of Hate: Understanding Hate Crimes*. New York: Routledge, 2001.

Pinedo, Isabel Cristina. *Recreational Terror: Women and the Pleasures of Horror Film Viewing*. Albany, NY: SUNY Press, 1997.

Pinkerton, A. F. *The Whitechapel Murders; or, An American Detective in London*. Chicago: Laird & Lee, 1888.

Pizzato, Mark. "Jeffrey Dahmer and Media Cannibalism: The Lure and Failure of Sacrifice." In *Mythologies of Violence in Postmodern Media*, ed. Christopher Sharrett, 85–118. Detroit, MI: Wayne State University Press, 1999.

Plagens, Peter. "Violence in Our Culture." *Newsweek*, 1 Apr. 1991, 46–52.

Plimpton, George. "The Story behind a Nonfiction Novel." *New York Times Book Review*, 16 Jan. 1966.

Pollard, Scott. "Cooper, Details, and the Patriotic Mission of *Twin Peaks*." *Literature/Film Quarterly* 21, no. 4 (1993): 296–304.

Ponce de Leon, Charles. *Self-Exposure: Human-Interest Journalism and the Emergence of Celebrity in America, 1890–1940*. Chapel Hill: University of North Carolina Press, 2002.

Porter, Bruce. "Mind Hunters." *Psychology Today*, Apr. 1983, 44–52.

Potter, Claire Bond. *War on Crime: Bandits, G-Men, and the Politics of Mass Culture*. New Brunswick, NJ: Rutgers University Press, 1998.

Powdermaker, Hortense. *Hollywood: The Dream Factory*. Boston: Little, Brown, 1950.

Powers, Richard Gid. *G-Men: Hoover's FBI in American Popular Culture*. Carbondale: Southern Illinois University Press, 1983.

———. *Secrecy and Power: The Life of J. Edgar Hoover*. New York: Free Press, 1987.

Prince, Stephen. "Graphic Violence in the Cinema: Origins, Aesthetic Design, and Social Effects." In Prince, *Screening* 1–44.

———. *Savage Cinema: Sam Peckinpah and the Rise of Ultraviolent Movies*. Austin: University of Texas Press, 1998.

———, ed. *Screening Violence*. New Brunswick, NJ: Rutgers University Press, 2000.

Puar, Jasbir K., and Amit S. Rai. "Monster, Terrorist, Fag: The War on Terrorism and the Production of Docile Patriots." *Social Text* 20, no. 3 (2002): 117–48.

Rapping, Elayne. "Aliens, Nomads, Mad Dogs, and Road Warriors: Tabloid TV and the New Face of Criminal Violence." In *Mythologies of Violence in Postmodern Media*, ed. Christopher Sharrett, 249–73. Detroit, MI: Wayne State University Press, 1999.

Red Dragon. Dir. Brett Ratner. Dino De Laurentiis Productions, 2002.

Rein, Irving, Philip Kotler, and Martin Stoller. *High Visibility: The Making and Marketing of Professionals into Celebrities*. Chicago: NTC Business Books, 1997.

Ressler, Robert K., Ann W. Burgess, and John E. Douglas. *Sexual Homicide: Patterns and Motives*. Lexington, MA: Lexington Books, 1988.

Ressler, Robert K., Ann W. Burgess, John E. Douglas, Carol R. Hartman, and Ralph D'Agostino. "Sexual Killers and Their Victims: Identifying Patterns through Crime Scene Analysis." *Journal of Interpersonal Violence* 1, no. 3 (1986): 288–308.

Ressler, Robert E., and Tom Schachtman. *I Have Lived in the Monster*. New York: St. Martin's Press, 1997.

———. *Justice Is Served*. New York: St. Martin's Press, 1994.

————. *Whoever Fights Monsters: My Twenty Years Tracking Serial Killers for the FBI.* New York: St. Martin's Press, 1992.

Reynolds, Michael. *Dead Ends.* New York: Warner, 1992.

Richardson, David. "Facts of Death." *Xposé* 24 (1998). http://profiler2.crosswinds.net/archives/press/article012.htm (site now discontinued).

Riordan, James. *Stone: The Controversies, Excesses, and Exploits of a Radical Filmmaker.* New York: Hyperion, 1995.

Robinson, Bryan. "Serial Killer Action Figures for Sale: Denver Sculptor's Serial Killer Action Figures Bringing in Profits and Raising Ire." *ABC News,* 25 Mar. 2002. http://abcnews.go.com/US/story?id=91786&page=1.

Robson, Ruthann. *Lesbian (Out)Law: Surviving under the Rule of Law.* Ithaca, NY: Firebrand Books, 1992.

Rojek, Chris. *Celebrity.* London: Reaktion Books, 2001.

Rosen, Ruth. "The Sinister Images of 'The X-Files.'" *Chronicle of Higher Education,* 11 Jul. 1997, B7.

Rosenbaum, Ron. "The FBI's Agent Provocateur." *Vanity Fair,* Apr. 1993.

Rosenberg, Scott. "Heightened Debate over Movie Violence." *San Francisco Examiner,* 6 Dec. 1992, D1, D7.

————. "New Cinema's Young Bloods." *San Francisco Chronicle,* 7 Feb. 1993, D2.

Rossi, C. T. "Guns—Not Political Correctness—Will Thwart Terrorists and Killers." *Free Congress Foundation,* 6 Aug. 2002. http://www.freecongress.org/commentaries/2002/020806CR.asp.

Rossmo, D. Kim. *Geographic Profiling.* Boca Raton, FL: CRC Press, 2000.

Rubin, Martin. "The Grayness of Darkness: *The Honeymoon Killers* and Its Impact on Psychokiller Cinema." In *Mythologies of Violence in Postmodern Media,* ed. Christopher Sharrett, 41–64. Detroit, MI: Wayne State University Press, 1999.

Rule, Ann. "Ann Rule's Newsletter." 1, no. 5 (1998).

————. Foreword to *Profiles in Murder: An FBI Legend Dissects Killers and Their Crimes,* by Russell Vorpagel (as told to Joseph Harrington), 9–10. New York: Plenum Trade, 1998.

————. *The I-5 Killer.* New York: Signet, 1988.

————. *Lust Killer.* New York: Signet, 1988.

————. *A Rose for Her Grave and Other True Cases.* New York: Pocket Books, 1993.

————. *The Stranger Beside Me.* New York: Signet Books, 1980.

Rumbelow, Donald. *Jack the Ripper: The Complete Casebook.* New York: Berkley Books, 1990.

Ruth, David E. *Inventing the Public Enemy: The Gangster in American Culture, 1918–1934.* Chicago: University of Chicago Press, 1996.

Safire, William. "Homeland Insecurity; Even If He Was Made in America, the D.C. Sniper Serves the Ends of Al-Qaida." *Pittsburgh Post-Gazette,* 15 Oct. 2002, A9.

Salisbury, Mark. "You Don't Know Jack." *Premiere,* Dec. 2000. http://www.premiere.com/Premiere/ShortTakes/1200/ripper.html (no longer available).

Sardis, Kristen. "Loose Talk: What the Stars Said This Week." *In Style*, 19 Jan. 2004, 8.

Satten, Joseph, Karl Menninger, Irwin Rosen, and Martin Mayman. "Murder without Apparent Motive: A Study in Personality Disorganization." *American Journal of Psychiatry* 117 (1960): 48–53.

Schechter, Harold. *Depraved: The Shocking True Story of America's First Serial Killer*. New York: Pocket Star Books, 1994.

———. *Fiend: The Shocking True Story of America's Youngest Serial Killer*. New York: Pocket Books, 2000.

———. "Skin Deep: Folk Tales, Face Lifts, and *The Silence of the Lambs*." *Literature Interpretation Theory* 5 (1994): 19–27.

Schechter, Harold, and David Everitt. *The A–Z Encyclopedia of Serial Killers*. New York: Pocket Books, 1996.

Scheuer, Jeffrey. *The Sound Bite Society: Television and the American Mind*. New York: Four Walls Eight Windows, 1999.

Schickel, Richard. *Intimate Strangers: The Culture of Celebrity*. New York: Fromm, 1986.

———. "Stars vs. Celebrities: The Deterioration of the Star System." In *The National Society of Film Critics on the Movie Star*, ed. Elisabeth Weis, 10–18. New York: Penguin Books, 1981.

Schlesinger, Philip, Graham Murdock, and Philip Elliott. *Televising "Terrorism": Political Violence in Popular Culture*. London: Comedia, 1983.

Schlesinger, Philip, and Howard Tumber. *Reporting Crime: The Media Politics of Criminal Justice*. Oxford: Clarendon Press, 1994.

Schmich, Mary T. "Police Tempted by Theory That 2 Women Are Highway Killers." *Chicago Tribune*, 30 Dec. 1990, 19–20.

Schmidt, Curtis B. "The Psychopathology of Saddam." *Denver Post*, 21 Oct. 2002, B7.

Schmidt, Martha A. "Dahmer Discourse and Gay Identity: The Paradox of Queer Politics." *Critical Sociology* 203 (1994): 81–105.

Schuster, Hal. *The Unauthorized Guide to the X-Files*. Rocklin, CA: Prima, 1997.

Schwartz, Anne. *The Man Who Could Not Kill Enough: The Secret Murders of Milwaukee's Jeffrey Dahmer*. New York: Carol, 1992.

Schwartz, Jerry. "Get Your Dose of Crime Stories without Cracking a Book: CBS Newsmagazine to Feature Summer Series Inspired by True-Crime Books." *Ottawa Citizen*, 16 Jul. 2001, D8.

Sears, Donald J. *To Kill Again: The Motivation and Development of Serial Murder*. Wilmington, DE: Scholarly Resources, 1991.

Sedgwick, Eve Kosofsky. *Epistemology of the Closet*. Berkeley: University of California Press, 1990.

Segrave, Kerry. *Women Serial and Mass Murderers: A Worldwide Reference, 1580 through 1990*. Jefferson, NC: McFarland, 1992.

Seidman, Steven. "Identity and Politics in a 'Postmodern' Gay Culture: Some Historical and Conceptual Notes." In *Fear of a Queer Planet: Queer Politics and Social Theory*, ed. Michael Warner, 105–42. Minneapolis: University of Minnesota Press, 1993.

Sekula, Allan. "The Body and the Archive." *October* 39 (1986): 3–64.

Seltzer, Mark. *Serial Killers: Death and Life in America's Wound Culture*. New York: Routledge, 1998.

"Serial Killer." [Transcript.] *48 Hours*. CBS. KPIX, San Francisco. 8 May 1991. 1–10.

Serial Killers. Alexandria, VA: Time-Life Books, 1992.

"Serial Killers Are as American as Apple Pie." *National Examiner*, 7 Jun. 1994, 7.

Seven. Dir. David Fincher. New Line, 1994.

Shnayerson, Michael. "Natural Born Opponents." *Vanity Fair*, Jul. 1996.

Shapiro, Marc. *All Things: The Official Guide to The X-Files, Volume 6*. New York: HarperEntertainment, 2001.

Sharrett, Christopher. Introduction to Sharrett, *Mythologies* 9–20.

———, ed. *Mythologies of Violence in Postmodern Media*. Detroit, MI: Wayne State University Press, 1999.

Shaviro, Steven. *The Cinematic Body*. Minneapolis: University of Minnesota Press, 1993.

The Silence of the Lambs. Dir. Jonathan Demme. Orion, 1991.

Sinclair, Iain. "Jack the Rip-off." *Observer*, 27 Jan. 2002. http://www.guardian.co.uk/Archive/Article/0,4273,4343762,00.html.

Sinclair, Marianne. *Those Who Died Young: Cult Heroes of the Twentieth Century*. New York: Penguin Books, 1979.

Skal, David. *The Monster Show: A Cultural History of Horror*. New York: Norton, 1993.

Slotkin, Richard. *Gunfighter Nation: The Myth of the Frontier in Twentieth-Century America*. New York: Atheneum, 1992.

Smith, Gavin. "Oliver Stone: Why Do I Have to Provoke?" *Sight and Sound* 4, no. 12 (1994): 9–12.

Smith, Joan. "Done to Death." *Guardian*, 8 Jan. 2002. http://www.guardian.co.uk/Archive/Article/0,4273,4330891,00.html.

Soar, Matthew. "Andrew Cunanan, in the Houseboat, with the Bloody Versace Scarf." *Jump Cut: A Review of Contemporary Media* 43 (2000): 48–55.

Socarides, Charles. *The Overt Homosexual*. New York: Grune & Stratton, 1968.

Sparks, Richard. *Television and the Drama of Crime: Moral Tales and the Place of Crime in Public Life*. Buckingham: Open University Press, 1992.

Speck. Dir. Keith Walley. Magic Hat Media, 2002.

Springhall, John. *Youth, Popular Culture, and Moral Panics: Penny Gaffs to Gangsta-Rap, 1830–1996*. New York: St. Martin's Press, 1998.

Srebnick, Amy Gilman. *The Mysterious Death of Mary Rogers: Sex and Culture in Nineteenth-Century New York*. New York: Oxford University Press, 1995.

Stacey, Jackie. *Star Gazing: Hollywood Cinema and Female Spectatorship*. New York: Routledge, 1994.

Stasio, Marilyn. "The Killers Next Door: We Can't Get Enough of Them." *New York Times Book Review*, 20 Oct. 1991, 46–47.

Steinem, Gloria. "Supremacy Crimes." *Ms. Magazine* online, 1 Aug. 1999. Archived at http://www.afsc.org/pwork/0106/010618.htm.

Steyn, Mark. "Muslim Ties Are No Surprise." *Chicago Sun-Times*, 27 Oct. 2002, 37.

Stone, Oliver. Introduction to *Natural Born Killers: A Novel*, by John August and Jane Hamsher, 7–12. New York: Signet, 1994.

Strean, Herbert S., and Lucy Freeman. *Our Wish to Kill: The Murder in All Our Hearts*. New York: St. Martin's Press, 1991.

Streib, Victor L. "Death Penalty for Lesbians." *National Journal of Sexual Orientation Law* 1, no. 1 (1999): 105–27.

Sugden, Philip. *The Complete History of Jack the Ripper*. New York: Carroll & Graf, 1994.

Surette, Ray. *Media, Crime, and Criminal Justice: Images and Realities*. 2nd ed. Belmont, CA: West/Wadsworth, 1997.

———. "Predator Criminals as Media Icons." In *Media, Process, and the Social Construction of Crime: Studies in Newsmaking Criminology*, ed. Gregg Barak, 131–58. New York: Garland, 1994.

Susman, Warren. *Culture as History: The Transformation of American Society in the Twentieth Century*. New York: Pantheon Books, 1984.

Suspect Zero. Dir. E. Elias Merhige. Intermedia Films, 2004.

"Talk of the Town." *New Yorker*, 15 Aug. 1977, 21–22.

Tally, Ted. "Coming Attractions." In *Plays from Playwrights Horizons*, 273–329. New York: Broadway Play Publishing, 1987.

Tapper, Jake. "Senate Report: FBI Still Unprepared." *Salon*, 3 Mar. 2003. http://www.salon.com/news/feature/2003/03/03/fbi/index.html.

Taubin, Amy. "Demme's Monde." *Village Voice*, 19 Feb. 1991.

———. "Killing Men." *Sight and Sound* 1, no. 1 (1991): 14–18.

Taylor, John. "Murder: The Ultimate Art Form." *Esquire*, Sep. 1994.

Ted Bundy. Dir. Matthew Bright. First Look Media, 2002.

Thaler, Paul. *The Spectacle: Media and the Making of the O. J. Simpson Story*. Westport, CT: Praeger, 1997.

"35 Murderers of Many People Could Be at Large, U.S. Says." *New York Times*, 28 Oct. 1983, A17.

Thomas, Ronald R. "The Fingerprint of the Foreigner: Colonizing the Criminal Body in 1890s Detective Fiction and Criminal Anthropology." *ELH* 61, no. 3 (1994): 655–83.

Tithecott, Richard. *Of Men and Monsters: Jeffrey Dahmer and the Construction of the Serial Killer*. Madison: University of Wisconsin Press, 1997.

Trachtenberg, Alan. *The Incorporation of America: Culture and Society in the Gilded Age*. New York: Hill & Wang, 1982.

"Tracked to Earth." *Chicago Daily News*, 30 Jul. 1895, 1.

"Transcript of NBC's Chat with Kim Moses and Ian Sander the Executive Producers and Bob Lowry, the Story Editor of 'Profiler.'" *NBC.com*, 8 Jan. 1997. http://profiler2.crosswinds.net/archives/press/transcript03.htm (site now discontinued).

Troyer, Lon. "The Calling of Counterterrorism." *Theory and Event* 5, no. 4 (2002). http://muse.jhu.edu/journals/theory_and_event/v005/5.4troyer.html.

Tucher, Andie. *Froth and Scum: Truth, Beauty, Goodness, and the Ax Murder in America's First Mass Medium*. Chapel Hill: University of North Carolina Press, 1994.

Turner, Frederick Jackson. *The Significance of the Frontier in American History*. Ed. Harold
    P. Simonson. New York: Continuum, 1990. First published 1893.

Uccella, Michaele, and Melanie Kaye. "Survival Is an Act of Resistance." In *Fight Back!*
    Feminist Resistance to Male Violence, ed. Frédérique Delacoste and Felice Newman,
    14–19. Minneapolis: Cleis Press, 1981.

"An Underground Market Moves to Mainstream America." *BusinessWeek Online*, 20 Nov.
    2000. http://www.businessweek.com/2000/00_47/b3708056.htm.

U.S. Five. *The Devil's Rood: A Group Novel about America's First Serial Killer*. Berkeley:
    Creative Arts, 1999.

U.S. Senate. *Hearing before the Subcommittee on Juvenile Justice of the Committee on the Judi-*
    ciary United States Senate, Ninety-Eighth Congress, First Session on Patterns of Murders
    Committed by One Person, in Large Numbers with No Apparent Rhyme, Reason, or Moti-
    vation, July 12, 1983. Serial No. J-98-52. Washington, DC: U.S. Government Printing
    Office, 1984.

"The Victim of a Ripper." *National Police Gazette*, 11 May 1895, 3.

Voloshinov, V. N. *Marxism and the Philosophy of Language*. Trans. Ladislav Matejka and
    I. R. Titunik. New York: Seminar Press, 1973.

Walkowitz, Judith R. *City of Dreadful Delight: Narratives of Sexual Danger in Late-*
    Victorian London. Chicago: University of Chicago Press, 1992.

Warren, Detective. *The Whitechapel Murders; or, On the Track of the Fiend*. New York:
    Munro's, 1888.

Warrick, Pamela. "Killer Approach to Nasty Letters." *Los Angeles Times*, 7 Apr. 1997, E1,
    E3.

Watney, Simon. *Policing Desire: Pornography, AIDS, and the Media*. London: Methuen,
    1987.

———. "Stellar Studies." *Screen* 28, no. 3 (1987): 110–14.

"Wealth of Clews Bewilders Police." *Chicago Daily News*, 26 Jul. 1895, 1.

Weber, Adna Ferrin. *The Growth of Cities in the Nineteenth Century*. Ithaca, NY: Cornell
    University Press, 1963. First published 1899.

Weber, Samuel. "Wartime." In *Violence, Identity, and Self-Determination*, ed. Hent De Vries
    and Samuel Weber, 80–105, 359–60. Stanford, CA: Stanford University Press, 1997.

Webster, William H. "Director's Message." *FBI Law Enforcement Bulletin* 55, no. 12
    (1986): 1.

"The Week." *Guardian Weekly*, 12–18 Oct. 2000, 2.

Weeks, Jeffrey. *Sex, Politics and Society: The Regulation of Sexuality since 1800*. 2nd ed.
    London: Longman, 1989.

Weinraub, Bernard. "Hollywood Is Silent on Film Violence." *New York Times*, 6 Jun. 1999,
    28.

Weis, Elisabeth, ed. *The National Society of Film Critics on The Movie Star*. New York:
    Penguin Books, 1981.

Wells, Carolyn. *The Technique of the Mystery Story*. Springfield, MA: Home Correspon-
    dence School, 1913.

Wertham, Frederic. *The Show of Violence*. Garden City, NY: Doubleday, 1949.

Weyr, Tom. "Marketing America's Psychos." *Publisher's Weekly*, 12 Apr. 1993, 38–41.

The Whitechapel Murders; or, The Mysteries of the East End. London: G. Purkess, 1888.

Whitman, Howard. *Terror in the Streets*. New York: Dial Press, 1951.

Wilkinson, Alec. "Conversations with a Killer." *New Yorker*, 18 Apr. 1994, 58–76.

Williams, Daniel E. "Rogues, Rascals, and Scoundrels: The Underworld Literature of Early America." *American Studies* 24, no. 2 (1983): 5–19.

Williams, Montagu. *Round London: Down East and Up West*. London: Macmillan, 1892.

Williams, Raymond. "Most Doctors Recommend." In *Raymond Williams on Television: Selected Writings*, ed. Alan O'Connor, 81–83. New York: Routledge, 1996.

———. *Television: Technology and Cultural Form*. New York: Schocken Books, 1975.

Willis, Sharon. *High Contrast: Race and Gender in Contemporary Hollywood Film*. Durham, NC: Duke University Press, 1997.

Wilson, Cintra. *A Massive Swelling: Celebrity Re-examined as a Grotesque Crippling Disease and Other Cultural Revelations*. New York: Viking, 2000.

Wilson, Colin. Introduction to *The Complete Jack the Ripper*, by Donald Rumbelow. Boston: New York Graphic Society, 1975.

Wilson, Colin, and Donald Seaman. *The Serial Killers: A Study in the Psychology of Violence*. New York: Carol, 1991.

Winn, Steven, and David Merrill. *Ted Bundy: The Killer Next Door*. New York: Bantam, 1980.

"Wuornos." *Wuornos Opera*, 23 Jun. 2004. http://www.wuornos.org.

"Yoder Is Fifth Known Victim of Louisiana Serial Killer." *TheNewOrleansChannel.com*, 18 Mar. 2003. http://www.theneworleanschannel.com/news/2047003/detail.html.

Young, Elizabeth. "*The Silence of the Lambs* and the Flaying of Feminist Theory." *Camera Obscura* 27 (1991): 4–35.

Zelizer, Barbie. "What's Rather Public about Dan Rather: TV Journalism and the Emergence of Celebrity." *Journal of Popular Film and Television* 17 (1989): 74–80.

Žižek, Slavoj. "Welcome to the Desert of the Real!" *South Atlantic Quarterly* 101, no. 2 (2002): 385–89.

INDEX

Kaplan Educational Centers, 272n14
Karpis, Alvin, 75
Kearney, Patrick, 282n12
Kehr, Dave, 142
Kellner, Douglas, 159, 170–71
Kemper, Edmund, 15
Kendall, Elizabeth, *The Phantom Prince*, 232, 279n2
Kensington Publishing, 175, 277n1
Kent, Constance, 191
Keppel, Robert: on Bundy as exemplary serial killer, 211; emphasis on the usual aspects of serial killers, 203; on the mobile serial killer, 80; *The Riverman: Ted Bundy and I Hunt for the Green River Killer*, 89, 218, 247
Kerrigan, Nancy, 124
Kessler, Ronald, 99
Kessler, William F., 70
Kidwell, Sue, 192
Killer: A Journal of Murder (Gaddis and Long), 262n17
"Killer Fonts," 266n14
Kilmer, Val, 247
Kinamore, Pam, 254
King, Barry, 121
King, Brian, *Lustmord: The Writings and Artifacts of Murderers*, 262n17
King, John, 57
King, Rodney, 124
Kingsley, Ben, 247
Klaprat, Cathy, 107
Kleinfield, N. R., 252
Knight, Peter, 154
Knox, Sara L., 252
Kohl, C. E., 60, 61
Kolarik, Gera-Lind, *Freed to Kill*, 229
Kolchak: The Night Stalker (TV show), 162
Kooistra, Paul, 19
Kosminski, Aaron, 37
Kotler, Philip, 260n9
Kozloff, Sarah, 147, 153–54
Kraft, Randy, 210, 218, 225, 227, 282n12
Krajicek, Richard, 13
Kramer, Hilton, 192
Krar, William, 245
Krause, Mary Ann, 91
Krueger, Freddy, 144
Krum, Sharon, 240

Lacy, Oliver, 227
Lacy, Suzanne, "In Mourning and in Rage," 233
Lane, Roger, 184
Lang, Fritz, 109
Langer, John, "Television's 'Personality System,'" 142
Larson, Erik, *The Devil in the White City*, 52
Lasch, Christopher, 11
Lawless, Lucy, 143
Lawson, W. B., *Jack the Ripper in New York; or, Piping a Terrible Mystery*, 45–46
Leach, Kimberly, 215
"Leather Apron"; or, The Horrors of Whitechapel, London, 1888, 33–34
Lecter, Hannibal, 144
"Lecter syndrome," 279n3
Lee, Derrick Todd, 254, 284n8
Leitch, Thomas M., 113–14
Lennon, John, 10
Leonard, John, 277n13
Leong, Ian, 274n7
Leopold and Loeb case, 70, 188, 277n2
lesbianism, history of association with violence, 230–33
Lesser, Henry, 16
Lesser, Wendy, 207
Levin, Jack, 259n4, 271n8
Levin, Jennifer, 127
Levine, Richard, 198
Levy, Emanuel, 107
Lewis, Dorothy Otnow, 211, 214
Lewis, Juliette, 123
Leyton, Elliott, 23–24
Licensed to Kill (film), 281n8
life insurance industry, 268n26
Lindberg, Gary, 64–65
Lindbergh, Charles, 73
Lindsay, Paul: *Freedom to Kill*, 272n15; *Witness to the Truth*, 97–98
Lindsey, Robert, 78, 80
Linedecker, Clifford, *The Man Who Killed Boys*, 282n11
Lipski, Israel, 40, 266n11
Livingstone, Dr. David, 48
Livingstone, Sonia, 146
Lodger, The (film), 108
Logan, Guy B. H., *Masters of Crime: Studies of Multiple Murders*, 37–38, 70, 267n19